CLASSI

# Revival: Times of Refreshing

# Why Revival Tarries

# In the Day of Thy Power

ISBN 0 85476 916 1

Published by
KINGSWAY PUBLICATIONS
Lottbridge Drove, Eastbourne, BN23 6NT, England.
Email: books@kingsway.co.uk

Designed and produced for the publishers by
Bookprint Creative Services, P. O. Box 827, BN21 3YJ, England.
Printed in Great Britain.

Reproduced from the original typesetting
of the single-volume editions.

# Revival
## Times of Refreshing

SELWYN HUGHES

KINGSWAY PUBLICATIONS
EASTBOURNE

# CONTENTS

# INTRODUCTION

One of the biggest and most vital issues facing the Church as it pushes open the door into a new century is this: Are we on the verge of one of the greatest spiritual revivals the world has ever seen? There are evidences that this is so.

In all the years that I have been a Christian I have never witnessed such a burden and expectancy for revival as I do at this moment among the true people of God. Wherever I go I meet prayerful Christians whose spirit witnesses with my own that a mighty Holy Spirit revival is on the way. The 1960's and 1970's were characterised by the word 'renewal'. Then in the eighties, the word began slowly losing currency, and another appeared to take its place — revival. And why? Because great and wonderful though renewal is, many are beginning to see that there are greater things in our Father's storehouse, and slowly but surely their faith is rising to a flashpoint.

Thirty-five years ago, CWR was founded in order to become a voice for revival. Some said at that time that the emphasis was ill-timed as the breath of the risen Christ was already blowing upon the Church in charismatic renewal. Thankful though I was for the showers of renewal that were falling, I still felt that God's call to me was to elevate the spiritual vision of the Church to focus its gaze on revival. At times, and because of the great things that were happening through *renewal*, the message I preached seemed to fall on deaf ears. Now, however, things are different. Almost daily I receive letters from ministers or church leaders that say something like this: "Our church is burdened for revival — how can we prepare ourselves for it?" God, so I believe, is about to send revival to His people — our task is to provide the prayer ramp over which His purposes can pass.

Selwyn Hughes

# CHAPTER ONE

# REVIVAL . . .
## What is it?

*". . . O Lord, revive thy work
in the midst of the years . . ."*

(Habakkuk 3:2, AV)

The Holy Spirit is witnessing to many parts of His Church that a spiritual revival is on the way. Probably no greater issue faces the Church at this moment than the issue of revival. Many are very confused about the subject so we must begin by carefully defining the term. We ask ourselves, therefore: What is revival? Before coming to a definite conclusion, it might be helpful if we were to look first at what it is not.

## Revival is not evangelism

Great damage has been done by people who insist on placing it in this category. During my first visit to the United States in 1961, I was asked by one group if I would preach at the 'revival' they would be having in their church in a few months' time. I was overwhelmed by what I thought was the faith of the leaders in believing that a revival would take place at a certain time in a certain week until I was informed that, in most American churches, the term 'revival' meant a series of evangelistic meetings, such as I am often invited to preach at in England. But to place revival on a par with evangelism is to misunderstand both its nature and its purpose.

Evangelistic crusades undoubtedly draw thousands to Christ, but, however effective they turn out to be, it will not be revival. Evangelism is the expression of the Church — something brought about by a combination of human and divine effort, but revival is an experience in the Church — something brought about by God alone. Evangelism is the work men do for God: revival is the work God does for men.

### Revival is not the restoration of backslidden Christians

There are times in Church life, such as during special conventions, large rallies, conferences, camps and 'deeper-life' meetings, that large numbers of lethargic Christians make a new and deeper commitment to Jesus Christ. This, of course, is highly desirable, and worthy of much praise and gratitude to God — but it is not revival. In one meeting at which I was present, about 500 Christians responded to an invitation to make a total commitment to Christ. Later, a report in a Christian newspaper stated: "Revival breaks out at a Deeper Life Conference." It was true that Christians had been individually re-vived, but in the classic sense of the word, it was not strictly a revival.

### Revival is not an unusual sense of God's presence resting upon a particular church or fellowship for a number of weeks or months

I have known churches where a great sense of God's presence predominates for a few weeks more than usual, and they come to speak of it as revival. Supernatural things may happen, such as they have never seen before, but in the strictest sense of the word, it cannot be described as revival. While the salvation of sinners, the restoration of backsliders, and an unusual sense of God's presence hovering over a congregation for a period of time are by-products of revival, these experiences by themselves do not necessarily constitute it. You can see people converted, renewed, restored, and yet fall short of revival. Revival includes all these things, yet it surpasses them all.

*Revival is . . .*

It is important to remember that any definition can never adequately describe the true nature of revival. "Revival in a definition," said one preacher, "is like David in Saul's armour — it just doesn't fit." Revival, like salvation, is grander and greater and more glorious than anything that can be said or written about it. Having said that, however, we must still struggle to find a working definition of the term. From the Old Testament we see that the word comes from the root meaning 'to live'. The basic idea contained in the word is the return of something to its true nature and purpose. G. Campbell Morgan put it this way: "Revival is the re-animation of the life of the believer (not the unregenerate as they are 'dead in sin') . . . there can only be revival where there is life to revive." A revival, then, is for Christians, not sinners. Sinners don't need revival: they need a resurrection.

Based on these thoughts, I believe the definition of Christmas Evans, the famous Welsh preacher, is the most effective I have ever heard. It is this: "Revival is God bending down to the dying embers of a fire that is just about to go out, and breathing into it, until it bursts again into flame." In revival, men and women come alive to the life of God. D.M. Panton describes it as "the inrush of divine life into a body threatening to become a corpse." The very word 'revival' suggests that once life existed in all its fullness, but, for some reason, it waned and became moribund. As you no doubt know, when the prefix 're' is used in a word, such as revival, reanimation, return, and so on, it simply means 'back again'. Revival, then, is the Christian Church going back again to the God–given norm. And what is that 'norm'? Nothing less than the experience of Pentecost.

Peter, in his second sermon, made it clear that when God's people repented of their sin, this would be followed by "times of refreshing from the presence of the Lord" (Acts 3:16). "This phrase," says J. Edwin Orr in his book *The Second Evangelical Awakening in Britain*, "is one of the best definitions of revival in the Bible." Isn't this what happens when true revival takes place? The Church returns to the glory and power that prevailed at Pentecost.

Picture the scene described in Acts 3. Except, of course, for the ministry of Jesus, no prophet had spoken in the nation of Israel for four hundred years. Spiritually the people were at an all-time low — broken, beggared and bankrupt. Then the Spirit came. Thousands were brought into a new and living relationship with God. It was a "time of refreshing from the presence of the Lord". Every revival contains some feature of the Day of Pentecost, for Pentecost is God's pattern of blessing for His Church.

# CHAPTER TWO

# REVIVAL . . .
## The Scriptural Pattern

*". . . Up to that time the Spirit had not been given, since Jesus had not yet been glorified."*

(John 7:39, NIV)

In Chapter 1, we said that the pattern for revival is based on the Pentecost experience. Why Pentecost? Why couldn't it be based on an Old Testament revival such as took place under the leadership of Nehemiah, Hezekiah or King David?

The pattern for Old Testament revivals, while powerful and reformative, did not contain enough ingredients upon which to construct a norm. The Holy Spirit — always the prime agent in any revival — worked in a limited capacity in Old Testament times. He came and went, providing temporary infusions of power for temporary tasks. Then again, He came upon people from the outside as opposed to residing permanently on the inside. Further, He could never fully reveal His true nature, for there was no perfect vehicle through whom He could manifest Himself.

John 7:37–44 draws all these strands of thought together into a single statement when he says that the Spirit could not be given until Jesus had been glorified. Why couldn't the Spirit be manifested on earth in all His fullness until Jesus had been glorified? Because only through the life and death of Jesus could God's power be properly seen and understood. Eternal power must be seen not only in the context of signs, wonders and miracles, but at work on a Cross, forgiving its enemies and triumphing over denial, betrayal and an ugly death. It must be seen in supreme modesty and humility — the modesty and humility Jesus showed, when, after triumphing over those who brought about His crucifixion, He chose not to appear in all His glory to make them cower before Him. The power that fell at Pentecost was Christlike power, which became, from that point, the pattern for all future manifestations of power. It is imperative that we grasp this truth, for so many Christians, when praying for revival, set their sights only on the Old Testament pattern. We can certainly learn many valuable lessons and find many challenges from the record of Old Testament revivals, but we must not make them our pattern. The pattern for revival is Pentecost.

The Spirit could not have been fully given in the Old Testament dispensation because this would have set the wrong pattern. The Spirit could not have been fully given in the day of Jesus' humiliation (His birth, life and death), for that, too, would have set the wrong pattern. He could only be given in the day of Christ's triumph — His arrival on the throne — for that alone could set the right pattern.

We must establish this principle in our lives. Our prayers and expectations for revival must be based upon the greatest manifestation of the Holy Spirit the world has ever known — Pentecost. Don't be intimidated by theologians who tell you that Pentecost was simply a one-off experience which God will never want to repeat. The revivals that have taken place in the last few hundred years all contain one or more of the ingredients that were present at Pentecost. In some the dominant feature has been conviction of sin, in others, abounding joy, and in others, amazing supernatural events. Perhaps the next revival will contain *all* the ingredients of Pentecost. Somehow, I think it will.

# CHAPTER THREE

# REVIVAL . . .
# An Extraordinary
# Happening

*" . . . there came a sound . . . as of
a rushing mighty wind . . . And
there appeared . . . tongues like as
of fire . . . "*

(Acts 2:2–3, AV)

Revival is an extraordinary work of God, producing extraordinary results amongst a large group of people. It is vitally important that we see revival in these terms otherwise we will fall for the popular notion of calling any special activity in the Church by that name.

It has been a long time since the English-speaking world has been visibly shaken by an extraordinary outpouring of the Spirit of God. Most of us have to acknowledge that we have never been part of a deep and powerful revival. That, however, shoud not stop us desiring it, for, with the Acts of the Apostles before us, together with the records of history, we are able to see that God has greater things in store for us than we are presently witnessing and experiencing. Our purpose must be to examine in more detail the ingredients of that first outpouring at Pentecost for there, as we said, we have the model of what God wants His Church to be.

A young Christian said to me some years ago, "I've been a Christian for three months, and as I read the Acts of the Apostles, I sense that something is wrong." "What do you think it is?" I asked. He said, "There seems to be too wide a gap between the Church of that day and the Church of today." He had spotted it. There is! "All revivals," said Dr Martyn Lloyd Jones, "are in some way a return to Pentecost. Every revival in history repeats some aspect of that first great outpouring." The more clearly we understand what happened at Pentecost, the deeper our desire will be for a revival based on God's great pattern — a work of God that is majestic, awesome, startling and extraordinary.

## Extraordinary physical occurrences

The first thing that strikes even the most casual reader of the second chapter of Acts is that the descent of the Spirit is accompanied by extraordinary physical occurrences. We read that God sent a "mighty rushing wind" and caused "tongues of fire" to rest on the disciples (Acts 2:2–3). Why, we ask ourselves, did God cause such strange physical occurrences to accompany the descent of the Spirit? The answer is quite clear — God called attention to Himself and His work through unusual physical phenomena.

Some say, of course, that the wind and fire were occurrences that took place only on the Day of Pentecost and were never repeated. That may be so, but similar supernatural happenings took place later in the book of Acts, e.g., Acts 10:44, Acts 19 — events that were most certainly on a par with what happened at Pentecost. The history of revivals, subsequent to the Acts of the Apostles, show that whenever God floods His Church with extraordinary power He usually accompanies it with unusual physical phenomena. Why He should do so is His own business: ours is to make sure that we do not quench the Spirit by our intellectualism and unwillingness to accept the supernaturalism that generally accompanies revival.

## Extraordinary preaching

One sermon, preached by Peter, resulted in three thousand souls coming into the kingdom of God (Acts 2:41). Richard Owen Roberts, in his book on revival, says that there are three kinds of preaching. (1) Mouth to ear preaching. This takes place when the words from the mouth of the preacher enter the ears of the hearer but go no further. (2) Head to head preaching. This is where the thoughts of the preacher influence the thoughts of the hearer, affecting the mind, but nothing more. (3) Heart to heart preaching. This is where something happens in the preacher's heart of so compelling a nature that it runs like quicksilver into the heart of the hearer, producing great and wonderful results. That was the kind of preaching that took place at Pentecost.

In revival, preachers experience an extraordinary dynamic flowing through their words. Simple statements and sentences bristle with a strange and unusual power. Men and women are cut to the quick with conviction. You may have heard preaching that has come very close to this, but, believe me, it is nothing compared to what one hears in revival.

## An extraordinary sense of God's holiness

Something of this is undoubtedly present in the Church at all times, but when revival comes, the sense of God's holiness is greatly heightened. Such was the sense of God's holiness in the early Church that on one occasion we read: "No-one else dared join them, even though they were highly regarded by the people" (Acts 5:13, NIV).

Every great move of God since Pentecost has contained this impressive ingredient. It is probably true to say that the very first evidence that revival is present is when men and women are gripped by a heightened sense of God's awesomeness and holiness. Conduct, that hitherto appeared respectable, now seems unbelievably wicked. Prejudices that characterised professing Christians for years are seen as grievous sins. Private indulgences, upon which people have looked with favour, suddenly seem to merit all the wrath of God. Prayerlessness, ignorance of Scripture, sins of omission, pride, self-centred living, long-forgotten sins against members of the Body of Christ, words carelessly spoken are no longer defended by a myriad of excuses, but are laid open before the God 'with whom we have to do'. People who thought themselves worthy of heaven stand amazed that they are not in hell.

## An extraordinary understanding of the Cross

I doubt whether Peter really understood the meaning of the Cross until it was revealed to him by the Spirit on the Day of Pentecost. Doubtless its meaning deepened for him as he waited with the others those ten days in the Upper Room, but the full understanding of it came only as the Holy Spirit revealed it to him on that first Day of Pentecost. Empowered by the Spirit, he was able to make its meaning clear to the crowd gathered before him, some of whom, no doubt, had actually been present at the Saviour's crucifixion. After Peter's sermon, such was their understanding of the Cross, they were "cut to the heart and said . . . 'Brothers, what shall we do?'" (Acts 2:37, NIV).

The Cross of Christ always takes on a new and precious meaning in times of revival. Awakened hearts see the Cross, not in general terms, but in personal terms. It is no longer "He died for the sins of the world", but "He died for *me*". The Cross becomes so personal that the wounds, bruises and stripes Jesus received, along with the insults, the taunts and the jeers, provoke deep personal sorrow that He had to endure such agony for "such a one as me". These stirrings in the hearts of revived Christians drive the soul to contemplate the Cross in a way never before known. All the devils in hell and all the wickedness on earth do not have the power to keep the awakened Christian from deeper consecration and devoted love to such a Saviour.

## *An extraordinary interest in prayer and in the reading of the Scriptures*

Prior to Pentecost the disciples — Jews to a man — no doubt spent a good deal of their time praying and pondering the Scriptures. After Pentecost, however, both prayer and the study of God's Word took on a new and greater meaning. So important did this become that they decided to abstain from their administrative tasks in order to give themselves continually to prayer and the ministry of the Word. If it be said that these men were the ministers of the Early Church, and as such were obligated to spend their time in this way, then consider the Christians of Berea of whom it was said that they "searched the scriptures daily, whether those things were so" (Acts 17:11).

In today's Church, many Christians are content to let their pastors or elders do the praying and studying for them, but in revival each Christian finds their heart leaping toward prayer and the perusal of the Word of God. They learn to appreciate not only the "sincere milk of the word" but the "strong meat" also, and delight in lengthy, reverent, searching study of God's Word, and in the application of its truths to their lives. Prayer, too, which prior to revival might have seemed a drudgery becomes pure delight. Those words of the hymn, "the sweet hour of prayer", become a precious reality. And when the allotted time for prayer is up, instead of relief that the chore is over, there is sorrow that the time has passed so swiftly. In revival, men and women enjoy, as Moffatt puts it in 1 Samuel 21:7 — being "detained in the presence of the Eternal."

## An extraordinary fervour and excitement

One has only to read the pages of the Acts of the Apostles to feel the throb of excitement and joy that characterised the early disciples. It surfaces in many places, one of which is in Acts 8:1-8.

The Early Church was excited about everything that was connected with God and His Kingdom. They were excited about Jesus, about the coming of the Spirit, about the establishing of His kingdom, and about His coming again. The dull apathetic attitude, which is present in so many churches today, was a thing unknown in the first century Christian community. They were gripped by intense earnestness and a spirit of expectation. The God that raised up Jesus from the dead had raised them also from their own graves of sin. The power that had elevated Christ to the heavens and placed Him at the right hand of the Father was working in them with all its quickening might.

In revival, Christians often have to defend themselves against the charge that they are drunk (Acts 2:13–14). And what are the marks of a man who is a little drunk? He is happy, hearty, jocular, exhilarated, genial and exuberant. Most of today's Christians do not come under the same dark suspicion as did our first century brothers and sisters, but it is hardly to our credit to stress such a distinction. We are more dignified, more sophisticated, more respectable and more sober — and more in need of revival.

# CHAPTER FOUR

# REVIVAL . . .
## Seen through History

*". . . I will pour out my Spirit on all people . . ."*

(Joel 2:28, NIV)

Having examined the ingredients of an extraordinary movement of God's Holy Spirit, we turn now to ask ourselves the question: Can we expect these same ingredients to be seen in the Church subsequent to Pentecost? I believe we can. In fact, God has been pleased to show us, in almost every century of the Church, that what He did at Pentecost, He can do again.

I want to examine with you some of the great revivals of history with a view to identifying in them the same characteristics that were present on the Day of Pentecost and in the life of the Early Church. Some might feel hesitant about looking outside the Bible for confirmation of what we are saying, but I believe there is a clear Biblical principle we can follow. God, knowing how easy it is for the human mind to forget even as great and significant an event as the crossing of the Jordan, commanded Joshua to raise up a memorial of twelve stones, so that when future generations asked what they meant, they could be told precisely what happened (Joshua 3:9 — 4:7). How sad it is that the great events of the past — even spiritual events — can be so easily forgotten. God has done great things for us in the past and if we ignore them, we do so to our peril. I propose to raise up before you some 'memorial stones' from some of the great revivals of history, in the hope that as you gaze at what God has done, you will draw fresh inspiration from it and move forward with renewed faith and greater expectancy.

Looking back can sometimes be a wasteful exercise, but not when we focus upon the great spiritual events of history. Dr Martyn Lloyd Jones once said, "So dulled is the human mind by sin that we would forget the death of Christ were it not for the fact that God has commanded us to remind ourselves of it regularly by breaking bread and drinking wine." We shall look together at some of the revivals of the past in order to see how every revival is, to some extent at least, a return to Pentecost.

In the previous chapter, we saw that one of the first noticeable features in an extraordinary move of God was *strange and unusual physical manifestations*. This was evidenced in a tremendous way during the 1859 revival in Ulster. The chief characteristic of this revival was, what has come to be called, the 'strikings down'. People would fall to the ground in the streets or in the fields and would lie there motionless for hours. When they recovered, they sensed that God had visited them, and they would worship Him and praise Him with great fervour and excitement. So astonishing was this physical phenomenon that crowds of non-Christians gathered where believers were present just to see these physical manifestations take place. Many were converted as they sensed that God was at work. Our human minds may find it difficult to accept such strange happenings, but we must face the fact that, in revival, God draws attention to Himself by unusual and inexplicable physical manifestations.

Almost every revival carries evidence of very ordinary preachers being transformed as the Spirit came upon them, but perhaps the most conclusive evidence of this is the record of what happened in 1904 to David Davies, a minister in the town of Swansea, South Wales. Prior to the revival, David Davies was known to be a fine Christian minister, but he was regarded by most as an extremely poor speaker. He would cough and splutter his way through a sermon, and, were it not for the consistent Christian character he bore, many would not have gone to listen to him. Then one day revival hit Swansea, and David Davies became a man transformed. He went into his pulpit the next Sunday, and the people could hardly believe their ears. Gone was the hesitancy and stuttering; instead he spoke with the most amazing authority and power. Following his message that Sunday, hundreds of men and women were converted to Christ and, week by week thereafter, David Davies wielded an exceptional ministry in the power and demonstration of the Spirit. When the revival simmered down the following year, the strange thing was that David Davies reverted to his previous hesitant style of preaching. This underlined, even more clearly, the fact that his anointed preaching was not the result of human effort, but a mighty manifestation of the Living God.

It would be impossible to find any revival in history where *an extraordinary sense of God's majesty and holiness* was not present. Just as God's awesomeness and holiness were made known to the Early Church, so they have been made known in every great spiritual awakening since.

One example of this is found in the great revival under Charles Finney in America during the mid-18th century. As Finney preached on such subjects as "The holiness of God" or "Sinners in the hands of an angry God", men and women were given such a revelation of God's holiness that the thought of remaining in a state of sinfulness became intolerable, and they would cry out: "O God, save me from myself and from my sin. Slay me, but do not let me persist another day in this awful condition." Some have put this down to Finney's eloquence and logic, but eloquence and logic, apart from the anointing of the Spirit, are utterly powerless to bring about lasting change in a human heart.

In one service in Northampton, Massachusetts, such was the anointing on Finney's message that the whole congregation of about five hundred people rose up as one man crying out: "O God, we are not worthy to stand in Your presence. Save us — or destroy us." Such was the revelation of God's holiness during the days of Finney that anyone who committed sin would make an instant confession of it. Christians, particularly, feared to enter a church with unconfessed sin in their hearts, unless, in front of the congregation, their sin might be made known.

In the previous chapter, we identified *a new insight into the Cross* as an ingredient of the first Pentecostal outpouring, and it has been present in every revival since.

One such revival in which the work of Christ on the Cross was most significantly underlined was that which took place under the ministry of Christmas Evans in North Wales during the mid-eighteenth century. Christmas Evans had always been an eloquent and forceful speaker, but when the revival came, it touched his tongue with an even greater eloquence and power. The main emphasis in all his preaching was the work of Christ on the Cross. One of his favourite texts was John 3:16, "For God so loved the world, that he gave his only begotten Son …" When he came to the part of his message that dealt with Christ's death on the Cross, his rugged features would take on a softness and a gentleness that had to be seen to be believed, and his voice, usually stern and demanding, became soft, mellow and persuasive.

A biographer says of him: "Thousands who heard Christmas Evans, having been content to wear the Cross as an ornament, now found themselves viewing it as the place on which Christ bore their own personal sins. The conviction was borne home to every man and woman, that their very own sins put Christ there. In every place he preached, multitudes would weep at the foot of the Cross, and end up wholly saved and redeemed." Can there be any movement of the Holy Spirit in which the Cross is not made prominent? Such a thing is unthinkable. It is as impossible as a river without a source, or a day without light.

Another common element in any revival is that of *an intense interest in prayer and the reading of the Scriptures*. This manifested itself at Pentecost, and it was demonstrated in the more recent revivals of history. A classic example is the revival which happened in Wales at the beginning of last century. When the fire fell, as the Welsh like to put it, one of the first indications that God was at work was evidenced by people's intense desire to pray and read the Bible. Meetings lasted from ten in the morning until twelve at night. There was little preaching. Singing, testimony, prayer and reading the Bible aloud were the predominant features. Coal miners, thousands of feet below the earth, would gather together during their food breaks, not to eat, but to pray and read the Scriptures aloud. Some would even gather at the pithead an hour before work in order to sing and pray. Often the manager and officials of the mine would join in.

This is characteristic not only of the Welsh revival, but of every revival. When God comes down upon His people in the way we are describing, it invariably happens that, instead of excuses for not praying and reading the Scriptures, revived Christians find no other activity so delightful and beneficial. Why should this be so? Simply because the revived Christian has fallen in love. The prime desire of every lover is to be with his beloved. He delights to talk to her, to spend time with her, to listen to her voice, to focus on her endless charm. And so it is with revival.

We consider now the last of these characteristics — *extraordinary fervour and excitement*. We have already spoken of the 1859 revival which, measured by its impact on both the Church and the world, was one of the greatest outpourings of God's Spirit since the Day of Pentecost. The 1859 revival is sometimes called the 'International Revival' because it broke out simultaneously in America, Ulster and many other places. Once people had repented of their sins, and had found perfect peace with God, it invariably happened that they would be filled to overflowing with deep and lasting joy.

Let no one think that revival is associated with gloom and heaviness and a downcast spirit. There is always a period of mourning for sin, but this is soon followed by waves of endless delight and joy. It is surely amongst the most tragic misrepresentations of truth when historians write that, in times of revival, Christians act like "dejected melancholiacs". It is a travesty of the true tradition of revival. Revival imparts an immense sense of well-being. It produces a witness in the hearts of believers that all is well within. It makes music inside the soul, and bestows a glad exuberance. Compare what I am saying with the dull, apathetic attitude which is common in many parts of today's Church. Only the Almighty can produce the change.

*O God, send a revival.*

# CHAPTER FIVE

---

# REVIVAL . . .
# When does it come?

*". . . for it is time to seek the Lord, until he comes . . ."*

(Hosea 10:12, NIV)

We must consider another important question in relation to the subject of revival, when does revival usually come? The answer is simple — when the Church is in declension, or at a low ebb spiritually. It is my belief that we are at such a place right now.

"But surely that cannot be," says someone. "After more than thirty years of charismatic Christianity, when thousands of Christians have been renewed, the Church at last has turned a corner. She is on the way to spiritual greatness and supremacy." Not so. Despite the renewal that has taken place and the great activity in the realm of evangelism — things for which we are indeed thankful — the reality is that, generally speaking, the Church in the West is on the decline. Every year denominations report great reduction in numbers, and the Church's influence in the world grows less and less.

The patient may have all the outward signs of good health, but when proper tests are given, the results show cause for deep concern. Don't be misled, I beg you, by the sabre rattling that goes on in today's Church. We sing, we shout, we hold occasional large meetings and conferences, but when it is all over, what impact have we made on society? Some perhaps, but far less than we ought. "Success," said someone, "is measured not by what we are, but by what we are, compared to what we could be." All the good we accomplish is nothing compared to what needs to be accomplished. The world laughs at our attempts to influence it. It sees us as weak, feeble and ineffectual.

As far as the Church in the West is concerned, there are signs that it is fast declining and losing its influence in the world. Why? We need to explore and face the issues concerned.

## Prayer

The Church of today, generally speaking, is a prayerless Church. Many churches go from week to week without a public prayer meeting of any kind. More upsetting is the fact that many individual Christians have no regular times of private prayer when they commune alone with God. There are exceptions, of course, but in general there is such a perfunctory attitude toward prayer that it is little less than scandalous. The public prayer meeting has often been called 'The Cinderella of the Church', and how fitting that description is of contemporary Christianity. How many churches do you know where as many attend the prayer meeting as the Sunday morning worship service?

"We wish revival would come to us as it came in the Hebrides," said a pastor to Leonard Ravenhill — author of *Why Revival Tarries*. "But revival didn't come to the Hebrides by wishing," said Ravenhill. "The heavens were opened and the mighty power of the Lord shook those islands because a group of people waited, tear-stained and travailing, before the throne of the living God." The birth of a child is preceded by months of burden and days of travail: so is the birth of revival. Jesus prayed for His Church, but then, to bring it to birth, He *gave* Himself in death. It was when Zion *travailed* that she brought forth children (Isaiah 66:8).

## Compromise

Another reason why the Church in the West is in a state of decline is because it has compromised its convictions. Why does the Church of the West not suffer for the faith? Dietrich Bonhoeffer said, "Suffering is the badge of the Christian." Luther said, "Suffering is one of the marks of the true Church." Paul said, "All who desire to live a godly life in Christ Jesus will be persecuted" (2 Timothy 3:12, RSV). And Jesus said, "If they persecuted me, they will persecute you" (John 15:20, NIV).

In the light of these statements, I ask again: why does the Church in the West not suffer for the faith? The ugly truth is that we tend to avoid suffering by compromise. Our moral lives are often not much higher than the standards of the world. Our lives do not challenge and rebuke unbelievers by their integrity and purity. The world sees nothing in us to despise. We are seldom bold to rebuke vice or speak out against the injustices in society. Issues like abortion on demand, homosexual practices and other abominations deserve our united condemnation, but many in the Church mind their own business lest people are offended. The Christian message is diluted to such an extent that we escape suffering by compromise.

Suppose we raised our standards, tightened our disciplines, and spoke out against the breaking of God's laws without fear or favour — what would happen? There would be a huge public outcry. We would be ridiculed, scorned and vilified in the press, on radio and on television. But, at the same time, the Church would be carried by God into a place of mighty spiritual revival.

*Finance*

Yet another evidence for the decline of today's Church is the way in which we rob God of His tithes and offerings. The Church will never be powerful until Christians recognise and understand the principles that govern financial giving. Giving must begin with tithes and offerings to God. No Christian can afford to neglect this. If we give to Him, He has promised that He will "open the windows of heaven" (Malachi 3:10). I am convinced, from the letters I receive, the people I talk to and the reports of others, that multitudes of Christians are robbing God through neglect of tithes and offerings. What is the tithe? The tithe is the first ten percent of our income. This belongs to the Lord. God encourages us to give offerings to meet special needs, but these offerings are above and beyond the tithe. Those who say that tithing is part of the law and does not apply today are quite wrong as the tithe was established before the law was given by Moses (Genesis 14:20), and tithing was reaffirmed by Christ in the New Testament (Matthew 23:23). God also promises that when we are faithful in our tithes and offerings, he "will prevent pests from devouring ... crops, and the vines ..." (Malachi 3:11, NIV).

I am convinced that many of the financial difficulties in which Christians find themselves are due to their failure to tithe. This might sound harsh and legalistic to some, but don't, I beg you, dismiss the principle on those grounds. I have seen it working in my own life and in the lives of many others. Our failure to give tithes and offerings to the Lord will prevent Him from "rebuking the devourer" for our sakes. We will be left to fend for ourselves.

## Worldliness

The Church is spiritually declining because of its worldliness. Some think of worldliness as attendance at cinemas, discos, bars, and so on. But worldliness is much deeper than that. You can refrain from attending theatres, cinemas, discos or watching television, and still be worldly. Worldliness is an attitude of mind — it means thinking like the world. And there is evidence that the Church has allowed itself to be squeezed into the mould of the world. Instead of letting Scripture be our standard and guide, we tend to form conclusions based on humanistic thinking — the way of the world. For example, take this issue — one supported not only by the world, but by large numbers of Christians also — that husbands and wives have equal rights and responsibilities in society. Not so, says the Bible. Both are equal before God, but both do not have equal responsibilities: "Wives, submit to your husbands as to the Lord. For the husband is the head of the wife as Christ is the head of the church, his body, of which he is the Saviour. Now as the church submits to Christ, so also wives should submit to their husbands in everything. Husbands, love your wives, just as Christ loved the church and gave himself up for her . . ." (Ephesians 5:22–25, NIV). Take another view held by the world and also by many Christians — the standard for all behaviour is love. No, says the Bible, the standard for behaviour is truth: "Now we know that God's judgment . . . is based on truth" (Romans 2:2, NIV). Take yet another popular view of life, and one supported by many Christians — marriages that are unhappy qualify for divorce. The answer, according to Scripture, is to overcome self-centredness and put one's own interests last: "Do nothing out of selfish ambition or vain conceit, but in humility consider others better than yourselves. Each of you should look not only to your own interests, but also to the interests of others" (Philippians 2:3–4,

NIV). Slowly but surely the Church in this generation is allowing its thinking to be cast in the mould of the world. Apostasy occurs when the world influences the Church. In revival, the Church influences the world.

## Unrepentance

What was the urgent note that characterised New Testament Christianity, but is scarcely heard in the Church today? Why, repentance of course! Time after time, in the Acts of the Apostles, the call to repentance was sounded. The preaching of the early apostles was dominated by this theme. The mandatory nature of repentance was woven throughout the entire fabric of the life and ministry of Jesus Himself, and its urgent necessity repeatedly proclaimed. But repentance is a missing note in today's Church. "Nowadays," says James Robinson, an American evangelist, "there is abroad an 'easy believism'. We tell people, 'Say this prayer after me and you will have the gift of eternal life, a mansion on the main street of heaven, a diamond-studded crown, and you will be ruler over five cities in the Millennium.'" An exaggeration? Well maybe, but there is still enough truth in it to hurt.

When men and women are not challenged to repent as they come into the Christian life, then they enter it with their ego still intact and dominant. Is it any wonder that we have so many Christians in the Church today who are argumentative, self-centred and rebellious? They never really surrendered their will when they entered the Christian life, and when any issue comes up between their will and God's will, they, never having learned the way of obedience and repentance, take a self-centred stance — one that is usually in opposition to the Almighty. A church which does not recognise the importance of repentance is a church that is rapidly in decline.

## Attitudes

Yet another of these signs is the *unloving attitudes of Christians toward one another*. Some time ago, I wrote to ten Christian leaders in Great Britain, asking if they would share, openly and frankly, where they saw the greatest need for concern in today's Church. All, with one exception, put at the top of his list the harsh, critical and unloving attitudes which Christians have one toward the other. A man I know, who travels the country visiting churches of all denominations, said: "The biggest single issue that muffles the voice of the Church is the hostile and unloving attitudes Christians have one toward another." The truth is that such unloving attitudes can never be entirely eliminated from the Church by powerful preaching, expert counselling, or by writing about it. These things can help, but the real answer lies in a mighty Holy Spirit revival that cleanses the Church of all its blemishes and impurities, and gives it once again a powerful voice in the world.

We must conclude our examination of the

signs and evidences of today's declining Church. Although, as we have been saying, there is a great deal of zeal and activity in today's Church, it has, nevertheless, the smell of decay upon it. This is evidenced in its general attitude of prayerlessness, its tendency to imbibe the attitudes of the world, its willingness to compromise, its disregard of God's principles of finance, its failure to preach and practise the truth of wholehearted repentance, and the unloving attitudes of Christians toward one another.

Our condition is desperate, but, take heart, for, as Peter Lewis says, "Revival comes to a desperate church not a triumphalist one."

# CHAPTER SIX

# REVIVAL . . .
# How does it
# Begin?

*". . . Will you not revive us
again, that your people may
rejoice in you?"*

**(Psalm 85:6, NIV)**

We turn our focus on another important question that has to do with the issue of revival: How do revivals begin? Quite simply, the answer is that revivals begin in the sovereign purposes of God. Man has little to do with them: they are initiated not on earth, but in heaven. There are many things that Christians, by dedicated and spiritual effort, can bring to pass in the Church, but revival is not one of them. We said earlier that evangelism, counselling, preaching, teaching, and other such things are work that men and women do for God. Revival is work that God does for men and women.

It is at this point — the sovereignty of God — that Christians tend to differ in their thinking about revival. One school of thought says: "Revival is a sovereign act of God, and there is absolutely nothing that man has to do with it. God sends revival when He wills and does not consult or confer with any of His creation." Another school of thought says: "Revival can happen any time the Church wants it — providing she is willing to pay the price." Charles Finney believed this. "Revival," he said, "can happen in the Church the moment we are prepared to meet God's conditions."

The truth, as is so often the case, is found, I believe, somewhere between these opposing views. Revival is a sovereign act of God in the sense that He alone can produce it, but it is transported to earth on the wings of fervent, believing prayer. Every revival in history — Pentecost included — began in heaven, but flowed into the Church across the ramp of intercessory prayer. This view, I believe, neither robs God of His sovereignty, nor man of his responsibility. I have thought long and hard on this matter, and I have come to the conclusion that there are two rails running through Scripture — one is the sovereignty of God and the other is the responsibility of man. If you keep to just one of those rails, you end up being derailed. Those who talk only of the sovereignty of God end up minimising the responsibility of man. Those who talk only of the responsibility of man end up minimising the sovereignty of God. When we move along both rails, making sure that we do not place a disproportionate emphasis on either truth, then we are more likely to arrive at sounder judgments and better conclusions.

A single statement by John Wesley, which I have quoted on numerous occasions, has helped me more than anything I have ever read to balance these great truths of the sovereignty of God and the responsibility of man. He said, "God does nothing redemptively in the world — except through prayer."

Can you see what he is saying? Whenever God wants to bring His redemptive purposes to pass here on earth, He does not move arbitrarily but respects the principle of prayer, which He Himself has established. He, therefore, touches the hearts of certain of His people to pray — it may only be a few — and thus proceeds to transmit His purposes along the ramp that prayer has built. God never acts against His nature. He would cease to be God if He did so. And His nature is to use, not ignore, the great principle of prayer which He has so wonderfully established in His universe.

So although, from the divine point of view, revival begins in the sovereign purposes of God, it would be true to say, I believe, that from the human point of view, it begins in the hearts of those who are burdened to see God work in an extraordinary way.

John Wallace, Principal of the Bible College I attended in my youth, used to say: "Before there can be a blessing, somebody has to bear a burden." He went on to illustrate it in this way: "Before deliverance came to the nation of Israel in Egypt, Moses had to bear a burden. Before the great temple of God was built, Solomon had to bear a burden. Before the sins of the world could be removed, Jesus had to bear a burden. *Before there can be a blessing, somebody has to bear a burden.*" This is one of the great principles of Scripture which can be traced right through the Bible from Genesis to Revelation. It can be seen at work, too, in the history of revival.

Before God comes from heaven to work in extraordinary ways, He places the burden of revival on the hearts of certain of His people. Why some should be selected to carry this burden and others not, I cannot say, except that it is a mystery we must ascribe to the sovereignty of God. One thing is sure, however, God never goes over the head of His Church to introduce redemptive changes in His universe. When revival comes to the West, it will come through the hearts of those who have been greatly burdened to pray.

But revival is not only a sovereign work of God: it is a sudden work of God. Revival begins without much preamble and without warning. Pentecost began in this way you remember: "When the day of Pentecost had *come . . . suddenly* a sound came from heaven like the rush of a mighty wind" (Acts 2:1–2, RSV). This is brought out very clearly in the book of Habakkuk (3:1–3). After the prophet has prayed for revival: "O Lord, revive thy work in the midst of the years," the next verse goes on to say: "God came from Teman, the Holy One from Mount Paran." The original Hebrew here, so I am told, conveys the impression of suddenness. Following Habakkuk's prayer, God came suddenly, and without warning, to revive and reinvigorate His people.

When revival came to Ulster in the nineteenth century — it came *suddenly*. When revival came to Wales in 1904 — it came *suddenly*. When revival came to the Hebrides in the middle of last century — it came *suddenly*. Study the record of any revival throughout history and you will find that God came to His people unheralded and unannounced. It sometimes happens that He imparts to a few people a sense of His approaching presence, but the actual breakthrough always comes with startling suddenness. Tonight we may go to sleep aware that the Church desperately needs revival, and wake up tomorrow to find ourselves right in the middle of it. Oh, that it may be so.

Revival also begins in the most unlikely places. Pentecost, you remember, began not in the majestic atmosphere of Solomon's Temple, but in an Upper Room. For some reason, God seems to delight in bypassing the places where we might expect revival to break out — in a splendid cathedral or at a large Christian conference — and causes His fire to burst out in a small prayer meeting where only a few are present. In fact, no revival has been an official movement of the Church. This is why revival always astonishes the Church — it flares up where it is least expected.

Have you ever heard of the Primitive Methodist revival in the 1800's? This began not on the historic sites of former Methodist accomplishments, such as in London or Bristol, but in a tiny hamlet on the hillside of Mow Cop near Stoke-on-Trent. Someone described it as the "least likely place in which a revival has ever broken out". And why? Because there were only a few grey, roughly built cottages situated there, inhabited by people with little intellectual ability or learning. The area was bleak, rugged and uninteresting. Nevertheless, this is the place God chose in which to manifest His power and glory. If ever the Church receives a blow to its pride, it is when God breaks forth in revival. He shows, in that act, how unimpressed He is with ornate buildings or exquisite architecture. When God came down to meet Moses in Midian, did He do so because Midian was a holy and sanctified place? No, He came not because it was holy, but to *make* it holy (Exodus 3:1–5).

One revival in North Wales in the eighteenth century began in the most unexpected way with the death of a highly-respected minister. As the crowds gathered at his funeral service, the Holy Spirit broke in and produced a mighty revival. The 1904 revival is connected with the name of Evan Roberts, but it really began in a meeting at which Evan Roberts was present, when a shy and timid 16 year-old girl stood up and blurted out, "I love Jesus Christ with all my heart."

Consider again the great revival which took place in New York in 1847. A Dutch business-man, Jeremiah Lanphier, advertised a midday prayer meeting in his office. At the first meeting, six people were present. So mightily did the Spirit work amongst those six, that within six months more than 100,000 businessmen were crowding into prayer meetings all over the city. In Uganda, a revival broke out when one Christian walked more than a hundred miles to ask the forgiveness of a Christian whom he had wronged twenty years previously.

The question is often asked by those who study the origin of revival: Why does God bypass organisations, committees and the well-oiled machinery of the Church in order to bring a revival to birth? He does it so that the glory might not be man's, but God's. The Almighty delights to be involved in situations where there is no doubt who is responsible for the victory which has been achieved. And revival is such a situation.

Revivals begin not only in the most unlikely places and in the most unexpected ways, but also with the most unassuming people. Don't think, when you read of famous names such as Charles Finney, Christmas Evans, and so on, that all revivals begin with such outstanding person-alities. In fact, although revivals have marked the history of the Church throughout its long course of almost twenty centuries, most of these began with unknown individuals. And those who were well-known, generally speaking, played little part in the revival until they themselves had passed through a time of deep repentance and inner cleansing.

Ever heard of James McQuilkee? I'll be surprised if you have. Yet he was a man whom God used mightily in the Ulster revival in 1859. Have you heard of David Morgan? God used him greatly in one of the revivals that shook Wales, yet prior to the revival he was known to no more than the five hundred or so people who lived in the small village where he was brought up. In researching this subject, I came up with names of men who never merited a mention in the usual books on revival, but who were used by God nevertheless to bring about His mighty purposes here on earth.

I am conscious, as I write, that within me is a tendency to try to explain why God works in this strange way, but the Spirit seems to be saying to my heart: "Don't try to explain my ways, for they are higher than your ways, and my thoughts higher than your thoughts. If you can explain a revival — then it is not a revival."

# CHAPTER SEVEN

---

# REVIVAL . . .
## What is its
## Purpose?

*"Praise be to his glorious name forever; may the whole earth be filled with his glory . . ."*

**(Psalm 72:19, NIV)**

What is the purpose of revival? Why does God send these periodic awakenings? Those who have made a special study of revival tell us that in every century of the Church, somewhere or other in the world, a revival containing one or more of the features of the first Pentecost has taken place. Again we ask: What is God's purpose behind these great awakenings? The primary purpose behind every spiritual revival is to bring glory to God's Name. Lose sight of this and you can miss your way regarding this great and important subject.

Many Christians are motivated to pray for revival because they are tired of the dull, apathetic condition of the Church, and long for the kind of meetings revival produces — meetings in which there is great spiritual fervour and excitement. There is no doubt that revival creates such an atmosphere, but if that is our primary motivation, then we have simply fallen prey to the age-old problem — self-centred interests.

But someone asks: Isn't it legitimate for Christians to enjoy themselves in God's presence, and to long for services which pulsate with divine power? Yes, of course it is — this is certainly a legitimate desire. The problem arises when that desire takes priority, for then your interests, and not God's, take pre-eminence. I say again, the primary purpose behind every spiritual revival is to bring glory to God's Name. When we make His goal our goal, then we bring ourselves in line with His infinite purposes. And when we are linked to His purposes, we are linked to His power. The main purpose of our being in the world, and in the Church, is not to enjoy ourselves, but to glorify God. God's glory is to be the goal — enjoyment the result. Reverse the order and you end up in conflict with God, and with the structure of the universe.

Some of the great theologians of the past, when laying down guidelines for the worship of the Church, asked the question: "What is the chief end of man?" With absolute accuracy and splendid conciseness, they answered: "Man's chief end is to glorify God, and to enjoy Him forever." Any pursuit of pleasure, even spiritual pleasure, apart from God who made us, is a violation of God's purpose in the creation of man, and a travesty of man's best interests. Man was not made for himself but for God.

"To pursue self-gratification to the abandonment of God," the theologians went on to say, "is to guarantee immediate disappointment and eventually total ruin." Now don't dismiss this as mere theological rhapsodising: it is an important point. The greatest need of the Church at this moment is to put God's interests first, and other interests second. Some may be prepared to pray earnestly for revival, fearing that if it doesn't come, their very way of life will be undermined or destroyed. Others may pray for revival motivated by a concern for loved ones who are in sin. Still others may pray for revival out of a concern for the bankrupt condition of the Church. But worthy as such aims may be, let it be understood that the primary reason why we should pray for and desire a spiritual revival is for the glory of God.

A second purpose for which God sends revival is to elevate His Church to the level of power it was always intended to enjoy. The history of the Church has been one of 'peaks and troughs'. At times it soars in the chariot of revival with the world at its feet. Other times it is beggared and bankrupt — the laughing stock of society. History records that 50 years after Pentecost, the Church began to lapse into lukewarmness and infidelity, and by the end of the first century had lost much of its spiritual supremacy. It stayed this way for over a century. Then at the beginning of the third century, God stepped in to revive His people. In subsequent centuries, this pattern of 'peaks and troughs' is clearly traceable. During one period the Church is up, in the next, it is down. Then when it looks as if it is finished and will never rise again, God graciously steps in and touches the hearts of His people in revival power.

Why should it be that with all the great ministries which God sets in the Church — gifted pastors, teachers, prophets, and so on — it should fall into periods of lukewarmness and declension?

There can only be one answer — the waywardness of the human heart. Such is the human condition that even the most spiritual people can allow their hearts to be turned away from God by things such as materialism and humanism. So wilful are their desires that the ordinary ministries of the Church cannot move them. It is at such times that God sends revival.

As we continue meditating on one of the reasons why God sends revival, to elevate His Church to the position it was always intended to enjoy, a question is raised which we will look at in greater detail later: Is the Church at present experiencing all that God intends for her? Hardly. Someone has described the Church here in Great Britain as 'a sleeping giant'. "But how can that be," asks someone, "when the Church in general is caught up in a tremendous amount of evangelistic activity for the last decade of the century. Isn't this evidence that the 'sleeping giant' has awakened?" Not necessarily. Any evangelistic concern is good and proper and has my support one hundred percent. When I use the term 'sleeping giant', I am using it in relation to what the Church could be doing, not in relation to what it is doing. When revival comes, the 'sleeping giant' will not just stir and awaken, but will move with such dynamic power and impact that it will make a mass evangelistic crusade look like a Sunday School picnic.

Imagine your church with every member living together in harmony, with not one sleeping Christian left, with every individual on fire for God, and with everyone intent on seeing the will of Christ accomplished. To this startling picture, add the power that produced such astonishing scenes on the Day of Pentecost. Now multiply this until it fills every church in every community, every town, every city in the nation. Unleash all this mighty power against the forces of sin and evil, THAT is revival!

God sends revival in order to arrest the attention of an unbelieving world. We have to face the fact that, at the moment, the world hardly recognises the presence of the Church. It pays lip service to it, of course, but deep down unbelievers regard the Church as a relic of the past — archaic and ineffectual. This finds expression in many ways. When a minister is portrayed in a play, he is invariably a stilted caricature of the real thing, a dyspeptic creature, who speaks in a silly, affected voice, and who is more non-Christian than Christian. It would be impossible to deny, of course, that occasionally one meets members of the clergy who come close to the caricature, but to reason from the particular to the general is foolish and absurd.

Another idea the world has of the Church is that we are a group of psychologically immature people needing a religious prop in order to face the challenge of living in a strife-torn world. But that isn't the worst of it. Men and women in the world project the weaknesses, the mistakes, the inadequacies of the Church on to God, and say:

"If there is a God, what kind of God can He be to give His Name to such a motley crowd as this?" Revival changes all that. It puts God right in the middle of His people, giving them a voice so powerful that when the Church speaks — the world sits up and listens. To those who say that the Church of Jesus Christ is weak and enervated, we can reply: "That is how it may look at present. But just wait — our God is on the way."

Permit me to ask you a personal question: Does it grieve you that we are living in a godless and morally bankrupt age? Does it grieve you that the Name of our God is ridiculed and blasphemed in almost every section of society? Does it grieve you that men scoff at the Bible, this matchless book which God brought into being by the power of His Holy Spirit, and regard it with no more interest than the works of Shakespeare?

The more I see and hear arrogant men denying or blaspheming the very God who gave them breath, the more I can understand and identify with the Psalmist in Psalm 46. The writer penned these words because he was conscious that all around him godless men were repudiating the Almighty by their blasphemous utterances and sinful lives, and he petitions God that such men might be silenced. The Psalmist implores God to do something, to come from heaven and stop the mouths of those who were ridiculing Him. He wants God to rise up and confront an unbelieving world and say: "Be still, and know that I am God" (Psalm 46:10, NIV).

Do not you, too, when you hear the Lord's Name taken in vain, spiritual concerns mocked and eternal issues flippantly treated, feel the way this Psalmist felt? If you are a Christian, and you don't, then, believe me, there is something deeply wrong with you. To hear sacred things treated with contempt and eternal matters trivialised without indignation is not possible to those who truly love God and serve His Son, the Lord Jesus Christ.

One of the purposes of God in sending revival is to make the world sit up and take notice. We turn again to the Day of Pentecost as a classic example of this. We read that when the Holy Spirit fell, the people who were in Jerusalem, together with all the strangers gathered there for the feast, came to where the disciples were, and said, "What does this mean?" They were arrested by the mighty outpouring of God's eternal power. That is always the case in revival — unbelievers, albeit out of curiosity, gather in the presence of the unusual and ask the question: "What does this mean?" (Acts 2:12, NIV).

As a boy I remember hearing a great preacher, who was converted in the 1904 Welsh revival, recounting his experience of conversion. "I was a drunkard and a down-and-out," he said, "but one night someone came into the pub where I was drinking and said, 'There's some strange things going on in the church down the road.

People are crying, falling on the floor, and all kinds of things are happening.' My friends and I went down to the church to scoff and have some fun. But when I entered the door it was as if I had been arrested. I sobered up immediately, and fell to my knees calling upon God to have mercy on my soul." And then he added some words which I have heard on numerous occasions in connection with revival: "I went to scoff but I stayed to pray."

Clearly, there is nothing the Church can do to produce such an impact and an effect. Evangelistic crusades, rallies, concerts can attract and appeal to the world, but only revival can arrest it.

# CHAPTER EIGHT

# REVIVAL . . .
## The Practical Effects

*"Thy people shall be willing in
the day of thy power . . ."*

(Psalm 110:3, AV)

We turn now to consider another important question in relation to revival: What are its results? We have already touched on some aspects of this, but now we examine the matter in greater depth.

Revival, as we have seen, results in greater power and purity in the Church. But what does this mean in practical terms? First, it means that long-standing habits of self-indulgence, that surrender neither to reason nor to God, will be broken when revival comes. The doors and walls of the prison of self, in which so many Christians are incarcerated, will be broken down by revival. The Lord who came to declare freedom to the captive will enable His people to be free indeed. Unconfessed sins that have been covered over for years will be brought to light. The interesting thing about the exposure of sin in times of revival is that the fear and shame which usually accompany such moments are thought of as nothing in comparison with the prospect of forgiveness and cleansing.

Second, it means that the plans and strategies of the Church are thrown into upheaval and disarray. Goals and ambitions once thought to be of the utmost spiritual importance are seen to be but temporal. God's timing, God's purpose, God's plans rule the day. Some church structures may collapse when revival comes, but are then rebuilt "according to the pattern shown in the Mount" (Hebrews 8:5, AV). Traditions may perish. Programmes may have to be abandoned and schedules rearranged. Well-rehearsed choir numbers may remain unsung for ever. Nothing is ever the same again in the Church when revival comes.

A third result of revival is the breaking of the will. When God moves from heaven in extraordinary power, all that stands in opposition to Him may be expected to be broken and cast aside. Pastors, elders and leaders will be broken by revival. Men who have preached interesting and eloquent sermons may discover their ministry has the value of "wood, hay and stubble". Sermons and messages which seemed satisfactory enough in previous days will never do for revival. God, the Master Workman, will break the congregation, too. Men and women, who had resisted Him and His Word, now find themselves pliant and ready to do His bidding. But the breaking always leads to a remaking. God not only pulls down — He builds up.

A fourth result of revival among the people of God is that holiness becomes the prime object of their lives. To be like Jesus often becomes the theme song of a revival. Christians are consumed with a desire to conform to Christ's image, and the principle of Romans 8:29 — "God decided that those who came to him . . . should become like his Son" (TLB) — becomes the dominating passion of their lives. The great truths of Scripture are no longer relegated to group discussions in church on a Sunday or in a mid-week house group, but are lived out on a daily basis and applied in every exigency of life. Revived people are truly a holy people.

A fifth result of revival is that Christians become greatly burdened for the souls of unbelievers. Prayer for the eternal welfare of those outside of Christ becomes a passion. Someone said that the word that is characteristic of revival is the word 'Oh'. It comes out continually in the prayers of those who agonize for the lost. "*Oh* God," they cry, "save those who are dying in sin." Nothing short of lasting conversions will satisfy the saints in a time of revival. They pray that the same liberating Spirit that broke and remade them will do the same in the hearts of their friends, families, acquaintances and people throughout the world. New converts are made without arm-twisting. No elaborate plans for follow-up are necessary as new converts stand on their own feet from the moment of conversion.

A sixth result of revival is that Christians begin to manifest the love of Christ toward one another. Those who have borne grudges or have gossiped about other Christians go to those they have wronged and ask for their forgiveness. Maintaining a clear conscience becomes a matter of paramount importance. Those who have sinned privately make their confession to God whom they have wronged. Those who have sinned publicly find the grace and strength to make a public confession. A watching world will look on in amazement as it sees Christians, who had hitherto lived hypocritical lives, now take their faith seriously. The light that shines in a revived Church cannot be put out. It shines more and more until the perfect day.

As we continue meditating on what we can expect to happen when revival comes, we turn our attention away from its effect upon the Church, and consider how it affects the wider community and ultimately the nation.

Some people say that revival is completely irrelevant to such issues as politics and socio-economics, but to hold such a view is to fly in the face of the facts. J. Edwin Orr in his book, *The Second Evangelical Awakening in Britain*, says that when revival came to Wales "drunkenness was immediately cut in half and many public houses went bankrupt. Crime was so diminished that the judges were presented with white gloves signifying that there were no cases of murder, assault, rape, robbery, or such like, to consider. The police became 'unemployed' in many districts. Stoppages occurred in coal mines, not due to unpleasantness between management and workers, but because so many miners became converted and stopped using foul language that the horses which hauled the coal trucks in the mines could no longer understand what was being said to them, and transportation ground to a halt."

In an age when so much is being said about the Church's duty to become involved in bringing about positive social and political changes, it is salutary to observe the tremendous effects which God's people have had upon society when they are in a state of revival. When the Church communicates her unique message in the power of the Holy Spirit, an improved society is always an early and inevitable result. Those who are not even converted sense a heightening of morality, and are strangely restrained and affected by it.

At this moment, thousands of Christians throughout the world are deeply concerned over the high rate of abortion. Despite our strongest protests, we seems powerless to get people to see that life begins at the moment of conception, and that to abort a foetus for any other reason than danger to the life of the mother is an offence in the eyes of God. Though the problem is one that did not affect previous generations to such a degree, and we have no statistics against which we can measure it, I believe, nevertheless, that revival in the Church would greatly affect the thinking of society in relation to this issue. The Holy Spirit flowing out from the Church into the world with power would, in my judgement, cause men and women to feel deeply uncomfortable about abortion. In no time, the laws governing abortion on demand would be changed.

Today subjectivism has taken the place of fixed principles of moral law. Instead of judging conduct on the basis of what God says we now say: "Let your conscience be your guide". But conscience, without the reinforcement of God's Word and the Holy Spirit, can excuse just as easily as it can accuse. Revival would not force men and women to act in ways that are consistent with God's demands in Scripture, but the light it would cast would make men think twice before embarking upon deeds of darkness.

Consider yet another social problem — divorce. In 1951-56 there were 146,186 divorces — an average of approximately 29,000 a year. In 1982, the divorce rate in Great Britain and Northern Ireland was 150,000. In two decades, the divorce rate had rocketed! At the end of the twentieth century the situation is such that if current rates of marital breakdown continue (based on the 1994/5 figures), 41% of all marriages will end in divorce and 28% of all children will experience divorce before they leave school.

What can be done about this problem? Very little, it seems. The Church can teach about the sanctity of marriage for all it is worth, but this seems to make little difference to a secular society. The community, as a whole, tends to make divorce easier and easier. Revival in the Church would, I believe, curb the rising divorce rate. Such would be the power that would flow through the Church, that its voice would be heeded, and its standards recognised and upheld.

Revival would restore a sense of destiny.

Prior to World War Two, the British people believed they had a special destiny in the world. Some aspects of the idea were, of course, quite insupportable. Those who said that whoever resisted Britain resisted heaven, and old memorial tablets in churches to admirals and generals declare this, were speaking from an imperialistic and not a spiritual perspective. Thankfully, most of that imperial pride has gone. Discerning people know that the only country with a future is the country which sets out to bring its purposes in harmony with the purposes of God.

One Christian historian believes that Britain could do that more swiftly than most other countries. The reasons given are these: "She has a longer history and experience of self-government, and long enjoyment of civil, political and religious liberty has given her a maturity of judgment in all these fields, which is still rare among men. Britain has had no civil war for 300 years. Tolerance, fair play and a freedom from frenzy mark the people. The nation has a high destiny still." A revival in the House of God would inevitably overflow into the Houses of Parliament. Revived Christians in government, and other high places, would speak with new power and new authority. Few, if any, would be able to resist the call to Biblical standards and morality. Yes, our country can be a great nation still — but nothing short of revival in the Church can accomplish it.

# CHAPTER NINE

# REVIVAL . . .
## Where it Begins

*"If my people, who are called by
my name, will humble
themselves and pray . . . and turn
from their wicked ways, then will
I hear . . ."*

(2 Chronicles 7:14, NIV)

Having spent the past eight chapters examining the various aspects of revival, we come now to what is perhaps the most important question of all: What is the way to revival? We said that revival is a sovereign act of God, and that the Church is unable to produce it, unable to explain it, and unable to control it. It is a glorious, majestic, mighty, awesome act of God in which He sweeps His Church from spiritual bankruptcy into spiritual riches.

The impression you may have from reading this book is that as revival is a sovereign act of God, and cannot be produced by anyone on earth, then the only thing the Church can do is sit back and wait for God to send it. Nothing could be further from the truth. Revival is most certainly a sovereign act of God, in the sense that only He can initiate it, but whenever God gets ready to revive His Church, He approaches those who are ready to listen to His voice, and instructs them on how to be the channel through whom His Spirit can flow from heaven to earth.

The instructions God gives to His people, when preparing them for revival, are crystallised in 2 Chronicles 7:14.

This verse has been described as "the final and finished formula on how to prepare for revival". It is so important that I propose to devote a whole chapter to it. Before we begin to look at it clause by clause, let me urge you to spend a few minutes memorising it. If you do, I promise you that this text will make more of an impact upon your life than anything else you have ever experienced.

"If my people, who are called by my name, will humble themselves and pray and seek my face and turn from their wicked ways, then will I hear from heaven and will forgive their sin and will heal their land."

We begin with the opening clause: "*If my people, who are called by my name* ... " The truth we have been stressing over and over is, once again, brought to our attention, revival begins with the people of God. To criticise and condemn unbelievers for their unbiblical standards and practices is beginning at the wrong place. Revival relates first to the people of God. Some believe that the term 'people of God' refers to all who have some kind of religious inclination. But the Almighty leaves us in no doubt as to whom He is addressing: "If my people, *who are called by my name.*" He is talking to those who know Him intimately, who have taken His Name upon themselves, and who are linked with Him in a family relationship.

What a responsibility it is to belong to the people of God. After all, whether we like it or not, people judge God by the impression we make upon them. If we fail, they don't reason with themselves and say: "He is only one in a million Christians — the others are a good deal better." No, they observe our way of life, evaluate our actions and our behaviour, and say: "If that's what serving God is like, then I want nothing to do with it." This is why God chooses to begin with His own people when He is about to bring His redemptive purposes to pass in history. Once the people of God are right, then it won't take long to put the world right.

"If my people, who are called by my name, will *humble themselves* ..." Humble themselves? Shouldn't prayer take priority of place here? There is good reason why God puts humility first. It is because pride is one of the biggest barriers to God having His way in His Church. Not for nothing did the old theologians put pride at the head of the list of the "seven deadly sins". "Pride," said Dr. W. E. Sangster, "is the primal sin. Little as we know of the life of the angels, there is evidence for believing that pride led to the revolt of Satan in heaven." It certainly is in the vanguard of any revolt we may make against the God of heaven.

Self-centredness is a blight that affects both the redeemed and the unredeemed. Because we are Christians, it does not mean that we are automatically protected from the disease of self-interest. How many times have you, even though you are a Christian, allowed yourself rather than God to have the benefit of the doubt over some spiritual challenge He gave you? When pride is present, then everything which comes up has an immediate self-reference. Me ... Me ... Me ... or I ... I ... I. There can be no real victory in any Christian's life until they have found victory over pride. The phrase, "humble yourselves", suggests that an act of the will is necessary. God can humble us, but how much more meaningful it becomes when we do it ourselves. Are you a proud person? Then do something today to trample on your pride. Pride has many evil characteristics, but its greatest evil is this — it blocks the way to revival.

"If my people, who are called by my name, will humble themselves *and pray* ..." But Christians *do* pray! But how much? How sincerely? How unselfishly? When did we last stay up late just to pray? When did we last get up early simply to pray? Many Christians go through their Christian life praying by rote, or praying only when they want something for themselves. This isn't the kind of praying God means when He lays down the conditions for revival.

One of the greatest definitions of prayer I know is this: prayer is co-operation with God. Consider what is meant by this phrase — co-operation with God. It is an exercise that links our faculties to our Maker to work out the intentions He had in mind in their creation. Prayer isn't bending God's will to ours, but bending our will to His. We work out the purposes which God has worked out for us.

I read the account of a man who sat and listened to an organist playing a beautiful melody. He said that, behind the organ, he could see a man striking upon bells the same notes the organ was playing. So in addition to the tones of the organ were the tones of the chimes, forming a beautiful accompaniment. Prayer is like that — it means we are striking the same notes as God. We thus become a part of a universal harmony — the music of the spheres. Our little notes are caught up and universalised. Prayer puts us in tune with the Infinite, and then Infinite power works through our finiteness. Milton summed it up when he said, "By small accomplishing great things."

God invites us not merely to pray, but to make the prayer time a deep encounter with Him. "If my people . . . will . . . pray *and seek my face* . . ." The kind of praying God looks for is not the brief, eager-to-get-it-over-with type, but the unhurried waiting before Him — the true seeking of His face. The Old Testament prophets knew how to pray like this. They came before God and laid hold on Him until something great and mighty happened.

Some time ago, when studying the great Biblical prayers such as the prayer of Moses (Exodus 32:31-32), the prayer of Abraham (Genesis 18:23-33) and the prayer of Daniel (Daniel 9:4-19), I made a fascinating and interesting discovery. I found that in all these prayers there were common elements. The prophets, when they prayed, all used the same principles to get God to respond. Now it follows that if we can discover these common elements, and weave them into our prayers, then their presence will greatly strengthen our petitions.

The first ingredient was selflessness. They put others first — themselves last. The second — boldness. They were so convinced of their cause that they had no fear in coming into His presence. The third ingredient was that of reasoned argument. Taking God's own words, and quoting them back to Him, was one of their greatest strategies. God loves to be reasoned with — "'Come now, let us reason together,' says the Lord . . ." (Isaiah 1:18, NIV). A fourth ingredient of the great Biblical prayers was that of being specific. They knew what they wanted, and they asked God straight out for it. All of these ingredients are in this great prayer of Isaiah:

"Look down from heaven and see
>from your lofty throne, holy and glorious.
Where are your zeal and your might?
Your tenderness and compassion are withheld
>from us.
But you are our Father,
>though Abraham does not know us
>or Israel acknowledge us;
you, O Lord, are our Father,
>our Redeemer from of old is your name.
Why, O Lord, do you make us wander from
>your ways and harden our hearts so we
>do not revere you?

Return for the sake of your servants,
>    the tribes that are your inheritance.
For a little while your people
>    possessed your holy place,
>    but now our enemies have trampled
>    down your sanctuary.
We are yours from of old;
>    but you have not ruled over them,
>    they have not been called by your name."
>    (Isaiah 63:15–19, NIV)

"If my people . . . will humble themselves and pray . . . *and turn from their wicked ways* . . ." Can it be true that God's people have wicked ways? Perhaps the Lord meant careless ways, or formal ways — surely not wicked ways? The Bible says wicked ways.

Perhaps we Christians have learned to so rationalise some of our actions and our behaviour that we do not realise quite how wicked they really are. The tendency in this day and age is to let ourselves off lightly whenever we have done wrong. We use such euphemisms as: "Well, the only one I hurt was myself", or: "It isn't all that important." But any violation of a Biblical principle is immensely serious. When we pass on a juicy bit of gossip concerning someone who has erred and strayed — that is a wicked way. When we criticise and condemn those who have the spiritual oversight over us, rather than bring them before God in prayer — that is a wicked way. When we wound others by our words or actions, and fail to ask their and God's forgiveness — that is a wicked way. When the acquisition of money dominates our thinking and crowds out eternal things — that is a wicked way. When we watch degrading films or read morally debilitating literature — that is a wicked way.

Can these things, and there are many others, go on in the hearts of those who claim to know the Way — God's own people, called by His Name? I am sorry to say they can. If we are guilty of any of these wicked ways, then let us, here and now, repent of them and have done with them. As the people of God, the world has a right to expect us to be different.

"If my people . . . will humble themselves and pray . . . and turn from their wicked ways, *then will I hear from heaven and will forgive their sin and will heal their land.*"

What a hope-filled promise! What a healing word! "I will hear . . . forgive . . . and heal." Do you believe that? Do you believe that as you prepare your heart through repentance and prayer, God will come again and restore the Church to its former glory? It may be a lot for some of you to believe, especially those of you who find yourselves in a lethargic local church. But not to believe it would make God a liar. Believe it then! With all your heart. Put your whole weight behind the promise. Humble yourself before God. Pray more — in private and in the public prayer meeting. If your church doesn't have a prayer meeting, then gently ask why this is so. Lay hold of the grace of God to get rid of everything in your life of which you know He disapproves. Hear His promise again. Even though you have memorised it, it will do you good to see it spelt out in full:

> "*If my people, who are called by my name, will humble themselves and pray and seek my face and turn from their wicked ways, then will I hear from heaven and will forgive their sin and will heal their land.*"

2 Chronicles 7:14, NIV

## CHAPTER TEN

# REVIVAL . . .
## A Personal Checklist

*"Search me, O God, and know my heart; test me and know my anxious thoughts."*

**(Psalm 139:23, NIV)**

Having explored this thrilling and important subject of revival, we need to spend these last few pages giving ourselves a spiritual check-up. It is so easy to allow truth to enter our minds without allowing it to affect our wills. After all, it is only what we act upon that we really believe. It is important to keep in mind, as you go through this check-up, that however deficient you are spiritually, God's love for you remains constant and certain. He loves you as you are, but He loves you too much to let you stay as you are — hence His gentle prodding toward maturity. I say again, it is extremely important that you keep this in mind, otherwise a check-up like this can be devastating, and thus countr-productive.

*I must ask myself:*
How long is it since I became a Christian? ☐
Have I grown steadily in that time? ☐
Was I ever further forward than I am now? ☐
Can I measure a degree of steady progress
in my spiritual understanding? ☐
I wonder how much of my life is left? ☐
Is my reading of the Scriptures a mere
duty, or is it a delight? ☐
Am I deeply conscious of the need for
more private and corporate prayer? ☐

Do I think more of a larger income than I do of my spiritual development? ☐

Am I a *deeply* spiritual person? ☐

Do I live day by day in conscious dependence on the Lord? ☐

Does the need for revival have much place in my prayer life? ☐

Have I hurt or wounded anyone and not yet apologised? ☐

How much time have I given in the past to acquainting myself with the history of revival? ☐

How much time am I prepared to give in the future? ☐

Do I give myself to God, then draw back when I realise just how much is involved? ☐

How do I feel about undertaking this spiritual check-up — challenged, bored, unconcerned? ☐

Do I grieve when I hear the name of Christ blasphemed, or have I grown insensitive to such things? ☐

When my non-Christian friends ask me about my interests, do I take the opportunity to share Christ? ☐

How long is it since I last shed tears over the condition of the world and the Church? ☐

Am I fighting a losing battle with evil thoughts? ☐

When did I last undertake a spiritual fast? ☐

If I was arrested for being a Christian, would there be enough evidence to convict me? □

Am I a faithful steward of the money that flows through my hands? □

Do I give at least one-tenth of my income to God? □

What do other members of my family think about my Christian life at home? □

Does my conscience function in the way God designed it — by objecting to evil and approving good? □

Do I watch degrading films in the cinema or on television? □

Am I dependent on alcohol to see me through life's problems and difficulties? □

Have I debts which are outstanding and well overdue? □

Am I honest in relation to my employer — giving my whole energy to my responsibilities, and remembering that I am not employed by an earthly employer, but by God? (Romans 13:1) □

Am I eager for revival? □

# CONCLUSION

# REVIVAL . . .
# Preparing the
# Way

*". . . Prepare the way for the Lord, make straight paths for Him."*

(Luke 3:4, NIV)

Nothing else but an extraordinary move of God can meet the urgent need of the Church and the world at this hour.

Evangelism, conferences, seminars, rallies, and the other activities of the Church, while important and necessary, are, however, inadequate in themselves to arrest the attention of an unbelieving world. *God must come down from heaven and visit us in mighty Holy Spirit power*. My personal conviction is that, in conjunction with His prepared people — *He will*.

I was greatly encouraged, when starting on this book, by some words of Bishop Wilberforce. This is what he wrote many years ago: "We look at some mighty estuary which the retiring tide has left bare of water. We see a vast expanse of sand and mud, with little trickling rivulets wearing their scarcely appreciable way through the resisting banks of that yielding ooze. The man who knows not the secrets of the tide, and the influence by which God governs nature would say: How can you expect to see that great expanse covered? But high in the heavens, the unseen Ruler has set the orb, which shall bring in her time, the tides of the surrounding ocean, and when the appointed moment comes, suddenly and sufficiently, the whole is covered by the rejoicing water, and again it is one silvery surface, sandless and mudless — *because the Lord has willed it.*"

My Christian friend, take heart. The unseen Ruler has willed the revival of His people. The day of His power is not far distant. But He looks to you and me to "prepare the way".

## PRAYER

Gracious Father, You have given me a commission — a commission to "prepare the way" for the coming revival. I am the wire along which Your power runs. Keep me connected and insulated. For Your praise and honour and glory. Amen.

# A SELECTIVE
# BIBLIOGRAPHY
# ON REVIVAL

Brian Edwards, *Revival! A people saturated with God* (Evangelical Press).

Eifion Evans, *Revival comes to Wales — the story of the 1859 revival in Wales* (Evangelical Press of Wales).

Eifion Evans, *The Welsh Revival of 1904* (Evangelical Press of Wales).

Charles G. Finney, *Finney on Revival* (Bethany House Publishers, USA; Nova Publishing, UK Distributor).

Martyn Lloyd-Jones, *Revival* (Marshall Pickering).

John Pollock, *Whitefield: the Evangelist* (Kingsway Publications).

Leonard Ravenhill, *Revival Praying* (Bethany House Publishers, USA; Nova Publishing, UK Distributor).

Emyr Roberts and R. Geraint Gruffydd, *Revival and its Fruit — two lectures* (Evangelical Library of Wales).

Richard Owen Roberts, *Revival* (Tyndale, USA; Scripture Press, UK Distributor).

Colin Whittaker, *Great Revivals* (Marshall Pickering).

Andrew Woolsey, *The Channel of Revival*, a biography of Duncan Campbell (The Faith Mission).

# WHY REVIVAL TARRIES

# *Why Revival Tarries*

LEONARD RAVENHILL

KINGSWAY PUBLICATIONS
EASTBOURNE

*To Martha, my gracious wife*

# CONTENTS

# FOREWORD

GREAT industrial concerns have in their employ men who are needed only when there is a break-down somewhere. When something goes wrong with the machinery, these men spring into action to locate and remove the trouble and get the machinery rolling again.

For these men a smoothly operating system has no interest. They are specialists concerned with trouble and how to find and correct it.

In the kingdom of God things are not too different. God has always had His specialists whose chief concern has been the moral breakdown, the decline in the spiritual health of the nation or the church. Such men were Elijah, Jeremiah, Malachi and others of their kind who appeared at critical moments in history to reprove, rebuke, and exhort in the name of God and righteousness.

A thousand or ten thousand ordinary priests or pastors or teachers could labor quietly on almost un-noticed while the spiritual life of Israel or the church was normal. But let the people of God go astray from the paths of truth and immediately the specialist appeared almost out of nowhere. His instinct for trouble brought him to the help of the Lord and of Israel.

Such a man was likely to be drastic, radical, possibly at times violent, and the curious crowd that gathered to watch him work soon branded him as extreme, fanatical, negative. And in a sense they were right. He was single-minded, severe, fearless, and these were the qualities the circumstances demanded. He shocked some, frightened others and alienated not a few, but he knew who had called him and what he was sent to do. His ministry was geared to the emergency, and that fact marked him out as different, a man apart.

To such men as this the church owes a debt too heavy to pay. The curious thing is that she seldom tries to pay him while he lives, but the next generation builds his sepulcher and writes his biography, as if instinctively and awkwardly to discharge an obligation the previous generation to a large extent ignored.

Those who know Leonard Ravenhill will recognize in him the religious specialist, the man sent from God not to carry on the conventional work of the church, but to beard the priests of Baal on their own mountaintop, to shame the careless priest at the altar, to face the false prophet and warn the people who are being led astray by him.

Such a man as this is not an easy companion. The professional evangelist who leaves the wrought-up meeting as soon as it is over to hie him to the most expensive restaurant to feast and crack jokes with his retainers will find this man something of an embarrassment, for he cannot turn off the burden of the Holy Ghost as one would turn off a faucet. He insists upon being a Christian all the time, everywhere; and again, that marks him out as different.

Toward Leonard Ravenhill it is impossible to be neutral. His acquaintances are divided pretty neatly into two classes, those who love and admire him out of all proportion and those who hate him with perfect hatred. And what is true of the man is sure to be true of his books, of this book. The reader will either close its pages to seek a place of prayer or he will toss it away in anger, his heart closed to its warnings and appeals.

Not all books, not even all good books come as a voice from above, but I feel that this one does. It does because its author does, and the spirit of the author breathes through his book.

A. W. Tozer

# PREFACE

Here is my simple offering of loaves and fishes—just plain diet, lacking the ice and spice of the wedding cake. Like a sailor I once saw pounding a soldier "because," said the sailor, "he insulted my mother," so my Lord is insulted and His Church slighted. And, believe me, under this double injury, I smart. The Church has many adversaries. Can my sword sleep, then, in my hand? Never!

I estimate that in the English edition alone, a million people read each issue of the "Herald of His Coming." Some of the chapters in this book are articles in old Heralds and have been read by millions. (I am neither ashamed nor proud of this.) There are a dozen other "Heralds" in Spanish, German, French, etc. Enough to say that through this paper, along with the "Alliance Witness" and other periodicals, God has seen fit to make non-academic essays a means of blessing to many. I pray that you gentle readers may be helped by them.

My sincere thanks to my esteemed friend and spiritual counselor, Dr. A. W. Tozer, for his kindness in writing the foreword. My unstinted praise to Mrs. Hines and her daughter, Ruth, for their fine work in typing and correcting the manuscripts. (All profits from this book go to overseas missions. May we live with eternity's values in view.)

Leonard Ravenhill

*No erudition, no purity of diction, no width of mental outlook, no flowers of eloquence, no grace of person can atone for lack of fire. Prayer ascends by fire. Flame gives prayer access as well as wings, acceptance as well as energy. There is no incense without fire; no prayer without flame.* —E. M. Bounds

*Bear up the hands that hang down, by faith and prayer; support the tottering knees. Have you any days of fasting and prayer? Storm the throne of grace and persevere therein, and mercy will come down.* —John Wesley

*Before the great revival in Gallneukirchen broke out, Martin Boos spent hours and days and often nights in lonely agonies of intercession. Afterwards, when he preached, his words were as flame, and the hearts of the people as grass.* —D. M. McIntyre, D.D.

*How many Christians there are who cannot pray, and who seek by effort, resolve, joining prayer circles, etc., to cultivate in themselves the "holy art of intercession," and all to no purpose. Here for them and for all is the only secret of a real prayer life—"Be filled with the Spirit," who is "the Spirit of grace and supplication."* —Rev. J. Stuart Holden

## CHAPTER ONE

## WITH ALL THY GETTING, GET UNCTION

THE Cinderella of the church of today is the prayer meeting. This handmaid of the Lord is unloved and unwooed because she is not dripping with the pearls of intellectualism, nor glamorous with the silks of philosophy; neither is she enchanting with the tiara of psychology. She wears the homespuns of sincerity and humility and so is not afraid to kneel!

The offense of prayer is that it does not essentially tie in to mental efficiency. (That is not to say that prayer is a partner to mental sloth; in these days efficiency is at a premium.) Prayer is conditioned by one thing alone and that is spirituality. One does not need to be spiritual to preach, that is, to make and deliver sermons of homiletical perfection and exegetical exactitude. By a combination of memory, knowledge, ambition, personality, plus well-lined bookshelves, self-confidence and a sense of having arrived—brother, the pulpit is yours almost anywhere these days. Preaching of the type mentioned affects men; prayer affects God. Preaching affects time; prayer affects eternity. The pulpit can be a shopwindow to display our talents; the closet speaks death to display.

The tragedy of this late hour is that we have too many *dead* men in the pulpits giving out too many *dead* sermons to too many *dead* people. Oh! the horror of it. There is a strange thing that I have seen "under the sun," even in the fundamentalist circles; it is preaching without unction. What is unction? I hardly know. But I know what it is not (or at least I know when it is not upon my own soul). Preaching without unction kills instead of giving life. The unctionless preacher is a savor of death unto death. The Word does not live unless the unction is upon the preacher. *Preacher, with all thy getting—get unction.*

Brethren, we could well manage to be half as intellectual (of the modern pseudo kind) if we were twice as spiritual. Preaching is a spiritual business. A sermon born in the head reaches the head; a sermon born in the heart reaches the heart. Under God, a spiritual preacher will produce spiritually minded people. Unction is not a gentle dove beating her wings against the bars outside of the preacher's soul; rather, must she be pursued and won. Unction cannot be learned, only earned—by prayer. Unction is God's knighthood for the soldier-preacher who has wrestled in prayer and gained the victory. Victory is not won in the pulpit by firing intellectual bullets or wisecracks, but in the prayer closet; it is won or lost before the preacher's foot enters the pulpit. Unction is like dynamite. Unction comes not by the medium of the bishop's hands, neither does it mildew when the preacher is cast into prison. Unction will pierce and percolate; it will sweeten and soften. When the hammer of logic and the fire of human zeal fail to open the stony heart, unction will succeed.

What a fever of church building there is just now! Yet without unctionized preachers, these altars will never see anxious penitents. Suppose that we saw fishing boats, with the latest in radar equipment and fishing gear, launched month after month and put out to sea only to return without a catch—what excuse would we take for this barrenness? Yet thousands of churches see empty altars week after week and year after year, and cover this sterile situation by misapplying the Scripture, "My word. . .shall not return unto me void." (Incidentally, this seems to be one of the very few texts that the dispensationalists forgot to tell us was written to the Jews!)

The ugly fact is that altar fires are either out or burning very low. The prayer meeting is dead or dying. By our attitude to prayer we tell God that what was begun in the Spirit we can finish in the flesh. What church ever asks its candidating ministers what time they spend in prayer? Yet ministers who do not spend two hours a day in prayer are not worth a dime a dozen, degrees or no degrees.

The church today is standing on the sidewalk, watching with fever and frustration, while the sin-dominated evil geniuses of Moscow strut the middle of the road, breathing out threatenings against "whatsoever things are lovely and of good report." Behind, follows the purple pageantry of papal Rome. Moreover, the devil has substituted reincarnation for regeneration, familiar spirits for the Holy Spirit, Christian Science for divine healing, the Antichrist for the true Christ, and the Church of Rome for the true Church.

Against these twin evils of Communism and Romanism, what has the Church to offer? Where is the supernatural? Both in the pulpit and in the press, somnolence seems to have overtaken religious controversy of late. Even Rome does not call us Protestants any more; we have just the juiceless name of non-Catholics! Significant, isn't it? Hell has no fury like that of this "Mother of Harlots" *when she is stirred.* But who now "earnestly contends for the faith once delivered to the saints"? Where are our unctionized pulpit crusaders? Preachers who should be fishing for men are now too often fishing for compliments from men. Preachers used to sow seed; now they string intellectual pearls. (Imagine a field sown with pearls!)

Away with this palsied, powerless preaching which is unmoving because it was born in a tomb instead of a womb, and nourished in a fireless, prayerless soul. We may preach and perish, but we cannot pray and perish. If God called us to the ministry, then, dear brethren, I contend that we should get unctionized. *With all thy getting—get unction,* lest barren altars be the badge of our unctionless intellectualism.

*Our praying, however, needs to be pressed and pursued with an energy that never tires, a persistency which will not be denied, and a courage which never fails.*                              *—E. M. Bounds*

*But ye, beloved, building up yourselves on your most holy faith, PRAYING IN THE HOLY GHOST.*
                                                        *—Jude*

*O that we were more deeply moved by the languishing state of Christ's cause upon the earth today, by the inroads of the enemy and the awful desolation he has wrought in Zion. Alas that a spirit of indifference, or at least of fatalistic stoicism, is freezing so many of us.*
                                                        *—A. W. Pink*

*Prayer was pre-eminently the business of his life.*
                                *—Biographer of Edwin Payson*

*Whole days and WEEKS have I spent prostrate on the ground in silent or vocal prayer.*   *—George Whitefield*

*All decays begin in the closet; no heart thrives without much secret converse with God, and nothing will make amends for the want of it.*           *—Berridge*

*It seemed to me as if he had gone straight into heaven, and lost himself in God; but often when he had done praying he was as white as the wall.*
                                                        *—A friend's*
*comment after meeting Tersteegen at Kronenberg.*

## CHAPTER TWO

## PRAYER GRASPS ETERNITY

NO man is greater than his prayer life. The pastor who is not praying is playing; the people who are not praying are straying. The pulpit can be a shop-window to display one's talents; the prayer closet allows no showing off.

Poverty-stricken as the Church is today in many things, she is most stricken here, in the place of prayer. We have many organizers, but few agonizers; many players and payers, few pray-ers; many singers, few clingers; lots of pastors, few wrestlers; many fears, few tears; much fashion, little passion; many interferers, few intercessors; many writers, but few fighters. Failing here, we fail everywhere.

The two prerequisites to successful Christian living are vision and passion, both of which are born in and maintained by prayer. The ministry of preaching is open to few; the ministry of prayer—the highest ministry of all human offices—is open to all. Spiritual adolescents say, "I'll not go tonight, it's only the prayer meeting." It may be that Satan has little cause to fear most preaching. Yet past experiences sting him to rally all his infernal army to fight against God's people praying. Modern Christians know little of "binding and loosing," though the onus is on us—"Whatsoever *ye* shall bind. . . ." Have you done any of this lately? God is not prodigal with His power; but to be much for God, we must be much with God.

This world hits the trail for hell with a speed that makes our fastest plane look like a tortoise; yet alas, few of us can remember the last time we missed our bed for a night of waiting upon God for a world-shaking revival. Our compassions are not moved. We mistake the scaffolding for the building. Present-day preaching, with its pale interpretation of divine truths, causes us to mistake action for unction, commotion for creation, and rattles for revivals.

The secret of praying is praying in secret. A sinning man will stop praying, and a praying man will stop sinning. We are beggared and bankrupt, but not broken, nor even bent.

Prayer is profoundly simple and simply profound. "Prayer is the simplest form of speech that infant lips can try," and yet so sublime that it outranges all speech and exhausts man's vocabulary. A Niagara of burning words does not mean that God is either impressed or moved. One of the most profound of Old Testament intercessors had no language—"Her lips moved, *but her voice was not heard.*" No linguist here! There *are* "groanings which cannot be uttered."

Are we so substandard to New Testament Christianity that we know not the historical faith of our fathers (with its implications and operations), but only the hysterical faith of our fellows? Prayer is to the believer what capital is to the business man.

Can any deny that in the modern church setup the main cause of anxiety is money? Yet that which tries the modern churches the most, troubled the New Testament Church the least. Our accent is on paying, theirs was on praying. When we have paid, the place is taken; when they had prayed, the place was shaken!

In the matter of New Testament, Spirit-inspired, hell-shaking, world-breaking prayer, never has so much been left by so many to so few.

For this kind of prayer there is no substitute. We do it—or die!

*A religion of mere emotion and sensationalism is the most terrible of all curses that can come upon any people. The absence of reality is sad enough, but the aggravation of pretence is a deadly sin.* —S. Chadwick

*It is well to get rid of the idea that faith is a matter of spiritual heroism only for a few select spirits. There are heroes of faith, but faith is not only for heroes. It is a matter of spiritual manhood. It is a matter of maturity.* —P. T. Forsyth

*When God intends great mercy for His people, the first thing He does is set them a-praying.*—Matthew Henry

*Truth without enthusiasm, morality without emotion, ritual without soul, are things Christ unsparingly condemned. Destitute of fire, they are nothing more than a godless philosophy, an ethical system, and a superstition.* —S. Chadwick

*The call of the Cross, therefore, is to enter into this passion of Christ. We must have upon us the print of the nails.* —Gordon Watt

*My need and Thy great fulness meet,*
*And I have all in Thee.*

—Unknown

*I have seen faces upon which the Dove sat visibly brooding.* —Charles Lamb on the Quakers

*Fervent in Spirit, serving the Lord.* —Paul

## CHAPTER THREE

# A CALL FOR UNCTION IN THE PULPIT

# — ACTION IN THE PEW!

WHEN a man who has crept along for years in conventional Christianity suddenly zooms into spiritual alertness, becomes aggressive in the battle of the Lord, and has a quenchless zeal for the lost, there is a reason for it. (But we are so subnormal these days that the normal New Testament experience seems abnormal.) The secret of this "jet-propelled fellow" we have just mentioned is that somewhere *he has had Jacoblike wrestlings with God and has come out stripped, but also "strengthened by the Holy Ghost!"*

There are two indispensable factors to successful Christian living. They are *vision* and *passion*. Men battle mountainous seas of human. carnal criticism and storm the flinty heights of devilish opposition to plant the cross of Christ amidst the habitations of cruelty. Why? Because they have caught a vision and contracted a passion.

Someone now warns us lest we become so heavenly minded that we are of no earthly use. Brother, this generation of believers is not, by and large, suffering from such a complex! The brutal, soul-shaking truth is that we are so earthly minded we are of no heavenly use.

Friend, if you were as good at soul-cultivation as you are in developing your business, you would be a menace to the devil; but if you were as poor in business matters as you are in soul, you would be begging for bread.

George Deakin drummed into my mind many years ago this fine bit of spiritual reasoning: A vision without a task makes a visionary; a task without a vision is drudgery; a vision with a task makes a missionary. Well said! Isaiah had a vision *when Uzziah died!* Maybe there is some person in your way blotting out the full vision of the Lord. Spiritual expansion is expensive and at times excruciating. Are you prepared for vision at this top-price demand—the loss of a friend or a career? There are no reduced rates for revolution of soul. If you only want to be saved, sanctified, and satisfied, then the Lord's battle hath no need of thee.

Isaiah had a vision in three dimensions. Note verses one to nine in the sixth chapter of Isaiah. Verse five, *WOE*, a word of *confession;* verse seven, *LO,* a word of *cleansing;* verse nine, *GO,* a word of *commission.*

It was an *upward* vision—he saw the Lord; an *inward* vision—he saw himself, and an *outward* vision—he saw the world.

It was a vision of *height*—he saw the Lord high and lifted up. A vision of *depth*—he saw the recesses of his own heart. And a vision of *breadth*—he saw the world.

A vision of *holiness*. Oh, beloved! How this generation of believers needs the vision of God in all His holiness! A vision of *hellishness*—"I am undone, . . . unclean!" and a vision of *hopelessness*—implied by the words "Who will go for us?"

In this hour—when the average church knows more about promotion than prayer, has forgotten consecration by fostering competition, and has substituted propaganda for propagation—this threefold vision is imperative.

"Where there is no vision the *people* perish." Where there is no passion the *church* perishes, even though it be full to the doors.

A world-famed preacher, who has been mightily used of God in the past few years in real revival (distinct and very different from mass evangelism), told the writer that he had a similar threefold vision. I can still see the solemn dread on that face as he spoke of hardly knowing whether he was having a dream or seeing a vision, not knowing whether he was in the body or transported; yet he could see a multitude that no man could number in a large abyss—surrounded by fire—locked in the "madhouse of the universe," *HELL*. This preacher has never been the same since. How could he be?

Could God entrust us with such a heartbreaking revelation? Have we graduated in the secret place of prayer and in the school of suffering so that our spirits are tempered to bear such a soul-sickening sight? Blessed is the man to whom the Lord can impart such a vision!

No man lives beyond his vision. Heavy-minded theologians can not break open the iron curtains of superstition and darkness behind which, for millenniums, millions have perished. Only men with less breadth of intellect, maybe, but with more depth of vision can do that.

To be spiritually minded is joy and peace. Yet to be statistically minded in addition can be very disturbing. Read this and weep:

JAPAN — The government there states that the population has passed the eighty-seven million mark. The nation is growing at the rate of one million one hundred thousand a year! This means that the non-Christian population of Japan has increased by five million in the past five years. Put this well up on your prayer list.

KOREA — Here are nine million people mostly refugees, homeless and almost foodless.

INDIA — Millions sit in darkness and in the shadow of death.

MIDDLE EAST — Here are a million Arab refugees.

EUROPE — She has eleven million "displaced persons." What a heartache for them!

CHINA — A third of a million escapees are from communist China, living in squatters' huts in Hong Kong.

To add to your burden and mine, there are fifteen million Jews; three hundred and fifteen million Mo-

hammedans; one hundred and seventy million Budd-
hists; three hundred and fifty million Confucianists
and Taoists; two hundred and fifty-five million Hin-
dus; ninety million Shintoists; and millions of others,
for whom Christ died and who are mainly unreached
with the blessed Gospel. Even church-conscious America has twenty-seven million youth under twenty-one
years of age who receive no Christian training, and ten
thousand villages that do not have a church building.
Almost a million persons in the world die each week
without Christ. *Is this nothing to you?*

This sin-swamped situation calls for unction in the
pulpit and action in the pew! Synthetic religion must
go. The Amen Corner has passed away with the model-
T Ford; the camp-meeting glory has vanished; zeal for
street meetings has evaporated.

Maybe—who knows?—God is more wroth with
America and England than He is with Russia! Is that
shocking? Then consider soberly that millions in Russia
have never heard a gospel message, never had a Bible,
and never listened to a spiritual broadcast. They would
go to a church if they could.

The repeated prayer that the sinner might have a
vision of hell may be entirely wrong. On the contrary,
he probably needs a vision of Calvary, with a suffering
Saviour pleading with him to repent; for after Calvary, why should he die? William Booth of the Salvation Army is quoted as saying that if he could do it,
he would have finalized the training of his soldiers
with twenty-four hours hanging over hell, to see its
eternal torment. Fundamentalism needs this awe-
striking vision again. The gusty, grandiloquent evangelist needs it most!

Charlie Peace was a criminal. Laws of God or man curbed him not. Finally the law caught up with him, and he was condemned to death. On the fatal morning in Armley Jail, Leeds, England, he was taken on the death-walk. Before him went the prison chaplain, routinely and sleepily reading some Bible verses. The criminal touched the preacher and asked what he was reading. "The Consolations of Religion," was the reply. Charlie Peace was shocked at the way he professionally read about hell. Could a man be so unmoved under the very shadow of the scaffold as to lead a fellow-human there and yet, dry-eyed, read of a pit that has no bottom into which this fellow must fall? Could this preacher believe the words that there is an eternal fire that never consumes its victims, and yet slide over the phrase without a tremor? Is a man human at all who can say with no tears, "You will be eternally dying and yet never know the relief that death brings"? All this was too much for Charlie Peace. So he preached. Listen to his on-the-eve-of-hell sermon.

"Sir," addressing the preacher, "if I believed what you and the church of God *say* that you believe, even if England were covered with broken glass from coast to coast, I would walk over it, if need be, on hands and knees and think it worth while living, just to save one soul from an eternal hell like that!"

My reader, because the Church has lost Holy Ghost fire, men go to hell-fire! We need a vision of a holy God. God is essentially holy. The cherubim and seraphim were not crying, "Omnipotent! Omnipotent is the Lord!" nor "Omnipresent! and Omniscient! is the Lord," but "Holy! Holy Holy!" This vast Hebrew concept needs to penetrate our souls again. If I make my bed in hell, if I take the wings of the morning—yet He is there. God compasses us in time; God, the inescapable God, awaits us in eternity. We had better be at peace with Him *here*, and be in the center of His will *now!*

To wait tremblingly before this thrice-holy One before we leave home for the day's work would be a mighty soul-stimulant. He who fears God fears no man. He who kneels before God will stand in any situation. A daily glimpse at the Holy One would find us subdued by His omnipresence, staggered by His omnipotence, silenced by His omniscience, and solemnized by His holiness. *His* holiness would become *our* holiness. Holiness-teaching contradicted by unholy living is the bane of this hour! "A holy minister is an awful weapon in the hands of God." So said Robert Murray McCheyne.

Before the experiences of the sixth chapter, Isaiah has a lot of woes for a lot of people. Now he sees himself and cries, "Woe is *me!*" "It's *me*, it's *me*, O Lord, standing in the need of prayer!" How true! Are there chambers of the mind with unclean pictures hanging in them? Have we skeletons in the cupboards of our hearts? Can the Holy Ghost be invited to take us by the hand down the corridors of our souls? Are there not secret springs, and secret motives that control, and secret chambers where polluted things hold empire over the soul? There are three persons living in each of us: the one we think we are, the one other people think we are, and the one God *knows* we are.

Unless we are desperate to get into real victory, we are so easy on ourselves and so hard on others! Self loves self, though it was said of Gerard Majella that by grace "he loved all men except Gerard Majella." Great possibility! But too often we hide ourselves from ourselves lest the sight of ourselves should sicken ourselves. Let us invite the searching eye of God to locate this corrupted, spotted, stinking Self in us. Let it be torn from us and "crucified with Him, [so] that henceforth we no longer serve sin" (Rom. 6: 6).

It will not do to call sin by some other name, saying, "The other fellow has a devilish temper; mine is just righteous indignation! She is touchy; my irritability is just 'a case of nerves.' He is covetous; I am expanding my business. He is stubborn; I have convictions. She is proud; I have superior tastes." There is a cover-up for anything if you want it that way.

But the Spirit will neither spare us nor cheat us if we will expose ourselves to His infallible scrutiny. Jesus said unto [the blind man], "What wilt thou that I should do unto thee? [He] said unto him, Lord, that I might receive my sight" (Mark 10: 51). Let us, too, pray for sight—upward, inward, and outward! Then like Isaiah, as we look *upward*, we will see the Lord in all His holiness; as we look *inward*, we will see ourselves and our need for cleansing and power; and as we look *outward*, we will see a world that is perishing and in need of a Saviour! "Search *me*, O God, and know *my* heart: try *me*, and know *my* thoughts: and see if there be any wicked way in *me*, and lead *me* in the way everlasting" (Psalm 139: 23, 24). Then only will there be *unction in the pulpit and action in the pew!*

*Do not we rest in our day too much on the arm of flesh? Cannot the same wonders be done now as of old? Do not the eyes of the Lord still run to and fro throughout the whole earth to show Himself strong on behalf of those who put their trust in Him? Oh, that God would give me more practical faith in Him! Where is now the Lord God of Elijah? He is waiting for Elijah to call on Him.*  —James Gilmour of Mongolia

*We know the utility of prayer from the efforts of the wicked spirits to distract us during the divine office; and we experience the fruit of prayer in the defeat of our enemies.*  —John Climacus

*When we go to God by prayer, the devil knows we go to fetch strength against him, and therefore he opposeth us all he can.*  —R. Sibbes

*I sought for a man.*  —Ezekiel 22:30

*Elias was a man.*  —James 5:17

## CHAPTER FOUR

## *WHERE ARE THE ELIJAHS OF GOD?*

TO the question, "Where is the Lord God of Elijah?" we answer, "Where He has always been—on the throne!" But where are the Elijahs of God? We know Elijah was "a man of like passions as we are," but alas! we are not men of like prayer as he was! One praying man stands as a majority with God! Today God is bypassing men—not because they are too ignorant, but because they are too self-sufficient. Brethren, our abilities are our handicaps, and our talents our stumbling blocks!

Out of obscurity, Elijah came on to the Old Testament stage, a full-grown man. Queen Jezebel, that daughter of hell, had routed the priests of God and replaced them with groves to false deities. Darkness covered the land and gross darkness the people, and they were drinking iniquity like water. Every day the land, fouled with heathen temples and idolatrous rites, saw smoke curling from a thousand cruel altars.

All this was among a people who claimed Abraham as their father, and whose forebears had cried unto the

Lord in their trouble and He had delivered them out
of all their distresses. How the God of Glory had departed! the salt had lost its savour! the gold had become dim! But out of this measureless backsliding, God
raised up a man—not a committee, not a sect, not an
angel—but a *MAN*, and a man of like passions as we
are! God "*sought for a man,*" not to preach, but "*to
stand in the gap.*" As Abraham, so now Elijah "*stood
before the Lord.*" Therefore the blessed Holy Spirit
could write the life of Elijah in two words: "*He
prayed.*" No man can do more than that for God or
for men. If the Church today had as many agonizers
as she has advisers, we would have a revival in a year!

Such praying men are always our national bene-
factors. Elijah was such. He had heard a voice, seen
a vision, tasted a power, measured an enemy, and,
with God as partner, wrought a victory. The tears he
shed, the soul agonies he endured, the groans he uttered, are all recorded in the book of the chronicles of
the things of God. At last Elijah emerged to prophesy
with divine infallibility. He knew the mind of God.
Therefore he—one man—strangled a nation and altered the course of nature. This "crag of a man" stood
as majestic and immovable as the mountains of Gilead,
as he shut up the heavens with a word. By the key
of faith, which fits every lock, Elijah locked heaven,
pocketed the key, and made Ahab tremble. Though it
is wonderful indeed when God lays hold of a man,
earth can know one greater wonder—when a man lays
hold of God. Let a man of God "in the Spirit" *groan*,
and God will cry out, "*Let me alone.*" We would like
Elijah's accomplishments, but not his banishments!

Brethren, if we will do God's work in God's way
at God's time with God's power, we shall have God's

blessing and the devil's curses. When God opens the windows of heaven to bless us, the devil will open the door of hell to blast us. God's smile means the devil's frown! Mere preachers may help anybody and hurt nobody; but prophets will stir everybody and madden somebody. The preacher may go *with* the crowd; the prophet goes *against* it. A man freed, fired, and filled with God will be branded unpatriotic because he speaks against his nation's sins; unkind because his tongue is a two-edged sword; unbalanced because the weight of preaching opinion is against him. The preacher will be heralded; the prophet hounded.

Ah! brother preachers, we love the old saints, missionaries, martyrs, reformers: our Luthers, Bunyans, Wesleys, Asburys, etc. We will write their biographies, reverence their memories, frame their epitaphs, and build their cenotaphs. We will do anything except imitate them. We cherish the last drop of their blood, but watch the first drop of our own!

John the Baptist did well to evade prison for six months. He and Elijah would not last six weeks in the streets of a modern city. They would be cast into a prison or mental home for judging sin and not muting their message.

Evangelists today are wide-eyed to the might of Communism, but tight-lipped at the menace of Romanism. America would shake from coast to coast in twenty-four hours if some preacher, anointed with the Holy Ghost, gave the Roman Catholic Church a broadside! In England we are worse. We stir national interest against the cruel, half-civilized Mau Mau (wicked enough!), but powwow with, and pander to, the Roman Catholic Church! These priests who dope men's souls, these idolatrous "masses," these Calvary-eclipsing prayers to Mary, these miserable millions cheated in life and in death by the greatest forgery Lucifer ever made—all these do not seem to stir us to tearful intercessions and godly jealousy, as identical circumstances stirred Elijah. The enemy has come in like a flood. Is there no Spirit-filled messenger today, armed with all the panoply of God, to lift up a standard against him? One place alone will keep the heart in passion and the eyes in vision—the place of prayer. This man Elijah, with a volcano for a heart, and a thunderstorm for a voice, came to the Kingdom for such a time as this.

The difficulties to world evangelism are legion. But difficulties give way to determined men.

> "Got any rivers you think are uncrossable?
> Got any mountains you can't tunnel through?
> God specializes in things thought impossible,
> And He can do what no other pow'r can do."

The price is high. God does not want partnership with us, but ownership of us.

Elijah lived with God. He thought about the nation's sin *like God*; he grieved over sin *like God*; he spoke against sin *like God*. He was all passion in his prayers and passionate in his denunciation of evil in the land. He had no smooth preaching. Passion fired his preaching, and his words were on the hearts of men as molten metal on their flesh.

But "the steps of a good man are ordered by the Lord" (Psalm 37: 23). The Lord said to Elijah, "Hide thyself," and again, "Show thyself." It would be wrong to hide when we should be rebuking kings for

His sake; it would be wrong to preach if the Spirit is calling us to wait upon the Lord. We must learn with David, "My soul, wait thou only upon God" (Psalm 62: 5). Who of us dares to invite the Lord to cut out all our props? God's ways are not our ways. His ways are "past finding out," but He reveals them unto us by His Spirit. God ordered Elijah to Cherith, then to Zarephath—to lodge at a swank hotel? No! No! This prophet of God, this preacher of righteousness, was commanded by the Lord to stay at the home of an impoverished widow!

Later, Elijah's prayer at Carmel was a masterpiece of concise praying. "*Hear me, O Lord, hear me, that this people may know that thou art the Lord God, and that thou hast turned their heart back again*" (I Kings 18: 37). E. M. Bounds is right in saying that short, powerful public prayers are the outcome of long secret intercession. Elijah prayed, not for the destruction of the idolatrous priests, nor for thunderbolts from heaven to consume rebellious Israel, but that the glory of God and the power of God might be revealed.

We try to help God out of difficulties. Remember how Abraham tried to do this, and to this day the earth is cursed with his folly because of Ishmael. On the other hand, Elijah made it as difficult as he could for the Lord. He wanted fire, but yet he soaked the sacrifice with water! God loves such holy boldness in our prayers. "Ask of me, and I shall give thee the heathen for thine inheritance, and the uttermost parts of the earth for thy possession" (Psalm 2: 8).

Oh! my ministering brethren! Much of our praying is but giving God advice! Our praying is discolored with ambition, either for ourselves or for our denomination. Perish the thought! Our goal must be God alone. It is His honor that is sullied, His blessed Son who is ignored, His laws broken, His name profaned, His Book forgotten, His house made a circus of social efforts.

Does God ever need more patience with His people than when they are "praying"? We tell Him what to do and how to do it. We pass judgments and make appreciations in our prayers. In short, we do everything except pray. No Bible School can teach us this art. What Bible School has "Prayer" on its curriculum? The most important thing a man can study is the prayer part of the Book. But where is this taught? Let us strip off the last bandage and declare that many of our presidents and teachers do not pray, shed no tears, know no travail. Can they teach what they do not know?

The man who can get believers to praying would, under God, usher in the greatest revival that the world has ever known. There is *no* fault in God. He is able. God *"is able to do. . .according to the power that worketh in us."* God's problem today is not Communism, nor yet Romanism, nor Liberalism, nor Modernism. God's problem is—dead fundamentalism!

*Revival and evangelism, although closely linked, are not to be confounded. Revival is an experience in the Church; evangelism is an expression of the Church.*
                                            —Paul S. Rees


*God never intended His Church to be a refrigerator in which to preserve perishable piety. He intended it to be an incubator in which to hatch out converts.*
                                            —F. Lincicome


*Lord, is it I?*                            —The Disciples


*Got any rivers you think are uncrossable?*
*Got any mountains you can't tunnel through?*
*God specializes in things thought impossible,*
*And He can do what no other pow'r can do.*


*God helps us seek popularity where it counts—at the court of God!*
                                            —Zepp

## CHAPTER FIVE

## REVIVAL IN A BONE YARD

*THE hand of the Lord was upon me, and carried me out in the Spirit of the Lord, and set me down in the midst of the valley which was full of bones...and, behold, there were very many...and lo, they were dry...And He said unto me... Prophesy upon these bones, and say unto them, O ye dry bones, hear the word of the Lord...So I prophesied as I was commanded...and the breath came into them, and they lived and stood upon their feet, an exceeding great army"* (Ezekiel 37).

Does history, sacred or profane, offer a more ridiculous picture than this? Here is hopelessness incarnate. Who ever had such a dumb audience? Preachers deal with possibilities, prophets with impossibilities. Isaiah had seen this nation full of wounds and putrifying sores; but disease had galloped on to death, death to disintegration, and now these disjointed bones spell out despair. Written over the whole situation in large capitals is *I-m-p-o-s-s-i-b-i-l-i-t-y.* Now obviously no faith is required to do *the possible;* actually only a morsel of this atom-powered stuff is needed to do *the impossible,* for a piece as large as a mustard seed will do more than we have ever dreamed of. Again and again God asks men to do not what they can, but what they can't. To prove that no sleight of hand does it but that they link their impotence to His omnipotence, the word *impossible* is dropped from their vocabularies.

Prophets are lone men: they walk alone, pray alone, and God makes them alone. For them there is no mold; their patent rights are with God, for the principle of divine selection is "past finding out." But let no man despair; let none of us say, however we may have been or have not been used, that we are too old. Moses was eighty when he took command of an enslaved and broken people. After George Mueller was seventy, he went around the world several times, and without the aid of radio preached to millions of people.

As for Ezekiel, he called no committee and sent out no prayer letter; he solicited no funds and loathed publicity. But this situation was a matter of Life and Death. (So is evangelism today—therefore, let every preacher beware lest his "theological-juggling" act send his hearer home saying, "He is a clever fellow!" and yet leave him in complete spiritual darkness.) To this mountain of bones, then, Ezekiel was asked to say, *"Be thou removed!"* So he said and so it was. Here was a curse—had he a cure? Here was death—could he bring life? This was no pretty declaration of doctrine. Dear believers, listen. The world is not waiting for a new definition of the Gospel, but for a new demonstration of the power of the Gospel. In these days of acute political helplessness, moral lawlessness, and spiritual helplessness, where are the men not of doctrine, but of faith? No faith is required to curse the darkness or give staggering statistical evidence that the dikes are down and a tidal wave of hellish impurity has submerged this generation. Doctrine?—we have enough and to spare, while a sick, sad, sin-sodden, sex-soaked world perishes with hunger.

At this grim hour, the world sleeps in the darkness, and the Church sleeps in the light; so Christ is "wounded in the house of His friends." The limping Church militant is derisively called the Church impotent. Yearly we use mountains of paper and rivers of ink reprinting dead men's brains, while the living Holy Ghost is seeking for men to trample underfoot their own learning, deflate their inflated ego, and confess that with all their seeing they are blind. Such men, at the price of brokenness and strong crying and tears, seek that they may be anointed with divine eyesalve, bought at the price of honest acknowledgment of poverty of soul. Years ago a minister put this sign outside of his church, "This church will have either a revival or a funeral!" With such despair God is well pleased, though hell is despondent. Madness, you say? Exactly! A sober church never does any good. At this hour we need men drunk with the Holy Ghost. Has God excelled Himself? Were Wesley, Whitefield, Finney, Hudson Taylor special editions of ministers? Never! If I read the Book of Acts aright, they were just the norm.

The atom bomb seems to have disturbed everything—except the Church. By overstating the sovereignty of God and blundering on in an atmosphere of stagnant dispensationalism, we safeguard our spiritual bankruptcy. All the while hell fills. With Communism in the world, Modernism in the churches, and Moderatism crippling the fundamentalist groups, will the Lord look in vain for a man to stand in the gap, as Ezekiel did? My preacher brethren, these days we are more fond of travelling than travailing, hence—no births. God send us, and that right early, a prophet out of step with a church which is out of joint.

The hour is too late for another denomination to be born. Right now, God is preparing His Elijahs for the last great earthly offensive against militant godlessness (whether political or wearing a mask of religion). The last great outpouring of revival, Holy Ghost born and operated, will be new wine bursting the skins of dried-up sectarianism. Hallelujah!

Note that Ezekiel was *Spirit-led*. As a man, he must have shuddered at the appalling sight of mountains of dry human bones. But pivoted on Ezekiel's faith was the destiny of thousands if not millions—pivoted on faith, mark you, not prayer. Many pray, but few have faith. What holy tremors must have rushed through his soul at this sight! Only heaven and hell were spectators. Surely if Ezekiel were living today, he would have had a press photograph of this! Next, with a love of statistics, he would have *counted* the bones; when things had begun to move, he certainly would have called others to see him operate (lest men fail to give him the right ranking with national evangelists!). Not so Ezekiel. Listen to this: "*I prophesied as I was commanded*" (there is the crux of the matter—he was a fool for God); "*O ye dry bones, hear the word of the Lord.*" Madness? Yes, insanity—of virgin purity! He said to the bones, "*Hear!*" though they had no ears! Ezekiel did as he was told. To save our faces, we of course modify God's commands, and so lose our faces. But Ezekiel obeyed; and God, as always, operated: "*there was a great noise.*" Well—*that* would suit us. But Ezekiel did not mistake commotion for creation, nor action for unction, nor rattle for revival.

With only *one* breath from His omnipotent lips, God *could* have raised this heap to life, but no—there were to be *many* operations. First, *"Bones came to-gether, bone to his bone."* (No mountain of bones now.) Such phenomena would almost put us into hysterics; not so Ezekiel. But what good are skeletons? Can these fight the battles of the Lord? At this stage would they bring honor to His Name? Too often today blind guides count "skeletons" who come to the altars —moved certainly, but not yet born. At their few, hot tears we exhort, "Believe this promise." But as yet they have no life. Even so, flesh must come upon the skeletons; then skin must cover the flesh. And the result is that we have a valley full of—corpses! Any good to God? Not yet. They have eyes but cannot see, hands but cannot fight, feet but cannot walk. So are those who are seeking—until this last thing happens: *"I prophesied again."* Ezekiel held on; he resisted doubt. Instead of being discouraged both at the skeletons and at the corpses, he took it that God was with him. Alone with God—he prevailed. *"He prophesied as commanded and the breath came into them and they L-I-V-E-D!"*

But who today can say, *"I prophesied as I was commanded, and they l-i-v-e-d"?* We boys can get crowds. Our slick advertising, artistry, and strutting —our radio, music, build up, and what have you— see to that. Why brethren, we don't even know whether or not He has commanded us to enter the ministry. Have we a pain in our hearts for perishing men? Does the toll of eighty-five people dying without Christ every minute turn our moisture into drought, take away our garment of praise, or give us the spirit of heaviness? Can we *at this moment* look up into the face of the living God (for He is looking down on us) and say, "Woe is unto me if I preach not the Gospel"?

Can we actually say, "The Spirit of the Lord God is upon me" anointing me to preach? Do we count in hell? I mean, Would demons ever say, "Jesus I know, and Pastor —— I know!" Or, as we preach, do they say, "But who are ye?"

The political crystal-gazers give us no cheerful predictions, and the world's senior statesmen are whistling to keep up their courage. John Citizen stands bewildered as a spectator, seeing the Russellites, the Millennial Dawnists, and Jehovah's Witnesses peddling their poison at his door. Christian Science—which is neither Christian nor yet scientific—jostles with the Roman Catholics and Seventh Day Adventists to claim their right to lead him to heaven. John Citizen has heard of the Gospel with the hearing of the ear, but his eyes have *never* seen and his soul has *never* felt the power of a divine visitation. He has every right to ask, "Where is their God?" What shall we answer him?

One of the most painful things I know is to face up to truth. We are well conditioned to doctrine. Most of us know what the average preacher will say next. But a razor is blunt, compared to Spirit-edged truth. Ministers, and others in different parts of the world, all seem to have the same note of mourning, because of the ineffectiveness to a lasting degree of modern evangelism (even though it be fundamental)—flash-bulb evangelism we might call it—brilliant for the moment, but ah! but...!

Maybe we have a breath of life—of revival—in the churches, but we are not getting awakenings amongst the godless millions. We do get special train-loads, mainly of believers or church-goers, to our mass evangelistic efforts, but we need a General Booth to get to the up-and-outs, as well as to the down-and-outs.

The old saints used to sing,

"Blest are the men of broken heart,
Who mourn for sin with inward smart."

Herein are three very vital issues: *Broken Hearts*, *Mourning*, and *Sin*. First, "a broken and a contrite heart God will not despise"; in fact, God only uses broken things. For example, Jesus took the lad's bread and brake it; then, and only then, could it feed the crowd. The alabaster box was broken; only then could its fragrance escape and fill the house—and the world. Jesus said, "This is My body which was broken for you." If such was the way the Master went, should not the servant tread it still? For in saving our lives, we not only lose *them*, but we lose other people's too.

And next, mourning for sin! Jeremiah cried, "Oh that my head were waters," while the Psalmist says, "Rivers run down my eyes continually." Dear brethren, our eyes are dry because our hearts are dry. We live in a day when we can have piety without pity. It is passing strange. When a couple of struggling Salvation Army officers wrote to William Booth telling him they tried every way to get a move and failed, he sent this terse reply, "Try tears!" They did. And they had revival.

Bible schools don't teach "tears." They really cannot, of course. This is Spirit-taught; and a preacher, however weighed d o w n with degrees and doctorates, has not gotten far unless he knows soul-bitterness over the sin of this day. A repeated cry of David Livingstone was, "Lord, when will the wounds of this world's sin be healed?" But are we grief-stricken in prayer? Do *we* soak *our* pillows, as John Welch did, in *our* soul travail? The scholarly Andrew Bonar lay on his bed on a Saturday night in Scotland and as people below tramped the streets from the taverns and shows, he used to call from his tortured heart: "Oh! they perish, they perish!" Alas, brethren, we have not so learned Christ. Many of us know only a slick, tearless, passionless, soulless round of preaching, which passes for the minister's office these days.

Thirdly, what of sin? "Fools mock at it," says the Book. (Only fools would so do.) The Schoolmen of the Church have classified "seven deadly sins." We know, of course, that they are wrong, for all sin is deadly. Those seven sins are the womb out of which seventy times seventy million sins have been born. They are "the seven heads" of *one* monster, which is devouring this generation at a terrifying rate. We face a pleasure-doped youth, who couldn't care less about God. Cocksure with a psuedo-intellectualism, and insulated with a cultivated indifference to spiritual things, they also, alas, flaunt the accepted standards of morality.

It would be comic, if it were not tragic, to read that a certain film star (who is closely associated with scanty dress) refused to see the premiere of her own picture because she was upset at some of the indecent strips in it. (There is a demand for this stuff, hence the supply.) Remember that in Greek mythology, Augeas was king of the Epeians and noted for his immense wealth of herds, including twelve white bulls, sacred to Helios. For many years the stable for these bulls remained uncleaned. Then Eurytheus imposed upon Heracles the task of cleaning out all his stalls in one day. This Heracles did by turning loose through them the rivers Alpheus and Peneus.

Even so, to our knees, O Christians! Desist the folly of sprinkling today's individual and international iniquity with theological rose water! Turn loose against this putrefaction those mighty rivers of weeping, of prayer, and of unctionized preaching until all be cleansed.

There is sin in the camp. There is treason today!
    Is it in me? Is it in me?
There is cause in our ranks for defeat and delay;
    Is it, O Lord, in me?
Something of selfishness, garments or gold,
Something of hindrance in young or in old,
Something why God doth His blessing withhold;
    Is it, O Lord, in me?
    Is it in me? Is it in me?
    Is it, O Lord, in me?

*Power from on high is the supreme need of today.*
*—C. G. Finney*

*If Christ waited to be anointed before He went to preach, no young man ought to preach until he, too, has been anointed by the Holy Ghost.    —F. B. Meyer*

*Beware of reasoning about God's Word — obey it.*
*—Oswald Chambers*

*I cannot work my soul to save,*
*  For that my Lord hath done;*
*But I will work like any slave,*
*  For love of God's dear Son.        —Unknown*

*Tell me in the light of the Cross, isn't it a scandal that you and I live today as we do?      —Alan Redpath*

*As soon as we cease to bleed, we cease to bless.*
*—Dr. J. H. Jowett*

## CHAPTER SIX

## REVIVAL TARRIES — BECAUSE

HARNACK defined Christianity as "a very simple but very sublime thing: To live in time and for eternity *under the eye of God* and by His help."

Oh that believers would become eternity-conscious! If we could live every moment of every day under the eye of God, if we did every act in the light of the judgment seat, if we sold every article in the light of the judgment seat, if we prayed every prayer in the light of the judgment seat, if we tithed all our possessions in the light of the judgment seat, if we preachers prepared every sermon with one eye on damned humanity and the other on the judgment seat—then we would have a Holy Ghost revival that would shake this earth and that, in no time at all, would liberate millions of precious souls.

The heady, high-minded, incontinent truce-breakers of this hour, the tottering of thrones, the smoldering fires of Communism, and the bid for world dominion that Rome makes should fill us with alarm. It has been well said that there are only three classes of people in the world today: those who are afraid, those who do not know enough to be afraid, and those who know their Bibles. Sodom, which had no Bible, no preachers, no tracts, no prayer meetings, no churches, perished. How then will America and England be spared from the wrath of the Almighty, think you? We have millions of Bibles, scores of thousands of churches, endless preachers—and yet what sin!

Men build our churches but do not enter them, print our Bibles but do not read them, talk about God but do not believe Him, speak of Christ but do not trust Him for salvation, sing our hymns and then forget them. How are we going to come out of all this?

Almost every Bible conference majors on today's Church being like the Ephesian Church. We are told that, despite our sin and carnality, we are seated with Him. Alas, what a lie! We are Ephesians all right; but, as the Ephesian Church in the Revelation, we have "left our first love!" We appease sin—but do not oppose it. To such a cold, carnal, critical, care-cowed Church, this lax, loose, lustful, licentious age will never capitulate. Let us stop looking for scape-goats. The fault in declining morality is not radio or television. The whole blame for the present international degeneration and corruption lies at the door of the Church! It is no longer a thorn in the side of the world. Yet, it has not been in times of popularity but of adversity that the true Church has always triumphed. It is passing strange that we are so "simple" as to believe that the Church is presenting to men the New Testament standard of Jesus by such a substandard of Christian living.

Why does revival tarry? The answer is simple enough—*because evangelism is so highly commercial-*

*ized*. The tithes of widows and of the poor are spent in luxury-living by many evangelists. The great crowds, great lines of seekers, great appreciation by the mayor, etc., are shouted to high heaven. All get publicity—except the love-offering! The poor dupes who give "think they do God service," while all they are doing is keeping a big-reputationed, small-hearted preacher living in Hollywood style.

Preachers who have homes and cottages by the lake, a boat on that lake, and a big bank balance, still beg for more. With such extortioners and unjust men, can God entrust Holy Ghost revival? These dear, doll-like preacher-boys no longer change their suits once a day, but two or three times a day. They preach the Jesus of the stable, but themselves live in swank hotels. For their own lusts they bleed the audience financially in the name of the One who had to borrow a penny to illustrate His sermon. They wear expensive Hollywood suits in honor of One who wore a peasant's robe. They feast on three-dollar steaks in remembrance of the One who fasted alone in the desert. Today an evangelist is not only worthy of his hire (so he thinks), but of compound interest. How fearful will all this be in the judgment morning!

Revival tarries *because of cheapening the Gospel*. We now have church hymns played strictly to dance tempo on our sacred records and over the radio, as well as in the churches. We have the precious blood of Jesus set to "boogie woogie" time. Imagine! We have the Holy Ghost syncopated! The platform has become a shopwindow to display our gifts, and the "visiting team" look like a mannequin parade. I would as soon expect a frog to sit down and play

Beethoven's Moonlight Sonata as expect to see some of the slick preachers of this hour preach with an anointing that would cause godly fear among the people. The evangelists today are very often prepared to be anything to anybody as long as they can get somebody to the altar for something. They glibly call out: "Who wants help? Who wants more power? Who wants a closer walk with God?" Such a sinning, repenting "easy believe-ism" dishonors the blood and prostitutes the altar. We must alter the altar, for the altar is a place to die on. Let those who will not pay this price leave it alone!

Revival tarries *because of carelessness*. At the altar, too little time is spent with those souls who come to do eternal business. The evangelist is happy seeing his friends; and while sinners groan at the altar, he is drinking in the rich cream of men's praises. Thus America and England are strewn with spiritual derelicts, confused and confounded.

Revival tarries *because of fear*. As evangelists, we are tight-lipped about the spurious religions of the day, as if there were more than one name whereby men must be saved. But Acts 4:12 is still in the Scriptures —"there is *none other name* under heaven." To the modern preacher, does this seem tinged with bigotry?

Elijah mocked the prophets of Baal and sneered with derisive scorn at their impotence. Better to run out in the dark (as Gideon did) and cut down groves to false gods—than fail to do the will of God. The Christless cults and deity-dishonoring mushroom religions of this midnight hour tempt the Lord God. Will no one sound the alarm? We are not Protestants any more—just "non-Catholics"! Of what and of whom do we protest? Were we half as hot as we think we are, and a tenth as powerful as we say we are, our Christians would be baptized in blood, as well as in water and in fire.

Wesley saw the doors of the English churches closed against him, and Rowland Hill says of him, "He and his lay-lubbers—his ragged legion of preaching tinkers, scavengers, draymen, and chimney sweepers, etc.—go forth to poison the minds of men." What scurrilous language! But Wesley feared neither men nor devils. If Whitefield was burlesqued on the English stage in the basest way, and if, in the New Testament, Christians were stoned and suffered every ignominy, how is it then, since sin and sinners have not changed, that we preachers no longer raise the wrath of hell? Why are we so icily regular, so splendidly null? We can have riots without revival. But in the light of the Bible and Church History, where can we have revival without riots?

Revival tarries *because we lack urgency in prayer*. A famed preacher entered a conference the other day with these words, "I have come to this conference with a great burden for prayer on my heart. Will those who will share this with me, please raise their hands; and let none of us be hypocrites." There was a good response. But later in the week when a half night of prayer was called, the big preacher went to bed. Not much of a hypocrite! Integrity has passed away! All is superficial! The biggest single factor contributing to delayed Holy Ghost revival is this omission of soul travail. We are substituting propaganda for propagation. How insane! The New Testament adds a valuable postscript concerning Elijah when James 5: 17

says "he prayed!" Had it not been for that, we should have seized the Old Testament story and, noting the omission of prayer, have said: "Elijah prophesied!"

We have not yet resisted unto blood in prayer; nay, we "do not even get a sweat on our souls," as Luther put it. We pray with a "take-it-or-leave-it" attitude; we pray chance prayers; we offer that which costs us nothing! We have not even "strong desire." We rather are fitful, moody and spasmodic.

The only power that God yields to is that of prayer. We will write about prayer-power, but not fight while in prayer. A title, undeniably true of the Church to-day, would be *We Wrestle Not!* We will display our gifts, natural or spiritual; we will air our views, political or spiritual; we will preach a sermon or write a book to correct a brother in doctrine. But who will storm hell's stronghold? Who will say the devil nay? Who will deny himself good food or good company or good rest that hell may gaze upon him wrestling, embarrassing demons, liberating captives, depopulating hell, and leaving, in answer to his travail, a stream of blood-washed souls?

Finally, revival tarries *because we steal the glory that belongs to God.* Listen to this and wonder: Jesus said, "I receive not honour from men." and, "How can ye believe, which receive honour one of another, and seek not the honour that cometh from God only?" (John 5: 41, 44). Away with all fleshly backslapping and platform flattery! Away with this exalting of "*My* radio program," "*My* church," "*My* books!" Oh, the sickening parade of flesh in our pulpits: "We are greatly privileged, etc." Speakers (who are there really *by grace alone*) accept all this, nay—even expect it! The fact is that when we have listened to most of these men, we would not have known they were great if they had not been announced so!

*POOR GOD!* He does not get much out of it all! Then why doesn't God fulfill His blessed and yet awful promise and spew us out of His mouth? We have failed. We are filthy. We love men's praise. We "seek our own." "O God, lift us out of this rut and this rot! Bless us with breakings! Judgment must begin with us preachers!"

*The Gospel is not an old, old story, freshly told. It is a fire in the Spirit, fed by the flame of Immortal Love; and woe unto us, if, through our negligence to stir up the Gift of God which is within us, that fire burns low.*
*—Dr. R. Moffat Gautrey*

*The greatest miracle of that day (Pentecost) was the transformation wrought in those waiting disciples. Their fire-baptism transformed them.*
*—Samuel Chadwick*

*The sign of Christianity is not a cross but a tongue of fire.*  *—Samuel Chadwick*

*The Gospel is a fact; therefore tell it simply.*
*The Gospel is a joyful fact; therefore tell it cheerfully.*
*The Gospel is an entrusted fact; therefore tell it faithfully.*
*The Gospel is a fact of infinite moment; therefore tell it earnestly.*
*The Gospel is a fact of infinite love; therefore tell it feelingly.*
*The Gospel is a fact of difficult comprehension to many; therefore tell it with illustration.*
*The Gospel is a fact about a Person; therefore preach Christ.*

*—Archibald Brown*

*True preaching is the sweating of blood.*
*—Dr. Joseph Parker*

## CHAPTER SEVEN

## IS SOUL-HOT PREACHING A LOST ART?

CENTURIES have passed since the Swiss Reformer Oecolampadius forged the phrase, "How much more would a few good and fervent men affect the ministry than a multitude of lukewarm ones!" The passing of time has not taken the sting from this statement. We need more "good and fervent preachers." Isaiah was one such, with his "woe" of confession—"Woe is me! for I am undone; because I am a man of unclean lips, and I dwell in the midst of a people of unclean lips." And Paul was another such, with his "woe" of commission—"Woe is unto me, if I preach not the gospel!" But neither of these ordained men had a larger concept of the magnitude of his task than had Richard Baxter of Kidderminster, England. Listen to him in answer to the taunts that he was idle: "The worst I wish you is that you had my ease instead of your labor. I have reason to take myself for the least of all saints, and yet I fear not to tell the accuser that I take the labor of most tradesmen in the town to be a pleasure to the body in comparison to mine, though I would not exchange it with the greatest prince.

"Their labor preserveth health, and mine consumeth it. They work in ease, and I in continual pain. They have hours and days of recreation; I have scarce time to eat and drink. Nobody molesteth them for their labor, but the more I do, the more hatred and trouble I draw upon me."

There is something of New Testament soul-culture about that attitude to preaching. This is the Baxter who ever sought to preach as "a dying man to dying men." A generation of preachers of his soul-caliber would rescue this generation of sinners from the greedy mouth of a yawning hell.

We may have an all-time high in church attendance with a corresponding all-time low in spirituality. It may have been that in the past liberalism was rightly cursed by many as the seducer of the people. Now T.V. is the scapegoat, getting the anathema of the preachers. Yet having said all this, and knowing that both indictments carry truth, may I ask us preachers a question: Have we to confess with one of old, "The fault, dear Brutus, is within ourselves"? To sharpen my scalpel and plunge it further into the quivering flesh of the pulpiteers: Has great preaching died? is soul-hot preaching a lost art? have we conceded to the impatient modern's snack-bar sermons (spiced with humor!) the task of edging men's jaded spiritual appetites? do we endeavor to bring "the powers of the world to come" into every meeting?

Consider Paul. With a powerful anointing of the Holy Spirit upon him, he went out to ransack Asia Minor, mauling its markets, stirring its synagogues, penetrating its palaces. Out he went, with the war cry of the Gospel in his heart and on his lips. Lenin is credited with coining the phrase, "Facts are stubborn things." See how right such a phrase is by looking at the achievements of this man Paul; then sicken at the compromise of our generation of Christians! Paul was not merely a citywide preacher but a citywide shaker, and yet he had time to knock on the doors along the street and to pray for lost souls in the street.

The playboys of yesterday are the payboys of evangelism. A top-line evangelist of my knowledge refused a contract of five hundred dollars a week for a four-weeks' preaching campaign. No wonder a modernist has declared that these men will weep for souls—if the price is right—aye, like Judas, they will be weeping when it is too late! May weakness in the pew be caused by wickedness in the pulpit?

I am increasingly convinced that tears are an integral part of revival preaching. Preacher brethren, this is the time to blush that we have no shame, the time to weep for our lack of tears, the time to bend low that we have lost the humble touch of servants, the time to groan that we have no burden, the time to be angry with ourselves that we have no anger over the devil's monopoly in this "end time" hour, the time to chastise ourselves that the world can so easily get along with us and not attempt to chastise us.

Pentecost meant *pain*, yet we have so much pleasure. Pentecost meant *burden*, yet we love ease. Pentecost meant *prison*, yet most of us would do anything rather than for Christ's dear sake get into prison. Perhaps Pentecost re-lived would get many of us into jail—Pentecost, I say, not Pentecostalism—and I am throwing no stones.

Imagine Pentecost in your church this Sunday:

*You* are endued as was Peter, and under your word, brother Ananias is slain and his wife soon stiff beside him! Would the moderns stand for that? Again, here is a Paul, smiting Elymas with blindness. In these days *that* would bring a court case against any preacher. And even prostration, which has accompanied almost all revival preaching, would "get us a bad name." Is not that more than our tender hearts could take?

I am appealing again, as at the beginning of this article, for majestic preaching. The devil wants us to major on minors. Many of us in the "Deeper Life" bracket are *hunting mice*—while *lions* devour the land! What happened to Paul while in Arabia I have never been able to find out. No one knows. Did he get a glimpse of the new heaven and the new earth and see the exalted Lord reigning over all? I still do not know; but this much is sure, that he altered Asia, jaundiced the Jews, riled the Romans, taught the teachers, and pitied prison jailors. This man Paul, and another preacher called Silas, dynamited the prison walls—with prayer—and cost the taxpayers a load in order that they might get about the Master's business.

Paul the bond-slave, Paul the love-slave, having settled that he was the hardest soul God would ever have to deal with, strode out to shake regions for God. On his day he brought "the powers of the world to come," stayed Satan, and outsuffered, outloved, and outprayed us all. Brethren, to our knees again, to rediscover apostolic piety and apostolic power. Away with sickly sermonizing!

*The Church has halted somewhere between Calvary and Pentecost.*        *—J. I. Brice*

*How shall I feel at the judgment, if multitudes of missed opportunities pass before me in full review, and all my excuses prove to be disguises of my cowardice and pride?*       *—Dr. W. E. Sangster*

*O Living Stream! O Gracious Rain!*
*None wait for Thee, and wait in vain.*     *—Tersteegen*

*Revival — the inrush of the Spirit into the body that threatens to become a corpse.*     *—D. M. Panton*

*A revival of religion presupposes a declension.*     *—C. G. Finney*

## CHAPTER EIGHT

## UNBELIEVING BELIEVERS

ONE of these days some simple soul will pick up the Book of God, read it, *and believe it*. Then the rest of us will be embarrassed. We have adopted the convenient theory that the Bible is a Book to be explained, whereas first and foremost it is a Book to be believed (and after that to be obeyed).

The fact beats ceaselessly into my brain these days that there is a world of difference between knowing the Word of God and knowing the God of the Word. Is it not true that with the coming round of Bible conferences we hear only old things repeated, and most likely come away without any increase in faith? Perhaps God never had such a set of unbelieving believers as this present crop of Christians. How humiliating!

Are we mesmerized by spiritual wealth? Perhaps a penniless seaman might be tantalized and tormented to sail over the Atlantic, knowing that beneath him lies the *Lusitania* with ten million dollars in her holds—his for the taking! The only barrier is a mile or two of water! Even so, the Bible, the Christian's checkbook from the Lord of glory, says: "*ALL* things are yours. . .and ye are Christ's; and Christ is God's." I am finding a healthy dissatisfaction these days with the poverty of us believers.

We rarely enter a prayer meeting without hearing the familiar phrase, "Lord, thou *canst* do this," (stating some particular need). But is *that* faith? No. That is but recognizing the attribute of God called omnipotence. I believe that the living, unchanging Lord of glory *can* change into solid gold this good-sized table at which I am typing. Changing water into wine or wood into gold is all within the compass of His power. But He changed water into wine *because of need*. Right now I could use a million clean dollars (and not a cent of it on myself) in a way that would not make me tremble or blush in "that great day"; and so I believe that there is genuine need. But, to say that He *can* do this does *not* change the wood; it therefore leaves me unsupplied. Yet when I move up and say, "He *will* change this table into gold," my problem is solved.

We *all* know that "the greatest of these [faith, hope, and love]" is *not* faith. But why overlook the lesser? Where is there pure faith these days? What a travesty of interpretation of genuine faith there is right now! A familiar cry is: "We believe that the Lord would have us broadcast over ten more radio stations; we are looking to Him to supply our needs; send us your letters before next week!" That may be faith *and hints*, but it is not being shut up to God alone. We Christians glibly quote, "My God shall supply *all* (tremendous word!) your need"; but really, do we believe it?

Without lessening its value, an appendix could be

added to Hebrews Eleven and could include Hudson Taylor (founder of the China Inland Mission), George Mueller, Rees Howells, and others who *"through faith"* did mighty works. In this perilous hour I am weary of all our mighty *talk* about our risen, wealthy LORD, and yet the trailing poverty of us sickly believers! God honors not wisdom nor personality but faith. *Faith* honors God. And God honors faith. God goes wherever faith puts Him. *Faith,* in a sense which I believe you will understand, localizes deity. *Faith* links our impotence to His omnipotence.

The scientific world has broken the *sound* barrier; the lax, lustful world around us screams out to us that men have broken the *sin* barrier; now, please God, may we move along and by simple, single-eyed faith, break the *doubt* barrier! Doubt delays and often destroys faith. Faith destroys doubt. The blessed Book does not say "if thou canst *explain* the Scriptures, all things are possible to him that explaineth." God being who He is will never be explained in time; nor, we think, will He try in eternity to explain either Himself or His ways. The Book which is as immutable as its Author says, "If thou canst *believe, ALL* (that unavoidable word again) things are possible to him that believeth."

We have often heard people say with a sense of injury (after they have been overlooked for a job they thought they were admirably suited for), "It is not *what* you know these days that matters, but *whom* you know." I do not pretend to know how real that reasoning is in the business world; but I am absolutely sure it is right in the spiritual realm. What we know *about* God these days is giving us a deep stream of shallow books and is filling our libraries. (We are not despising true learning, and certainly not that wisdom which comes from above.) But *what* we know is one thing; *whom* we know is quite another. Paul had nothing, but yet "possessed *all* things." Sublime paradox! Blessed poverty! This blessed man was loaded spiritually. Building Christ's empire and writing the oracles of the Lord never unbalanced him. Yet despite Paul's uncomparable record, we find him toward the end of the journey still longing for more: "That I may know him, and the power of his resurrection, and the fellowship of his sufferings, being made conformable unto his death."

Much of the barrier to believers' translating the promises of God into fact before the eyes of men is that wretched thing called *self*. But Paul remembered when his old King Self was *dethroned and*—what is more—*crossed out* on a cross (Gal. 2: 20). Then Christ was enthroned. And before we can be clean and ready for Him to control, self-seeking, self-glory, self-interest, self-pity, self-righteousness, self-importance, self-promotion, self-satisfaction—and whatsoever else there be of self—must die. *Who* a man is is not important; *What he knows* does not matter; but *what he is* to the inscrutable God is what matters. If we displease God, does it matter whom we please? If we please Him, does it matter whom we displease? What we can *be* in union with Christ is one thing; but what we *are* is quite another. I am terribly dissatisfied with what I am. If you "have arrived," then pity your weaker brother and pray for me.

There is a faith that is just natural, intellectual, and logical; there is a faith that is spiritual. What good is it to preach the Word, if, as we present it, there is no kindling faith to make it live? "The letter killeth."

Shall we add death to death? The greatest benefactor of this generation will be the person who brings down on this strutting but stricken protestantism the inestimable power of the Lord. The promise still stands: "The people that do know their God shall be strong and do exploits." If any of us knows God, "then watch out, Lucifer!"

*Until self-effacing men return again to spiritual leadership, we may expect a progressive deterioration in the quality of popular Christianity year after year till we reach the point where the grieved Holy Spirit withdraws—like the Shekinah from the temple.*
                                                *—Dr. A. W. Tozer*

*No man is ever fully accepted until he has, first of all, been utterly rejected.*            *—Author unknown*

*No boasting for me ... none! — except in the Cross of our Lord Jesus Christ, by which the world has been crucified to me and I crucified to the world.*
                                *—Gal. 6:14 (Moffatt's Tran.)*

*If I had a thousand heads I would rather have them all cut off than to revoke.*            *—Luther, at Diet of Worms*

*I fear not the tyranny of man, neither yet what the devil can invent against me.*
                                *—John Knox, in "A Godly Letter"*

*The business of the truth is not to be deserted even to the sacrifice of our lives, for we live not for this age of ours, nor for the princes, but for the Lord.*
                                                *—Zwingli*

## CHAPTER NINE

*WANTED —*

*PROPHETS FOR A DAY OF DOOM!*

PAUL'S head is already halfway into the lion's mouth. What of it? Before Agrippa this daring, dauntless disciple Paul has neither nerves nor reserves! He can be no "tongue-in-cheek" preacher anytime, or anywhere. Physical courage will make a man brave one way; and moral courage, which despises men's opinions whosoever they be, will make a man brave another way. Both these types of courage made Paul a *Christian Daniel* in a Roman "den of lions." Men may try to destroy a prophet's body, but they can *not* destroy the prophet.

The clock creeps up to midnight as I write, and a peep through the window reveals a sky of velvet blackness. Transfer this into the realm of politics and it is a sky without a guiding star. Put that midnight sky in the realm of morals and you must multiply it to gross darkness. Come now to the realm of religion; count your T.V. audiences for top-line evangelists; tell me how many "big tops" are operating in evangelism at the moment; quote me the "converts" of all last year's Gospel efforts; and when you are done, I shall shout, with the roar of a tornado, "The moon of revival has not yet risen on this hell-bound, Christ-rejecting, speeding-to-judgment generation." We don't "sit at ease" in Zion any more. We have gone past that; we just sleep. In the church, pillars have given place to pillows.

As I began to say, Paul, as he stands before Agrippa, has his head half into the lion's mouth. With an awareness that the feet of pallbearers are not far away, he now "turns on the heat" until that wretched immoral King Agrippa stammers, "Thou almost persuadest me to be a Christian." Then Festus, a mere guest, forgets his manners and barges in with "Paul, thou art beside thyself; much learning doth make thee mad." Paul parries, "I am not mad, noble Festus." (I think the tone of his voice infers that the listening sinners *are* mad.)

But tell me, today when we preach the everlasting gospel, does anybody think that we are "raving" (as Rotherham translates *mad*) or going "insane" (as Weymouth translates it)? On the contrary, we have our love-offering in view, our big name to defend, our crowds to consider, and our extent of days to think over, don't we?

The Methodists in England have just finished their "Yearly Corporation of the People Called Methodists," a thing that John Wesley formed in 1784. It was held in Newcastle, England (1958). In spite of the colossal efforts of mass evangelism in the past two years and the boasted "lasting value of much follow-up work," it was acknowledged almost with tears that "the evangelistic candle" is almost guttered out. There are men among them large of mind, large of heart, and large of vision. Peep into the debating hall. Yes, there on his feet is Edwin Sangster—scholar, theologian, author, and now head of Methodism's Home Missions. He is not refuting the charge that Methodism is sick and (some add) nigh unto death. The man is moved and moving. Listen to him. I quote: "We are combatting something deep in the soul of the nation. For this deep malady, we need some deep X-ray therapy that we have not found." He adds, "I think, with passion, that agnosticism is flourishing in Britain in place of the great religious revival for which Methodists so fervently hoped. Last year church members in Methodism fell lower than for 13 years, and no less than 100,000 children ceased to attend Sunday schools." (I chip in here, Could T.V. be a real factor in this declension?) "Every year for the last twelve years the number of ministers has declined; it fell by 276 in the past year." (Dr. Sangster wrote some twenty years ago, *Can Methodism be Reborn*, knowing even then there was some canker at the heart.) Let Edwin Sangster finish his tormenting lament: "We thought that, even if our numbers were smaller, we could count on the total conviction of the people who came. But even those in the pews are having their battle for faith."

And Methodists in England are not alone in their perplexed plight. Tell me, Australians, Is the position like that with you? And what of the Church in South Africa? Any declension? In America we have an all-time high in church attendance; but that goes for Jews, Catholics, Jehovah's Witnesses, too; and do not forget the jails are full to overflowing, and the divorce mills are jammed to standing room only.

Men—benign, but bad and bloody— rule in many of the high places of the earth. "Uneasy lies the head that wears the crown." The cry of the slaughtered dead must be "Dost Thou not judge and avenge our blood on them that dwell on the earth?" The cry of "the living" (I mean those *really alive* with God-indwelt life) must be, "Avenge me of mine adversary. And shall not God avenge his own elect, which cry to him day and night?" Surely the hour is approaching when grace is impossible, when vengeance is inevitable.

To whom much has been given much will be demanded. Millions walk in darkness because they have no light; but the democracies are great offenders in that they have had light, but snuffed it out with the "bushel of business" or the "bed of idleness." Surely this Sodom-like sin must merit Sodom-like judgment. "This was the iniquity of thy sister Sodom," says Ezekiel 16: 49—"pride, fulness of bread, and abundance of idleness." We need prophets for this day of doom— holy men of God—to speak "as they are moved by the Holy Ghost." If He does not still move preachers, then we had better close down. But *He does* move them.

Neither Gideon nor anyone else gets into trouble because of his visions. It is actions that bring down the wrath of the offended powers. Let a Gideon slip out at midnight and cut down the groves of Baal; then hell releases its fury. Let John the Baptist call the priests "*vipers*" and rail at Herod's adultery, and he has signed his own death warrant. Certainly we need prophets for this day of doom, for look at the mounting interest in the false cults. *Newsweek*, Aug. 4th, 1958, says that Homer Knorr, president of the Watch Tower Bible and Tract Society, will take the Yankee Baseball Stadium this week, for 150,000 Witnesses will gather for a convention (their biggest ever—a sign of their growth). This eight-day conference will end with the baptism of 4,600 fanatical ministers, who are unpaid and would compass sea and land with their Christ-denying, man-concocted, Bible-twisting religion, to make another convert sevenfold more the child of hell. This makes you *think*—particularly after the above quotation of the all-time low in England of men for the ministry.

Can this organized but paralyzed system called Christianity cumber the earth much longer? Is Sangster right when he says we have not found an answer for the deep malady affecting the nation? (Would it not be more correct to say that we have scorned the old-time method of proclaiming repentance and regeneration and sanctification?) Tucked away in my heart is a stirring consolation; I share it with you. When God-given, heaven-sent revival does come, it will undo in weeks the damage that blasphemous Modernism has taken years to build. By the gale of the Spirit, the deceptive doctors of divinity will see swept away "the house which they built upon the sand" of human interpretations of the Bible. The head of humanity is sick and the heart faint. In the scheme of men, we are at the end of the line. Everything is "laid on" now for the superblast of the ages that will slice the earth in atomic destruction. Hell enlarges her mouth for the spoil which the filthy modernists have prepared as they have bartered the blood of Christ for "a mess of pottage" ("higher criticism"—so-called). With swollen heads and shrunken hearts, they will look at their folly.

Arm of the Lord, awake! put on strength! This is the hour for revival. This is the hour of doom. Where are the men of God? Prophets *may* have miracles, but they *must* have a message. In their own way, the bewildered worldlings are saying, Is there any word from the Lord? They know there is no intelligent word from any other source. Because God cannot lie, therefore Joel 2 and Malachi 3 will be fulfilled. "The Lord whom ye seek shall *suddenly* come to His temple." What comfort there! This moment drought; the next, deliverance. Ten minutes before John the Baptist arrived—no one knew that he was there. As it *was*, so I am sure it *will be*. God will get some man's ear and heart and will. Men, hidden in secret at this very moment, will utter soon, in the Spirit's might, the burning truths that this people must hear. Their words will burn as molten metal. With long patience, God awaits.

But when He arises, "Who may abide the day of his coming?" At the operation of the Spirit, men at this moment "drawing iniquity with a cart rope," will bend as corn before the wind. The Kremlin will tremble at the news of a supernatural operation in China. May God precipitate revival in China, Russia, Germany, etc.—lands scorched with the fire of militant Communism. For one reason, they need it so greatly; for another, our free nations need to be provoked, as Jonah was with Nineveh. Pharaoh finally wilted—under the assault of the ten plagues; and under Moses the prophet, the Israelites were led to victory. Today we have ten other new plagues—more sinister and effective and mighty than those (because world-wide and not confined just to Egypt); yet even these new plagues have not melted the heart of modern man but made it militantly wicked.

Have we no modern Moses? Can we suffer this generation to perish in the slave camp of moral bondage—and sit idly by, doing nothing about it? Are we to be mesmerized spectators, while Lucifer, with millions chained to his infernal chariot, sweeps many souls down the "broad way" to everlasting darkness? We need to rediscover the secret of those blessed men of whom the Word says, "They subdued kingdoms, [and] stopped the mouths of lions"—(that "lion" who goeth about today "seeking whom he may devour"). For this day of doom our pale, pathetic, paralyzed protestantism needs God-filled and God-guided men. Wanted — prophets of God!

*A baptism of holiness, a demonstration of godly living is the crying need of our day.    —Duncan Campbell*

*To bring fire on earth He came;*
  *Kindled in some hearts it is,*
*But O that ALL might catch the blaze,*
  *And ALL partake the glorious bliss.*

*The baptism of the heaven-descended Dove,*
*My heart the altar, and Thy love the flame.*
                                    *—George Croly*

*Come as the fire, and purge our hearts*
  *With sacrificial flame;*
*Let our whole soul an offering be*
  *To our Redeemer's Name.    —Andrew Reed*

*The same church members who yell like Comanche Indians at a ball game on Saturday sit like wooden Indians in church on Sunday.    —Vance Havner*

*There can be no revival when Mr. Amen and Mr. Wet-Eyes are not found in the audience.*
                                    *—C. G. Finney*

## CHAPTER TEN

*FIRE BEGETS FIRE*

M EN of prayer must be men of steel, for they will be assaulted by Satan even before they attempt to assault his kingdom.

Praying which is merely putting in a request sheet to the Ruler of the Universe is but the smallest side of this many-faced truth. Like everything else in the Christian's life, prayer can become lopsided. Prayer is no substitute for work; equally true is it that work is no substitute for prayer. In his masterly but little-known work, *The Weapon of Prayer*, E. M. Bounds says, "It is better to let the work go by default than to let the praying go by neglect." Again he says, "The most efficient agents in disseminating the knowledge of God, in prosecuting His work upon the earth, and in standing as a breakwater against the billows of evil, have been praying church leaders. God depends upon them, employs them, and blesses them."

Surely revival delays because prayer decays. Nothing do Satan or hell fear more than praying men. But to live well you don't have to live long. A man

only twenty-eight years old may die a hundred years
old in wisdom. The dragonfly rends his husk and har-
nesses himself in a clean plate of sapphire mail for a
pilgrimage to the dewy fields *lasting but a few days;*
yet no flowers on earth have a richer blue than the
color of his cuirass. So in the spiritual sphere, the
richest garments of the soul are spun on the looms of
prayer and dyed in the travail that fills up the sufferings of Christ. Fellow missionaries envied Henry
Martyn's spirituality. One says of him, "Oh to be able
to emulate his excellences, his elevation of piety, his
diligence, his superiority to the world, his love for
souls, his anxiety to improve all occasions to do souls
good, his insight into Christ and the heavenly temper!"
These are the secrets of the wonderful impression he
made in India. Martyn says of himself, "The ways
of wisdom appear more sweet and reasonable than
ever, and the world more insipid and vexatious." "The
chief thing I mourn over," he adds, "is my want of
power and lack of fervour in secret prayer, especially
when I plead for the heathen. In proportion to my
light, warmth does not increase within me." Does
anybody feel like casting the first stone at Henry
Martyn? Would we not all have to say that in
intercession we lack "heat"?

By its very nature, fire begets fire. If other com-
bustible material is about, fire will only spread its
kind. "See how great a matter a little fire kindleth."
*Fire* can never make *ice*, the *devil* certainly cannot
make *saints;* neither can prayerless pastors produce
warriors of intercession; yet one spark from an anvil
may set a city on fire. From one candle, ten thousand
others may take a light! From the matchless prayer
life of David Brainerd, outstanding stars in the firma-

ment of soul-winners have caught their initial light (like Carey, Payson, etc.).

William Carey read Brainerd's life story, and a dynamo started within the young soul-winner's breast, finally landing him on India's coral strand. At the flame of Brainerd's molten soul, the candle of Edward Payson's heart was lighted under God. Thus from just the diary of the pain-wracked, cowhide-clad apostle to the North American Indians, Payson caught the motivating inspiration, and began at twenty a prayer life that almost eclipsed Brainerd's. To add yet another soul-kinsman of Brainerd's, another master of prayer, who tottered into his grave at the "ripe old age" of twenty-nine years, we speak of Robert Murray McCheyne. This giant in prayer was first magnetized to this "greatest of all human offices that the soul of man can exercise" by reading about Brainerd.

Then another soul, the great Jonathan Edwards, watched Brainerd (while his daughter Jerusha wept), as the tides of consumption grew greater over Brainerd's body. Godly Edwards wrote: "I praise God that in His providence Brainerd should die in my house so that I might hear his prayers, so that I might witness his consecration, and be inspired by his example." When Brainerd was dying, Wesley was in about the prime of his spiritual conquest. Listen to Master Wesley talking to his conference in England. (Bear in mind here the other chapter where I quoted Dr. Sangster at this year's (1958) Methodist Conference in England.) Wesley said, "What can be done to revive the work of the Lord where it has decayed?" And then the relentless, tireless evangelist, who shook three kingdoms, answered his own question by saying, "Let every preacher read carefully the life of David Brainerd."

So there we have it. Let's line them up: Payson, McCheyne, Carey, Edwards, Wesley—men of renown, yet all kindled by one flame, and all debtors to the sickly but supplicating Brainerd.

The conflict of the ages is upon us. This unbiblical distorted thing called the church, that mixes with the world and dishonors its so-called Lord, has been found out for what it is, a fraud. The true Church is born from above. In it there are no sinners, and outside of it no saints. No man can put another's name on its member's roll; and no man can cross another's name off that roll. This Church—of which, bless the Lord, there is still a small remnant in the world—lives and moves and has its being in prayer. Prayer is its soul's sincere desire.

As the first atom bomb shook Hiroshima, so prayer alone can release that power which would shake the hearts of men. This cultured paganism at our doors, those idol temples, those fear-gripped, sin-mesmerized millions can only be moved *to* God as the Church is moved *of* God for their lost condition. With every possible guile that he knows, the devil would snatch us from the closet of prayer. For in prayer man is linked with God, and in that union Satan is baffled and beaten. Well he knows this; and so, if the closet is shut tightly, the mind is invaded with legitimate cares or with imaginations as big or more real than life. Here we need to plead our main defense—the blood. Another useful way to offset wandering thoughts and to help concentration is to pray audibly or to give some utterance at least, though it need not be loud.

Having thus moved and gained the mastery over Satan, our next power is in the "exceeding great and precious promises of God." Here we are on concrete foundation. Here are our trading currencies with heaven. Here God is pledged, and longs to hear us honor Him. Here we may be engaged in warfare not *with* God but *against* principalities, for Satan delights in loss no more than any other being. Souls of men are his treasures. Damned souls, doubting souls, drunk souls, disobedient souls, sick souls, religious souls, souls of the young, souls of the old, and all souls outside of the regenerationg power of the Spirit are mastered by him, though the degrees of his mastery vary. Souls, in various degrees of spirituality, are special targets for his fiery arrows, but the "shield of faith" will brush them all off and, bless the Lord, leave us all unscathed. Prayer is not for defence. The shield of faith is for that. Prayer is our secret weapon. (It seems secret to many of the Lord's people. Who of us, despite all that we have read, claims to know much about this masterly work of prayer?) We do not conquer Satan by prayer; Christ conquered him two thousand years ago. Satan fools and feints, blows and bluffs, and we so often take his threats to heart and forget "the exceeding greatness of God's power to usward." The Master Pray-er said, "I give you power over all the power of the enemy." That is the victory. The soul is drawn out in prayer. True prayer is a time-eater. In the elementary stages, the clock seems to drag; later, as the soul gets used to the holy exercise, time flies when we pray. Prayer makes the soul tender. Notice, we never pray for folks we gossip about, and we never gossip about the folk for whom we pray! For prayer is a great detergent. I am aware that the blood is the great soul-cleanser. But in prayer, if there is anything within of condemnation, the blood drawn from Emmanuel's veins will speak by the Spirit in mighty cleansing.

Satan would have us increase even in Bible knowledge, I believe, as long as we keep from prayer, which is the exercise of the instruction we have received through the Word. What use is deeper knowledge if we have shallower hearts? What use is greater standing with men if we have less standing with God? What use is personal physical hygiene if we have filthiness of the mind and of the spirit? What use is religious piety if we have soul carnality? Why strut with physical strength if we have spiritual weakness? Of what use is worldly wealth if we have spiritual poverty? Who can take comfort in social popularity if he is unknown in hell? Prayer takes care of all these spiritual maladjustments.

The soul that would be free from the false spiritual reckoning of this hour will need to steel itself to a closer walk with God, a calm and heavenly frame of mind. The aspirant for spiritual wealth and for the ear of God will know much loneliness and will eat much of "the bread of affliction." He may not know too much about family or social opposition; on the other hand, he may. But this is sure, he will know much of soul conflict, and of silences (which may create misunderstandings), and of withdrawal from even the best of company. For lovers love to be alone, and the high peaks of the soul are reached in solitude. The poet says,

"I heard a call, 'Come follow,'
    That was all.

Earth's joys grew dim,
My soul went after Him,
I rose and followed—
   That was all.
*Will you not follow
If you hear His call?*"

Could a mariner sit idle if he heard the drowning cry?
Could a doctor sit in comfort and just let his
    patients die?
Could a fireman sit idle, let men burn and give
    no hand?
Can you sit at ease in Zion with the world around
    you DAMNED?

                 —Leonard Ravenhill


Give me the love that leads the way,
The faith that nothing can dismay,
The hope no disappointments tire,
The passion that will burn like fire,
Let me not sink to be a clod:
Make me Thy fuel, Flame of God.

               —Amy Wilson Carmichael


...among whom ye shine as lights in the world;
holding forth the word of life....     —Phil. 2: 15, 16


Ye are the light of the world....     —Matthew 5: 14

## CHAPTER ELEVEN

## WHY DON'T THEY STIR THEMSELVES?

AMERICA cannot fall—because she is already fallen! This goes for Britain, too. She cannot go into slavery—because her people are fettered at the moment in the chains of self-forged, self-chosen moral anarchy. Here are millions, diseased morally, with no longing for healing. Here are men paying for shadows at the price of their immortal souls, men who not only reject the Substance, but who openly sneer at and caricature it.

An unprecedented tidal wave of commandment-breaking, God-defying, soul-destroying iniquity sweeps the ocean of human affairs. Never before have men in the masses sold their souls to the devil at such bargain prices. "There is none... that stirreth up himself to take hold of Thee" (Isa. 64: 7). What hell-born mesmerism holds them? How does the spell bind? Who brainwashed them? Why don't they wake and stir themselves?

Directed by the devil, the world has given a new

injection to the flesh. One of the signs of "the last days" is that "men are lovers of pleasures." (Note that it is in the plural.) And where is hell's broth stewed? In the breweries of the world. It is a lame argument that in some cases government subsidies are granted to help the breweries keep men employed. Breweries are maternity clinics that breed men-slayers operating with guns, and men driving on the highways while drunken. Courts deal with the *fruit* of liquor; revival would slay this deadly tree at the *roots*.

The mad merry-go-round of sensuality is filled with millions awaiting their turn for initiation into iniquity. When wrong is so sweet a morsel, the sin-soaked, sex-slain youth could not care less about doing right. One crowded hour of glorious "life"—so they argue—is worth a gamble on the speculation of the theologians' so-called "eternity."

Look for one bitter moment. Could anything be less intelligent and unmanly than a drinking match? The prize winner is the last man still standing on his feet when all others, grunting like hogs, have fallen to the floor, unconscious in drink. This is a sport not of stone-age men of the Baliem Valley, but of the new intellectuals, satiated in body, stained in soul, and recklessly abandoned to iniquity!

Loaded with lechery, gutted with gambling, damned in drink, such men (who are adult in body, but moral imbeciles) whine out Lord Byron's lament:

> "I now have ashes where once I had fire,
> The soul in my body is dead;
> The thing I once loved, I now merely admire,
> My heart is as gray as my head."

If the Church had something vital and victorious to offer, these men who choose golf clubs by day and night clubs by night might be drawn from these fleshpots.

Since in their freedom men will not heed God, will He have to enslave to Communism the mighty millions of America that they might have time to remember His *day*, His *way*, and His *Son?* Better to die bound in body and free in spirit than free in body and bound in soul!

We stand aghast when we see fine men magnetized by science, but mystified by the Christian religion. When these have forsaken faith, they feed on films and football. In the light of "a thousand years being as one day," it has taken science a matter of mere seconds to bring us from the chuck wagon to the station-wagon, and from the covered-wagon to the Sputnik.

But after admitting that science does hold and attract when it drills a hole two miles deep into the earth for oil, and if there is none, does the same thing in the sea (as off the shores of Mexico)—let us seriously consider that science has diabolic and deadly forms too—even lobotomization!

*Lobotomization* is the inhuman, devil-inspired surgery spawned by science. As you consider science in this guise, be imaginative and yet a realist! For years this horrible operation on the brain has been a weapon in the hands of dictators. Hitler used it on millions of his own flesh and blood. Stalin is said to have turned over ten million of his slaves into living Zombies with this simple operation, which takes only five minutes to perform. Afterwards the victim is said to be irrevocably insane.

The patient is strapped to an operating table, the straps tight and very strong. Electrodes are attached to the temples, three jolts of electricity are shot through the patient's brain, enough to start violent convulsions which finally give way to anesthetic coma. The doctor then takes his leucotomes (ice-pick-like instruments) and inserts them under the patient's eyelids. With a hammer he drives through the eye sockets into the fore part of the brain, severing the prefontal lobes of the brain from the rest of it. The result?—A Zombie (for want of a better word).

Fifteen Zombies can be made by science in ninety minutes. To add to this, we have the alarming news that there are probably 100,000 lobotomized people in the United States, according to George Conitz in Liberty League News. When enlightened men dehumanize other men in this fashion, it is time to stop and ask if the great Goddess of Science has not received too much veneration from men.

Keeping those lobotomized millions in mind, meditate on this from the pen of famed Bertrand Russell, whose "Principles of Logic" has made him the uncrowned king of modern philosophers: "Man now needs for his salvation only one thing: to open his heart to joy, and leave fear to gibber through the glimmering darkness of a forgotten past. He must lift up his eyes and say: 'No, I am not a miserable sinner; I am a being who, by a long and arduous road, has discovered how to . . . master natural obstacles, how to live in freedom and joy, at peace with myself and, therefore, with all mankind.' "

Would it be hard to persuade yourself that this "false prophet" of peace is dedicated to deception, consciously or otherwise? The same Bertrand Russell has trouble in trying to accept the incarnation. But would the relatives of the massacred Hungarians think his message a gospel of hope?

This is an hour in need of burning hearts, bursting lips, and brimming eyes! If we were a tenth as spiritual as we think we are, our streets would be filled each Sunday with throngs of believers marching to Zion—with sacks on their bodies and ashes on the shaking heads, shaking at the calamity that has brought the Church to be the unlovely, unnerved, unproductive thing that she is!

If we wept as much in the prayer closet as devout Jews have done at the Wailing Wall in Jerusalem, we would now be enjoying a prevailing, purging revival! If we would return to apostolic practice—waiting upon the Lord for apostolic power—we could then go forth to apostolic possibilities! This is the hour when we are asked over and over again, "Is everybody happy?" God's purpose for us is not happiness, but holiness! Soberness has given way to silliness, even though Paul in writing to Titus warns both young and old, "Be sober."

We surely need again to climb Calvary's hill on our knees, to survey the wondrous Cross in an attitude of humiliation and adoration. The Church must first repent; then the world will break! The Church must first weep; then our altars will be filled with weeping penitents.

At the very pinnacle of his power, William James, a Professor of Medicine at Harvard University, was struck down by a mysterious malady. His nerves were upset. He had insomnia and deep depression, but knew no cure for himself. He dashed off to Europe. Would Berlin have the answer? No door of hope opened. What about Vienna? The same answer. Might not Paris shelter a cure? But the panacea was not there.

Despair was heightening. London was near, but his call was but an echo. Scotland had eminent sons in this field. But there was no balm in this Gilead either. Back to America he came, the thought of suicide dancing in his brain. At last a man of prayer and of great faith for healing was recommended. Faith healing was anathema to William James, the distinguished philosopher and famed psychologist. His acute mind and mental training strongly protested against going this way. But needs must. James went. The simple, unlettered man of God put his humble hands on William James' head, who later said, "I felt a mysterious energy thrilling and tingling through my body which was followed by a sense of peace; I knew I was healed!" To cure the raging ills of this maddened world, the "Abana of Science" and the "Pharpar of Politics" are more attractive to our stubborn wills and warped intellects than the wondrous Cross. But for mankind to be made whole, we shall have to be as humble as William James was by getting back to the Cross of Jesus and its life-giving stream.

*I have need of nothing.*         *—Laodicean Church*


*Their iniquity: pride, fulness of bread, and abundance of idleness.*         *—Ezek. 16: 49*


*Is the Spirit of the Lord straightened? Are these His doings?*         *—Micah 2: 7*


*The Church that is man-managed instead of God-governed is doomed to failure. A ministry that is college-trained but not Spirit-filled works no miracles.*
        *— Samuel Chadwick*


*The man whose little sermon is "repent" sets himself against his age, and will for the time being be battered mercilessly by the age whose moral tone he challenges. There is but one end for such a man—"off with his head!" You had better not try to preach repentance until you have pledged your head to heaven.*
        *—Joseph Parker*

## CHAPTER TWELVE

## THE PRODIGAL CHURCH

## IN A PRODIGAL WORLD

TO take an over-all view of the Church today leaves one wondering how much longer a holy God can refrain from implementing His threat to spue this Laodicean thing out of His mouth. For if there is one thing preachers are agreed upon, it is that this is the Laodicean age in the Church.

Yet while over our heads hangs the Damoclean sword of rejection, we believers are lean, lazy, luxury-loving, loveless, and lacking. Though our merciful God will pardon our sins, purge our iniquity, and pity our ignorance, our lukewarm hearts are an abomination in His sight. We must be hot *or* cold, flaming *or* freezing, burning out *or* cast out. Lack of heat and lack of love God hates.

Christ is now "wounded in the house of His friends." The Holy Book of the living God suffers more from its exponents today than from its opponents!

We are loose in the use of scriptural phrases, lopsided in interpreting them, and lazy to the point of impotence in appropriating their measureless wealth. Mr. Preacher will wax eloquent in speech and fervent in spirit, serving the Lord with vigor and perspiration to defend the Bible's inspiration. Yet that same dear man a few breaths later with deadly calmness will be heard rationalizing that same inspired Word by outdating its miracles and by firmly declaring: "This text is *not* for today." Thus the new believer's warm faith is doused with the ice water of the preacher's unbelief.

The Church alone can "limit the Holy One of Israel," and today she has consummate skill in doing it. If there are degrees in death, then the deadest I know of is to preach about the Holy Ghost without the anointing of the Holy Ghost.

In praying, we assume the unpardonable arrogance of crying for the blessed Spirit to come with His grace—but not with His gifts!

This is the day of a restricted and relegated Holy Ghost, even in fundamentalist circles. We need and say that we want Joel 2 to be fulfilled. We cry, "Pour out Thy Spirit upon all flesh!" yet add the unspoken caution, "but don't let *our* daughters prophesy, or *our* young men see visions!"

"Oh, my God! if in our cultivated unbelief and our theological twilight and our spiritual powerlessness we have grieved and are continuing to grieve Thy Holy Spirit, then in mercy spue us out of Thy mouth! If Thou canst not do something with us and through us, then please, God, do something without us! Bypass us and take up a people who now know

Thee not! Save, sanctify, and endue them with the Holy Ghost for a ministry of the miraculous! Send them out 'fair as the moon, clear as the sun, and terrible as an army with banners' to revive a sick Church and shake a sin-soddened world!"

Ponder this: God has nothing more to give to this world. He gave His only begotten Son for sinners; He gave the Bible for all men; He gave the Holy Ghost to convict the world, and equip the Church. But what good is a checkbook if the checks be unsigned? What good is a meeting, even if it be fundamental, if the living Lord is absent?

We must rightly divide the Word of truth. The text *"Behold, I stand at the door and knock"* (Rev. 3: 20), has nothing to do with sinners and a waiting Saviour. No! Here is the tragic picture of our Lord at the door of His own Laodicean Church trying to get in. Imagine it! Again, in the majority of prayer meetings, what text is more used than "Where two or three are gathered together in My Name, there am I in the midst"? But too often He is *not* in the midst; He is at the door! We sing His praise, but shun His person!

With a stack of books beside us and marginal notes in Bibles for props, we have almost immunized ourselves from the scorching truth of the changeless Word of God!

I do not marvel so much at the patience of the Lord with the stonyhearted sinners of the day. After all, would we not be patient with a man both blind and deaf? And such are the sinners. But I do marvel at the Lord's patience with the sleepy, sluggish, selfish Church! A prodigal Church in a prodigal world is God's real problem.

Oh, we bankrupt, blind, boasting believers! We are *naked* and don't know it. We are *rich* (never had we more equipment), but we are *poor* (never had we less enduement)! We have need of nothing (and yet we lack almost everything the Apostolic Church had). Can He stand "in the midst" while we sport unashamedly in our spiritual nakedness?

Oh, we need the fire! Where is the power of the Holy Ghost that slays sinners and fills our altars? Today we seem much more interested in having churches air-conditioned t h a n prayer-conditioned. "Our God is a consuming fire." God and fire are inseparable; so are men and fire. Every single one of us is now treading a path of fire—hell-fire for the sinner, judgment-fire for the believer! Because the Church has lost Holy Ghost fire, millions go to hell-fire. .

The prophet Moses *was called by* fire. Elijah *called down* fire. Elisha *made* a fire. Micah *prophesied* fire. John the Baptist cried, "He shall *baptize* you with the Holy Ghost, and *with fire.*" Jesus said, "I am come to *send fire* on the earth." If we were as scared to miss *fire* baptism as we are to miss *water* baptism, we would have a flaming Church and another Pentecost. The "old nature" may dodge the *water* baptism, but it is destroyed in the *fire* baptism, for He shall "burn up the chaff with unquenchable fire." Until they were fire-purged, the miracle-working disciples who beheld His resurrection glory, were held back from ministering the Cross.

By what authority do men minister these days at home or overseas without an "upper room" experience? We have no lack of preachers of prophecy, but we are pitiably short of *prophetic* preachers. We make no plea for spiritual predictors and sensational prognosticators. There is now little scope left to foretell, for we have the Book and the unveiling of the Lord's mind in it. But we do need men to *forthtell*. No man can monopolize the Holy Ghost, but the Holy Ghost can monopolize men. Such are the prophets. They are never expected, never announced, never introduced —they just arrive. They are sent, and sealed, and sensational. John the Baptist "did no miracles"—that is, no rivers of derelict humanity swept down on him for his healing touch. But he raised a spiritually dead nation!

One marvels at our unblushing evangelists who announce that they have just had a wonderful revival with thousands thronging the altars, and then add, to soothe the staid fundamentalists, "but there was nothing sensational and no disorder." But can there be an earthquake without sensation? Or a tornado without disorder? Did Wesley's scorching ministry cause no upheaval? The Church in England slammed every door in the face of *"a man sent from God whose name was John"*—Wesley. But these "religious Canutes" did not keep back the tide of Holy Ghost revival.

This blessed man, Wesley, went away from Oxford University, having "failed completely," *conspicuously* is his own word (even with the brain of a scholar, the fire of a zealot, and the tongue of an orator), to lead others to the Lamb. Then came May the 24th, 1738, when John Wesley at an Aldersgate Street prayer meeting, was born of the Spirit; later he was filled with the Spirit. In thirteen years this fire-baptized man shook three kingdoms. And Savonarola shook Florence in central Italy until the face of "the mad monk" became a terror to the Florentines of his day, and a thing of derision to the religionists.

Brethren, in the light of the "bema seat," we had better live six months with a volcanic heart, denouncing sin in places high and low and turning the nation from the power of Satan unto God (as John the Baptist did) rather than die loaded with ecclesiastical honours and theological degrees and be the laughing stock of hell and of spiritual nonentities. Lampooning "liquor barons" and cursing corrupt politicians bring no fire down upon our heads. We can do both of these, and keep our heads and our pulpits. Prophets were martyred for denouncing false religion in no vague terms. And when we too see "lying religion" cheating men in life and robbing loved ones in death, or when we see priests leading them to hell under the banner of a crucifix, we should burn against them with holy indignation. Later, maybe, to lead the way to a Twentieth Century Reformation, we shall burn on martyr fires.

With tears, view this news: "Palsied Protestantism now hears the Roman Catholic priests commending Protestant evangelists!" In all conscience, could you picture the same religionists applauding a Luther, or sponsoring a Savonarola? "Oh! God, send us prophetic preaching that searches and scorches! Send us a race of martyr-preachers—men burdened, bent, bowed and broken under the vision of impending judgment and the doom of the unending hell of the impenitent!

Preachers make pulpits famous; prophets make prisons famous. May the Lord send us prophets—terrible men, who cry aloud and spare not, who sprinkle nations with unctionized woes—men too hot to hold, too hard to be heard, too merciless to spare. We are tired of men in soft raiment and softer speech who use rivers of words with but a spoonful of unction. These know more about competition than consecration, about promotion than prayer. They substitute propaganda for progagation and care more for their church's happiness than for its holiness!

Oh in comparison with the New Testament Church we are so sub-apostolic, so substandard! Sound doctrine has put most believers sound asleep, for the letter is not enough. It must be kindled! It is the letter *plus the Spirit* which "giveth life." A sound sermon in faultless English and flawless interpretation can be as tasteless as a mouthful of sand. To rob Rome and cripple Communism we need a fire-baptized Church. A blazing bush drew Moses; a blazing Church will attract the world, so that from its midst they will hear the voice of the living God.

*Let me burn out for God. After all, whatever God may appoint, prayer is the great thing. Oh, that I may be a man of prayer!* —Henry Martyn

*Love is kindled in a flame, and ardency is its life. Flame is the air which true Christian experience breathes. It feeds on fire; it can withstand anything, rather than a feeble flame; but when the surrounding atmosphere is frigid or lukewarm, it dies, chilled and starved to its vitals. True prayer MUST be aflame.* —E. M. Bounds

*O for a passionate passion for souls,*
  *O for a pity that yearns!*
*O for the love that loves unto death,*
  *O for the fire that burns!*
*O for the pure prayer-power that prevails,*
  *That pours itself out for the lost!*
*Victorious prayer in the Conqueror's Name,*
  *O for a PENTECOST!*
                              —Amy Wilson Carmichael

## CHAPTER THIRTEEN

## *WANTED —*

## *A PROPHET TO PREACH TO THE PREACHERS!*

TO attempt to measure the sun with an inch tape could hardly be more difficult than attempting to measure John the Baptist by our modern standards of spirituality. At Jordan the anxious crowd asked concerning the newborn child, "What manner of child shall this be?" They were told, "He shall be *great* in the sight of the Lord."

Today we are prodigal with the use of this word "great," for we mistake *prominence* for *eminence*. In those days God was wanting not a priest nor a preacher, but men. There were plenty of men then, as now; but all were too small. God wanted a *great* man for a *great* task!

John the Baptist probably had not one qualification for the priesthood, but he had every quality to become a prophet. Immediately before his coming there had been four hundred years of darkness without one ray of prophetic light—four hundred years of silence without a "Thus saith the Lord"—four hundred years of progressive deterioration in spiritual things. With a river of beasts' blood for its atonement and with an overfed priesthood for its mediator, Israel, God's favored nation, was lost in ceremony, sacrifice and circumcision.

But what an army of priests could not do in four hundred years, one man "sent of God," *John the Baptist*, God-fashioned, God-filled, and God-fired, did in six months!

I share the view of E. M. Bounds that it takes God twenty years to make a preacher. John the Baptist's training was in God's University of Silence. God takes all His great men there. Though to Paul, the proud, law-keeping Pharisee of colossal intellect and boasted pedigree, Christ made a challenge on the Damascus road, it needed his three years in Arabia for emptying and unlearning before he could say, "God revealed Himself in me." God can fill in a moment what may take years to empty. Hallelujah!

Jesus said, "Go ye!" but He also said, "Tarry until!" Let any man shut himself up for a week with only bread and water, with no books except the Bible, with no visitor except the Holy Ghost, and I guarantee, my preacher brethren, that that man will either break up *or* break through and out. After that, like Paul, he will be known in hell!

John the Baptist was in God's School of Silence, the wilderness, until the day of his showing forth. Who was better fitted for the task of stirring a torpid nation from its sensual slumber than this sun-scorched, fire-baptized, desert-bred prophet—sent of God with a face like the judgment morning? In his eyes was the light of God, in his voice was the authority of God, and in his soul was the passion of God! Who, I ask, could be greater than John? Truly "he did no miracle," that is, he never raised a dead man; but he did far more—he raised a dead nation!

This leathern-girdled prophet with a time-limit ministry so burned and shone that those who heard his hot-tongued, heart-burning message, went home to sleepless nights until their blistered souls were broken in repentance. Yet John the Baptist was *strange in doctrine*—no sacrifice, ceremony, or circumcision; *strange in diet*—no winebibbing nor banqueting; *strange in dress*—no phylacteries nor Pharisaic garments.

Yes, but John was great! Great eagles fly alone; great lions hunt alone; great souls walk alone—alone with God. Such loneliness is hard to endure and impossible to enjoy unless God-accompanied. Truly John made the grade in greatness. He was great in three ways: *great in his fidelity* to the Father—training long years, preaching short months; *great in his submission* to the Spirit—he stepped and stopped as ordered; *great in his statements* of the Son—declaring Jesus, whom he had never seen before, as "the Lamb of God who taketh away the sin of the world."

John was a *"Voice."* Most preachers are only echoes, for if you listen hard, you will be able to tell what latest book they have read and how little of *the* Book they quote. To reach the masses we need a Voice —a heaven-sent prophet to preach to *preachers!* It takes broken men to break men. Brethren, we have equipment but not enduement; commotion but not creation;

action but not unction; rattle but not revival. We are dogmatic but not dynamic!

Every epoch has been initiated by fire; every life, whether of preacher or prostitute will end with fire—judgment fire for some, hell-fire for others! Wesley sang, "Save poor souls out of the fire and quench their brands in Jesus' blood." Brethren, we have only *one mission*—to save souls; *and yet they perish!* Oh! think of them! Millions, hundreds of millions, maybe over one thousand million eternal souls, need Christ. Without Eternal Life they perish! Oh! the shame of it! the horror of it! the tragedy of it! "Christ was not willing that *any* should perish." Preachers, people go by the millions to hell-fire today because we have *lost Holy Ghost fire!*

This generation of preachers is responsible for this generation of sinners. At the very doors of our churches are the masses—unwon because they are unreached, unreached because they are unloved. Thank God for all that is being done for missions overseas. Yet it is strangely true that we can get more "apparent" concern for people across the world than for our perishing neighbors across the street! With all our mass-evangelism, souls are won only in hundreds. Let an atom bomb come and they will fall by the thousands into hell.

To say that the sin of today has no parallel is without foundation. Jesus said, "As it was in the days of Noah, so shall it be also in the days of the Son of man." We find a graphic picture of Noah's time in Genesis 6: 5, "God saw...the wickedness of man was great in the earth, and that every imagination...of his heart was only evil continually." So it was, evil without exception, *every* imagination; evil without mixture, *only* evil; evil without intermission, evil *continually*. As it was, so it is! Sin today is both glamorized and popularized, thrown into the ear by radio, thrown into the eye by television, and splashed on popular magazine covers. Church-goers, sermon-sick and teaching-tired, leave the meeting as they entered it—visionless and passionless! Oh God, give this perishing generation ten thousand John the Baptists—to tear away the bandages put over our national and international sins by politicians and moralists!

Just as Moses could not mistake the sight of the burning bush, so a nation could not mistake the sight of a burning man! God meets fire with fire. The more fire in the pulpit the less burning in hell-fire. John the Baptist was a new man with a new message. As a man accused of murder hears the dread cry of the judge, "Guilty!" and pales at it, so the crowd heard John's cry, "*Repent!*" until it rang down the corridors of their minds, stirred memory, bowed the conscience and brought them terror-stricken to repentance and baptism! After Pentecost, the onslaught of Peter, fresh from his fiery baptism of the Spirit, shook the crowd until as one man they cried out: "Men and brethren, what shall we do?" Imagine someone telling these sin-stricken men, "Just sign a card! Attend church regularly! Pay your tithes!" No! A thousand times NO!

Unctionized by the Spirit's might, John cried, "*Repent!*" And they did! Repentance is not a few hot tears at the penitent form. It is not emotion or remorse or reformation. Repentance is a change of mind about God, about sin, and about hell!

Nature's two greatest forces are fire and wind, and

these two were wedded on the Day of Pentecost. Thus, just like wind and fire, that blessed "upper room" company were irresistible, uncontrollable, unpredictable— Then their fire started missionary fires, quenched the violence of fire, lit martyr fires, and started revival fires!

Two hundred years ago, Charles Wesley sang
"O that in me the sacred fire
Might now begin to glow,
Burn up the dross of base desire,
And make the mountains flow!"

Dr. Hatch cried,
"Breathe on me, Breath of God,
Till I am wholly Thine,
Until this earthly part of me
Glows with Thy fire divine."

Holy Ghost fire both destroys, purifies, warms, attracts, and empowers.

Some Christians cannot say when they were saved. But I never knew a man yet who was baptized with the Holy Ghost and Fire and was unable to say when it happened. Such Spirit-filled men shake nations for God, like Wesley who was born of the Spirit, filled with the Spirit, and lived and walked in the Spirit.

An automobile will never move until it has ignition —fire; so some men are neither moved nor moving because they have everything except fire.

Beloved brethren, there is to be a special judgment for preachers; they shall receive the greater condemnation (James 3: 1). Can it be possible that as they stand condemned before the bar of God, men will turn on some and say, "Preacher, if you had had Holy Ghost fire, I should not now be going to hell-fire." Like Wesley, I believe in the need for repentance in the believer. The promise of the Father is for *you*. Just now, on your knees in that lonely mission station, or by your chair in that comfortable home, or in the pastor's study crushed and almost ready to give up, make this your prayer:

> To make my weak heart strong and brave,
>     Send the fire.
> To live a dying world to save, send the fire.
> Oh, see me on Thy altar lay
> My life, my all, this very day;
>     To crown the offering now, I pray:
>         Send the fire!
>
> —F. de L. Booth-Tucker

We have a cold church in a cold world *because the preachers are cold*. Therefore, "Lord, send the Fire!"

*No hat will I have but that of a martyr, reddened with my own blood.*
*—Savonarola, when rejecting a cardinal's hat*


*Apostolic preaching is not marked by its beautiful diction, or literary polish, or cleverness of expression, but operates "in demonstration of the Spirit and of power."*
*—Arthur Wallis*


*There are three things I would have liked to have seen. They are these: 1. Jesus in the flesh.*
*2. Imperial Rome in its splendor.*
*3. Paul preaching.* *—Augustine*


*Most joyfully will I confirm with my blood that truth which I have written and preached.*
*—John Huss on the stake*


*The primary qualification for a missionary is not love for souls, as we so often hear, but love for Christ.*
*—Vance Havner*

## CHAPTER FOURTEEN

## AN EMPIRE BUILDER FOR GOD

HAD Saul met only a preacher and heard only a sermon on the Damascus road, he might never have been heard of again. *But he met Christ!* (Sermons and preachers can be avoided—they often are—but Christ can never be avoided.) Right there that day Saul's philosophy of life was met with Life Himself. This fire-eating religious zealot met the fire-baptizing Lord; and as a result, when Saul was changed, civilization took a turn for the better. (May it please Thee to do this again, Lord, today!) Though in his own sight, a rigid, lawkeeping, blameless Pharisee, Paul soon began to declare himself to be the chief of sinners in the sight of God. No wonder, for he was to the infant church what Herod was to the infant Christ— turning darkest hell into yet darker despair.

A man with an experience of God is never at the mercy of a man with an argument, for an experience of God that costs something is worth something, and does something. Paul's was not an experiment that day; it was an experience. Yet his encounter with the

Holy One that day must have been as terrorizing as it was transforming. He had a blinding vision of the Lord "above the brightness of the [noonday] sun." Thereafter Paul was blind to all earthly honor. "They shall not honor me who would not honor Thee," said F.W.H. Meyer. Saul's collision with Christ suddenly shattered his dream of intellectual kingship and beggared his earthly prospects. Thus stricken, he stepped down yet further to another ordeal with God—-the stripping in the Arabian desert (of which things his lips are sealed).

And somewhere this empire-builder for Christ, with his colossal intellect and wonderful pedigree, accepted his Lord not only in substitution, but also in identification—"*I died* [in Him]." (To this truth we all render glib lip-service.) Paul also triumphantly affirms, "He *l-i-v-e-t-h* in me!" Grasp this truth with both hands. If we so testified, would friends shoot out the lip of mockery at us? This sold-out servant-of-the-Saviour arose from the ashes of his burned-up self to be the New Testament Samson, lifting off its hinges the gates of history, and turning Calvary's cleansing stream into the foul stables of Asian corruption. Blessed man!

Having found peace with God, Paul made war on all that was godless. He charmed the intelligentsia of Athens on his sweet lyre of the Gospel, ending his song abruptly by grasping the resurrection-trumpet, only to send the Athenians scattering—scarred and scorched by its truth.

But what made this man laugh at the frowning crags of Asia's barriers? Why did he die daily? What reason is there for his unmatched list of fortitude

(II Cor. 11)? Wherein is the rational explanation that he should carry an oversized burden? The answer is not from any wild guess or imagination, but from the well-kept diary of his soul. Staggering as it is, he goes on record as saying, "[It is] not I, but Christ liveth in me" (Gal 2: 20). Ponder it! He does not declare that he believes in the virgin birth, or that he is sure the Lord rose again from the dead—though of course, he believed this—but "Christ is now living in me!" From the sickening depth of depravity ("no more I ...but sin that dwelleth in me," Rom. 7: 17), he is now asserting from the height of spirituality, "Not I, but Christ liveth in me" (Gal. 2: 20). Precious exchanged life!

Paul's was an *exemplary life*. He was not a guidepost, but a guide. Listen to him, "Those things which ye have heard and seen in me, do" (Phil. 4: 9). He was indeed a "living epistle."

Paul's was an *exceptional life*. Would anyone be stupid enough to claim that Paul's self-abnegation is ours? Is it not rather true of us, "All seek their own"? He was exceptional in that he wrote so many epistles, and founded so many churches. But read the list again in II Cor. 11. Is he trying to outsuffer the martyrs, or make a safe claim to be listed with the saints? Not a bit of it! Place, pedigree, and privilege are but dung that he may win Christ, and by his abiding obedience be found in Him. He was exceptional in suffering, which was often by the choice of others, but exceptional in prayer, too, which was by his own choice. If more were strong in prayer, more would be suited to suffer. Prayer develops bone as well as groan, sinew as well as saintliness, fortitude as well as fire.

Paul calls the Holy Ghost as a witness that he could wish himself *"accursed"* for his brethren (Rom. 9: 3). Madam Guyon prayed almost an identical prayer. Brainerd and John Knox were "men of like passions." When, brother, (or where), did we ever hear such a prayer offered in a prayer meeting? We cannot have big results from our small praying. The law of prayer is the law of harvest: sow sparingly in prayer, reap sparingly; sow bountifully in prayer, reap bountifully. The trouble is we are trying to get from our efforts what we never put into them.

Paul's was an *expanding life*. Many of us, alas, are happy to get the scraps that are left over from another man's ministry. But Paul built upon no man's foundation (I Cor. 3: 10), for his brain was not so steeped in dogma that it became an ecclesiastical machine, merely grinding out the mysteries of metaphysics. He spent no wearying hours speculating upon Daniel's image. Neither did he hide away in some spiritual laboratory dissecting truth or labelling theological capsuls, nor yet complimenting himself on his ability to polish words for future creeds. The reason for this is as clear as the noonday.

Paul wrote no "Life of Christ"; He demonstrated it by his *"I am a debtor"* (Rom. 1: 14). If humanly possible at all, his soul's honor was pledged to erase that debt. The cost might be prison, for it were better that he should be "the prisoner of the Lord" *for a few years* than that his fellow men should be the devil's prisoners in hell *forever*. Paul was committed to a complete and costly consecration: "Henceforth let no man trouble me" (Gal. 6: 17). Paul was sold out to God. Every beat of his heart, every thought of his mind, every step of his feet, and every longing of his soul—all were for Christ and the salvation of men. He upset synagogues, had revivals and riots—either one or the other, sometimes both. (We seem to have neither.)

Though his revival party let him down—"all men forsook me" (II Tim. 4: 16), he dropped into the "everlasting arms" and went on. He escaped assassination; but with his daily bread he had daily death. for he said, *"I die daily"* (I Cor. 15: 31). Magnificent misery his!

The fruits of the Spirit were upon Paul; the gifts of the Spirit operated through him. He held citywide revivals while he patched tents to pay expenses! My brother preachers, aren't we a chicken-hearted group by the side of. Paul? Sometimes he almost starved! yet. when the table was full, he fasted. He wished everyone blessing, yet could wish himself accursed. With his revolutionary living and riotous theology, this "spectacle before men," this Christian filled with the Holy Ghost, is the redemptive counterpart of the fanatical devotee of the political religion of atheistic Communism. "People consumed by the inner fire of the Spirit are the counterpart in human life of the smashed atom which releases cosmic forces."

Paul, transformed, transported, and soon to be transplanted, reveals that we all could be "like him." Hear him as he stands before Agrippa—"I would to God, that not only thou, but also all that hear me this day were both almost, and altogether as I am, except these bonds." He does not say that he wishes all would write as he has done. Nor does he say that all would found churches by his example. Paul does not say "as I *did*," but, "as I myself *am*" (I Cor. 7: 7). The

Spirit that filled Paul can so fill us that we, like him, can be identified with Christ in sacrifice if not in service.

Where will this end with you, my brother? I do not know. (Neither do angels or men.) But where it all *begins* is in an Exchanged Life whereby we no longer live—*but Christ lives in us*. Paul lived gloriously and died triumphantly because in sacrifice and suffering he identified himself with Christ. So can we live and die, if we but will.

*The only saving faith is that which casts itself on God for life or death.* —Martin Luther

*...That is why, at every point in history where the Church of Christ has been carried on some wave of revival back to reality and self-consecration, thousands of men and women have rediscovered Paul, and have thrilled again to the music of his message.* —Dr. J. S. Stewart

*Tearless hearts can never be the heralds of the Passion.* —Dr. J. H. Jowett

*Oh! for a heart that is burdened!
Infused with a passion to pray;
Oh! for a stirring within me;
Oh! for His power every day.
Oh! for a heart like my Saviour,
Who, being in an agony, prayed.
Such caring for OTHERS, Lord, give me;
On my heart let burdens be laid.
My Father, I long for this passion,
To pour myself out for the lost—
To lay down my life to save others—
"To pray," whatever the cost.
Lord, teach me, Oh teach me this secret,
I'm hungry this lesson to learn,
This passionate passion for others,
For this, blessed Jesus, I yearn.
Father, this lesson I long for from Thee —
Oh, let Thy Spirit reveal this to me.* —Mary Warburton Booth

## CHAPTER FIFTEEN

## BRANDED — FOR CHRIST!

IN a certain sense all men are strangers to one another. Even friends do not really know each other. For to know a man, one must know all the influences of heredity and environment, as well as his countless moral choices that have fashioned him into what he is. Yet, though we do not really know one another, tracing the course of a man's life sometimes offers rich reward, particularly when we see the great driving forces which have motivated him. For instance, how greatly your life and mine would be benefited if we could experience the same surge of Christ-life that moved Saul of Tarsus, later called Paul, and plumb even a little the hidden depths of the meaning in his words, "I bear in my body the marks of the Lord Jesus" (Gal. 6:17)!

One thing is sure about these words—they were an acknowledgment of Christ's ownership. Paul belonged to the Lord Jesus Christ—body, soul and spirit. He was *branded for Christ*. When Paul claimed to bear in his body the five wounds of the Lord, he was claiming no "stigmata," as did Saint Francis of Assisi in 1224 A.D. It is not a bodily identification by outward imitation that Paul was speaking of, but a spiritual identification by inward crucifixion. He had been "crucified with Christ" (Gal. 2: 20).

The marks of Paul's inward crucifixion were plainly evident. First of all, Paul was *branded by devotion to a task*. If, as tradition says, Paul was only four feet six inches in height, then he was the greatest dwarf that ever lived. He out-paced, out-prayed, and out-passioned all his contemporaries. On his escutcheon was blazed: "One thing I do." He was blind to all that other men gloried in.

Likewise, Calvin suffered vituperation because he sat all day over his *Institutes*—with never a flourish of his mighty pen to tell us of the glories of the Alps. And Pascal was bitterly criticized because apart from the immortal soul of man, he could see no scenery anywhere worth looking at. And by the same token, the Apostle Paul might be castigated for saying not a word about Grecian art or the splendor of the Pantheon. His was a separation to spirituality.

After the Athenian clash on Mars Hill, he poured contempt on the wisdom of this world, dying daily to the temptation to outwit and out-think the wise. His task was not that of getting over a viewpoint, but of overcoming the legions of hell!

Somewhere, most likely in Arabia, Paul's personality had been transfigured. Never, after that, was he listed as a backslider. He was too occupied with going on. It would have vexed his righteous soul to hear a congregation sing, "Prone to wander, Lord, I feel it!"

Unsponsored, unwelcomed, unloved—made little difference to Paul. On he went—blind to every jewel of earthly honor, deaf to every voice of siren-ease, and insensitive to the mesmerism of worldly success.

Paul was also *branded by humility*. Moths could not corrupt this God-given robe. He never fished for praise with humility's bait, but in the long line of sinners put himself first (where we would have put him last). The old Welsh divine said that if you know Hebrew, Greek and Latin, do not put them where Pilate did at the head of Christ—but put them at His feet. "What things were gain to me," says Paul, "these things I count as loss for Christ."

What a hearts-ease is the virtue of humility—the great joy of having nothing to lose! Having no opinion of himself, Paul feared no fall. He might have swaggered in the richly embroidered robes of the chancellor of a Hebrew school. But in the adornment of a meek and quiet spirit he shines with more luster.

Next, Paul was *branded by suffering*. Consider the things he mentions in Romans eight: famine, peril, nakedness and sword (these belonging to acute discomfort in the body), and tribulation (perhaps of the mind), distress, persecution (of the spirit). Of all these sufferings the "little" minister partook.

This wandering Jew "made war" on all that made war on God and on the children of men. This prince of preachers and his foe, the prince of hell, spared each other no beatings. It was a free-for-all and no holds barred!

Look closely at Paul! that cadaverous countenance, that scarred body, that stooped figure of a man chas-

tened by hunger, kept down by fasting and ploughed
with the lictor's lash; that little body, brutally stoned at
Lystra and starved in many another place; that skin,
pickled for thirty-six hours in the Mediterranean Sea!
*Add* to this list danger upon danger; *multiply* it with
loneliness; *count* in the one hundred and ninety-five
stripes, three shipwrecks, three beatings with rods, a
stoning, a prison record, and "deaths" so many that the
count is lost. And yet if one could add it all up, it must
be written off as nothing, because Paul himself thus
consigned it. Listen to him: "Our light affliction, which
is but for a moment. . . ." That's contempt of suffering,
if you like!

Furthermore, Paul was *branded by passion*. A man
must be in the dead center of God's will and walking
the tightrope of obedience to call upon the Holy Ghost
to bear witness to his witness. Yet Paul does this in
Romans, chapter nine, verse one.

Oh, that from this wondrous flame every living
preacher might capture just a little light! Beatings
could not cast the flame out of him; fastings and
hunger could not kill it; nor misunderstanding and
misrepresentation quench its fire; waters could not
drown it, prisons break it; perils could not arrest its
growth. On and on it burned, until life ebbed from his
body.

The living Christ who was within Paul (Gal. 2: 20),
as manifested by his soul-passion, was at once the despair of hell, the capital for enlarging the Church, and
cheer to the heart of the Saviour (who was seeing the
travail of His soul and was being satisfied).

Paul was *branded by love*. When Paul experienced

becoming a "man in Christ," he developed the capacity for love. (Only maturity knows love.) How Paul loved! First and supremely, Paul loved his Lord. Then he loved men, his enemies, hardship, and even soul-pain. And he must have loved this latter particularly, else he would have shirked prayer. Paul's love carried him to the lost, the last, and the least. What scope of love! Mars Hill with its intellectuals, the synagogues with their religious traditionals, the market places with their prodigals—all these he yearned over and sought for his Lord. Love like a mighty dynamo pushed him on to attempt great things for God. Not many have prayed as this man prayed. Maybe McCheyne, John Fletcher, and mighty Brainerd, and a few others have known something of the soul-and-body mastering work of intercession motivated by love.

I remember standing by the Marechale once as we sang her great hymn:

> There is a love constraining me
> To go and seek the lost;
> I yield, O Lord, my all to Thee
> To save at any cost!

That was not just a lovely sentiment. It cost her prison, privation, pain, and poverty.

Charles Wesley seemed to be reaching on tiptoes when he said, "Nothing on earth do I desire, but Thy pure love within my breast!" More recently Amy Carmichael uttered the heartfelt prayer, "Give me a love that leads the way, a faith which nothing can dismay!" These men and women were certainly on the trail of the apostolic secret of soul-winning.

Great soul-winners have always been great lovers

of men's souls. All lesser loves were only conquered
by the greater Love. Great love to the Lover of their
souls drove them to tears, to travail, and to triumph.
In this evil hour, dare we love less?

> Let me love Thee, love in mighty
> Swaying realms of deed and thought;
> By it I can walk uprightly,
> I can serve Thee as I ought.
> Love will soften every trial,
> Love will lighten every care;
> Love unquestioning will follow,
> Love will triumph, love will dare!

Without any of their choosing, millions will be
branded for the Antichrist one day. Shall we shrink
to bear in our bodies, our souls, and our spirits our
Owner's marks—the marks of Jesus? Branding means
pain. Do we want that? Branding means carrying
the "slur" of the servant. Will we choose to be branded—for Christ?

*I have begotten you through the gospel.*     *—Paul*

*O brother, pray; in spite of Satan, pray; spend hours in prayer; rather neglect friends than not pray; rather fast, and lose breakfast, dinner, tea, and supper — and sleep too — than not pray. And we must not talk about prayer, we must pray in right earnest. The Lord is near. He comes softly while the virgins slumber.*
    *—Andrew A. Bonar*

*It was seven years*
*. . . before Carey baptized his first convert in India.*
*. . . before Judson won his first disciple in Burmah.*
*. . . that Morrison toiled before the first Chinaman was brought to Christ.*
*. . . declares Moffat, that he waited to see the first evident moving of the Holy Spirit upon his Bechuanas of Africa.*
*. . . before Henry Richards wrought the first convert, gained at Banza Manteka.*
    *—A. J. Gordon*

*Prayer—the soul's blood.*     *—George Herbert*

## CHAPTER SIXTEEN

## "GIVE ME CHILDREN OR I DIE!"

R EVIVAL is imperative, for the sluice gates of hell have opened on this degenerate generation. We need (and we say that we want) revival. Yet, though slick, shallow saints of this hour would have heaven opened and revival delivered on the slot-machine method, God has not mechanized His glorious power to fit our time-geared religious machinery.

"We wish revival would come to us as it came in the Hebrides," said a pastor recently. But fellow servant, revival did not come to the Hebrides by wishing! The heavens were opened and the mighty power of the Lord shook those islands because "frail children of dust. . .sanctified a fast and called a solemn assembly," and waited tear-stained, tired, and travailing before the throne of the living God. That visitation came because He who sought for a virgin in which to conceive His beloved Son found a people of virgin purity in those souls of burning vision and burdened passion. They had no double motive in their praying. No petitions were colored with desire to save the face of a failing denomination. Their eye was single to God's glory. They were not jealous of another group who was outgrowing them, but jealous for the Lord of Hosts, whose glory was in the dust, the "wall of whose house was broken down, and whose gates were burned with fire."

To draw the brooding Holy Ghost, a church group fundamentally sound in the Bible is not in itself a decoy. Beloved, we have thousands of such groups over the world. A girl of seventeen years and a boy of the same age may be equipped physically to parent a child, and even legally married. But does *that* in itself jusify their offspring coming? Would they have financial security to cover all the need? And would they be mentally mature enough to train a child in the way he should go? Revival would die in a week in some "Bible" churches, for where are the "mothers in Israel" to care for them? How many of our believers could lead a soul out of darkness into light? It would be as sensible to have spiritual births in the present condition of some of these churches as to put a newborn babe into a deep freeze!

The birth of a natural child is predated by months of burden and days of travail; so is the birth of a spiritual child. Jesus prayed for His Church but then to bring it to spiritual birth He *gave* Himself in death. Paul prayed "night and day. . .exceedingly" for the Church; moreover, he *travailed* for the sinners. It was when Zion travailed that she brought forth." Though preachers each week cry, "Ye must be born again," how many could say with Paul "Though ye have ten thousand instructors in Christ, yet have ye not many fathers: for in Christ Jesus *I have begotten* you through the gospel"? So he fathered them in the faith. He does not say that he merely prayed for them; he implies that he *travailed* for them. In the past century if the physical birth rate had been as low as the spiritual birth rate, the human race would now be almost extinct. "We must pray to live the Christian life." we say; whereas the truth is that we must live the Christian life to pray. "If ye abide. . .ye shall ask" (i.e., pray). I know that "asking" includes making our requests for the salvation of loved ones. but prayer is more than asking. Prayer, surely, is getting us into subjection to the Holy Ghost so that He can work *in and through us*. In the first chapter of Genesis every thing that had life brought forth its kind. Then in regeneration should not every really born-again soul bring others to birth?

We evangelists get a lot of credit—and very often take what is not ours at all. A woman in Ireland who prays for hours, prays each day for this poor stammerer. Others tell me "Never a day passes but what I lay hold of God for you." They have brought to birth many that are credited to me, whereas I very often only act as the midwife. In the judgment we shall be amazed to see big rewards go to unknown disciples. Sometimes I think we preachers who catch the eyes of the public will be among those rewarded the least. For instance, I know men who today preach sermons which they preached twenty years ago—which no longer gender life. Such preachers used to pray; one of these admitted to me some time ago, "No, brother, I do not pray as much as I used to, but the dear Lord understands." Aye, He understands all right, but He does not excuse us because we are busier than He wants us to be.

It is true that science has alleviated some of the

suffering that our mothers knew in childbirth; but science will never shrink the long slow months of child-formation. In the same way we preachers have also found easier methods of getting folk to our altars for salvation or for the filling with the Holy Ghost. For salvation, folk are permitted just to slip up their hand and, presto! the groaning at the altar is eliminated. For the filling with the Holy Ghost, men are told to "Just stand where you are while the evangelist prays for you, and you will be filled." Oh, the shame of it! Brother, before the miracle takes place, *true* revival and soul-birth still demand travail.

As the coming babe dislocates the body of the mother, so does the growing "body" of revival and soul-travail dislocate the Church. The mother-to-be wearies more as the time of the birth draws near (often spending sleepless but not tearless nights); so the lamps of the sanctuary burn the midnight oil as distressed, sin-carrying intercessors pour out their souls for a nation's iniquities. The expectant mother often loses desire for food and, in the interests of the one she will bear, denies herself certain things; so denial of food and a consuming love to lie quiet before the Lord seizes believers shamed by the barrenness of the Church. As women in pregnancy hide from public gaze (or used so to do) as the time of deliverance draws near, so those in travail of soul shun publicity and seek the face of a holy God.

It is very obvious that Jacob loved Rachel far more than he loved Leah, but yet the "woman's delight" was with Leah, for she had children. Consider how Jacob served fourteen years for Rachel, and yet that splendid devotion was no comfort to the woman stricken with barrenness. Undoubtedly Jacob proved his love by loading her with jewels, as the custom of the day was; but external nonentities were comfortless. And though Rachel was beautiful to look upon, for her sonless state she found no compensation in her own beauty or the admiration of others. The terrible truth remained that Leah had four laughing lads about her skirts; but at unfruitful Rachel men mocked and women shot out the lip. I can imagine Rachel—with eyes more red from weeping than ever Leah's were, and with hair dishevelled and voice hoarse with groaning—coming before Jacob, annoyed about her sterility, humiliated to despair by her condition, and crying with a piercing cry, "Give me children or else I die!" (Gen. 30: 1). That cry tore his heart as a sword would tear his flesh.

To spiritualize this, her praying was not routine but desperate, for she was gripped with grief, stunned with shame, and bowed low in barrenness. Preacher, if your soul is barren, if tears are absent from your eyes, if converts are absent from your altar, then take no comfort in your popularity; refuse the consolation of your degrees or of the books you have written! Sincerely but passionately invite the Holy Ghost to plague your heart with grief because you are spiritually unable to bring to birth. Oh, the reproach of our barren altars! Has the Holy Ghost delight in our electric organs, carpeted aisles, and new decorations if the crib is empty? Never! Oh that the deathlike stillness of the sanctuary could be shattered by the blessed cry of newborn babes!

There is no pattern for revival. Though babes are everywhere born by the same process, how different the babes themselves are—all new! no repeats! By the very same process of soul-grief and protracted prayer and burden because of barrenness, revivals of all ages have come—yet how different the revivals themselves have been!

Jonathan Edwards lacked no congregations and had no financial worries. But spiritual stagnation haunted him. The blemish of birth bankruptcy so buckled his knees and smote his spirit that his grief-stricken soul clung to the mercy seat in sobbing silence until the Holy Ghost came upon him. The Church and the world know the answer to his victorious vigil. The vows he made, the tears he shed, the groans he uttered are all written in the chronicles of the things of God. Edwards, Zinzendorf, Wesley, etc., were spiritual kinsmen (for there is an aristocracy of the Spirit, as well as of the flesh). Such men despised hereditary honors and sought the accolade of the Holy Ghost.

Political and military histories are wrapped up around individual men. History is sprinkled with the names of men who invested themselves with certain power and often made the world to tremble. Think of that evil genius Hitler. What kings he overthrew! what governments he tottered! what millions of graves he filled! To our age he was a bigger scourge than ten plagues. Hitler had one thing to do, and—he did it! The Bible says that in the last days when wicked men do wickedly, "the people that do *know their God* shall be strong and do exploits." Not those who sing about God, not those who write or preach about God, but they that *know their God* shall be strong and do exploits. Not talking about food will fill the stomach; not speaking of knowledge will make us wise; not talking of God means that the energies of the Holy Ghost are within us. We do well to ponder the fact that revival comes as a result of a cleansed section of the Church, bent and bowed in supplication and intercession. It views an age shackled with false religion and sickened at the sight of perishing millions; then they wait—perhaps days, weeks, and even months until the Spirit moves upon them, and heaven opens in revival blessing.

Women of the Bible who had been barren brought forth its noblest children: *Sarah*, barren until ninety years of age, begat Isaac; *Rachel's* cutting cry, "Give me children or I die!" was answered, and she bore Joseph, who delivered the nation. *Manoah's wife* bare Samson, another deliverer of the nation. *Hannah*, a smitten soul, after sobbing in the sanctuary and vowing vows and continuing in prayer, ignored Eli's scorn, poured out her soul, and received her answer in Samuel, who became the prophet of Israel. The barren and widowed *Ruth* found mercy and bare Obed, who begat Jesse, the father of David, of whose line came our Saviour. Of *Elizabeth*, stricken in years, came John the Baptist, of whom Jesus said there was no greater prophet born of women. If shame of childlessness had not subdued these women, what mighty men would have been lost!

As a child conceived suddenly leaps to life, so with revival. In the sixteenth century Knox parodied Rachel's prayer, crying, "Give me Scotland or I die!" Knox died, but while Scotland lives, Knox will live. Zinzendorf, chagrined and shamed at the loveless, fruitless state of the Moravians, was melted and motivated by the Holy Ghost until—*suddenly* revival came at about eleven o'clock on the Wednesday morning of August 13, 1727. Then began the Moravian revival, in which a prayer meeting was born that we are told lasted one hundred years. From that meeting came a missionary movement that reached the ends of the earth.

The Church of our day should be pregnant with passionate propagation, whereas she is often pleading with pale propaganda. To be sure, methods of child delivery have altered with the advance of science; but again we say that science, that darling of the doctors, cannot shrink the nine months of child-formation. Brethren, we are beaten by the time element. The preacher and church, too busy to pray, are busier than the Lord would have them be. If we will give God time, He will give us timeless souls. If we will hide in our soul-impotence and call upon His name, He will bring forth our light as the noonday. The Church has advisers by the carload. But where are her agonizers? Churches, boasting an all-time high in attendance, might have to admit an all-time low in spiritual births. We can increase our churches without increasing the kingdom. (I know a family where all the children are adopted. Many of us preachers have more adoptions than births.) The enemy of multiplication is stagnation. When believers lacking births become burdened, and when soul-sterility sickens us, then we will pulsate with holy fear, and pray with holy fervor, and produce with holy fertility. At God's counter there are no "sale days," for the price of revival is ever the same —travail.

Surely this ruined race requires reviving. I am fully aware that there are those who in their sleepiness will swing back on the sovereignty of God and say, "When He moves, revival will come." That is only half-truth. Do you mean that the Lord is happy that eighty-three people per minute die without Christ? Have you fallen for the idea that the Lord is now willing that *many* should perish? Do you dare to say—what to me is little less than blasphemy—that when God decides to lift up His heel and scatter His enemies, then a mighty visitation will come? Never! Quote *part* of a text and you can make the Bible say anything. For instance, "God is able to do exceeding abundantly above all that we ask or think." Stop the verse there, and it means "God is *able* to do it, but as yet He is not bothered so to do." This verse, misquoted, leaves the lack of revival on the steps of God's throne. But finish the text... "able to do—according to the power *that worketh in us*," and it means that the channel is blocked; it means God cannot get through to this age because of lack of power in the Church. So lack of revival is *our* fault.

Finney said: "God is one pent-up revival"; so we can have revival "according to the power that worketh in us," for we "shall receive power *after that the Holy Ghost is come upon* [us]." This is not power merely to do miracles, for *before* Pentecost they did miracles and cast out devils. Nor is it just power to organize, power to preach, power to translate the Scriptures, power to enter new territories for the Lord. All this is good. But have we Holy Ghost power—power that restricts the devil's power, pulls down strongholds and obtains promises? Daring delinquents will be damned if they are not delivered from the devil's dominion. What has hell to fear other than a God-anointed, prayer-powered church?

Beloved, let us put away all trifling. Let us forget denominational issues. Let us "give ourselves *continually to prayer* and to the ministry of the Word," "for faith cometh by hearing." Shamed at the impotence of the Church, chagrined at the monopoly the devil holds, shall we not cry with tortured spirits (and mean it): *"Give me children, or else I die!"* Amen.

*Christian men and women, self-renunciation is the cardinal ethic of the Christian Church.*

*—Dr. Charles Inwood*

*"Now I leave off to speak any more to creatures, and turn my speech to Thee, O Lord. Now I begin my intercourse with God which shall never be broken off. Farewell, father and mother, friends and relations! Farewell, meat and drink! Farewell, the world and all delights! Farewell, sun, moon, and stars! Welcome God and Father! Welcome sweet Lord Jesus, Mediator of the New Covenant! Welcome Blessed Spirit of Grace, God of all Consolation! Welcome Glory! Welcome Eternal Life! Welcome Death!"* Dr. Matthew MacKail *stood below the gallows, and as his martyr cousin writhed in the tautened ropes, he clasped the helpless jerking legs together and clung to them that death might come the easier and sooner. And so, with Christ was Hugh MacKail "with his sweet boyish smile." "And that will be my welcome," he said; "the Spirit and the Bride say, Come."*

*—The martyrdom of Hugh MacKail, a Covenanter*

## CHAPTER SEVENTEEN

## *"THE FILTH OF THE WORLD"*

WHAT is "the filth of this world"? (I Cor. 4: 13).
Is it the womb of evil of which the national
syndicated crime is born? Is it the evil genius operating the international upheaval? Was it Babylon? Is it
Rome? Is it sin? Has a tribe of evil spirits been located
bearing this repulsive title? Is it V.D.?

A thousand guesses at this question might provide
a thousand different answers with not one of them
correct. The right answer is the very antithesis of our
expectation. This *"filth of this world"* is neither of
men nor of devils. It is not bad, but good—nay, not
even good—but the very best. Neither is it material,
but spiritual; neither is it of Satan, but of God. It is
not only of the Church, but a saint. It is not only a
saint, but the saintliest of saints, the Kohinoor of all
gems. *"We apostles,"* Paul says, *"are the filth of this
world."* Then he adds insult to injury, heightens the in-
famy, and deepens the humiliation by adding "[and we
apostles are] *the offscouring of all things"* (I Cor.
4: 13).

Any man who has so assessed himself "filth of the earth" has no ambitions—and so has nothing to be jealous about. He has no reputation—and so has nothing to fight about. He has no possessions—and therefore nothing to worry about. He has no "rights"—so therefore he cannot suffer any wrongs. Blessed state! He is already dead—so no one can kill him. In such a state of mind and spirit, can we wonder that the apostles "turned the world upside down"? Let the ambitious saint ponder this apostolic attitude to the world. Let the popular, unscarred evangelist living in "Hollywood style" think upon his ways.

Who then hurt Paul far more than his one hundred and ninety-five stripes, his three stonings, and his triple shipwrecks could ever hurt him? The contentious, carnal, critical, Corinthian crowd. This Church was split by carnality—*and cash!* Some had rocketted to fame and become the merchant princes of the city. So Paul says, "*Ye* have reigned as kings without us." Ponder the glaring contrasts in I Cor. 4: 8: "*Ye* are full, *ye* are rich, *ye* have reigned as kings without us." "*We* are fools; *we* are despised; *we* both hunger and thirst and are naked" (verse 10). The blessed compensation is in verse 9, "*We* [apostles] are made a spectacle unto the world, and to angels, and to men."

It was not hard for Paul to claim after all this that *he* was "less than the least." Then, Paul pointed all this truth against those whose faith had lost its focus. These Corinthians were full, but not free. (A man escaped from his cell is not free who still drags his chain.) Paul is not grieved that they have superabundance and he nothing. He groans that their wealth has brought weakness of soul. They have comfort, but no cross; they are rich, but not reproached for Christ's sake. He does not say they are not Christ's, but that they are seeking a thornless path to heaven. He declares, "I would to God *ye* did reign, that *we* also might reign with you." If they were actually reigning, then Christ would have come, the millennium would have been there, and, Paul adds, *"We* would be reigning *with you."*

But who wants to be thus dishonored, despised, devalued? Such truth is revolutionary and upsetting to our corrupted Christian teaching. Can we *delight* in being esteemed fools? Is it *easy* to see our names cast about as an evil thing? Communism levels men down; Christ levels men up! True Christianity is far more revolutionary than Communism (though of course, bloodless). The bulldozers of socialism have tried to "push over" the hills of wealth and "fill in" the valleys of poverty. They thought that by education they could "make the crooked places straight"—by an act of parliament and a mere waving of the political wand, the millennium, so long delayed, could be brought in. But those changes in Russia have been merely a change of bosses with the underdog still the bottom dog. Today plenty of people are rich by making others poor, but Paul said he was *"poor, yet making many rich."* Thanks be unto God! the bag of Simon Magus still gets no attention from the Holy Ghost! If we have not yet been taught how to esteem "the mammon of unrighteousness," how shall we be entrusted with the "true riches"?

And so Paul, bankrupt materially and socially, was bracketed with the choice few who are listed "as the "filth of the world." Certainly this helped him understand that, as filth, he would be trodden under foot by men. Even though he could answer the philosophers, Stoics, and Epicurians on Mars Hill, yet for Christ's sake he was willingly rated a *"fool."* To Jesus, the world's antagonism was fundamental and perpetual.

Brethren, is this our choice? What irks us more than to be *classified with unlearned and ignorant men?* —though an unlearned and ignorant man wrote "the Revelation," which still baffles the learned. We are suffering today from a plague of ministers who are more concerned that their *heads should be filled* than that their *hearts be fired.* If a preacher leans toward headiness, let him spend his years of schooling *before* he enters the pulpit. Once he gets there, he is in it for life. Added degrees will not matter, because twenty-four hours a day are not sufficient for him to bear the names of his flock before the Great Shepherd, or fulfill the parallel responsibility of preparing their soul-food. The fact, then, is that spiritual things are spiritually (*not psychologically*) discerned. Neither God nor His judgments have changed. By His prerogative, there are still things withheld from the prudent and "revealed unto babes." And babes, brethren, have no colossal intellects! The Church of this hour boasts an all-time high in the I.Q. of its ministry. But hold on a minute before we triumph in the flesh. We are also having an all-time low in spiritual births, for the devil shudders not, Brother Apollos, at your verbal Niagaras!

The line of demarcation from the world is distinct, deliberate, and discredited. Bunyan's pilgrims passing through Vanity Fair were a spectacle. In dress, speech, interest, and sense of values, they differed from the worldlings. Is this so in our lives today?

During the last war a British general said, "We must teach our men to hate, for what men hate they will fight." We have heard much (though not half enough) about perfect love; but we also need to know how to "be angry and sin not." The Spirit-filled believer will hate iniquity, injustice and impurity; and he will militate against all of them. Because Paul hated the world, the world hated Paul. We, too, need this disposition of opposition.

Stanley wrote his "Darkest Africa," and General Booth his "Darkest England" amidst crushing opposition. The former saw the tall, impenetrable forest, with its lurking leopards, subtle snakes, and denizens of the darkness. Booth saw the English streets as God saw them—the lurking lust, the sewers of sin, the greed of gambling, the peril of prostitution—and he raised an army for God to fight them. Our front streets are now mission fields. Forget culture, for a well-mannered, nicely groomed and soft-spoken lady may be as far from God as the Mau Mau mother with her grass skirt. Our cities are alive with impurity. A Christian, dreaming before his television night by night, has a dead brain and a bankrupt soul. He would do better to persuade God to let him quit this world if he is so out of touch with this lax, loose, licentious age that blindness of the sinner no longer tears his soul. Every street is now a river of devilry, drink, divorce, darkness, and damnation. If you are taking a stand against all this, marvel not, brethren, that the world hate you. If ye were of the world, the world would love its own.

Paul declares in good round English, "The *world* is crucified unto me." Is this far beyond twentieth century Christians? Gologtha witnessed many crowds who came to see the humiliation of its malefactors. There was carnival at the Cross; there was mockery at misery. But who went the next morning to view the victims? The first callers were vultures—to peck out their eyes and strip their ribs; then dogs ate the limbs which hung from these hapless victims. Thus distorted, and decorated with his own entrails, the felon was a fright. Even so, to Paul, the crucified world was as unattractive as that!

Well might we, too, inwardly quake and with trembling lips repeat this phrase, *the world is crucified to me*. Only when we are thus "dead to the world and all its toys, its idle pomp and fading joys" can we feel the freedom that Paul knew. The plain fact is that we followers of Christ *respect* the world and its opinions and appreciations and qualifications. A modern critic says that we believers have *gold* for our god and *greed* for our creed. (Only those who are guilty will get mad at that quip!) On the other hand, in this year of grace, I do know some saints on both sides of the Atlantic who wear clothes that others have cast off, and so turn all their dollars and dimes (or pounds and pence) into grist for God's mill. With his strong emphasis on separation, one wonders that Paul ever got any converts at all.

This blessed man, to whom the world was crucified, was considered "mad." Moreover, Paul so presented his message that others sought his death, for their "craft was in danger!" Such blessed apostles, with their healthy, holy *disregard for the world* and its men, shame us.

> "They climbed the steep ascent to heaven
>     Through peril, toil and pain;
>  O God, to us may grace be given
>     To follow in their train."

Soon it will be "Farewell mortality, welcome eternity." Here's wishing you, beloved believer, a year of sacrificial service for Him who was our sacrifice. May we too, finish our course with *joy*.

*Brethren, it is just so much humbug to be waiting for this, night after night, month after month, if we ourselves are not right with God. I must ask myself — "Is my heart pure? Are my hands clean?"*
             *—Comment from the Hebrides' Revival*

*My soul, ask what thou wilt,*
  *Thou canst not be too bold;*
*Since His own blood for thee He spilt,*
  *What else can He withhold?*          *—Unknown*

*The place of prayer,*
  *O fruitful place!*
*The Spirit hovers there;*
  *For all embodiments of grace*
*Are from the womb of prayer.*          *—Harold Brokke*

*Revival is no more a miracle than a crop of wheat. Revival comes from heaven when heroic souls enter the conflict determined to win or die—or if need be, to win and die! "The kingdom of heaven suffereth violence, and the violent take it by force."*          *—Charles G. Finney*

*God's cause is committed to men; God commits Himself to men. Praying men are the vice-regents of God; they do His work and carry out His plans.*
             *—E. M. Bounds*

*Prayer is the sovereign remedy.*          *—Robert Hall*

*Prayer is the acid test of devotion.* *—Samuel Chadwick*

## CHAPTER EIGHTEEN

## PRAYER AS VAST AS GOD

GOD-GRIPPED prophets of old had a sensitive awareness of the enormity and unpopularity of their task. By pleading their own inefficiency and inadequacy, these care-bowed men sought to escape the delivering of their burdened souls. Moses, for instance, sought to evade a nation-wide commitment by pleading a stammering tongue. Yet note how God evaded his evasion by supplying a spokesman in Aaron. Jeremiah, too, reasoned that he was but a child. Yet in Jeremiah's case (as in Moses'), the human objection was not sustained. For men of divine selection were not sent to the council chambers of human wisdom—to get their personalities polished or their knowledge edged. But God somehow trapped His man and closeted him with Himself. If according to Oliver Wendell Holmes, a man's mind, stretched with a new idea, can never go back to its original dimensions, then what shall we say of a soul that has heard the whisper of the Eternal Voice? "The words that I [the Lord] speak unto you, they are spirit, and *they are life*" (John 6: 63). Our preaching is much diseased today by borrowed thoughts from the brains of dead men rather than from the Lord. Books are good when they are our guides, but bad when they are our chains.

Just as in atomic energy, modern scientists have touched a new dimension of power, so the Church has to rediscover the unlimited power of the Holy Spirit. To smite the iniquity of this sin-soaked age and shatter the complacency of slumbering saints, something is really needed. Vital preaching and victorious living must "come out of" sustained watches in the prayer chamber. Some one says, "We must *pray* if we want to live a holy life!" Yes, but conversely, we must *live a holy life* if we want to pray. According to David, "Who shall ascend into the hill of the Lord? He that hath clean hands, and a pure heart" (Ps. 24: 3, 4).

The secret of praying is praying in secret. Books on prayer are good, but not enough. As books on cooking are good but hopeless unless there is food to work on, so with prayer. One can read a library of prayer books and not be one whit more powerful in prayer. We must learn to pray, and we must pray to learn to pray. While sitting in a chair reading the finest book in the world on physical health, one may waste away. So one may read about prayer, marvel at the endurance of Moses, or stagger at the weeping, groaning Jeremiah, and yet not be able to stammer the ABC's of intercessory prayer. As the bullet unspent bags no game, so the prayer-heart unburdened gathers no spoil.

"In God's name, I beseech you, let prayer nourish your soul as meals nourish your body!" said the faithful Fenelon. Henry Martyn spake thus: "My present deadness I attribute to want of sufficient time and tranquility for private devotion. Oh that I might be a man of prayer!" A writer of old said, "Much of our praying is like the boy who rings the door bell, but then runs away before the door is opened." Of this we are sure: The greatest undiscovered area in the resources of God is the place of prayer.

Who can tell the measure of God's power? One might estimate the weight of the world, tell the size of the Celestial City, count the stars of heaven, measure the speed of lightning, and tell the time of the rising and setting of the sun—but you cannot estimate prayer power. *Prayer is as vast as God* because He is behind it. Prayer is as mighty as God, because He has committed Himself to answer it. God pity us that in this noblest of all employments for the tongue and for the spirit, we stammer so. If God does not illuminate us in the closet, we walk in darkness. At the judgment seat the most embarrassing thing the believer will face will be the smallness of his praying.

Here is a majestic passage from the venerated Chrysostom: "The *potency of prayer* hath subdued the strength of fire; it hath bridled the rage of lions, hushed anarchy to rest, extinguished wars, appeased the elements, expelled demons, burst the chains of death, expanded the gates of heaven, assuaged diseases, repelled frauds, rescued cities from destruction, stayed the sun in its course, and arrested the progress of the thunderbolt. Prayer is an all-sufficient panoply, a treasure undiminished, a mine which is never exhausted, a sky unobscured by clouds, a heaven unruffled by the storm. It is the root, the fountain, the mother, of a thousand blessings." Are Chrysostom's words mere rhetoric, to make a commonplace thing look superlative? The Bible knows nothing of such cunning.

Elijah was a man skilled in the art of prayer, who altered the course of nature, strangled the economy of a nation, prayed and fire fell, prayed and people fell, prayed and rain fell. We need rain, rain, rain! The churches are so parched that seed cannot germinate. Our altars are dry, with no hot tears of penitents. Oh for an Elijah! When Israel cried for water, a man smote a rock, and that flinty fortress became a womb out of which a life-giving stream was born. "Is anything too hard for the Lord?" God send us a man that can smite the rock!

Of this let us be sure, the prayer closet is not a place merely to hand to the Lord a list of urgent requests. Does "prayer change things"? Yes, but prayer *changes men*. Prayer not only took away the reproach of Hannah, but it changed her—changed her from a barren woman to a fruitful one, from mourning to rejoicing (I Sam. 1: 10; and 2: 1), yes, changed her "mourning into dancing" (Ps. 30: 11). Perhaps we are praying that we might dance when we have never yet mourned. We choose the garment of praise while God says, (Isa. 61: 3), *"unto them that mourn [I give] the garment of praise for the spirit of heaviness."* If we would reap, the same order is true, for "he that goeth forth and *weepeth*, bearing precious seed, shall doubtless come again with *rejoicing*, bringing his sheaves with him" (Ps. 126: 6).

It took a *heartbroken, mourning* Moses to cry, "Oh, this people have sinned a great sin...Yet now, if thou wilt forgive their sin—; and if not, blot me, I pray thee, out of thy book which thou hast written" (Ex. 32: 31, 32)! It took a *burdened, pain-gripped* Paul to say, "I have great heaviness and continual sorrow in my heart. For I could wish that myself were accursed from Christ for my brethren, my kinsmen according to the flesh" (Rom. 9: 2, 3).

If John Knox had prayed, "Give me success!" we would never have heard of him; but he prayed a self-purged prayer—"Give me Scotland, or I die!"—and his prayer scored the pages of history. If David Livingstone had prayed that he might split Africa wide open, as proof of his indomitable spirit and skill with the sextant, his prayer would have died with the wind of the forest; but he prayed, "Lord, when will the wound of this world's sin be healed?" Livingstone lived in prayer, and literally died upon his knees in prayer.

For this *sin*-hungry age we need a *prayer*-hungry Church. We need to explore again the "exceeding great and precious promises of God." In "that great day," the fire of judgment is going to test the *sort*, not the *size* of the work we have done. That which is born in prayer will survive the test. Prayer does business with God. Prayer creates hunger for souls; hunger for souls creates prayer. The understanding soul prays; the praying soul gets understanding. To the soul who prays in self-owned weakness, the Lord gives His strength. Oh that we were men of like prayer as Elijah —a man subject to like passions as we are! Lord, let us pray!

*On a tablet in a large church seating 1,000 people, this inscription was placed in memory of John Geddie: "When he landed in 1848 there were no Christians here; when he left in 1872 there were no heathen."*
　　　　　*—Memorial to John Geddie, the "father" of Presbyterian Missions in the South Seas*


*From the day of Pentecost, there has been not one great spiritual awakening in any land which has not begun in a union of prayer, though only among two or three; no such outward, upward movement has continued after such prayer meetings declined.*
　　　　　*—Dr. A. T. Pierson*

## CHAPTER NINETEEN

## AS THE CHURCH GOES, SO GOES THE WORLD

FOR this midnight hour, *incandescent* men are needed. On the day of Pentecost, the flame of the living God became the flame of the human heart to that glorious company. The Church *began* with these men in the "upper room" agonizing—and today is *ending* with men in the supper room organizing. The Church began in revival; we are ending in ritual. We started virile; we are ending sterile. Charter members of the Church were men of heat and no degrees; today many hold degrees, but have no heat! Ah, brethren, flame-hearted men are the crying need of the hour!

Men need to be a pillar of fire—God-guided men to lead a misguided people; passionate Pauls to stir timid Timothys; men of flame to outshine and out-burn men of name! We need knights of prayer to lead nights of prayer. We need true *prophets* to warn of false *profits*, "for what shall it profit a man, if he shall gain the whole world and lose his own soul?" (Mark 8: 36).

In this end time the rockaby-baby attitude of many

conference preachers is a tragedy. The cry should be "Blow the trumpet in Zion, sanctify a fast, call a solemn assembly...; let the priests, the ministers of the Lord, weep!" (Joel 2: 15–17).

Compared to a heart that has known the fire of the Lord and allowed that fire to go out, the ice-clad peaks of the Alps are warm. Metal is molten only while the fire burns; remove the fire and the metal is solid. Even so, a human heart without the heat of heaven is an iceberg.

If the Spirit is absent, the preacher's study becomes a laboratory for dissecting doctrine and developing lifeless dogma. Teaching needs anointing; truth must be trenchant; and comfort must kindle.

Inspired men are desperately needed! Believers with Spirit-generated souls are indispensable to this degenerate generation. The gale of end-time iniquity will blow out a mere human flame and as a dry reed cracks in a storm, will snap fleshly sectarianism's feeble candle. At the moment a rushing mighty wind of false religion and lukewarm Christianity is lashing the world. Warned of false fire by fireless men, we too often settle for no fire at all!

Unable to detect what is flesh and what is Spirit, the religionists of the hour are heralding with banner headlines a new boom in spirituality. The good has again become the enemy of the best. (The wise will understand.) Be alarmed! The conflict gets stiffer! This is the night of blight and plight. God help the nations, ruined with *man-made* religion, cursed with *man-made* cults, and doomed with *man-made* doctrine! Was there ever such an evil hour? Reiterated effort is the price we have to pay for progress.

As the Church goes, so goes the world! If the watchmen sleep, the enemy takes the city! The preacher should give at least one day a week to prepare his sermons and yet another day to prepare the preacher to preach the prepared sermons. Inspiration is as mysterious as life, for both are God-given. Life begets life by its very nature. By the same token, inspired men inspire.

We need Joshuas to lead the Lord's people into the Promised Land of Spirit-empowered living. Like Israel, we have escaped Egypt and Pharaoh (which in our experience means the world and Satan), but failed at Kadesh-Barnea. What should be a stepping stone can become a stumbling block. What should be a gateway can become a goal. What could be a thoroughfare can become a terminal.

"Blind unbelief is sure to err and scan God's works in vain." Have we come out of the poverty of the world, but not yet entered into the Canaan of His riches?

Think of it! For forty years these chosen people had no miracles and no answers to prayer—nothing but deaths, droughts and darkness. And all because of unbelief. "The giants are too great for us!" was their cry (Num. 13: 17–33). Today this is our cry. "Look at the might of this; measure, if you can, the strength of that!" Our reply should be, "Lord, I pray thee, open. . .eyes!" (II Kings 6: 17). "Is the Lord's arm shortened that He cannot save" (Isa. 59: 1)? Shall we but consider Him as the God of the past, the God of prophecy, but not the God of the present?

Peter's Pentecost sermon was as scorching as it

was searching. Truth became alive. *"This is that which was spoken by the prophet Joel!"* (Acts 2: 16). The inspired writer soon found that "this sword of the Lord" had a new edge so that the listeners were cut to the heart.

Men are ever saying that in these trying days people need comfort. Agreed—many do need comfort. The sick, the sad, and the suffering are in this bracket. However, let none fail to realize that to keep silent while a house is burning is criminal. He is no comforter who lets his neighbor sleep as he watches a criminal move to the door with a gun. (In this hour this is not overdrawing the picture of the peril.)

Before the men of straw of our day, who decry our blood-honoring, incarnation-believing, hell-fire evangelism, shall we wilt? To do this would reveal us as sawdust-Caesars. The legions of hell are great; but the legions of heaven are greater. The devil is mighty; God is Almighty. The stakes are high. The price and prize are great!

Some declare that in America Patrick Henry did more to pave the way for freedom and liberty than any other man in its history. Hear him, fired with passionate devotion for his people, as he speaks at the Virginia Convention, March 23, 1775: "Is life so dear or peace so sweet as to be purchased at the price of chains and slavery? Forbid it, Almighty God! I know not what course others may take. But as for me, give me liberty —or give me death!" Could Cato or Demosthenes surpass that oratorical gem? Can we translate it?

The fearful bondage and slavery that exists in the world today and threatens the rest of mankind is no fairy story! Though Communism may conquer the world (terrible and unimaginable as that might be), to the true child of God there is a greater horror—eternity for the unrepentant in an endless hell!

Perhaps we should get near Patrick Henry's language this way: "Is life's span so dear and are home comforts so engrossing as to be purchased with my unfaithfulness and dry-eyed prayerlessness? At the final bar of God, shall the perishing millions accuse me of materialism coated with a few Scripture verses?

"Forbid it, Almighty God! I know not what course others may take; but as for me, *GIVE ME REVIVAL* in my soul and in my church and in my nation—*or GIVE ME DEATH!*"

*Whatsoever thou shalt bind on earth shalt be bound in heaven.*                                                    —*Jesus*

*Your adversary the devil, . . . resist, steadfast in the faith.*                                                    —*Peter*

*Submit. . . to God. Resist the devil, and he will flee from you.*                                                    —*James*

*The more God's people reckon with the devil in their praying, the more they will taste of the liberty of the Spirit in dealing with the issues of life.*
—*F. J. Perryman*

*Lord, even demons are subject unto us in Thy name.*
—*The Seventy*

*O Hell, I see thee surging round;*
*But in my Lord a cleft I've found,*
*A solid, sure abiding place*
*From which my enemy I face,*
*As here with Thee at God's right hand,*
*I on Thy Calvary-Victory stand.*          —*Unknown*

*Should all the hosts of death*
*And powers of hell unknown*
*Put their most dreadful forms*
*Of rage or malice on,*
*I shall be safe; for Christ displays*
*SUPERIOR POWER and guardian grace.*
—*Isaac Watts*

## CHAPTER TWENTY

## KNOWN IN HELL

SOME preachers master their subjects; some subjects master the preacher; once in a while one meets a preacher who is both master of, and also mastered by his subject. The Apostle Paul, I am sure, was in that category.

Look at Paul in Ephesus (Acts 19). Seven men were attempting to use a religious formula over a Gadara-type of victim. But slinging theological terms or even Bible verses at devil-possessed men is as ineffective as snowballing Gibraltar in the hope of removing it. One man, demon-controlled, was an easy match for these seven silly sycophants. While the seven sons of Sceva fled into the streets, shirtless and shamed, the man filled with an unholy spirit increased his wardrobe with seven suits. And so, the seven wounded, fearful men told their own tale, for God turned their folly to the glory of Christ, so that His name was greatly feared and magnified. Spooky spiritists were converted; Jews and Greeks were saved; at a public bonfire, cult books to the value of fifty thousand pieces were burned. Surely that was making the wrath of man to praise Him! Listen, too, to the testimony of the demon, "Jesus I know, *AND PAUL I KNOW*, but who are ye?" (Acts 19: 15). This is the highest praise that earth or hell affords—to be classified by the enemy as one with Jesus.

But how did Paul get that way? Why did demons know Paul? Had they beaten him too, or had he beaten them? Consider for a moment this man Paul. God and Paul were on intimate terms. Revelations were granted him. His servants were angels; at his finger tips were earthquakes. His Spirit-powered words shattered the fetters from the soul of a spirit-bound girl, whom men had snared as a fortuneteller. In Corinth, this mighty man Paul drained a part of the Slough of Despond, and there on the devil's doorstep established a church. Later, he snatched souls from under the nose of Caesar, right from Caesar's own household. And before kings Paul was at home, for he said, "I count myself happy King Agrippa!" Paul also stormed the intellectual capital of the world (Mars hill) with resurrection truth and thereby routed their learned. While Paul lived, hell had no peace.

But what was Paul's armory? Where did he edge his blade? Paul more than once uses the phrase "I am persuaded," and therein lay his secret. Revealed truth held him like a vise. The Word, like the Lord, was immutable. Paul's anchor was cast in the depths of God's faithfulness. His battleaxe was the Word of the Lord; his strength was faith in that Word. So the Spirit alerted Paul to the coming strategy of the devil. Paul was not ignorant of his devices; therefore hell suffered. Even when men willed to assassinate Paul, an informer uncovered the plot, and men and demons were foiled.

Spirituality that saves men from hell and keeps men from vulgar sins is wonderful, but, I believe, elementary. When Paul went *to* the Cross, the miracle of conversion and regeneration took place; but later when he got *on* the Cross, the greater miracle of identification took place. That I believe is the masterly argument of the Apostle—to be dead *and* alive at the same time. "Ye *are* dead," Paul wrote the Galatians. Suppose we try this on ourselves first. Are we *dead?*— *dead* to blame or praise? *dead* to fashion and human opinion? *dead* so that we have no itch for recognition? *dead* so that we do not squirm if another gets praised for a thing that we engineered? Oh sweet, sublime, satisfying experience of the indwelling Christ by the Spirit! We, too, can sing with Wesley:

> *Dead* to the world and all its toys!
> Its idle pomp and fading joys!
> Jesus, my glory be!

Yes, Paul was *dead*. Then he added, "Nevertheless *I live*, yet not I." Christianity is the only religion in the world where a man's God comes and lives *inside* of him. Paul no longer wrestled with flesh (neither his own nor any other man's); he wrestled "against principalities, against powers, against the rulers of the darkness of this world." Does that shed any light on why this demon said, *"And Paul I know"?* Paul had been wrestling against the demon powers. (In these modern days, this art of binding and loosing that Paul knew is almost forgotten or else ignored.) On the last lap of his earthly pilgrimage, he declared, "I have fought a good fight." Demons could have said amen to that statement, for they suffered more from Paul than Paul suffered from them. Yes, Paul was *known in hell*.

Another anchor that held this soul undaunted was the wrath of a holy God upon sin. "Knowing the terror of the Lord he persuaded men" (II Cor. 5: 11). Paul accounted men as *lost!* The other night I saw a picture thrown onto a screen; but in its blurred state it had no meaning. Then the operator's hand reached out and focussed the slide. What a difference! Even so, we Christians need the Divine Hand to sharpen the picture of the lostness of men to our eternity-dimmed eyes. Because Paul loved His Lord with a perfect love, he also hated sin with a perfect hatred. Thus he saw men not only prodigals but also rebels—not just drifters from righteousness but conspirators in wickedness, who *must* be pardoned *or* punished. With the fierceness of Love's intensest blaze, he burned at the injustice of men subordinate to demon power. His watchword was "This one thing I do." He had no side issues, no books to sell. He had no ambitions—and so had nothing to be jealous about. He had no reputation—and so had nothing to fight about. He had no possessions—and therefore nothing to worry about. He had no "rights"—so therefore he could not suffer wrong. He was already broken—so no one could break him. He was "dead"—so none could kill him. He was less than the least—so who could humble him? He had suffered the loss of all things—so none could defraud him. Does this throw any light on why the demon said, "Paul I know"? Over this God-intoxicated man, hell suffered headaches.

Yet another anchor to the spirit of this saint was the efficacy of the blood of Jesus, and so the ability of Christ to save *fully*. "*ALL* have sinned and come short of the glory of God." Yes! But Christ is *able to save* to the uttermost *ALL* who come unto God by Him. Oh that the world might know the all-atoning Lamb!

With Paul there was no limited atonement. Zealot he was and wanted to be. In the light of an eternal hell what were perishing things of clay? And in our present day what are honors among men? or what are the schemes of hell? Right now *men are LOST*, as well as after they die. Right now men are being swept into the vortex of a sewer of gross iniquity which ultimately will suck them down to an *ETERNAL HELL*. Is this true? Paul was convinced that it was. Then, "oh arm of the Lord, awake; put on strength" (Isa. 51: 9). "Make me Thy battleaxe and Thy weapons of war," I hear Paul say.

Another anchor for Paul was the blessed assurance that "to be absent from the body was to be present with the Lord" (II Cor. 5: 8). No soul-sleep here ! No interminable intermediate state! Out of life into life! At the thought of *eternity*, language is beggered and imagination staggered. Paul could "write off" stripes, imprisonments, fastings, weariness, and painfulness as *"light* affliction"—recompensed by the fact "so shall we ever be with the Lord." All the "shot and shell" of demons was wasted against Paul. Do you wonder now that one of them said, "And Paul I *know*"?

The final truth as an anchor to Paul's soul was *"WE MUST ALL APPEAR* before *the judgment seat of Christ"* (II Cor. 5: 10). Living with eternity's values in view took the sting out of this oncoming test too. Living "right," here on earth (I do not mean just living righteously, but living after the pattern set in the Holy Word) takes care of the hereafter. Paul was so conformed to the image of the Son that he could say, "What things ye have both learned, and received, and heard, *and seen in me, do"* (Phil. 4: 9). To copy copies is not normally safe, but it is safe to copy Paul, for he was *fully* surrendered, *wholly* sanctified, *completely* satisfied, yea, "complete in Christ."

Do you still wonder why a demon said, "And Paul I know"? I don't.

# STUDY QUESTIONS

## Chapter One

1. Why is prayer less attractive than many other types of ministry?
2. How are logic and zeal meaningless apart from "unction"?
3. In what way is prayer your primary means of obtaining resources to share God's truth?

## Chapter Two

4. Is it true that "Satan has little cause to fear most preaching"? Why or why not?
5. How does prayer changes what effort and words cannot?
6. What percentage of your prayer is done privately?

## Chapter Three

7. How many people do you know that are "so heavenly that they are of no earthly good," and how many who are "so earthly they are of no heavenly good"? Based on your experience, which represents real trouble for the Church?
8. What are the problems with the idea of being content with having been saved and sanctified?
9. Are you willing to endure life-altering agony and suffering to receive God's vision and passion?

## Chapter Four

10. Is it possible to have passion without prayer?
11. What must we be willing to give up in order to obtain the mind of Christ?

12. Would you prefer God to have partnership with you or to have ownership of you?

## Chapter Five

13. Why is it true that contemporary evangelists—that is, all present-day disciples of Christ—have the same ability to reach a dying world as did those followers of the 1st century?
14. What does the term "useful brokenness" mean to you? Does it make sense—or do you see the two terms as mutually exclusive? Can you justify your answer when you hold it up to your specific life situations/choices?
15. What walls and dams are you prepared to open so that the waters of healing and growth might flow once again?

## Chapter Six

16. What things would change immediately in our world if the Church lived constantly "in the light of the judgment seat"?
17. With today's push toward "tolerance" and "pluralism" in mind, can we still teach that a person is only acceptable to God through Jesus Christ? How will your answer affect your life?
18. What will you do if you are rejected or slandered because of your stand for truth?

## Chapter Seven

19. How do humility and confession relate to Spirit anointing?
20. Consider Paul before Damascus—then consider him afterward, turning the world upside-down. What do you

think he must have been willing to endure in the wilderness of Arabia?

21. Is it ever right to turn down a preaching opportunity because of issues related to money?

## Chapter Eight

22. How are doubt and unbelief similar or different? In what ways can doubt damage faith?

23. Why is saying "Lord, You can do this" not an example of faith?

24. What parts of "self" do you recognize as hindering your union with Christ?

## Chapter Nine

25. What would it take for modern-day prophets of God to be considered "mad" and "insane" by the world?

26. Is this "insane boldness" reserved for those with the gift of prophecy? Why or why not?

27. Are you willing to proclaim the truth even at the cost of your own life?

## Chapter Ten

28. How can men be made of steel and yet be flexible enough for God to have His way?

29. Why is prayer a weapon rather than a defence?

30. Would Satan tremble if he considered your prayer life?

## Chapter Eleven

31. How does sin lobotomize people's minds and hearts?

32. What is the difference between joy and "silliness"?

33. At what times in your daily life is your focus more on the things of this world than on eternity?

## Chapter Twelve

34. What is the problem with requesting the coming of the Holy Spirit while questioning His gifts?
35. Why is the Church in worse shape than the world?
36. What would you change immediately if you had six months to live?

## Chapter Thirteen

37. What is the long-term difference between being alone and being lonely? Which of the two will remain, and which need not?
38. Why are we often more willing to pray for and contribute to people around the world than to help the people across the street?
39. If someone came to you and said, "I want to repent but I don't know how," what would you tell him/her?

## Chapter Fourteen

40. How would the world today respond to the God-breathed preaching of Paul?
41. What decisions did Paul have to make in order that He might be fully broken for the glory of God?
42. What decisions are you willing to make so that you might be of service?

## Chapter Fifteen

43. What marks people who are "branded by devotion"?
44. What was Paul's method for dealing with humiliation and pain?

45. To you, who are "the lost, the last, and the least"? What are you willing to sacrifice to reach them with Christ's love?

## Chapter Sixteen

46. Is it possible to be too busy to pray? If so, is it possible to be praying too much to be busy?
47. Does our spiritual childlessness come more from sterility or from lack of union with God? Or both?
48. What limits do you place on how long you fervently pray for something that remains unfulfilled?

## Chapter Seventeen

49. Who today could rightly call themselves "the filth of the world"?
50. Is it true that if the world affirms or accepts us, it is proof we are not preaching the truth?
51. In what areas of life are you still in harmony with the world?

## Chapter Eighteen

52. What things stain the Church today and keep it from approaching God with a pure heart and clean hands?
53. In the realm of prayer, are we most concerned with the changing of God, the changing of circumstances, the changing of others, or the changing of ourselves?
54. If the final judgment were today, would you be confident in or ashamed of your prayer life?

## Chapter Nineteen

55. Have we, the Church, been so compromised that we can no longer recognize empty or counterfeit spirituality?

56. Are we insisting on remaining in the wilderness because the beauty and the challenge of Canaan are more than we wish to bear?

57. Do you proclaim peace and comfort when they are not present? Is it more important to you to be a peacemaker or a peacekeeper?

## Chapter Twenty

58. Is it possible for people today to have the same type of anointing as was given Paul?

59. How does the church live and minister today as though we believe everything the Bible says about eternity is true? In what ways do we fall short?

60. If you knew eternity was to face you in the next moment, what would you immediately change about your actions and interactions?

# IN THE DAY OF THY POWER

# In the Day of Thy Power

ARTHUR WALLIS

KINGSWAY PUBLICATIONS
EASTBOURNE

To the memory of my father
REGINALD WALLIS

through whose life and ministry I was drawn to
Christ, and through whose early death I was called
to the work of an evangelist, this, my first book, is
affectionately dedicated.

"He, being dead, yet speaketh."

# FOREWORD

From his many writings Arthur Wallis, the Christian states-
man, will be remembered supremely for his book *In the Day of
Thy Power*. When he died unexpectedly in September 1988,
almost all who paid tribute to him both in writing and at a
thanksgiving service made mention of the book.

I recall its publication in 1956: it was the most talked about
evangelical book and possibly one of the most influential. It
made us hunger and thirst for a fresh outpouring of the Spirit.
It marked the beginning of all nights of prayer for revival in
scores of towns and cities. Arthur Wallis was a forerunner,
"The voice of one that crieth: 'The King is coming! Prepare
for the King.'"

Some saw the worldwide growth of renewal as a partial
answer to those prayers; other pointed to the restoration
movement, but in the hearts of God's people there remains a
conviction that there is something more, something greater
than we have so far experienced, a divine visitation. I am
happy to call it revival.

This new edition of *In the Day of Thy Power* is welcome not
only because it is a spiritual classic but because the publication coincides with a fresh expectancy. In the author's
words, "Above the incessant noise of human activity we have
'heard the sound of marching' that tells us God is on the
move."

Since the book's first launch some 20000 new Christian
books have been published in Britain. Few, perhaps less than
fifty, have made the impact this book has. To read it is to share
a burden, an experience, a vision; to discover something of the

heart of the author and, more significantly, the heart of God.

That its ministry continues after more than thirty years is no surprise. In a day of instant books, written in weeks to meet a commercial publishing deadline, and forgotten almost as quickly, it is a glorious example of a literary work which was not hastily written but allowed to grow to maturity before publication, and on which there has since rested a heavenly anointing.

I have said elsewhere that if in heaven, as on earth, I live in a small cul-de-sac of twelve houses, I would like Arthur Wallis to be my neighbour. Meanwhile, on this earth, I pray that his book will help us to realise afresh that revival is the product of prevailing prayer prompted by the Holy Spirit.

Edward England

Crowborough,
Sussex
Christmas 1988

# CONTENTS

If you would make the greatest success of your life, try to discover what God is doing in your time, and fling yourself into the accomplishment of His purpose and will.

SELECTED.

# FOREWORD

IT is with very real pleasure that I accede to the request of my friend, Arthur Wallis, to write a foreword to his book "In the Day of Thy Power". I first met the author on the Island of Lewis in the autumn of 1951. The fellowship of that hour and the impression made linger with me as a most fragrant memory.

Mr. Wallis's book is a powerful plea for the recognition of the supernatural in the realm of revival. While recognizing man's responsibility as the human agent, attention has been called again and again to the utter futility of human effort apart from the mighty manifestation of divine power.

How many today are really prepared to face the stark fact that we have been out-manœuvred by the strategy of hell, because we have tried to meet the enemy on human levels by human strategy? In this we may have succeeded in making people church-conscious, mission-conscious, or even crusade-conscious, without making them God-conscious. This book will, I trust, act as a corrective to help to bring the church back to a true recognition of the basic fact that revival must ever be related to righteousness, and that the way to a revived church is still the way of repentance and true holiness. What I saw of the movings of God in the Hebrides during the past few years is in keeping with the revival called for in this book, and that is why I consider its publication now to be most timely.

Readers will do well to ponder the contents of Chapter Two, "A Sign Spoken Against". Here Mr. Wallis cuts right across the popular approach and appeal. How arresting are his words: "If we find a revival that is not spoken against we had better look again to ensure that it is a revival."

The effect upon the world of the divine operation in the regeneration of the soul is still the same, "To the Jews a stumbling block, and to the Greeks foolishness"; but the divine appeal does

not change, "If any man will come after Me, let him deny himself
and take up his cross and follow Me." There is no other way,
and that is the truth this book proclaims, and my prayer is that
God may use it to speed the day for which we long, when "the
desert shall rejoice and blossom as the rose".

DUNCAN CAMPBELL

# PREFACE

THE church has been blessed with many volumes on the subject of revival. Most of these are historical accounts of the revivals of the past. They rehearse the righteous acts of the Lord, and are precious documents to all who long to see a movement in our day. Those that unfold the spiritual principles are few by comparison, and are mostly written from the historical standpoint : that is, they expound the laws of revival from the histories and illustrate from Scripture. The design of this book has been to expound the principles of revival from Scripture and illustrate from the histories. For the sake of accuracy the numerous Scripture quotations are taken from the English Revised Version. I readily acknowledge the debt I owe to those other works on the subject and I have quoted freely from them.

That four chapters in a work of this nature should be devoted to the subject of prevailing prayer will be no surprise to those who have learned from Scripture and history what is the road to every true revival. The Ulster Awakening of 1859 may be traced back, so far as such things can be traced on the human side, to the reading by a young man of *George Müller's Narrative*. Faith was quickened in his heart, and when news reached him of the great American Awakening (1858) he said to himself : "Why may we not have such a blessed work here, seeing God did such things for Mr. Müller simply in answer to prayer?" Thus began the revival prayer-meeting at Kells where the movement commenced. Similarly, one of the springs of the 1904 Awakening in Wales may be traced to the reading of Andrew Murray's book, *With Christ in the School of Prayer,* by a hungry minister, and the subsequent transformation of his spiritual life. It would be impossible to estimate the influence exerted on revival movements all over the world during the past hundred years by Charles Finney's lectures on prayer in his *Revivals of Religion.* At the heart of every revival is the spirit of prayer.

I am most grateful to Mr. Duncan Campbell, whose name will always be associated with the recent Lewis Awakening, for consenting to write the Foreword. He is one of the very few in these Islands who have laboured in the midst of a general outpouring of the Spirit. I must also record my thanks to Miss L. Rutty and Mrs. G. Roberts for their labour of love in the typing of the MSS, to Mr. Geoffrey Williams of the Evangelical Library, London, for every facility and encouragement in the work of research, and to those friends who read the MSS and offered valuable suggestions. Conscious of its limitations, I commend the book to God, Who has ever chosen the weak things to be the instruments of His power. If, according to His abundant mercy, He should deign to use its message in any measure to awaken the church to the need and possibilities of this hour, to Him shall be all the glory for ever and ever. Amen.

ARTHUR WALLIS

*Talaton, Devon.*
April 1956

# INTRODUCTION

"And it shall be in the last days, saith God, I will pour forth of My Spirit . . . and your young men shall see visions" (Acts 2:17*).

"Write the vision, and make it plain upon tables, that he may run that readeth it" (Hab. 2: 2).

## I

IT was springtime in the year 1938. A boy in middle teens stood in the little schoolroom adjoining Moriah Chapel, in the small Welsh mining town of Loughor, Glamorganshire. A strange feeling of awe and wonder filled his heart, for this was the very room that witnessed the beginnings of that great outpouring of the Spirit, the Welsh Revival of 1904. He listened to his host and guide, himself a convert of the revival, speak of those memorable days when the hardest hearts were melted by the presence of the Lord, and when the hills and valleys rang again with the songs of Zion. It was almost too wonderful to be true, but it created questions deep down in his heart for which he could find no answer. If God can achieve such mighty things in times of revival, and if the spiritual labours of fifty years can be surpassed in so many days when the Spirit is poured out, why, he wondered, is the church today so satisfied with the results of normal evangelism? Why are we not more concerned that there should be another great revival? Why do we not pray for it day and night?

The boy returned to his home in England. The questions that had puzzled him were temporarily forgotten, crowded out by many other youthful interests, but an indelible impression had been made upon his soul. The fires of that 1904 Awakening, burning still in many a Welsh breast, had lit a flame in his young heart. In that corner of South Wales which had been the heart of the Welsh Revival a strange longing had filled his soul: "O God, wilt Thou not do it again?"

## II

It was autumn in the year 1951. In the largest Island of the Outer Hebrides, Lewis and Harris, a young man was travelling

* Scripture quotations are from the Revised Version unless otherwise stated and the reference is usually to the first verse only of the quotation.

along the narrow, winding road leading to the village of Barvas. The surrounding countryside was bare and bleak, strewn with rocks and boulders, and marked here and there with the familiar peat-banks. At length the village itself came into view, with its irregular clusters of crofters' cottages and bungalows. With intense interest he gazed at the plain, stone-built kirk standing alone just beyond the edge of the village. He felt again something of the awe and wonder he had experienced as a boy in the little school-room at Loughor. It was here that God had come down in power in December 1949. This parish church had witnessed the beginning of the Lewis Awakening. True, there had not been the widespread, sweeping movement of the Welsh Revival. In scope it had been a local movement, confined to scattered villages of Lewis and Harris and some of the adjoining islands. But the marks of heaven-sent, Spirit-wrought revival were all there. God *had* done it again.

Thoughts flooded into the visitor's mind. If God had sent revival to Lewis was He unwilling to do it elsewhere? Was God using these favoured isles as a sort of spiritual arena in which to demonstrate in miniature that He could and would "do it again"? Was this awakening, away in the Western Isles, the harbinger of a modern era of spiritual revival? The visitor seemed to find an answer in his heart to these questions as quickly as they came to him, nor had he to wait long for some confirmation of his inner convictions.

Later he enjoyed the warmth of true Scottish hospitality in the homely manse at Barvas. The following morning, while alone upon his knees, the Lord spoke to him. It was as though he was looking across a vast open prairie to where, on the far horizon, a small fire was burning. It seemed to be coming slowly, very slowly nearer. The scene faded from view. Again he saw the prairie, but now the fire was very much nearer, and stretching like a continuous wall right across the prairie as far as the eye could see. Slowly, inexorably, the wall of flame and smoke moved forward till again the picture faded from view.

Then it seemed as though a vast and endless desert stretched away to the horizon. There in the far distance some small dazzling object lay on the sand, shining like a star. As he watched, it grew larger and larger, filling out with blue as it did so, till even the shining framework was eclipsed by the blue, and there in the midst of the desert was a lake of water. Almost at once there came back to his mind a rendering of Isaiah 35 verse 7 he had heard quoted only the previous day. "And the mirage shall become a pool, and the thirsty ground springs of water" (R.V. margin).

When he rose from his knees he opened his Bible and commenced to read Isaiah 43. The word of the Lord seemed to fall upon him with greater authority and power than anything God had said to him before. Like a great rain from heaven the word seemed to descend upon his thirsty soul: "I, even I, am the Lord; and beside Me there is no Saviour. . . . I will work, and who shall let it? . . . Thus saith the Lord, which maketh a way in the sea, and a path in the mighty waters; . . . Remember ye not the former things, neither consider the things of old. Behold, I will do a new thing; now shall it spring forth; shall ye not know it? I will even make a way in the wilderness, and rivers in the desert."

### III

Perhaps the reader will forgive the recounting of these personal reminiscences, since they present the background for the writing of the book, and provide some explanation for its appearance. The message of the following pages has flowed out of God's personal dealings with the writer in regard to revival. The vision and the burden have been the mainspring of the book. Throughout its preparation there has been a sense of the quiet compelling of the Spirit, and it is this that has brought it through many hindrances and delays to see the light of day.

Behind the message that follows is the solemn conviction that grows ever clearer with the passing of the days, that we are surely moving towards a day of God's power. "His going forth is as certain as the dawn; and He shall come unto us as the rain, as the latter rain that watereth the earth" (Hos. 6: 3*). How soon this may be we cannot say, "For the vision is yet for the appointed time, and it hasteth toward the end, and shall not lie: though it tarry, wait for it; because it will surely come, it will not delay" (Hab. 2: 3). Our concern is to see that we are a people willing in the day of His power.

* A modern rendering.

God hath had it much on His heart, from all eternity, to glorify His dear and only begotten Son; and there are some special seasons that He appoints to that end, wherein He comes forth with omnipotent power to fulfil His promise and oath to Him : and these times are times of remarkable pouring out of His Spirit, to advance His kingdom; such a day is a day of His power.

JONATHAN EDWARDS.

## CHAPTER ONE

## WHAT IS REVIVAL?

"God came. . . . His glory covered the heavens, and the earth was full of His praise. . . . He stood, and measured the earth; He beheld, and drove asunder the nations: And the eternal mountains were scattered, the everlasting hills did bow; His goings were as of old" (Hab. 3:3).

THERE was never a day in which the term "revival" needed to be more carefully defined. It has come to be used in relation to spiritual things so widely and so loosely that many are perplexed to know what it does mean. To some prejudiced or misinformed people the term is synonymous with excessive emotionalism and mass hysteria. It is to be hoped that the following pages will be a sufficient answer to such a slander on the work of the Holy Spirit. Others use the word to describe a successful evangelistic mission. When they tell us that their church is "having a revival", we understand them to mean that a gospel campaign is being conducted there. This use is possibly a relic of days when the Spirit was working widely, and one had only to arrange such a mission to witness a quickening amongst the believers and an ingathering of the lost. Today it is otherwise, but in any case to use the term thus is misleading.

Some, adhering closely to the etymology of the word, use it to describe a personal reviving of the believer by the Holy Spirit. If an individual or group is quickened in holiness and brought into a place of blessing, that is what they call "revival", even if there is little extension of the work. Similarly others, whose emphasis is more on a definite experience of the Spirit, will claim that when an individual or group has been filled with the Spirit they have "got revival", regardless of whether there are any repercussions outside their circle. In so far as revival always involves the reviving of individual believers these views are true, but as definitions of revival they are inadequate.

We cannot go to the Bible to see how the word "revival" is used, for it is not found there, although it contains many examples and types of revival, and unfolds all its principles. The nearest

Scriptural equivalents are "revive" (or quicken), and "reviving",
but these may be applied to individual quickening, and are not
always synonymous with what has come to be called, by common consent down the centuries, "religious revival". It might be
well if those who wish to describe what is simply a quickening
work amongst believers would use those Scriptural expressions,
"revive" and "reviving", and distinguish them from "revival",
which includes and yet exceeds them. Revival is more than big
meetings. It is more than religious excitement. It is more than the
quickening of the saints, or their being filled with the Holy Spirit.
It is more than a great ingathering of souls. One may have any
one of these without revival, and yet revival includes them all.

There is a wealth of difference between missions or campaigns
at their best and genuine revival. In the former man takes the
initiative, it may be with the prompting of the Spirit; in the latter
the initiative is God's. With the one the organization is human;
with the other it is divine. There is no intention here of disparag-
ing the work of missions, or of denying that God has owned
them to the conversion of multitudes, but it must be made clear
that they do not constitute revival. Missions may be a part of the
continuous programme of evangelism which is the task of the
church, but revival is a thing of special times and seasons. Revival
may of course break out during a mission, but when it does so
certain features will appear which are peculiar to revival, and
certain features will disappear which are characteristic of missions. However, while revival tarries, the normal evangelism of
the church must continue, but let us keep the distinction clear.

The meaning of any word is determined by its usage. For a
definition of revival we must therefore appeal to the people of
God of bygone years, who have used the word with consistency
of meaning down the centuries, until it began to be used in a
lesser and more limited sense in modern times. Numerous writings
on the subject that have been preserved to us will confirm that
revival is divine intervention in the normal course of spiritual
things. It is God revealing Himself to man in awful holiness and
irresistible power. It is such a manifest working of God that
human personalities are overshadowed, and human programmes
abandoned. It is man retiring into the background because God
has taken the field. It is the Lord making bare His holy arm, and
working in extraordinary power on saint and sinner.

The God of the Old Testament saints and prophets was the God of revival. In chapter 63 of his prophecy, Isaiah, recalling how God's people had rebelled and grieved His Holy Spirit (verse 10), longs for a manifestation of His zeal and mighty acts (verse 15). He looks upon the downtrodden sanctuary and cries out, "Oh that Thou wouldest rend the heavens, that Thou wouldest come down, that the mountains might flow down at Thy presence . . . to make Thy name known to Thine adversaries, that the nations may tremble at Thy presence! When Thou didst terrible things which we looked not for, Thou camest down . . . " (Isa. 64: 1–3). Habakkuk also, living in a day when God's judgments were already being poured out upon His people for their sin, pleads for revival, "O Lord, revive Thy work in the midst of the years, in the midst of the years make it known; in wrath remember mercy"(3: 2). Then in vision he perceives the answer to his prayer; he sees God on the move (verse 3), manifesting His power and glory (verses 3–6). He sees the tents of Cushan in affliction, and even nature itself moved at the divine presence (verses 7, 10, 11) as the Lord marches through the land in indignation, going forth for the salvation of His people (verses 12, 13).

At the end of the Old Testament story we find God still pleading with the remnant through His servant Malachi, and promising revival at this eleventh hour if His people would pay the price: "Bring ye the whole tithe into the storehouse . . . and prove Me now herewith, saith the Lord of Hosts, if I will not open you the windows of heaven, and pour you out a blessing, that there shall not be room enough to receive it" (3: 10). One might refer to Zechariah, to Joel, and to many another prophet, who brought to dark days a ray of hope in the promise of revival. How many saints in that bygone age could have testified to the value of this great expectation that filled their lives, in the words of David: "I had fainted, unless I had believed to see the goodness of the Lord in the land of the living" (Ps. 27: 13).

In the New Testament the true motive-force of revival is seen in clearer light as we find it associated with the pouring out of the Spirit. In its historic setting as the birthday of the church, Pentecost was unique, and there were factors in that remarkable event that have never been repeated. But as a specimen outpouring of the Spirit, Pentecost was unique only in being the first.

Peter declared on that memorable day, "This is that which hath been spoken by the prophet Joel; And it shall be *in the last days,* saith God, I will pour forth of my Spirit upon all flesh" (Acts 2: 16). It is to be noted that Peter, speaking under inspiration, was led to alter the Joel prophecy (2: 28) from "it shall come to pass afterward" to "it shall be in the last days". This wonderful promise relates then to a period of time, "in the last days", not just to a moment of time, such as the day of Pentecost. It is equally clear from the words that Peter quotes that the prophecy had but a partial fulfilment on that day. There was evidently more to come. All the years of the church's history have been "in the last days", and thus it has pleased the Lord down those years at special seasons to fulfil this prophecy.

There is further evidence in the New Testament that God never intended to confine the outpouring of the Spirit to one historic day. In Acts 10 verse 45 the remarkable event at Cæsarea is described by Luke as an outpouring of the gift of the Holy Spirit. Paul writing to Titus uses the same word as did Peter when quoting Joel : "the Holy Spirit, which He *poured out* upon us richly" (Titus 3: 5, 6).

True revivals have ever been marked by powerful and often widespread outpourings of the Spirit. Many many times the preaching had to cease because the hearers were prostrate, or because the voice of the preacher was drowned by cries for mercy. Who will deny that these were outpourings of the Spirit? Who could find a more appropriate description of such scenes than the words of Luke : "The Holy Spirit fell on all them which heard the Word"? (Acts 10: 44). David Brainerd recorded the beginning of the wonderful movement among the American Indians in 1745 thus : "The power of God seemed to descend upon the assembly 'like a rushing mighty wind' and with an astonishing energy bore down all before it. I stood amazed at the influence that seized the audience almost universally, and could compare it to nothing more aptly than the irresistible force of a mighty torrent. . . . Almost all persons of all ages were bowed down with concern together, and scarce one was able to withstand the shock of this surprising operation."

Revival can never be explained in terms of activity, organization, meetings, personalities, preachings. These may or may not be involved in the work, but they do not and cannot account for the effects produced. Revival is essentially a manifestation of God; it has the stamp of Deity upon it, which even the unregenerate and uninitiated are quick to recognize. Revival must of necessity make an impact upon the community, and this is one means by which we may distinguish it from the more usual operations of the Holy Spirit. The marks of revival will be considered more fully in a later chapter.

Persons are very ready to be suspicious of what they have not felt themselves. It is to be feared many good men have been guilty of this error. . . . These persons that thus make their own experience their rule of judgment, instead of bowing to the wisdom of God, and yielding to His Word as an infallible rule, are guilty of casting a great reflection upon the understanding of the Most High.

JONATHAN EDWARDS.

Can you find in your hearts to be like the Jews, who prayed and longed for the coming of the Messias, and when He came, rejected and crucified Him, because He came not in the way their prejudices led them to look for Him?

JAMES ROBE.

## CHAPTER TWO

## A SIGN SPOKEN AGAINST

"Behold, this Child is set for the falling and rising up of many in Israel; and for a sign which is spoken against . . . that thoughts out of many hearts may be revealed" (Luke 2: 34).

THUS spoke the aged Simeon as he held the long-promised Saviour in his arms. Thirty years elapsed and then the prophecy was fulfilled as Christ stood in manhood in the synagogue at Nazareth with the roll of the book in His hand. "The Spirit of the Lord is upon Me," He read, "because He anointed Me to preach the gospel. . . ." (Luke 4:18). Then He began to preach, applying the word in the power of the Spirit to the consciences of His hearers. Soon their wonder gave place to wrath, and they "cast Him forth out of the city, and led Him unto the brow of the hill . . . that they might throw Him down headlong" (verse 29). Thus from the time that He commenced to preach and work in the power of the Spirit, He became "a sign spoken against . . . that thoughts out of many hearts might be revealed".

It has been thus with every servant of God whose ministry was endued with power. It has been thus with every movement of God by which the church has progressed since its inception at Pentecost. It has been thus with every genuine revival—"a sign spoken against . . . that thoughts out of many hearts may be revealed". The mighty operation of the Spirit will always uncover and draw forth into the open the antagonism of the natural or carnal mind which is "enmity against God". He whom God chooses to be an instrument in revival may expect to be a continual target for the malice of Satan, who never seems to lack willing hands or lips to do his work, in the church as well as out of it. Many know of the contribution of Jonathan Edwards to the New England Revival in the seventeen hundreds; few know that he was ultimately compelled to resign from the church so signally blessed through his labours. Many know of William Burns, under whose ministry revival broke out in R. M. McCheyne's church in Dundee, and elsewhere; few know of the gruelling he received in defending that work before a committee of his fellow ministers. So it was with Finney and many others. If we find a revival that is not spoken against, we had better look again to ensure that it is a revival.

We must pause a moment and answer some of the objections that are always brought against revival. When God pours out the Spirit these arguments are sure to occur again, and there will be no time to deal with them then. There is little that can be said to those who wilfully blind their eyes to the facts, and whose antagonism to the work of the Spirit would seem to derive more from the enmity of the heart than the reasonings of the head. Some, however, speak against revival out of ignorance. They have never experienced it, do not know what it is, and are prejudiced against it from the outset. Influenced by enemies of the work, their opinions are based on hearsay. The effective cure for such, if they are willing, is to go and see for themselves.

Others object to revival because they consider that it is always accompanied by excesses and other undesirable features. That there is a tendency for such to occur where care is not exercised, and that at times excesses have occurred, cannot be denied. No one would pretend to claim that every revival burns with a smokeless flame. But let us test the depth of the argument. Would these critics suggest that the early church ought never to have sold their possessions that distribution might be made to those in need, because this was abused by Ananias and Sapphira? Should the young churches have refrained from eating the Lord's supper, because in some places, e.g., Corinth, the ordinance had been abused? Ought there to have been no Reformation because occasionally Protestants gave way to excessive zeal and wrongs were perpetrated? The picture must be seen in perspective, and the evils must be weighed against the overall good. "After drought, the copious rains often deluge the land and sweep away bridges, and otherwise do very much harm. But no one is so alarmed by the evils of rain, as to desire a continuation of the drought" (Wm. Patton, D.D.).

There are always some who are desirous of revival until it comes, and then they bitterly oppose it, because it has not come in the way they anticipated. The instrument that God used, or the channel through which the blessing flowed, was not what their convictions had led them to expect. They looked to see an Eliab or an Abinadab chosen for this great work, but the Lord, who "looketh on the heart", chose a David. They thought that their own local church, their own fellowship which was so scriptural and right, would see the beginning of the work, but God chose to work elsewhere, and this became to them a stumbling-block. To all who handle the work of revival, this should be a solemn warning of the great danger of yielding to jealousy and prejudice, which blind the eyes, harden the heart, and hinder the Spirit.

Then the manner of the Spirit's working or the manifestations through which God chose to exhibit His power may have been contrary to their expectations or foreign to their experience. They brought the glorious work of the Spirit to the bar of their own judgment, and there condemned and denied it. As the Jews rejected their Messiah because He did not fit in with their plans, or fulfil their preconceived ideas, so these also reject the manifestation of God in revival. Thus it becomes, as in the case of the Lord, "a sign spoken against", and those who thus speak inevitably reveal, by their opposition to the work of the Spirit, the thoughts of their hearts. Let all beware of an attitude which presumes to dictate to the Almighty how He shall conduct His work. This must be considered further when discussing supernatural manifestations in revival.

To be distinguished from the objectors just considered, there is another class, with many good, earnest people among them, who do not speak against revival itself, but against the *expectation* of it. They readily acknowledge the need of it, and that should it come it would do much good, but deny that God is ready to meet that need and do that good. Some take this view because they do not see any evidence in the church or the world to encourage the hope. Others do not see any evidence in Scripture, but rather that the very reverse of revival is to be expected in these last days. We would ask the former what evidence do they look for among believers and unbelievers to indicate a coming movement? What are the outward signs of the advent of revival for which they look in vain? It is a crucial question, and a later chapter (XIV, The Sound of Marching) must be devoted to answering it.

Those who argue from Scripture say, "Are we not approaching the end of the age? And do not the Scriptures teach that in the last days perilous times shall come, and that things in the world are to wax worse and worse? How, then, can we look for revival, and a great ingathering of the lost, when God has predicted the very opposite?" It is to be noted here that this argument, which was so prevalent among believers a few years ago, is not being vented so much of late, because facts too big to ignore are disproving the theory. Great evangelistic drives, which we must be careful to distinguish from revival, but for which we must thank God, are reaping in a manner that has not been witnessed since the beginning of the century. Let those who yearn for that deeper and greater work of revival be careful not to criticize what God is pleased to bless. While God is smiling, who are we to frown? It is not a question of whether we approve of every method being used, but whether we have hearts as large as Paul's, who could say, "In every way . . . Christ is proclaimed; and therein I rejoice, yea, and will rejoice" (Phil. 1: 18). If the apostle could do this even when motives were doubtful (verses 17, 18), how much more should we when it is merely a question of what we judge to be doubtful methods.

But let us return to this objection. It is based on 2 Timothy 3 and other like passages, where we are told that "in the last days grievous times shall come. For men shall be lovers of self", etc. and that "evil men and impostors shall wax worse and worse, deceiving and being deceived". The passage teaches, what is affirmed elsewhere in Scripture, that moral conditions in the world are to deteriorate in the end times, that men will be lovers of pleasure more than lovers of God, cloaking their sin with a form of godliness that denies the power. But why should this forbid revival? Was it not in grievous and perilous times that the church was born? God found it needful then to demonstrate His power and pour out His Spirit. If the gathering out of the church is to be consummated in a greater time of world turmoil, how much more needful that God should again act in power to safeguard His rights, complete His church, and vindicate His Name.

History abounds with instances of where the desperate plight of man has called forth all the mightier working on the part of God. Again and again the history of revival has been the history of God's intervention to retrieve what was hopeless. Furthermore, the prophetic word warns us that Satanic agents are going to deceive by signs and wonders (Matt. 24: 24). Is the Lord then to withhold His power, and so give the Devil the monopoly in the realm of the supernatural? Are the Moses and Aarons of these last days to hold their rods while "the magicians of Egypt" cast down theirs and turn them into serpents? Should we not expect the servants of God to do as much, and more—that their rods should swallow up those of "the magicians" as they did of old, according to the promise, "Greater is He that is in you than he that is in the world"? (1 John 4: 4). The same Book that warns us that "iniquity shall abound", also reminds us that "where sin abounded, grace did abound more exceedingly" (Rom. 5: 20). Man's extremity is God's opportunity. Is there widespread rejection of God's law? Then "it is time for the Lord to work, for they have made void Thy law" (Ps. 119: 126).

Others who oppose any expectation of revival argue in this manner : "Revival must begin in the church, but the Scriptures foretell that *in the church* there is to be the falling away prior to the return of Christ, the love of the many is to wax cold, and the Laodicean spirit will prevail. We see these things already being fulfilled; how then can we expect revival?" The first two predictions we cannot deny, and must be careful not to overlook; but the third is based on the assumption that the letter to the Church in Laodicea (Rev. 3: 14) describes the state of the church in these end times. It is doubtful whether this can be proved, though it may be true. However, let us take the objection as it stands. It involves the question as to what is the divine purpose in these recorded predictions of departure and decline. For example, is the picture we have of the lukewarm church of Laodicea presented to us as an example to follow or a state to condone? Did God intend that we should argue in favour of the Laodicean spirit, or resign ourselves fatalistically to it, because we believe we are in the end times?

It must be remembered that predictions as to departure are accompanied by predictions as to judgment which is the consequence of departure. Christ says to the lukewarm Laodiceans, "I am about to spue thee out of my mouth" (Darby). But again and again we find that prophecies of coming judgment were uttered that they might so move the hearers as to make it possible for the judgment to be averted, or at least deferred. There is such a thing as God repenting Him of the evil He thought to do, and doing it not, as in the case of Nineveh (Jonah 3: 10), when God revoked the prophecy of Jonah concerning its overthrow. When

Daniel interpreted the vision of Nebuchadnezzar, which was a prediction of God's judgment upon him, he did not counsel the king solemnly to await his punishment, but to take action which might avert it. "Wherefore, O king, let my counsel be acceptable unto thee, and break off thy sins by righteousness, and thine iniquities by shewing mercy to the poor; *if there may be a lengthening of thy tranquillity*" (Dan. 4: 27).

If God has foreseen and predicted a tendency on the part of the church in the latter days to decline in faith and devotion, He has not forewarned us of it that we may apathetically await its fulfilment, but that we may be forearmed and strive together to avert it. There is no more effective way of achieving this than by preparing our hearts and pleading with God for genuine revival. There is nothing more calculated to arrest the downward spiritual trend, and set a lukewarm church on fire than a mighty awakening of the Holy Spirit.

God's dealings with Israel, "written for our admonition" (1 Cor. 10: 11), both illustrate and confirm the argument. When spiritual decay set in with the death of Solomon and the division of the kingdom, God constantly warned His people of the consequences of departure, and predicted coming judgment which was ultimately fulfilled. We find nevertheless that the history of decline is punctuated by some outstanding spiritual revivals through godly kings and fearless prophets who turned the people back to God. These men did not argue, as some Christians do today, that departure and judgment were prophesied and could not be averted, therefore a widespread turning to God was not to be contemplated. God had not revoked His promises. He was still the God of revival, if they would fulfil the conditions. "If My people, which are called by My Name, shall humble themselves, and pray, and seek My face, and turn from their wicked ways; then will I hear . . . forgive . . . and heal" (2 Chron. 7: 14). This promise had actually been given for a time of judgment (verse 13). They took God at His word, sought earnestly His face, and in their day saw the turn of the tide.

Towards the close of Judah's history as an independent kingdom there came to the throne the boy, Josiah. The temporary eclipse of the nation in captivity for its sin was not to be deferred much longer, and in fact began in the reign of his son, Jehoahaz. Nevertheless through the obedience to God of this young king there took place a powerful revival which pulsated through every vein of the nation. The word of the Lord ran and was glorified. Sin and idolatry were purged from the land (2 Kings 23: 4–20). The passover was kept as it had never been kept since the time of Samuel (2 Chron. 35: 18), and all the days of Josiah the people departed not from following the Lord (2 Chron. 34: 33). Josiah had fulfilled the conditions and God had kept His promise : "Because thine heart was tender, and thou didst humble thyself before God, *when thou heardest His words against this place* . . . and hast rent thy clothes, and wept before Me; I also have heard thee, saith the Lord" (2 Chron. 34: 27). Notice the phrase italicized. It was the prophecy of coming judgment that produced in Josiah's heart a desire for revival, not a dumb resignation to fate.

Those who long for a movement in these last days need not hide away these divine predictions, as though they constituted an embarrassing contradiction to the promise of revival. Let us rather bring them out into the open and make them, for ourselves and for others, both a powerful warning and an incentive, as did Josiah. For these very prophecies that are often used as objections to revival should drive us to our knees in humble earnest prayer, that God may pour out His Spirit, revive His Church, and save the lost. "Many there be that say, who will show us any good? Lord, lift Thou up the light of Thy countenance upon us" (Ps 4: 6).

Finally, there are those who object to the expectation of revival because, they assert : "The church should not be looking for revival, but for the return of Christ". Of course the church should be looking for the return of Christ, but is it? Dare we begin to claim that the people of God are ready and waiting for their returning Lord? How can they be when, in the main, they are carnal, sleepy, worldly, lukewarm? "He that hath this hope set on Him purifieth himself, even as He is pure" (1 John 3: 3). And it is certain that the church is largely in this state, not because it is preparing and pleading for revival, but because it is not doing so. In revival the church is awakened, carnality and worldliness are slain, the lukewarm are made hot, and the people of God begin to purify themselves. There is nothing calculated to incite preparation for and expectation of the return of Christ so much as revival.

The re-emphasis throughout Wales of the blessed truth of Christ's return was one of the direct results of the 1904 Awakening. One who was himself prominent in the movement wrote: "In the whole of the Welsh pulpit, anterior to 1904, one knew of but two ministers who held and taught the truth of the pre-millennial, personal advent of our Lord. . . . But mark the divine miracle. The revival came. And with it, a great light. . . . The writer's own testimony is but an instance of that of thousands. Never can he forget the occasion, the place, nor the day when, alone with God, the truth flashed into his heart. He had heard no preaching, nor had he read any book on the subject. . . . At that moment, however, a conviction was wrought in his heart that the Lord was coming; that He was coming quickly; that indeed He *must* come, and that apart from His coming, there seemed no hope for the world" (*Rent Heavens* by R. B. Jones). The hope of revival is not a substitute but a supplement to the hope of His coming. The prospect of His appearing unto them that look for Him makes revival imperative.

The final and conclusive answer to these and many other such objections to the possibility of revival, is the answer of facts; and no theory, however plausible, can stand if it is contradicted by the facts. If, as is asserted, God is not willing to pour out His Spirit in revival because He has predicted that things in the world are going to wax worse, or that faith will decline in the church, or because He would have us looking for the return of Christ, then these arguments must apply universally and continuously; they can admit of no exceptions. We cannot for example apply such arguments to Britain and not to Africa; or to North America and not to South America. Since we are all at the same point in the dispensation, they must apply equally everywhere and all the time. Now it is evident to any student of revival that throughout this century up to the present time there have been in different parts of the world definite and unmistakable outpourings of the Spirit. The Awakening in Lewis and Harris in 1949, or the more recent outpourings in the Belgian Congo, to mention two recent examples, give the lie to the suggestion that God is not willing. The theory must beat a hasty retreat before the irresistible advance of the facts.

There are some, alas, who do not wish to be acquainted with the facts; who have only eyes to see and ears to hear what goes on in their own circle or within their own fellowship of believers. Nevertheless, let those who know the facts publish them abroad without fear, for there is nothing more calculated to create expectancy for revival than the news of it. "They shall speak of the glory of Thy kingdom, and talk of Thy power; to make known to the sons of men His mighty acts" (Ps. 145: 11). "The works of the Lord are great, sought out of all them that have pleasure therein" (Ps. 111: 2). But those who do not appear to find any pleasure in them, would do well to heed the apostolic warning: "Beware therefore, lest that come upon you, which is spoken in the prophets; Behold, ye despisers, and wonder, and perish; for I work a work in your days, a work which ye shall in no wise believe, if one declare it unto you" (Acts 13: 40). From this negative aspect, the objections to revival, let us move on to the positive side, the promise of revival.

Vastly more was wrapt up in the descent of the Holy Spirit than the church has yet experienced, or than the world has yet seen; and the Spirit Himself thus reveals that while the Christian centuries are "the last days", and Pentecost began the wonder, we today, standing in the last of the last, are on the edge of a second and more tremendous upheaval of the Holy Spirit. . . . So in linking up ourselves with myriads of Christians throughout the globe in praying for world-revival, world-evangelism and the world-return of our blessed Lord, we are praying for solid coming facts, and therefore know that we are praying according to the will of God; we are praying for that in which we may have sudden and glorious part; and we are praying for the world the biggest blessing it will ever have on this side of the great White Throne.

D. M. PANTON.

## CHAPTER THREE

## THE LATTER RAIN OF PROMISE

"And I will cause the shower to come down in its season; there shall be showers of blessing" (Ezek. 34:26).

"WHAT are the prospects of revival?" asked the writer of an aged servant of God. "They are as bright as the promises of God," was the swift reply. No truer answer could have been given. We know that there are to be those in the last days who shall say of the hope of Christ's coming, "Where is the promise?" (2 Pet. 3:4). Even so there are those today who question the expectancy of revival, because they cannot see in God's Word any ground for such a hope. "Where", they would ask us, "is the promise of revival?" If, however, they are right in implying that there is no promise, then they must be asked to explain why, down the centuries of the church's history, God's people have been led and moved to plead with Him to do what He has never promised to do, and why He has done it again and again in answer to their burdened prayers. But is there no promise?

Already some of the great revival promises of the Old Testament have been quoted. They could be easily multiplied. Let us take the familiar chapter 35 of Isaiah as an example: "The wilderness and the solitary place shall be glad; and the desert shall rejoice, and blossom as the rose. It shall blossom abundantly, and rejoice even with joy and singing; the glory of Lebanon shall be given unto it, the excellency of Carmel and Sharon: they shall see the glory of the Lord, the excellency of our God. Strengthen ye the weak hands, and confirm the feeble knees. Say to them that are of a fearful heart, Be strong, fear not: behold, your God will come with vengeance, with the recompence of God; He will come and save you. Then the eyes of the blind shall be opened, and the ears of the deaf shall be unstopped. Then shall the lame man leap as an hart, and the tongue of the dumb shall sing: for in the wilderness shall waters break out, and streams in the desert. And the glowing sand shall become a pool, and the thirsty ground springs of water" (verses 1–7).

It may be objected, however, that these Old Testament prophecies refer to national Israel, and find their fulfilment in a dispensation other than this age of the church. It is not disputed that this may be the primary application of many such passages, but we surely make a great mistake when we confine such glorious promises to their immediate and literal fulfilment. God never intended that we should limit His word in this way, by restricting His precious promises to dispensational pigeon-holes, for He has not done so Himself, as we shall see when dealing presently with the Joel prophecy. When the Spirit of God causes these Old Testament promises to come alive in the hearts of His children, and gives them faith to appropriate them in prayer and plead them before His face, until He answers from heaven in revival, who are we to suggest that this is a misapplication of God's promises to Israel? The outcome is conclusive evidence that God does not think so. "I will pour water upon him that is thirsty, and floods upon the dry ground" (Isa. 44: 3 A.V.) was one of the promises constantly pleaded in the recent Lewis Awakening, and God responded to such pleading. It has been so with almost every revival.

The promise of revival, however, is not confined to the Old Testament. The verse just quoted, "I will pour water upon him that is thirsty, and floods upon the dry ground", has its New Testament counterpart: "If any man thirst, let him come unto Me and drink . . . as the [O.T.] Scripture hath said, out of his belly shall flow rivers of living water" (John 7: 37, 38). The teaching in both passages is the same, and it is the whole principle of revival: the personal thirst—assuaged by the water of the Spirit—resulting in an overflow of blessing.

Next in order there is the statement of Peter on the day of Pentecost referred to in the opening chapter: "In the last days, saith God, I will pour forth of My Spirit upon all flesh" (Acts 2: 17), where he relates the Joel prophecy to the age of the church. This must be considered more fully in a moment. There are the further words of Peter in his address in the porch of the Temple: "Repent ye therefore, and turn again, that your sins may be blotted out, that so there may come seasons of refreshing from the presence of the Lord; and that He may send the Christ" (Acts 3: 19, 20). The order set forth here is important. Firstly, repentance and turning to God; secondly, seasons of refreshing from His presence; thirdly, the return of Christ. Here is the promise of revival, "seasons of refreshing", *before* the return of Christ, and as definite as the promise of the return itself.

The latter half of Joel 2, from which Peter quoted on the day of Pentecost, applies primarily to the time of Israel's national restoration. It relates to a day when Israel has responded to the call of the Lord (verses 12–17) and her people have turned to Him with all their heart. He will then have pity upon them, and cause that they should be no more a reproach among the nations (verses 18, 19). After He had driven away from them "the northern army" (verse 20), He would bless their land by restoring the former rain and the latter rain that "the floors shall be full of wheat, and the fats shall overflow with wine and oil" (verses 23, 24), and they would know that the Lord was in the midst of them (verse 27). *After* this, the Lord promised to pour out His Spirit on all flesh, in the familiar prophecy, quoted by Peter at Pentecost (verses 28–32).

These prophecies of the restoration of the rain and of the outpouring of the Spirit which was to follow come within the space of six verses. They must both be taken literally or both figuratively. We cannot take one literally and spiritualize the other without doing violence to the passage. Plainly, the promise of the outpouring of the Spirit can only be literal, therefore the promise of the former and latter rain must be also taken literally to mean that those special seasons of rain in Palestine to which the Jewish farmer looked in order to obtain maximum fertility from the soil, are to be restored in full measure, as in the beginning, and that this is to take place at the time of Israel's national restoration. But "afterward", as Joel says, these natural and temporal blessings were to be followed by their spiritual counterpart—there was to be an outpouring of the Spirit, not upon selected ones here and there, as in Old Testament days, but upon all flesh. This was to be accompanied by wonders in the heavens and in the earth, and was to precede "the great and terrible day of the Lord" (verses 30, 31). There would be a calling on the name of the Lord for deliverance (verse 32), and all this was to be when God should bring again the captivity of Judah and Jerusalem (3:1) as promised.

It is evident from consideration of these factors that the prophecy, as we find it here in Joel, has *not* been fulfilled, and must await that day when world-wide blessing shall come through national Israel turning to God, when "all Israel shall be saved" (Rom. 11: 26) and "a land shall be born in one day", and "a nation be brought forth at once" (Isa. 66: 8). Paul expressed it thus: "If the casting away of them [the nation of Israel] is the reconciling of the world, what shall the receiving of them be, but life from the dead?" (Rom. 11: 15). However, the wonderful fact is that Peter declared on the day of Pentecost, *"This is that* which was spoken by the prophet Joel", and then changing the word "afterward", he continued, *"In the last days* . . . I will pour forth of My Spirit". The inspired Apostle thus revealed that Joel's prophecy had an earlier application to the age of the church, "the last days", which began with Pentecost. It is a feature of Old Testament prophecy, that there is very often a secondary fulfilment as well as the primary and literal one. The primary fulfilment is of necessity an exact fulfilment of the prophecy in every detail. The secondary fulfilment which usually precedes and anticipates the primary, will be but a partial fulfilment. Failure to recognize or acknowledge this duality in prophecy has led to much confusion.

Joel thus predicts for Israel, at the time of her national restoration, the return of the former and latter rain in Palestine, bringing abundant temporal blessing, to be followed by a glorious "latter rain" of the Spirit. Peter reveals by inspiration what could not otherwise have been known from the passage in Joel, that the promised "latter rain" of the Spirit was also to apply to the age of the church; that hidden away in that Old Testament prophecy was a secret purpose of God, to pour out His Spirit during this age and before the time of Israel's national restoration, and that this began with the outpouring at Pentecost. "Upon all flesh" indicates that the outpouring was to be unrestricted—as to sex, "sons and daughters" (Acts 2: 17); as to age, "young men and old men" (2: 17); as to race, "to you and to your children [Jews], and to all that are afar off [Gentiles]" (2: 39).

It hardly needs to be asserted that the history of Israel in the Old Testament has a spiritual application to the church. Who has not seen that the redemption from Egypt, the wanderings in the wilderness, the entering of the Promised Land have a fulfilment in Christian experience? The New Testament confirms this again and again, for it is packed with Old Testament allusions to illustrate and enforce New Testament truths (viz. 1 Cor. 10). It now remains to show that the promised outpouring of the Spirit referred to by Peter at Pentecost was prefigured by the rain that God promised He would pour out upon the land in response to the obedience of His people.

When the nation was about to enter Canaan, God said through Moses, "The land, whither ye go over to possess it, is a land of hills and valleys, and drinketh water of the rain of heaven. . . . And it shall come to pass, if ye shall hearken diligently unto My commandments which I command you this day, to love the Lord your God, and to serve Him with all your heart and with all your soul, that I will give the rain of your land in its season, the former rain and the latter rain, that thou mayest gather in thy corn, and thy wine, and thine oil" (Deut. 11: 11–14). It is clear from this passage that the harvest was dependent upon the rain, and that the rain was promised by God, contingent upon their obedience.

There are many references in Scripture to the long "dry season" in Palestine which commences in April and lasts until October, leaving the ground parched and the cisterns almost empty. Only those who have experienced this "dry season" in the East can appreciate the great longing which fills the hearts of all for the coming rain. How graphic are David's words in this connection : "My soul thirsteth for Thee, my flesh longeth for Thee, in a dry and weary land, where no water is" (Ps. 63: 1; cf. Isa. 32: 2; 35: 7). The rainy season usually commences about the end of October with light showers that soften the ground (Ps. 65: 10), and then continues with heavy intermittent falls often lasting for two or three days, throughout November and December. These heavy falls were called in Scripture "the former [or early] rain" (Heb. yoreh or moreh). The farmer depends upon the former rain to render the rocklike soil suitable for ploughing and sowing. A native of Palestine has written in this connection, "When the rains have come in sufficient quantities, he must begin to plough. He may have to plough in the face of hail and snow, storm and tempest, but plough he must, for if he does not plough and sow with the early rains, he will not reap after the latter rains" (Prov. 20: 4; Eccles. 11: 4) (Samuel Schor).

When these heavy falls are over, lesser showers still continue intermittently. "At no period during the winter do they entirely cease" (Smith's Dictionary). With the approach of the harvest,

however, the heavy rain would return to swell the grain and fruit
in preparation for the time of reaping. This was known as "the
latter rain", meaning the rain of ingathering, which was very
similar in character to the "former rain", for both are described
by the word "geshem", meaning gushing rain. "Let us now fear
the Lord our God, that giveth rain [geshem], both the former and
the latter, in its season; that reserveth unto us the appointed
weeks of the harvest" (Jer. 5: 24; cf. Joel 2: 23, 24, Hos. 6: 3).
We see from this that the former and latter rains are distinguished
from various other kinds of rain spoken of in Scripture (in all
ten different Hebrew words are used) by their own distinctive
names, and by the description "geshem"* or "gushing rain", that
pours down in copious falls. It is also clear that the former and
latter rains could not be expected at any time, for they had their
appointed seasons. Finally, both were related to the long-looked-
for harvest, for without them there would be neither sowing nor
reaping.

On the face of it, the similarity between this rainy season of
Canaan and the age of the church is striking. Just as that season
was heralded by preliminary showers that soon gave way to the
copious falls of the former rain, so in the ministries of John the
Baptist (when there "went out unto him Jerusalem, and all
Judaea, and all the region round about Jordan" Matt. 3: 5), and
of Christ, (when "there followed Him great multitudes from
Galilee and Decapolis and Jerusalem and Judaea and from beyond
Jordan" Matt. 4: 25), we see distinct movements of the Spirit
which told all those looking for the consolation of Israel that the
season of drought was over, and that a new and glorious season
of rain had come. At the outset of His ministry the Lord said,
"Thou shalt see greater things than these" (John 1: 50), and at
its conclusion, "Greater works than these shall [ye] do" (John
14: 12). The former rain was at hand, and Pentecost marked its
commencement. "In the last days, saith God, I will pour forth
of My Spirit." The outpourings continued throughout that first
century, gradually decreasing in power and frequency as time
elapsed and faith and spirituality declined. However, all through
the ensuing centuries of the dark middle ages, the showers continued here and there, now and again. Such histories as Broad-
bent's *Pilgrim Church* make it clear that at no point, not even in

* Not used exclusively of the latter rain.

the darkest days, did the rain of blessing entirely cease, though the heavier outpourings of revival were few and far between. Since the Reformation there have been outpourings more distinct and frequent.

The latter rain is in preparation for the day of harvest; it is the last epoch of the rainy season prior to the final ingathering. But when and what is the harvest? In the parable of the tares the Lord explained that "the harvest is the end of the age" when "the Son of man shall send forth His angels, and they shall gather out of His kingdom all things that cause stumbling, and them that do iniquity" (Matt. 13: 39, 41). It will be the time when the word shall come to the One "like unto a son of man" sitting upon the white cloud, "Send forth Thy sickle, and reap: for the hour to reap is come". He will then "cast His sickle (viz. angels; Matt. 13: 39, 41) upon the earth", and the earth shall be reaped (Rev. 14: 14-16). The harvest is clearly associated in Scripture with the coming of Christ at the end of the age.

It has been shown that this age of the church is the time of rain. We may look upon Pentecost as the commencement of the former rain, for it was during those first and powerful effusions of the Spirit that the gospel was spread throughout the civilized world, and the ground prepared for the final harvest. Before the age concludes with the personal return of Christ at harvest time we must expect the latter rain of promise, or the rain of ingathering. How can the day of reaping come before this final season of the outpouring of the Spirit, so vital for the final maturing of the spiritual harvest? Just as the rainy season of Canaan concluded with the same kind of rain as it began, the "geshem" or heavy rain, so should we expect before the coming of Christ a season of mighty outpourings, eclipsing all that the church has experienced since the Reformation, and only comparable in character and in power with the former rain of the early church.

James puts the matter beyond doubt when he says, "Be patient therefore, brethren, until the coming of the Lord. Behold, the husbandman waiteth for the precious fruit of the earth, being patient over it, until it receive the early and latter rain. Be ye also patient; stablish your hearts: for the coming of the Lord is at hand" (Jas. 5: 7, 8). Do we long for the day of harvest? Do we grow impatient for the coming of the Lord? It is as though the apostle would curb our restless spirits, and enjoin us to be patient by reminding us that the heavenly Husbandman has been waiting all through the long seasons, waiting for the fulfilment of His purposes, waiting for the precious fruit of the earth at the time of harvest. We must be imitators of "the God of patience", who has been waiting so much longer than we have. The Husbandman knows, and those also who labour as His servants should know, that before the final harvest day can dawn at the coming of the Lord the fruit of the earth must receive the early and the latter rain. If we in this day can look backward to the former rain, we have still to look forward to the latter rain, the final epoch of the age, prior to the day of harvest.

Leaving aside for a moment the testimony of Scripture on this point, one has only to survey with unprejudiced eye the harvest-fields of God's kingdom, one has only to examine the spiritual condition of that which is growing up unto the harvest to be convinced of the absolute necessity of the latter rain of the Spirit before the fruit of the earth can be mature for harvesting. If it has been shown that there is in the word of God a promise of revival for us today, if there is any evidence that we are, in the purpose of God, moving into the era of the latter rain, then let us heed the word of God to Israel, let us do what they shall do in a coming day : "Ask ye of the Lord rain in the time of the latter rain, even of the Lord that maketh lightnings; and He shall give them [geshem] showers of rain" (Zech. 10: 1).

> Pour down Thy Spirit once again, dear Lord;
> Our cry goes up to Thee for "latter rain";
> Unite Thy people as the "heart of one",
> And Pentecostal days shall come again !
>                                   E. M. GRIMES.

The quiet conversion of one sinner after another, under the ordinary ministry of the gospel must always be regarded with feelings of satisfaction and gratitude . . .; but a periodical manifestation of the simultaneous conversion of thousands is also to be desired, because of its adaptation to afford a visible and impressive demonstration that God has made that same Jesus who was rejected and crucified, both Lord and Christ.

WILLIAM REID.

CHAPTER FOUR

## THIS IS THE PURPOSE

"This is the purpose that is purposed upon the whole earth:
and this is the hand that is stretched out upon all the nations.
For the Lord of Hosts hath purposed, and who shall disannul it?" (Isa. 14: 26).

GOD has always worked by means of revivals. Since the
dawn of human history His purposes have progressed by
sudden and mighty movements of the Spirit. "The world
of mankind has not advanced by evolution but by revolution;
that is, by violent upheavals of society. Many changes have taken
place rapidly, changes that make the ordinary events of history
appear commonplace by contrast. Eden, the Flood, the Exodus
period and the Captivity era are Old Testament illustrations of
these revolutionary epochs, while Pentecost is the conspicuous
New Testament example. Our Christian era is marked by many
such times of religious transformation. The Renaissance and Protestant Reformation in the fifteenth century changed the whole
thought and life of Europe. Modern history dates from them"
(P. V. Jenness).

While all must acknowledge this principle in the workings of
God, some may ask, "Why has God chosen to work in this way?
Would it not be more satisfactory for the work of God to progress
quietly and steadily, without the stimulus of such excitement and
upheaval as are produced in seasons of revival?" It should not be
necessary to justify the ways of God before His people; nevertheless, in doing so, the underlying reasons for revival may perhaps
be more clearly set forth. Revival as a method of God's working
may be justified from the standpoint of divine strategy, first *to
counteract spiritual decline*, and then *to create spiritual momentum*. Then revival may be justified from its results, by examining
its effects in relation to *the saints, the sinners* and *the Godhead*.
Firstly, let us see its place in divine strategy.

*Counteracting Spiritual Decline*

If the work of God could have been maintained and extended down the centuries in steady spiritual power, revivals would have been unnecessary as a counteracting agent, but this, as we know, has been far from the case. "A revival of religion presupposes a declension" (Finney). Decline and decay are inherent in fallen nature and are not confined simply to the physical and moral realm, but invade and influence even the spiritual. This is writ large not only in the history of Israel, but also across the pages of the New Testament and the subsequent history of the church. It has pleased God to counteract this deadly tendency to departure by working at special seasons and places in extraordinary power.

It is a well-established fact that when the Spirit of God is working powerfully the spiritual results are usually deep and abiding. Souls saved or blessed in powerful revivals are, on the whole, more likely to continue steadfastly than is the case at other times. There is more connection between the manifestation of God's power and spiritual steadfastness than some have realized. The history of Israel in the time of the Judges illustrates this very vividly. "And the people served the Lord all the days of Joshua, and all the days of the elders that outlived Joshua, *who had seen all the great work of the Lord,* that He had wrought for Israel . . . and there arose another generation after them, which knew not the Lord, nor yet the work which He had wrought for Israel. And the children of Israel did that which was evil in the sight of the Lord, and served the Baalim" (Judges 2: 7, 10, 11).

It would not be good for these displays of God's power to be other than occasional. It would not make for spiritual health that the Lord's people should live on them. Nevertheless, in times of spiritual declension there is perhaps nothing more calculated to stay the rot, wean the heart from earth and attract it to heaven, and produce spiritual steadfastness than to experience such a mighty work of God. Again and again spiritual situations and conditions that seemed beyond recovery have been transformed by such a working of the Spirit. One recalls the pithy definition of revival as "the inrush of the Spirit into a body that threatens to become a corpse"! (D. M. Panton). If "counteracting spiritual decline" was the only purpose achieved by God in such seasons,

His method would be abundantly justified. It is after all but the sound military principle that the best method of defence is attack.

## Creating Spiritual Momentum

There is another well-known military principle known as *concentration of force*, according to which a commander will husband his reserves, concentrate them at a strategic point, for a vital blow at the crucial moment. He will thus hope to break through the enemy defences and so produce momentum or advance where all was static. A powerful thrust of this sort may well achieve what routine patrolling, skirmishing, or harassing tactics could never effect. It is thus with revival : it is designed to achieve what the quieter workings of the Spirit do not.

There was once an ancient reservoir in the hills that supplied a village community with water. It was fed by a mountain stream, and the overflow from the reservoir continued down the stream-bed to the valley below. There was nothing at all remarkable about this stream. It flowed on its quiet way without even disturbing the boulders that lay in its path or the foot-bridges that crossed it at various points. It seldom overflowed its steep banks, or gave the villagers any trouble. One day, however, some large cracks appeared in one of the walls of the old reservoir, and soon afterwards the wall collapsed, and the waters burst forth down the hillside. They rooted up great trees; they carried along boulders like playthings; they destroyed houses and bridges and all that lay in their path. The stream-bed could not now contain the volume of water, which therefore flowed over the countryside, even inundating distant dwellings. What had before been ignored or taken for granted now became an object of awe and wonder and fear. From far and near people who in the usual way never went near the stream, hastened to see this great sight.

In picture language this is revival; in fact it is the sort of picture language that Scripture uses to convey the irresistible power of God. Often in the period just preceding the movement, the stream of power and blessing has been unusually low. The people of God and the work of God have been "in great affliction and reproach", despised or ignored by those around them. In response, however, to the prayers of a burdened remnant God has been quietly heaping the flood. The watchful eye has seen "a cloud as small as a man's hand". The listening ear has caught "the sound of abundance of rain". Then suddenly, when the majority had no expectation of it, God opened the windows of heaven and poured out the blessing so that in the channels of organized Christianity there was not room enough to receive it. Like the river that issued from the sanctuary in the vision of Ezekiel (chap. 47), the waters that were at first to the ankles are before long, in the full tide of revival, "waters to swim in". The flood of life and blessing has now become an object of awe and wonder. Works of darkness and strongholds of Satan that have long resisted the normal influences of the Spirit are swept away. Stubborn wills that have long withstood the overtures of the gospel, the pleadings and the prayers of loved ones, now bend and break before the irresistible flow of the Spirit, to be engulfed themselves and borne along in the stream of blessing.

What God has said of a coming time of judgment and revival for Israel and the earth, is in measure true of all such displays of God's power : "So shall they fear the name of the Lord from the west, and His glory from the rising of the sun : for *He shall come as a rushing stream*, which the breath of the Lord driveth" (Isa. 59: 19). Thus does God see fit to use revival to create spiritual momentum, to accomplish in days what could never otherwise be achieved in years of normal Christian activity. We must not, however, in our zeal for revival disparage what is achieved in the quieter seasons, for God has His purposes in these times also. The patrolling and the harassing and the limited advances are all essential to the big offensive. "The day of small things" (Zech. 4: 10) is preparatory and supplementary to "the day of [God's] power" (Ps. 110: 3), and we must not despise it.

We should not be surprised to discover that it has been in times of spiritual revival that most of the forward movements of the church have been born. The great missionary advance of the last century derived its momentum from the widespread revivals that blessed America and Britain during those years. Ever since the light was almost eclipsed in medieval times, God has been working to recover the situation, and to restore to the church the light, the purity, and the power which are her birthright, and which characterized her in the first century. The affairs of God's house must be re-established as He instituted them at the beginning. The ways of apostolic Christianity must be recovered, or the church of the latter days will never ride the storms that already threaten to engulf her. God has used revivals to this end.

During such times new light has broken from the sacred page, and out of such times new expressions of the church have evolved, recovering in most cases something more of the mind of God. Only when the new truth became central, and the work was built around it, instead of around Christ; only when the believers became more diligent in holding fast the new truth than in "holding fast the Head", did the movement become denominational and sectarian. Although the revivals of the future will surely reveal that there is yet more land to be possessed in this respect, let us never forget what we owe to the spiritual momentum derived from the movements of the past, and let us be ready to walk in whatever new light may break forth when once again God is pleased to manifest His power and glory. It must now be shown that the ways of God in revival are yet further vindicated by the effects produced.

## The Saints

Clearly it is the saints, not the sinners, that are primarily involved in revival. The quickening of the saints is the root, while the saving of the sinners is the fruit. Therefore, to see the primary effects of revival we must look at the church. Isaiah sounded a reveille call to the people of God in the familiar words, "Awake, awake, put on thy strength, O Zion; put on thy beautiful garments, O Jerusalem, the holy city" (52: 1). Revival marks the awakening of the church; indeed such a time is commonly termed "an awakening". When asleep one is out of touch with the world of reality. The church asleep is out of touch with the world of spiritual reality, and needs to be awakened.

The argument in favour of an awakening grows stronger as the end of the age approaches, for Paul himself said, "knowing the season, that now it is high time for you to awake out of sleep : for now is salvation nearer to us than when we first believed. The night is far spent, and the day is at hand: let us therefore cast off the works of darkness, and let us put on the armour of light" (Rom. 13: 11). Here is the primary effect of revival—the church awakes, casts off the works of darkness that have blanketed her in her slumber, and puts on the armour of light. The assertion that we cannot have an awakening in these days is but the Devil's lullaby to hush the church to sleep.

"Awake, awake, put on thy strength, O Zion." Asleep, the church of Christ is impotent; awakened, she clothes herself with spiritual strength. The power that began to flow at Pentecost is inexhaustible, and is as much available now as then, but only an awakened church can claim her birthright and go forth "clothed with power from on high" (Luke 24: 49). No one can deny that the people of God today are largely denuded of this power. It is a characteristic effect of revival that Zion puts on her strength. It is doubtful if the power is ever renewed in a widespread manner save in times of revival.

"Awake, awake . . . put on thy beautiful garments, O Jerusalem, the holy city." The church asleep is not only denuded of power but also of holiness. Only when the people of God are awakened are they clothed with the beautiful garments of practical righteousness. Is there not a need of holiness today? Is there not a downward tendency on the part of individual believers seen in lukewarmness toward the Lord, compromise with the world, and complacency as to themselves? Then there is an undoubted need of an awakening. Holiness is not optional but obligatory. God demands it. Without it no man shall see the Lord (Matt. 5: 8; Heb. 12: 14). But revival is a time when God comes and rains righteousness upon us (Hos. 10: 12). If there is no revival of righteousness, there is no revival at all.

It is characteristic of revivals that they have been seasons when sins that have long hindered blessing are exposed, confessed, and forgiven. Relationships, wrecked by pride, envy, and evil-speaking are wonderfully restored when the hearts of the saints melt in the fires of revival. As Jonathan Edwards wrote of the 18th-century New England Awakening, "Abundance has been lately done at making up differences, and confessing faults one to another, and making restitution; probably more within these two years, than was done in thirty years before." It is at such times that Zion awakes and puts on her beautiful garments, displaying to a wondering world "the excellencies of Him Who called [her] out of darkness into His marvellous light" (1 Pet. 2: 9). Revival issues in an awakened church clothed with the power and holiness of her risen Head. The church dormant becomes the church militant. Then indeed may her Beloved declare, "Thou art beautiful, O my love, as Tirzah, comely as Jerusalem, terrible as an army with banners" (Song 6: 4). Is not this effect on the church sufficient justification for revival? Does it not provide ample reason why we should all be thirsting for revival?

## The Sinners

When God finds His people willing, when they have been forged into an instrument He can use, He will begin to work in power upon the consciences of sinners. Revival involves two awakening cries: God crying to man, "Awake, awake . . . O Zion" (Isa. 52: 1), and man crying to God, "Awake, awake, put on strength, O arm of the Lord; awake, as in the days of old" (Isa. 51: 9). When the voice of the Lord has awakened the church, the voice of the church will awaken the Lord, and the power of God will be manifested in the saving of sinners. "Then the Lord awaked as one out of sleep, like a mighty man that shouteth by reason of wine. And He smote His adversaries backward" (Ps. 78: 65). When it has seemed that for a long time the Almighty has slumbered, the cry of the church pierces the heavens, "Let God arise, let His enemies be scattered; let them also that hate Him flee before Him" (Ps. 68: 1). Then does the Lord go forth to war, and His "arrows are sharp . . . in the heart of the King's enemies" (Ps. 45: 5). There is deep and widespread conviction amongst the lost. "The sinners in Zion are afraid; trembling hath surprised the godless ones. Who among us shall dwell with the devouring fire? Who among us shall dwell with everlasting burnings?" (Isa. 33: 14).

Out of this deep conviction multitudes are born into the kingdom. Wherever there comes this awful sense of God's presence stealing over the hearts of men, the fountains of the great deep are broken up. Gone is the voice of the sinner who inwardly debates whether or not he will patronize the Son of God: "Christ is knocking at my sad heart, shall I let Him in? . . . Shall I bid Him for ever depart,—or shall I let Him in?" Instead we hear the heart-wrung sob: "Depth of mercy! can there be mercy still reserved for me? Can my God His wrath forbear? Me, the chief of sinners, spare?" Conversions take place without any appeals, and tend to be clear cut and decisive. As in the early church, many born again in revival are at once filled with the

Spirit and became effective for God. Whether in meetings or out of them, whether through personal dealing or without it, men and women, broken over their sin, find their way to Christ.

When God thus moves in power He wrests the initiative from Satan. Sin no longer stalks the land in triumph but hides its head in shame. It is not unusual for social evils to be swept away and industrial problems solved overnight. Drink saloons, places of amusement, and dens of iniquity have often had to close through lack of patronage. Magistrates have been known to take a holiday, and the jails to be nearly empty. Everywhere there seems to be one topic of conversation, the things of eternity. On the faces of the people there is a spirit of inquiry or of concern. They are asking, "What meaneth this?" or, "What shall we do?" Every stratum of society has been affected, and the widespread indifference of the masses is a thing of the past. Such are the effects upon sinners, and are they not sufficient justification for revival? Do they not provide a powerful reason, if we have any concern for the souls of men, why we should all be thirsting for revival?

### The Godhead

Finally, there is the fruit of revival as it affects the Godhead. Important as were the other two, here is an effect which exceeds in importance the other two combined, for in a sense it includes them. In a day when the power of God is in great measure restrained, and when it would seem that the Lord hides His face, it is nothing strange to most believers that men should live in rebellion against Him; they come to expect it. It is the usual thing that men of the world should treat their Creator with indifference or contempt. The prevalent attitude towards God, unexpressed perhaps yet real, amounts to this, "Depart from us; for we desire not the knowledge of Thy ways. What is the Almighty, that we should serve Him? And what profit should we have, if we pray unto Him?" (Job 21: 15). While repudiating this attitude for oneself, one may unconsciously become accustomed to it in others, and think of it as inevitable.

Thank God indeed for the thousands who have not bowed the knee to Baal, but where are the Elijahs who have been "very jealous for the Lord God of Hosts" because the people have forsaken His covenant, thrown down His altars, and—if words have power to kill—slain His prophets with the sword? Where are "the priests, the ministers of the Lord [who] weep between the porch and the altar"? (Joel 2: 17). Where are those who yearn to see the God of heaven, so long robbed of His crown rights, manifesting His power and glory, and vindicating His Name? To those who feel for God, it is intolerable that men should continue to treat Him thus.

> Yet saints their watch are keeping,
>   Their cry goes up, "How long?"
> And soon the night of weeping
>   Shall be the morn of song.
> S. J. STONE.

It is of course true that the full answer to this longing, wrought in the heart by the Spirit, must await that day when every knee shall bow to Christ, and every tongue confess that He is Lord (Phil. 2: 10), and the pierced hand shall hold the sceptre of the universe and the government shall be upon His shoulder. Revivals, however, have always been times when God has vindicated His honour before the eyes of men in an extraordinary degree. They are seasons when men are made to know, though they be as proud and as powerful as Nebuchadnezzar, "That the Most High ruleth in the kingdom of men, and giveth it to whomsoever He will . . . and all the inhabitants of the earth are reputed as nothing : and He doeth according to His will in the army of heaven, and among the inhabitants of the earth : and none can stay His hand, or say unto Him, What doest Thou?" (Dan. 4: 32, 35).

As with God, so with Christ. Everywhere we see evidence of the bitter enmity which Satan bears to the Son, who gave His blood for the life of the world. This age, blinded by its god, has not revoked the tragic decree, "We will not that this Man reign over us" (Luke 19: 14); nor has it ceased to ask, whether in fear or in scorn, the question, "What have we to do with Thee, Thou Jesus of Nazareth?" (Mark 1: 24).

> Our Lord is now rejected,
> And by the world disowned,
> By the many still neglected,
> And by the few enthroned.
> EL NATHAN.

Nevertheless the promise still stands—"He shall see of the travail of His soul, and shall be satisfied" (Isa. 53: 11). In that word "satisfied" there are depths eternal, and consolations that outweigh even the agonies of Gethsemane and Golgotha. This was "the joy that was set before Him" when He "endured the cross, despising shame" (Heb. 12 : 2).

Nearly two millenniums have passed and still He waits. Is it not strange that many who profess so much seem to care so little? Where are those with Paul's passion for the glory of Christ, who can say with that apostle, "I hold not my life of any account, as dear unto myself, so that I may accomplish my course, . . . to testify the gospel of the grace of God"? (Acts 20 : 24). Or again, "I am ready not to be bound only, but also to die . . . for the name of the Lord Jesus"? (Acts 21 : 13). Where are those with an intense longing that the Saviour may be satisfied with the fruit of His suffering? You may expect to find them praying for revival, for that is a time when multitudes bow the knee before Him, and clamour to confess Him Lord. It is then that they will joy before Him "according to the joy in harvest, as men rejoice when they divide the spoil" (Isa. 9 : 3). For Him it is a precious foretaste of that final harvest when "a great multitude, which no man could number" shall stand before the throne (Rev. 7 : 9).

As for the Comforter, who is the Holy Spirit, men's attitude to Him is no less grievous. Cults abound that deny both His deity and His personality. How true was the word of Christ to the apostles concerning this One, whose presence was to mean more to them than His own, "the world . . . beholdeth Him not, neither knoweth Him" (John 14 : 17), and we might add, "and many believers know Him not either". If we asked some who have truly believed, "Did ye receive the Holy Spirit when ye believed?" (Acts 19 : 2) they would have to confess, "We don't know about the Holy Spirit", or "We thought that He was the same as Christ". How seldom is that gracious unseen Presence truly recognized, relied upon, or given His rightful place in the church which He established. How often is He grieved and hindered because the people of God prefer human organization and the methods of the world, to that which costs more than money to secure—His own gracious presence and power. But revival ever brings a fresh emphasis upon the person and work of the Holy Spirit. It is a time when believers thirst and are filled, and when the Spirit Himself reasserts His rights, and is given the reins in the worship and service of the church.

So revival has its repercussions even in the realm of the Triune God. It is a time when the rights of humanity give way to the rights of Deity. "God is not only the *source* of revival—'Wilt *Thou* not revive us again?'—but He is also the *end* of revival—'that Thy people may rejoice in *Thee*' (Ps. 85: 6 A.V.). Revival comes from God and leads to God, that He may be 'all in all', and that man may learn that of himself he is nothing" (Philip Hughes). Here is the transcendent effect of all revival, and the fulfilment of its highest purpose: "The loftiness of man shall be bowed down, and the haughtiness of men shall be brought low: and THE LORD ALONE SHALL BE EXALTED IN THAT DAY" (Isa. 2: 17). If we have a jealous desire for the glory of Father, Son, and Holy Spirit, should we not all be thirsting for revival?

The antecedents, accompaniments, and results of revivals are always substantially the same as in the case of Pentecost.

CHARLES FINNEY.

Come as the wind, with rushing sound
    And Pentecostal grace,
That all of woman born may see
    The glory of Thy face.

A. REED.

## CHAPTER FIVE

## DISTINCTIVE FEATURES (I)

"This is that which hath been spoken by the prophet Joel;
And it shall be in the last days, saith God, I will pour forth of
My Spirit upon all flesh" (Acts 2:16).

THERE are certain characteristics that mark this divine activity we call "revival", and distinguish it from other and more normal operations of the Spirit. Some have already been mentioned, but it will now be necessary to set them forth in order, and consider them in their relation to the whole. As Pentecost was the first distinctive outpouring of the Spirit, a careful examination of that great event will reveal the distinctive features of every subsequent outpouring. Let Acts 2 be the text-book.

### Divine Sovereignty

This first mark is implicit in the statement, "When the day of Pentecost was now come". Every genuine revival is clearly stamped with the hallmark of divine sovereignty, and in no way is this more clearly seen than in the time factor. The moment for that first outpouring of the Spirit was not determined by the believers in the upper room but by God, who had foreshadowed it centuries before in those wonderful types of the Old Testament. "The slaying of the paschal lamb told to generation after generation, though they knew it not, the day of the year and week on which Christ our Passover should be sacrificed for us. The presentation of the wave sheaf before the Lord 'on the morrow after the sabbath' (Lev. 23:11–16) had for long centuries fixed the time of our Lord's resurrection on the first day of the week. And the command to 'count from the morrow after the sabbath, from the day that ye brought the sheaf of the wave offering, seven sabbaths', determined the day of Pentecost as the time of the descent of the Spirit. . . . They tarried in prayer for ten days, simply because after the forty days of the Lord's sojourn on earth subsequent to His resurrection, ten days remained of the 'seven sabbaths' period" (A. J. Gordon).

But there was something more than the fulfilling of prophecy in the choice of the day of Pentecost for the great outpouring. It was a strategic moment which God had foreseen would give to the event of that day the maximum possible effect. God saw to it that this mighty outpouring of the Spirit was felt throughout the world of that day, for the feast had brought to Jerusalem "Jews, devout men, from every nation under heaven" (Acts 2: 5). Not only the day, however, but the time of day had been appointed by God, that the mocking charge, "they are filled with new wine" (verse 13) might be easily rebutted, seeing it was but "the third hour of the day" [9 a.m.] (verse 15).

Similarly God has His time for every subsequent outpouring, a time that must surely be related to a thousand other plans He has on foot, and therefore a time that He alone can determine. It has already been mentioned that God promised His people Israel, if they were obedient, the rain of their land, but only "*in its season*" (Deut. 11: 13–17; Ezek. 34: 26). It would not help the spiritual harvest that God desires if we could have the outpouring of the Spirit any time or all the time; any more than it would have helped their harvest if the Israelites could have had the former and latter rain at any time or all the time. "Ask ye of the Lord rain." When?—"In the time of the latter rain" (Zech. 10: 1). A sober view of the sovereignty of God will not lessen a God-given burden, or discourage fervent praying in the Spirit, but it may deliver us from extravagance in which some have erred, or despondence in which some have failed, in their quest for revival.

It may seem strange to go to Charles Finney for an example of the sovereignty of God in revival, as that great revivalist tended to overlook this aspect in battling against the hyper-Calvinism of his day. However, he once recounted: "While I was in Boston on one occasion, a gentleman stated that he had come from the capital of Nebraska, and he had found prayer meetings established throughout all the vast extent of country over which he had travelled. Think of that—a region of 2,000 miles, along which the hands of the people were lifted up to God in prayer! From north to south, till you come within the slave territory, a great and mighty cry went up to God that He would come down and take the people in hand and convert souls; and He heard, and everybody stood astounded." Such a vast, unorganized, and yet co-ordinated prayer movement cannot be explained except that God in His sovereignty had taken the initiative. What is true of the promise of future blessing for Israel, is true also of the promise of revival, "I the Lord will hasten it in its time" (Isa. 60: 22).

It has been said of the Welsh Revival, "The outpouring of the Spirit came dramatically with precision, in the second week in November, 1904, on the same day—both in the north and in the south." Undoubtedly there were those in both regions who had met the conditions and were ready for God to work, but we cannot account for this strange co-ordination apart from that divine strategy which lies behind the sovereign ways of God. In the 1859 Revival that spread to many parts of the British Isles, there was an immediate movement in some places when Christians met to pray and fulfil God's conditions. In other parts, however, although it would appear that the preparation of heart and burden of prayer were quite as real, the believers were kept waiting for one or even two years. It is significant that when revival came after a longer waiting period, the work was often deeper and more widespread. "Behold, He withholdeth the waters, and they dry up; again, He sendeth them out, and they overrun the earth" (Job 12: 15). The same principle is seen in the great variety of manifestations that have accompanied different movements. God is sovereign, and His sovereignty is revealed not only in the *timing* of every revival movement, but in the *manner* and *measure* of the Spirit's working.

Where believers have been encouraged by God to expect revival, and where they have with all their hearts sought to prepare themselves and pray through, but the blessing has been delayed, there is a danger of giving way to despondence, or undue introspection. Let such remember that if He has promised, then "God is not a man, that He should lie; neither the son of man, that He should repent: hath He said, and shall He not do it? Or hath He spoken, and shall He not make it good?" (Num. 23: 19). Let such be emboldened to "hold on" by a sober view of the sovereignty of God, and the immutability of His purposes. "The Lord of Hosts hath sworn, saying, Surely as I have thought, so shall it come to pass; and as I have purposed, so shall it stand. . . . For the Lord of Hosts hath purposed, and who shall disannul it? and His hand is stretched out, and who shall turn it back?" (Isa. 14: 24, 27). Let them wait *on* the Lord, and wait *for* the Lord, and they shall not be ashamed (Isa. 49: 23).

### Spiritual Preparation

This feature was also in evidence, for "they were all together in one place" (verse 1). How these believers in the upper room had reached this state of preparedness is shown in Chapter 1, where we find that they "all with one accord continued steadfastly in prayer" (verse 14). The word of God presents to us side by side the two foundation stones of every revival—the sovereignty of God and the preparedness of man. Because we cannot understand how they harmonize is no reason for emphasizing one at the expense of the other. There is an extreme view of the sovereignty of God that argues, "If God wills to send revival it will come. Nothing that we do can effect this, so why need we be concerned?" The word of God and history teach us that such an attitude of indifference and fatalism must be abandoned before revival can be expected. If the blessing comes then we may be sure that somewhere someone has met the conditions and paid the price. Such a view of divine sovereignty ignores the conditions of spiritual preparedness.

There is also an extreme emphasis on spiritual preparedness that ignores the fact of divine sovereignty; it suggests that God is at our beck and call, and that we can have revival any day we care to pay the price, much as we can have electric light the moment we care to turn the switch. The word of God gives us the proper balance by presenting, as here in the first verse of Acts 2, the two aspects side by side. Similarly David declared, "Thy people offer themselves willingly in the day of Thy power" (Ps. 110: 3). The day of His power is determined by God alone, and emphasizes His sovereignty; but in that day His people have met the conditions by being ready and willing, which reveals the fact of spiritual preparation. God reminds us of His sovereignty when He declares, "I will cause the cities to be inhabited, and the waste places shall be builded . . . I the Lord have spoken it, and I will do it"; but He adds, "For this moreover will I be inquired of by the house of Israel, to do it for them", reminding us of the conditions that must be fulfilled (Ezek. 36: 33–37).

War is not all attack, but there is a strategic moment for offensive action. The place, the time, and the manner of any attack are of crucial importance in the interests of the campaign as a whole; therefore such matters are not left to the soldier in the fighting line, but are determined beforehand by the supreme commander in the conference room. He alone can see the whole picture and keep his hand upon the whole situation. If, however, the plans made at the highest level are to be carried through successfully, the soldier in the line must be fully prepared for all that is involved. Revival, as we have seen in the previous chapter, is a strategic attack by God upon the strongholds of Satan. The place, the time, and the manner of working are in the sovereign hands of the Lord the Spirit; but His subordinates, through whom He works, must be spiritually prepared when God's zero hour strikes.

How clearly these two important factors are set forth in the promised rain of Canaan. Divine sovereignty was seen in that the rain was confined to its God-appointed "season", but it was also strictly conditioned by the obedience of the people. "If ye shall hearken diligently unto My commandments which I command you this day, to love the Lord your God, and to serve Him with all your heart and with all your soul, that I will give the rain of your land in its season" (Deut. 11: 13). God declared with equal emphasis and on the same occasion, that if on the other hand they turned aside and served other gods and worshipped them, He would "shut up the heaven, that there be no rain, and that the land yield not her fruit" (verses 16, 17).

How spiritual preparedness, or the absence of it, may influence God's working is vividly illustrated by the visit of the Saviour to Nazareth. "He could there do no mighty work . . . and He marvelled because of their unbelief" (Mark 6: 5, 6). What this spiritual preparation involves, and how it may be effected, is a subject so large and so important that it must be considered separately.

### Suddenness

Here is the third feature, "And *suddenly* there came. . . ." (verse 2). Since revival may be likened to a strategic attack, it is plain that, as in the realm of human conflict, so in the spiritual, the effect of every attack is heightened by the surprise factor. In revival God works suddenly and unexpectedly. Often even the mass of believers are taken unawares, while wonder and astonishment grip the hearts of unbelievers. It was so at Pentecost where we read of those who came together, "They were all amazed and marvelled" (verse 7), and again, "They were all amazed, and were perplexed" (verse 12). As to Christians being taken by surprise, Charles Finney often noticed it and remarked, "They would wake up all of a sudden, like a man, just rubbing his eyes open, and running round the room pushing things over, and wondering where all this excitement came from. But though few knew it, you may be sure there had been somebody on the watch-tower, constant in prayer till the blessing came." How vital it is for the ears of the saints to be open to the voice of God in these days, for He speaks first to those whose ears are attuned to Him, and then He acts suddenly. "Surely the Lord God will do nothing, but He revealeth His secret unto His servants the prophets" (Amos 3:7). God's methods have not changed down the centuries: it may be the sound of marching in the tops of the mulberry trees, it may be a tiny cloud arising out of the sea; such insignificant tokens are all that is needed for the listening ear or the watchful eye. "I have declared the former things from of old; yea, they went forth out of My mouth, and I shewed them: *suddenly* I did them, and they came to pass" (Isa. 48:3); "Behold, the former things are come to pass, and new things do I declare: before they *spring forth* I tell you of them" (Isa. 42:9).

In 2 Chronicles 29 there is a detailed account of the revival that took place under Hezekiah. The house of the Lord was cleansed and the people were moved to offer sacrifices and thank-offerings in such abundance that the few priests who had sanctified themselves could not handle them, and they had to be assisted by the Levites. Scripture records, "Hezekiah rejoiced, and all the people, because of that which God had prepared for the people: for the thing was done *suddenly*" (verse 36). Who knows all that God is preparing for His people in these days? May we not be found unsanctified, and so unfitted for the work, when the day of God's power shall dawn.

The effect of the sudden working of the Spirit in revival is very striking in the conviction of sinners. Often without any preparatory concern or even thought for spiritual things, a sinner will be suddenly seized with overwhelming conviction of sin. "But God shall shoot at them; with an arrow suddenly shall they be wounded . . . and all men shall fear; and they shall declare the work of God, and shall wisely consider of His doing" (Ps. 64: 7, 9). Describing the course of the Ulster '59 Revival at Ballymena and elsewhere, John Shearer writes of some who "were suddenly pierced as by a sharp sword, and their agonized cry for help was heard in the streets and in the fields. Here, for example, is a farmer returning from market in Ballymena. His mind is wholly intent upon the day's bargain. He pauses, takes out some money, and begins to count it. Suddenly an awful Presence envelops him. In a moment his only thought is that he is a sinner standing on the brink of hell. His silver is scattered, and he falls upon the dust of the highway, crying out for mercy" (*Old Time Revivals*).

### Spontaneous Working

With the brevity and simplicity characteristic of Scripture we are shown in four words the source of the outpouring, "there came *from* heaven" (verse 2). This provides the fourth feature of revival; it is *spontaneous* because it is "not forced or suggested or caused by outside agency" (Oxf. Dict.). It is the result of a divine and not a human impulse. In language plain to all, it cannot be "worked up". It is true that spiritual conditions must be met before revival can be expected, but fulfilled conditions do not provide the motive force of revival. At Pentecost it was "the windows of heaven", not the windows of the upper room, that were opened. The source of the blessing was the heart of God, not the heart of man. It cannot be too strongly emphasized that such "seasons of refreshing" have always come "from the presence of the Lord" (Acts 3: 19). We may believe that during those ten days of waiting there were revived hearts in that upper room, but there was no revival; there were empty vessels, but no outpouring. When it came, it came direct from heaven and found in that waiting band a channel through which to flow.

A missionary, recounting what he had seen of the 1860 Revival in South India, wrote, "Man seems to have little part in it, the Spirit's work is all predominant, fulfilling that blessed promise, 'I will work'." Another who wrote of the 1904 Revival stated,

"The hidden springs of the Awakening in Wales lay deep in the heart of God", and this is where we may find the springs of every awakening. The origin of all revival must be traced back, further than human factors and fulfilled conditions, to the heart of the Eternal that yearns to bless, and to bless superabundantly. "God *so* loved . . . that He gave" and "He that spared not His own Son . . . shall He not also with Him freely give us all things?"

Once again the rain of Canaan, with the remarkable accuracy of Scripture types, aptly illustrates this very feature of revival. Contrasting Egypt, which typifies the world, with Canaan, which speaks of that which is heavenly, God said: "For the land, whither thou goest in to possess it, is not as the land of Egypt, from whence ye came out, where thou sowedst thy seed, and wateredst it with thy foot, as a garden of herbs; but the land, whither ye go over to possess it, is a land of hills and valleys, and drinketh water of the rain of heaven" (Deut. 11: 10, 11). Egypt was stamped with the workmanship of the creature; it was "as a garden of herbs", carefully laid out, planned and arranged. Canaan, on the other hand, was stamped with the workmanship of the Creator; for everywhere the eye was refreshed and delighted with the unorganized order of creation, it was "a land of hills and valleys".

Egypt's fertility, as dependent upon water as was Canaan's, was watered with the foot. In other words, a simple device worked by the foot, which can still be seen in Egypt today, pumped water from the Nile, and conveyed it by a system of irrigation channels to where it was required. Thus the supply of water was dependent upon human energy and ingenuity, and a dirty supply it was when men had finished manipulating it, and it had reached the thirsty soil. But the heavenly country—oh, how different—"a land that drinketh water of the rain of heaven". Canaan was made fruitful by that which came down in all its freshness and purity from above. God had designed that it should be dependent upon the heavens for water, and if these were shut up, the spiritual reason must be sought out and the matter rectified; there was no suggestion of devising any artificial substitute.

It was said of redeemed Israel that they "turned back in their hearts unto Egypt" (Acts 7: 39). Someone has put it thus: "It was one thing to get the people out of Egypt, but quite another to get Egypt out of the people." Said the prophet, "Woe to them that go down to Egypt for help . . . but they look not unto the Holy One of Israel, neither seek the Lord" (Isa. 31: 1). This tendency of going back for assistance into the land whence we have come out, of borrowing from the world and its ways, is as evident today as ever. There are still too many who have more confidence in the working of the foot to produce results, than in the bowing of the knee. This spontaneous feature of revival, however, cuts right across this human tendency. There is no mightier corrective to worldly methods in Christian service than a heaven-sent revival. Who would want to continue to work the pump when the heavens are pouring down a copious rain?

A movement bears this mark of spontaneity when men cannot account for what has taken place in terms of personalities, organization, meetings, preachings, or any other consecrated activity; and when the work continues unabated without any human control. As soon as a movement becomes controlled or organized, it has ceased to be spontaneous—it is no longer revival. The course of the 1904 Welsh Revival has been outlined thus: "God began to work; and then the Devil began to work in opposition; and then God began to work all the harder; and then man began to work, and the revival came to an end." It is most needful in times of revival that a careful watch should be kept so that nothing should gain a foothold which is not of the Spirit, but great care must be taken not to interfere with what is evidently the work of God. When God is working let man keep his hands off. Many a revival has ended through human interference.

## God-Consciousness

Here is another conspicuous feature that characterizes revival. "There came . . . a sound as of the rushing of a mighty wind . . . there appeared unto them tongues . . . like as of fire" (verses 2, 3). Wherever the Spirit of God is poured out saints and sinners alike are made acutely aware of the presence of the Almighty. The spirit of revival is the consciousness of God. Just as the "light from heaven, above the brightness of the sun" struck down the zealous Pharisee, Saul of Tarsus, and brought him to his knees, convicted and repentant (Acts 26), so does the Eternal Light, in days of revival, burst upon the slumbering consciousness of men with much the same result. On the day of Pentecost God manifested His presence first to those in the upper room, and then to the multitude who had gathered outside, who were soon "pricked in their heart" (Acts 2: 37), until that strange, mysterious influence from heaven had spread over the whole city, "and fear came upon every soul" (verse 43).

The effects of such manifestations of God are twofold : men are made aware both of His power and of His holiness. What awe must have come to the hearts of that waiting band, as they listened to that "sound as of the rushing of a mighty wind"— what a sense of the irresistible power of God! But there was also the appearance of "tongues parting asunder, like as of fire". Fire typifies the activity of God's holiness in relation to sin; fire consumes and fire purifies. When the Spirit came upon Christ it was not as the fire, but "as a dove", for there was no sin in Him, as the Father then declared, "Thou art My beloved Son; in Thee I am well pleased" (Luke 3: 22). But here the tongues like as of fire sat upon each of them, bringing not only a sense of the infinite holiness of God, but of the activity of that holiness in dealing with all that was unholy in themselves.

This manifestation of God in power and holiness was intensely personal. The sound of the wind appeared to bear down upon them until it filled the very house where they were sitting. The tongues of fire parted asunder and sat upon each one of them. It was God moving in power and holiness, and moving toward *them*; they themselves were the objects of God's activity. Here is an outstanding feature of revival, and it is not difficult to see why it results in overwhelming conviction both among the saved and the lost, whenever there is unjudged sin. Those waiting hearts in the upper room were doubtless cleansed and prepared for the coming of the Spirit, consequently there is no evidence of conviction, though no doubt there was a deeper work of purging accomplished by the fire of the Spirit. Usually, however, it is otherwise. At such times man is not only made conscious that God is there; but that He is there, as it seems, to deal with him alone, until he is oblivious of all but his own soul in the agonizing grip of a holy God.

If these facts are borne in mind the extraordinary effects of past revivals will not seem incredible. The ruthless logic of Jonathan Edwards' famous discourse, *Sinners in the hands of an angry God* (from Deut. 32: 25), preached in his usual plain and undemonstrative manner, at Enfield, New England, in 1741, could never have produced the effect it did had not God been in the midst. "When they went into the meeting-house the appearance of the assembly was thoughtless and vain; the people scarcely conducted themselves with common decency", recorded Trumbull, but he goes on to describe the effect of the sermon : "the assembly appeared bowed with an awful conviction of their sin and danger. There was such a breathing of distress and weeping, that the preacher was obliged to speak to the people and desire silence that he might be heard." Conant says, "Many of the hearers were seen unconsciously holding themselves up against the pillars, and the sides of the pews, as though they already felt themselves sliding into the pit."

Similar is the scene described by Charles Finney when he preached in the village school-house near Antwerp, N.Y. "An awful solemnity seemed to settle upon the people; the congregation began to fall from their seats in every direction and cry for mercy. If I had had a sword in each hand, I could not have cut them down as fast as they fell. I was obliged to stop preaching." Of course the measure of conviction is not often so overwhelming as this, and varies even with different individuals affected on the same occasion, but the explanation is always the same, the manifestation of God in holiness and power.

This strange sense of God may pervade a building, a community, or a district, and those who come within its spell will be affected. At the beginning of the 1904 Awakening near the town of Gorseinon a revival meeting was in progress throughout the night. A miner, a somewhat hardened notorious case, returning from his shift about 4 a.m. saw the light in the chapel and decided to investigate. As soon as he opened the chapel door he was overwhelmed by a sense of God's presence, and exclaimed, "Oh, God is here!" He was afraid either to enter or depart, and there on the threshold of the chapel a saving work began in his soul.

No town in Ulster was more deeply stirred during the 1859 Revival than Coleraine. It was there that a boy was so troubled about his soul that the schoolmaster sent him home. An older boy, a Christian, accompanied him, and before they had gone far led him to Christ. Returning at once to the school, this latest convert testified to the master, "Oh, I am so happy! I have the Lord Jesus in my heart." The effect of these artless words was very great. Boy after boy rose and silently left the room. On investigation the master found these boys ranged alongside the wall of the playground, everyone apart and on his knees! Very soon their silent prayer became a bitter cry. It was heard by those within and pierced their hearts. They cast themselves upon their knees, and their cry for mercy was heard in the girls' schoolroom above. In a few moments the whole school was upon its knees, and its wail of distress was heard in the street outside. Neighbours and passers-by came flocking in, and all, *as they crossed the threshold*, came under the same convicting power. Every room was filled with men, women, and children seeking God.

Similar stories could be told of the 1858 American Revival. Ships as they drew near the American ports came within a definite zone of heavenly influence. Ship after ship arrived with the same tale of sudden conviction and conversion. In one ship a captain and the entire crew of thirty men found Christ out at sea and entered the harbour rejoicing. Revival broke out on the battleship "North Carolina" through four Christian men who had been meeting in the bowels of the ship for prayer. One evening they were filled with the Spirit and burst into song. Ungodly shipmates who came down to mock were gripped by the power of God, and the laugh of the scornful was soon changed into the cry of the penitent. Many were smitten down, and a gracious work broke out that continued night after night, till they had to send ashore for ministers to help, and the battleship became a Bethel.

This overwhelming sense of God, bringing deep conviction of sin, is perhaps the outstanding feature of true revival. The manifestation of it is not always the same. Sometimes it is predominantly the unconverted who are convicted, as in the cases quoted. At other times it is Christians or professing Christians, as in the revivals in Manchuria and China (1906–9) under Jonathan Goforth; or the recent awakening in the Belgian Congo (1953). But the explanation is always the same. Of the revival in Northampton, Mass., Jonathan Edwards wrote: "In the spring and summer, A.D. 1735, the town seemed to be full of the presence of God. It never was so full of love, nor so full of joy, and yet so full of distress, as it was then." To cleansed hearts it is heaven, to convicted hearts it is hell, when God is in the midst.

## Anointed Vessels

Here is a further vital feature—"they were all filled with the Holy Spirit". In times preceding revival it is common to find among believers of various persuasions a fresh emphasis on the person and work of the Holy Spirit. Many have been lost in a maze of theological controversy. Others have moved for years in the rut of traditional interpretation, concerned with an explanation rather than an experience, a definition instead of a dynamic. But with those stirrings of the Spirit that are the precursor of revival, there is born in many such hearts a wholesome dissatisfaction with that vague and mystic view of being filled with the Spirit that leaves one in the dark as to what it is, how it comes, and whether or not one has received it. There is not scope here to deal with this important subject as it needs to be dealt with, but let us briefly mention three important facts regarding the anointing of the believer with the Holy Spirit that emerge from this and other parallel cases in the New Testament.

Firstly, the anointing was *a definite experience*. It had to be, for the risen Christ had left the believers of the upper room with a promise and a command : the promise was that of the Spirit coming upon them, "Ye shall be baptized with the Holy Spirit not many days hence" (1 : 5); and the command was that they were to "wait for the promise" (1 : 4) to be fulfilled, "tarry ye . . . until" (Luke 24 : 49). Apart from the expectation of a definite experience they could not have obeyed the command to "tarry . . . until". However, they took their Lord at His word, they waited, and in due time the promise was fulfilled. They knew that they had received the promised Holy Spirit, and very soon others knew also that something remarkable had taken place.

These who but a few days before had slunk into the upper room and bolted the door for fear of the men who had murdered their Master, are now standing in the open and alleging that this Jesus is alive, and accusing their hearers of His murder. Peter, who a month and a half before had denied his Lord at the jibe of a servant-girl, now stands before the multitudes in the very city where He was crucified, and asserts that God had made this Jesus "both Lord and Christ". Certainly something very definite has happened to these believers. Every other instance in the New

Testament of individuals being filled with the Spirit confirms that it is a definite experience. There may or may not be emotional accompaniments. There may or may not be striking manifestations, but it is the birthright of every child of God to receive that anointing, and to know that he (or she) has received it.

Secondly, the anointing was a *dynamic experience*. It was not given that they might enjoy a spiritual uplift. It was not given primarily that they might be more holy. It was given to make them powerful and effective for God. Through it they would be "clothed with power from on high" (Luke 24: 49). "Ye shall receive power, when the Holy Spirit is come upon you: and ye shall be My witnesses," said the Saviour (Acts 1: 8). As the Father had sent Him, so was He sending them (John 20: 21), and it was in view of this commission that He breathed on them as a symbolic act, and commanded them to receive the Holy Spirit, which they did on the day of Pentecost. Thenceforth they were to be like their Lord, "anointed . . . with the Holy Spirit and power" (Acts 10: 38). Being filled or anointed with the Spirit is always related to spiritual service. This alone can make the fearful believer a courageous and effective witness for Christ. It does not result in all becoming evangelists or great soul-winners. The gifts bestowed may vary with each individual (1 Cor. 12), and this is in the hands of the same Spirit "dividing to each one severally even as He will" (1 Cor. 12: 11). But with each there is an imparting of power, and an equipping to function for God in whatever way He may choose.

Finally, it was a *desired experience*, intensely desired. It was then, and still is, born out of soul thirst. It is the experience of the one who cannot do without it. "If any man thirst, let him come unto Me, and drink" (John 7: 37). "I will pour water upon him that is thirsty" (Isa. 44: 3). Thirst is a more intense desire than hunger, and in the realm of the Spirit "thirst" is the word that God has used to illustrate the desire that should characterize His people. How ready the Lord is to satisfy the longing soul, and to lead His people to the "fountains of living water". Child of God, are you thirsty to be filled with the Spirit?

Characteristically revival is a time when large numbers of believers are filled with the Spirit. Such an event, as here at Pentecost, may set off a revival. Charles Finney received a mighty anointing of the Spirit on the evening of the day of his conversion.

As a result a revival broke out the following day in Adams, N.Y., the town where he lived. When the waiting vessel cannot contain the abundance of the heavenly anointing, there must of necessity be floods upon the dry ground, and such are often the beginning of revival. Said Finney, "Many times great numbers of persons in a community will be clothed with this power, when the very atmosphere of the whole place seems to be charged with the life of God. Strangers coming into it and passing through the place will be instantly smitten with conviction of sin, and in many instances converted to Christ."

God has not only said, "I will pour water upon him that is thirsty, and streams upon the dry ground", but also "I will pour My Spirit upon thy seed, and My blessing upon thine offspring" (Isa. 44: 3). Both are blessedly true of revival, for it is then that God not only pours out His Spirit upon the church, but also upon the seed and offspring of the church, so that new-born souls are at once filled with the Spirit and become effective for God. A revival will often increase in power and influence in this way.

The waiting on of young and older people at the close of each meeting, and the anxious asking of so many "what to do"; the lively singing of the praises of God, which every visitor remarks; the complete desuetude of swearing and of foolish talking in our streets; the order and solemnity at all hours prevailing; the voice of praise and prayer almost in every house; the cessation of the tumults of the people; the consignment to the flames of volumes of infidelity and impurity; the coming together for divine worship of such a multitude of our population day after day; the large catalogue of new intending communicants giving in their names, and conversing in the most interesting manner on the most important subjects; not a few of the old careless sinners and frozen formalists awakened and made alive to God; the conversion of several poor colliers, who have come to me and given a most satisfactory account of their change of mind and heart—are truly wonderful proofs of a most surprising and delightful revival. The public-houses, the coal-pits, the harvest reaping fields, the weaving loom-steads, the recesses of our glens, and the sequestered haughs around, all may be called to witness that there is a mighty change in this place for the better.

AN OBSERVER OF THE KILSYTH REVIVAL, 1839.

## CHAPTER SIX

# DISTINCTIVE FEATURES (II)

"The tree is known by its fruit" (Matt. 12:33).

**T**HERE are yet further features of this Pentecostal outpouring which may help us to recognize outpourings of the Spirit today.

## Supernatural Manifestation

This mark of revival is suggested by the phrase, "they began to speak with other tongues, as the Spirit gave them utterance" (Acts 2:4). Of course, strictly speaking all the operations of the Spirit are supernatural. The most ordinary conversion of a sinner is a supernatural work, but it may not be *manifestly* so. Here is meant that which is in the eyes of men manifestly supernatural, and which can be accounted for in no other way. It is that which produces in the hearts and minds of onlookers the reaction described here, "they were all amazed, and were perplexed, saying one to another, What meaneth this?" (verse 12).

In considering this particular manifestation of speaking with tongues it is needful to avoid unhealthy extremes. Some who expound the giving of the Spirit at Pentecost are careful to avoid any mention of this strange phenomenon, as though it had no real significance. Others, however, can see nothing else in the chapter; to them it is the be-all and the end-all. Some insist that this gift of tongues is now extinct, others that it is the indispensable proof of the filling of the Spirit. Neither view is supported by Scripture or by history. It was not the only proof of the filling of the Spirit in apostolic times (Acts 8:14–17; 9:17–19; 1 Cor. 12:30); it is not the only proof today. At the same time God has never withdrawn this or any other gift. It is true that tongues with prophecies and knowledge are to cease, but not till "that which is perfect is come" (1 Cor. 13:8–10).

Revival always seems to bring with it a temporary return to apostolic Christianity. Never is the church nearer to the spirit and power of the first century than in times of revival. An eyewitness described the New England Revival of the 18th century thus: "The apostolical times seem to have returned upon us." Thus we must not be surprised to discover that God uses such times to restore spiritual gifts which many have thought were confined to the days of primitive Christianity. Such a conservative work as the *Devotional Commentary* contains this note on the verse "Quench not the Spirit" (1 Thess. 5: 19): "In the early church the influence of the Holy Spirit in the utterances of individual believers was fully recognized. He is set before believers as the source of various gifts (1 Cor. 12), and conspicuously of gifts of utterance (Acts 2: 4). In times of spiritual blessing these gifts are more especially manifest. It has been so in every great revival from the days of Wesley and Whitefield to the days of Evan Roberts. Such gifts, coming indeed from the Spirit, are not to be quenched, put out, like a lamp no longer needed or a fire that meant danger. Nor must such utterances—'prophesyings', not necessarily predictive, but claiming to be of divine impulse—be despised. They are, indeed, commended by St. Paul (1 Cor. 14: 1, 39). They are to be received with respect and yet with intelligent discrimination."

It is not suggested that the exercise of such supernatural gifts is confined to times of revival; nor is it maintained that God only bestows them during such seasons, for the facts are otherwise. It is only asserted, as a fact beyond dispute to those who accept the testimony of history, that the renewal of such gifts, together with various other signs and wonders, are a prominent feature of revival. God is sovereign in all these things. Let the creature beware of imputing folly to the Creator, or of dictating to Him how He shall conduct His work. If God-sent revival is characterized by elements altogether new to our experience and which we cannot understand, if there are dreams and visions, tongues and interpretations, revelations and trances, prophesyings and healings, tremblings and prostrations, let us remember that God said that "signs" would accompany the outpouring of the Spirit (Acts 2: 17–19), and that it has almost always been so.

God uses such signs as a divine authentication of the truth of the gospel, even as Nicodemus said to Jesus, "We know that Thou art a teacher come from God: for no man can do these signs that Thou doest except God be with him" (John 3: 2). Thus it was with His disciples who "went forth, and preached everywhere, the Lord working with them, and confirming the word by the signs that followed" (Mark 16: 20). "God also bearing witness with them, both by signs and wonders, and by manifold powers, and by gifts of the Holy Spirit, *according to His own will*" (Heb. 2: 4). We would do well to ponder that last phrase, for it emphasizes that such matters rest solely in the hands of God. Nevertheless the fact remains that during those early days it pleased God to employ signs and wonders in nearly every great ingathering of souls to bring the people together and prepare their hearts for the truth. The first recorded prayer of the church was that "signs and wonders may be done" (Acts 4: 30). This was an invincible weapon against persecution. It may be that God will consummate this age as He commenced it.

Perhaps the most common sign in times of revival has been the prostration of convicted souls. It was common in the Wesley–Whitefield Revivals. Lady Huntingdon wrote to Whitefield regarding the cases of crying out and falling down at the meetings, and advised him not to remove them, as had been done, for it seemed to bring a damper on the meeting. She wrote : "You are making a mistake. Don't be wiser than God. Let them cry out; it will do a great deal more good than your preaching." Wesley in his journals dated July 7th, 1739, recorded a conversation with Whitefield on this subject, whose objections were evidently founded on misrepresentations of fact. "But the next day he [Whitefield] had an opportunity of informing himself better : for no sooner had he begun . . . to invite all sinners to believe in Christ, than four persons sunk down close to him, almost in the same moment. One of them lay without either sense or motion. A second trembled exceedingly. The third had strong convulsions all over his body, but made no noise, unless by groans. The fourth, equally convulsed, called upon God, with strong cries and tears. From this time, I trust, we shall all suffer God to carry on His own work in the way that pleaseth Him."

In the 1860 Revival in Tinevelly, South India, the main instrument God used was a native evangelist called Aroolappen,* a disciple of A. N. Groves. The movement began in the Brethren assemblies in which he had laboured, later spreading to other communities. Aroolappen wrote of the beginning of the movement as follows: "From the 4th May to the 7th the Holy Spirit

* See Bibliography—*History and Diaries of an Indian Christian.*

was poured out openly and wonderfully. Some prophesied and rebuked the people: some beat themselves on their breasts severely, and trembled and fell down through the shaking of their bodies and souls. . . . They saw some signs in the air. They were much pleased to praise God. Some ignorant [uninstructed] people gave out some songs and hymns that we never heard before. . . . *All the heathen marvelled, and came and saw and heard us with fearful minds.*"

This man of God wrote again later, "In the month of June some of our people praised the Lord by unknown tongues, with their interpretations. In the month of July the Spirit was poured out upon our congregation at Oleikollam, and above 25 persons were baptized. They are steadfast in prayers. . . . Some missionaries admit the truth of the gifts of the Holy Spirit. The Lord meets everywhere one after another, though some tried to quench the Spirit."

Henry Groves, son of A. N. Groves, writing in the *Indian Watchman* for July, 1860, gives a fuller account of this movement, and of how two poor native women received visions which led to days of deep conviction of sin, after which they found peace. The husband of one of them bitterly attacked his wife while she was under conviction, and accused her of being demon-possessed. Soon after he himself fell into a trance while out in the fields in which someone appeared to him and told him to read Revelation 1 and to tell others "I am coming quickly". He returned to the house weeping and under deep conviction, soon afterwards finding peace. These converts went forth to tell their neighbouring heathen what God had done for their souls.

Henry Groves continues his account: "The day following when Aroolappen was engaged in prayer, he says, the spirit of prophecy was given to some there, and a little boy said that in a certain village, which he named, about a mile distant, the Spirit of God had been poured out. Within a quarter of an hour, some men and women came from that village, beating their breasts in great fear and alarm of conscience. They fell down and rolled on the ground. This continued a short time; they all asked to have prayer made for them, after which they said with great joy, 'The Lord Jesus has forgiven our sins', and clapping their hands together, in the fulness of their hearts' gladness, they embraced and kissed one another. For nearly three days this ecstatic joy appears to have lasted. They ate nothing, except a little food taken in the evening, and passing sleepless nights, they continued the whole time in reading of the word, in prayer and in singing praises to the Lord. Of some it is said, 'they lifted up their eyes to heaven and saw blood and fire and pillars of smoke, and, speaking aloud, they told what they had seen.' "

Several missionaries, at first sceptical or even opposed to the movement, were won over when they saw the fruit of it, and were compelled to acknowledge that the work was of God, though some remained dubious of the revival phenomena. One declared, "I do not know that there has been one single case, where one, whom my dear native brethren and myself have considered really influenced, has fallen back." Another wrote, "What God is now doing in the midst of us was altogether beyond the expectations of missionaries and other Christians : who can say what manifestations the Spirit of God will or will not make of His power?"

It is strange, yet all too often true, that when the Spirit of God is working in supernatural power in revival, unbelievers will often be more quickly convinced that this work is wrought of God, than some believers. No doubt there always have been and always will be the prejudiced and sceptical among the people of God, who in unbelief would limit the Holy One of Israel; who cannot bear to think of the Almighty working outside the range of their own finite understanding, or beyond the bounds of their own limited experience. They would have revival, but only if it comes along the quiet orderly lines of their own preconceived ideas. Where it is otherwise they will attribute the work to the flesh, or where this does not provide adequate explanation, to the Devil. Of course there is always the possibility of satanic intrusion, or of the admixture of the flesh in such times of blessing, but this calls for a spirit of discernment, not a spirit of prejudice; the ability to "prove the spirits, whether they are of God" (1 John 4: 1), not the wholesale, out-of-hand condemnation of them, which must often result in quenching the Spirit (1 Thess. 5: 19). There is a general tendency to err on the side of prejudice, suspicion and unbelief; and this attitude is nowhere countenanced in the New Testament. Where there is doubt, let there be a patient waiting upon God until the true character of the work is manifest, for the tree will be known by its fruit. Let all take heed. If we indulge in hasty criticism we may be speaking against the Holy Spirit;

if we oppose we may "be found even to be fighting against God".

Finally, let us ponder these words from the *Church Missionary Intelligencer* (1860) on the Tinevelly Revival, written after the work had revealed its true character: "We believe that an unreadiness to recognize the extraordinary operations by which the Holy Spirit is now revealing Himself here and there, is too much a characteristic of the church generally. There are thousands in the ministry of the Church of England, there are multitudes in other denominations, whose conceptions of the work of the Holy Spirit are greatly narrowed, in consequence of their not having given due attention to the admirable accounts on record of the various revivals, enjoyed, since the days of the Reformation, in Europe and America. A very peculiar responsibility is resting upon all at this day, in consequence of the many proofs afforded of the readiness of the Holy Spirit to do things transcending the narrow limits of our ordinary experience. When the Son of Man cometh shall He find faith on the earth? When He is prepared to bless the church with unwonted tokens of His nearness, with new discoveries of His majesty and grace, will He be met by a proportionate faith? . . .

"Let us not put our views of decorum and of order above the mighty operations of the Spirit. When He comes forth in His glory, it is as it were a judgment day; there is an overwhelming revelation of sin and of danger; and we can no more expect men to act under such circumstances in accordance with ordinary rules of decorum, than we could expect men aroused from their beds by an earthquake to avoid every demonstration of a noisy or alarming character. Perhaps it behoves us all to surrender our very imperfect views of the power and majesty of the Holy Spirit, and prepare for something grander, more awful and more revolutionary than we have yet witnessed."

## Divine Magnetism

"And when this sound was heard, *the multitude came together*" (verse 6). In chapter 37 of his prophecy, Ezekiel records his vision of the valley of dry bones, over which he was commanded by God to prophesy; he says, "I prophesied as I was commanded: and as I prophesied, there was a noise . . . and the bones came together . . ." (verse 7). Similarly at Pentecost there was a divine magnetism at work, and the "dry bones" were drawn irresistibly together to where God was working in power. On this occasion God used the supernatural manifestation as the magnetic agent, "when this sound was heard", and this is very often the case in seasons of revival. Sometimes, however, this strange drawing is apparent even where there is no outward manifestation. This would seem to have been the case when Paul and Barnabas visited Antioch-in-Pisidia, when "almost the whole city was gathered together to hear the word of God" (Acts 13: 44).

During the early days of the recent Lewis Awakening, there was a remarkable movement in the village of Arnol. There had been no response during the first few meetings, and a time of prayer was convened in a house at the close of an evening meeting. As one man was praying all present became aware that prayer had been heard, and that the Spirit of God was being poured out upon the village. They left the house to discover that the villagers also were leaving their cottages and making their way, as though drawn by some unseen force, to one point in the village. There they congregated and waited, and when Mr. Duncan Campbell commenced to preach, the word took immediate effect. In a few days that small community had been swept by the Spirit of God, and many souls had been truly converted to God.

It is constantly the complaint of the evangelist that the unconverted, pleasure-loving masses will not come to hear the gospel. Although there have been exceptions, it is still true that many city-wide campaigns attract but a small proportion of those they are designed to reach, and though one rejoices that some do come and that some are saved, the needs of the masses remain largely untouched. The majority of those converted in such meetings are those with church connections or who have been interested by Christian friends. One must admire the energy and thoroughness with which attempts are made to alter this situation. Large sums are spent on advertising and publicity of every kind. Witness marches are conducted through the streets. The meetings themselves are not lacking in varied items and features calculated to appeal. If all this did not reach the godless masses the time before, then it is only ground for trying again with greater thoroughness or more imagination. If it is found that the proportion of spurious decisions is high, then it must be reduced by more careful training of the inquiry room workers, and by greater diligence in following up each case.

There is no intention here of destructively criticizing such evangelistic drives. Rather let us thank God for all that they achieve in making Christ known and leading souls to repentance. Though God blesses and uses them according to the proportion that faith and prayer are exercised, it is important to realize their limitations. As we survey the situation, we may well inquire with Gideon, "And where be all His wondrous works which our fathers told us of?" (Judges 6: 13). Is this all that God can do in the face of the appalling need on every hand? Are we for ever shut up to the obvious limitations of modern evangelism? Must we never hope to see that mightier working that truly touches the masses at every level and compels them to face the implications of the gospel? Shall there never be a day of God's power, when our organization, and publicity, and inquiry room technique shall be superseded by the resistless power and faultless control of the Holy Spirit?

Of course God expects us to do our part in drawing souls under the sound of the gospel. It required no outpouring of the Spirit to bring Simon Peter to Jesus, it needed only the invitation of Andrew, his brother (John 1: 41, 42). But where the normal means are failing to achieve the necessary end, it is of no avail to adopt the extra special means. If the natural means do not succeed we must look to the supernatural. On Carmel Elijah's fervent pleading left the people unmoved. "How long halt ye between two opinions?" was his challenge; but "the people answered him not a word" (1 Kings 18: 21). But when God answered by fire instantly the people were on their faces. What the strivings of man cannot achieve is but the work of a moment to the outpoured Spirit. We may be sure that when God begins to work the people will be there, drawn not by invitation or persuasion, but by that divine magnetism that operates in revival.

It may be necessary for us to cease from our own endeavours in order to enlist the mighty intervention of God. It is possible to be so busy with what we are doing, that we are oblivious of that mightier work that God is waiting to do, if we will but give Him the opportunity. When we are brought to seek His face, and acknowledge, as did Jehoshaphat, "We have no might against this great company . . . neither know we what to do: but our eyes are upon Thee", then we may expect Him to answer us likewise, "the battle is not yours, but God's . . . Ye shall not need to fight in this battle: set yourselves, stand ye still, and see the salvation of the Lord with you" (2 Chron. 20: 12–17).

### Apostolic Preaching

"But Peter . . . lifted up his voice, and spake forth unto them" (verse 14). When we speak of "apostolic preaching" we do not mean that of apostles only, but the kind of preaching that was characteristic of that first century, and of revivals down the years. Although many souls are saved in revival apart from preaching, such times have nearly always been characterized by the powerful proclamation of the truth. Sometimes the outpouring has come through such preaching; at other times, as here, the preaching has come through the outpouring. There is a rugged grandeur about the apostolic preacher which recalls the fearless prophet of Old Testament days. They were clothed with the same power and impelled by the same boldness, for their torches were lit from the same holy fire. Neither was popular, but both were mighty to the pulling down of strongholds. "When a prophet is accepted and deified, his message is lost. The prophet is only useful so long as he is stoned as a public nuisance calling us to repentance, disturbing our comfortable routines, breaking our respectable idols, shattering our sacred conventions" (A. G. Gardiner). Of such a character was the apostolic preacher. Peter's address on this occasion reveals all the main features of apostolic gospel preaching.

The primary design was to lead souls to repentance. A glance at the message of the New Testament preachers, John the Baptist, the Lord Himself, and the Apostles, will confirm that "repent" was one of the great words in their gospel vocabulary. They were not out merely to obtain many "decisions" but rather to "turn many to righteousness" (Dan. 12: 3). The difference in emphasis is important. The true index of their success was not in the counting of heads or hands, but in the revolutionizing of lives and even communities, men and women turned "from darkness to light, and from the power of Satan unto God" (Acts 26: 18). Since repentance was to them the fundamental condition of conversion, they did not set out at once to "get results" but to produce conviction of sin, without which there could be no solid foundation for a soul-saving work.

Under the ministry of these early preachers people did not decide to become Christians simply because this was a desirable or respectable thing to do, or because Christianity appeared more attractive, and to offer better dividends than living for the world. There was no suggestion that salvation was just a course of expediency, an insurance policy for eternity, or a good bargain that any sensible man ought to make with his God. No, indeed; they were led to repent because they saw their desperate plight. They were convicted of their shameful rebellion against God, Whose laws they had broken and Whose Son they had crucified. They were indeed "weighed in the balances and found wanting". They were lost and undone, and more than ready, when a loving Saviour was presented to them, to flee to Him for refuge against the wrath of a holy God.

There is so much emphasis today on believing, receiving, deciding, and so little on the vital step of repenting. We need to beware of reducing conversion to a technique, for a person can be persuaded to go through the motions of accepting Christ while the conscience remains unawakened, the will unmoved, and so the heart unchanged. If the soil is shallow the seed may germinate, but it will be without root, and so "he endureth for a while; and when tribulation or persecution ariseth because of the word, straightway he stumbleth" (Matt. 13: 21). The apostles felt that their labour was in vain if their converts did not stand fast (1 Thess. 3: 5–8).

How was it that this apostolic preaching produced such deep and abiding results? Because these men dealt faithfully with the question of sin, that the conscience might be aroused (Acts 2: 23, 36). Because they urged upon their hearers the imperative necessity of immediate repentance to God (verse 38). Because they preached baptism in accordance with their commission from Christ (Matt. 28: 19; Mark 16: 16), as that which was to accompany and seal that act of repentance (verse 38). And because they demanded that all this should be followed by "doing works worthy of repentance" (Acts 26: 20). With the exception of the controversial question of baptism, these features have always characterized revival preaching.

"It was, I believe, a precept of John Wesley's to his evangelists, in unfolding their message, to speak first in general of the love of God to man; then, with all possible energy, and so as to search conscience to its depths, to preach the law of holiness; and then, and not till then, to uplift the glories of the gospel of pardon and of life. Intentionally or not, his directions follow the lines of the epistle to the Romans" (Moule on Romans).

It was said that Charles Finney in dealing with souls had a fixed principle never to tell a man how to get right with God until he could no longer look him in the face. Only when his conscience had been so thoroughly awakened that he hung his head in shame over his sin, did he consider that he was ripe to be told the way of salvation. We may say that Finney went too far, but do we go far enough? It is vain to urge men to go to the Physician so long as they remain unconvinced that they are dangerously ill. A Puritan writer, Thomas Goodwin, remarked in this connection, "Traitors must be convicted and condemned ere they are capable of a legal pardon; as sentence must be pronounced before a legal appeal can be made." When we try to foist a pardon on the rebel who has not been apprehended or convicted, we invite him to trample it underfoot. Bearing in mind this design, to produce conviction with a view to repentance, let us notice four characteristics of apostolic preaching revealed in Peter's address.

It was *spontaneous* preaching, as spontaneous as the outpouring that produced it. Christ had promised, when they should have to stand before governors and kings, "It shall be given you in that hour what ye shall speak. For it is not ye that speak, but the Spirit of your Father that speaketh in you" (Matt. 10: 19, 20). This word seemed to have a fulfilment in the seizing of many other unexpected opportunities of preaching Christ. It is remarkable that this masterly address of Peter that led to the conversion of three thousand souls, should have been impromptu. No one would deny that there is a place for the prepared and deliberate presentation of the gospel, but too many have lost sight of that unpremeditated, inspirational preaching which is so characteristic when the Spirit of God is working in power.

Charles Finney wrote in his autobiography: "For some twelve years of my earliest ministry, I wrote not a word; and was commonly obliged to preach without any preparation whatever, except what I got in prayer. Oftentimes I went into the pulpit without knowing upon what text I should speak, or a word that I should say. I depended on the occasion and the Holy Spirit to suggest the text, and to open up the whole subject to my mind; and certainly in no part of my ministry have I preached with greater success and power. If I did not preach from inspiration I don't know how I did preach. It was a common experience with me . . . that the subject would open up to my mind in a manner that was surprising to myself. It seemed that I could see with intuitive clearness just what I ought to say; and whole platoons of thoughts, words, and illustrations came to me as fast as I could deliver them."

Recounting the revival at Evan Mills, Finney wrote : "I had not taken a thought with regard to what I should preach. The Holy Spirit was upon me, and I felt confident that when the time came for action I should know. As soon as I found the house packed I arose and, without any formal introduction of singing, opened upon them with these words : 'Say ye to the righteous that it shall be well with him; for they shall eat the fruit of their doings. Woe to the wicked ! it shall be ill with him; for the reward of his hands shall be given him.' The Spirit of God came upon me with such power, that it was like opening a battery upon them. For more than an hour the word of God came through me to them in a manner that I could see was carrying all before it. It was a fire and a hammer breaking the rock, and as the sword that was piercing to the dividing asunder of soul and spirit. I saw that a general conviction was spreading over the whole congregation."

Although God has His times for this mightier work of the Spirit, as Matt. 10: 19 suggests, the vision of it needs to be recaptured. The gift of spontaneous preaching enables the evangelist to seize unexpected opportunities, as did Peter here at Pentecost and at the Temple Gate (Acts 3: 12); also Paul on Mars Hill (Acts 17) and on the steps of the castle in Jerusalem (Acts 22); and it gives maximum scope to the Spirit of God to produce conviction and lead to repentance. Far from encouraging laziness, such a manner of preaching demands incessant prayerfulness and constant meditation and feeding upon the word. Clearly, it is only possible "in the Spirit", and this anticipates our next feature of this apostolic preaching.

It was *anointed* preaching. Peter was "filled with the Spirit"; there was the explanation of his power. This feature has already been considered, and we need only touch on it now in its relation to public preaching. Christ had promised His followers that through the coming of the Spirit they would receive power to be His witnesses (Acts 1: 8), and that the Spirit would work through them to convict the world of sin and of righteousness and of judgment. It is strange, in view of the explicit promise of Christ, that many busily engaged in the preaching of the gospel seem to have no concern that they do not see that power operating in their ministry, nor any desire to seek and obtain it.

Apostolic preaching is not marked by its beautiful diction, or literary polish, or cleverness of expression. It has laid aside "excellency of speech or of wisdom"; it has no confidence in "persuasive words of wisdom" but operates "in demonstration of the Spirit and of power", so that the faith that it kindles in the heart does "not stand in the wisdom of men, but in the power of God" (1 Cor. 2: 1–5). It was said of Savonarola, the great Italian Reformer, that "nature had withheld from him almost all the gifts of the orator", and yet he was mighty through the power of the Spirit. Said A. J. Gordon of him : "When we read of his intense and enrapt communion with God, his unconquerable persistence in seeking the power of the Highest, till 'his thoughts and affections were so absorbed in God by the presence of the Holy Spirit, that they who looked into his cell saw his upturned face as it had been the face of an angel', we are not amazed at the character and effects of his preaching—so pathetic, so melting, so resistless that the reporter lays down his pen with this apology written under the last line—'Such sorrow and weeping came upon me that I could go no further.' "

There can be no substitute whatever for the anointing of the Spirit; it is the one indispensable factor for the effective proclamation of God's message. The apostolic preacher is first and foremost the man who can say with his Master, "The Spirit of the Lord is upon Me, because He hath anointed Me to preach the gospel" (Luke 4: 18 A.V.).

It was also *fearless* preaching. This feature is directly related to that which we have just considered. "They were all filled with the Holy Spirit, and they spake the word of God with boldness" (Acts 4: 31). These first Christians had been wonderfully liberated from "the fear of man that bringeth a snare". They gave their hearers the truth, the whole truth, and nothing but the truth.

There was no watering down the stern demands of divine holiness, no modifying the eternal severities to appeal to the natural man. The apostolic preacher was like Noah "a preacher of righteousness". He did not shun to set forth the changeless laws of a holy God, because he knew that "by the law cometh the knowledge of sin" (Rom. 3: 19, 20), and that this is the instrument that the Spirit of God uses to reveal that "all have sinned and come short of the glory of God" (verse 23).

Whitefield said of Griffith Jones, a Welsh evangelist of his day, that his preaching possessed "a grasp on the conscience". Such a ministry requires a proclamation of the holiness of God and the sinfulness of sin, and such a fearless application of the divine law as probes the conscience and leaves the hearer standing guilty before God. Such preaching does not generalize about sin and sinners, but focuses on the individual conscience and fearlessly declares, "Thou art the man". It was said of Gilbert Tennent, a contemporary of Jonathan Edwards, and mightily used in the New England Revival, "He seemed to have no regard to please the eyes of his hearers with agreeable gesture, nor their ears with delivery, nor their fancy with language; but to aim directly at their hearts and consciences, to lay open their ruinous delusions, show them their numerous, secret, hypocritical shifts in religion, and drive them out of every deceitful refuge wherein they made themselves easy, with the form of godliness without the power. . . . His preaching was frequently both terrible and searching" (Prince's *Christian History*).

Here Peter charged his hearers with the crime of crucifying their Messiah. They may not have been personally present, but they were personally responsible, for they had consented to His death. Emphatically he spoke of "This Jesus Whom ye crucified" (verse 36). Little wonder that we then read, "Now when they heard this, they were pricked in their heart." Fearless preaching like this was calculated to produce conviction, or to stir up the bitterest animosity. It usually did both. Many preachers today are so tactful, so careful lest they should offend, that they achieve little or nothing. How different were the "shock tactics" of the apostolic preacher, as we listen to his burning words in temple court (Acts 3: 13–15) or Jewish Council (Acts 4: 8–11; 7: 51–53); well might he say, "I truly am full of power by the Spirit of the Lord, and of judgment, and of might, to declare unto Jacob his transgression, and to Israel his sin" (Mic. 3: 8). Such preaching, by making indifference impossible, sets the hearers in one of two camps. It is calculated to produce a revival or a riot.

Finally, it was *Christ-centred* preaching. Having explained to the astonished multitudes that this which they saw and heard was the outpouring of the Spirit promised in Joel, Peter took them at once to "Jesus of Nazareth". He did not at once assert His deity, but found a common basis in what they already knew and believed concerning Him, in facts which were beyond contradiction —"a man approved of God unto you by mighty works and wonders and signs." It was a principle of these apostolic preachers to find common ground with their hearers and to work from that. They commenced with what was assuredly believed and accepted, and from that basis they argued their case, point by point, persuading the multitudes that this Jesus was the Christ.

In the story of the Ethiopian eunuch we read that Philip "preached unto him Jesus" (Acts 8: 35). He did not preach *about* Jesus, he preached *Jesus*; his message was a proclamation, a setting forth of the person of Jesus the suffering Messiah, yet Son of God. Paul's determination was ever to know nothing among men "save Jesus Christ, and Him crucified" (1 Cor. 2: 2), and so vividly had he set Him forth to the Galatian churches that he could remind them—"before your very eyes, Jesus Christ has been portrayed, crucified" (Gal. 3: 1, Darby). The risen Lord had explained to His disciples before He ascended into heaven why it behoved "the Christ to suffer these things, and to enter into His glory" (Luke 24: 26). He had opened their minds to the full significance of the cross and the resurrection in the plan of redemption, "that repentance and remission of sins should be preached in His Name unto all the nations" (Luke 24: 45–47), and so in these aspects they set forth Christ in their preaching.

The very corner stone of apostolic preaching, however, was the witness to the resurrection. Everything hinged on the fact that the Crucified One was alive. If He had indeed risen all His claims to be the "Sent One" of God, the long-promised Messiah, were authenticated and beyond dispute, and men found themselves under a cloud of divine wrath, guilty of the greatest crime of all time. "Ye denied the Holy and Righteous One, and asked for a murderer to be granted unto you, and killed the Prince of Life" (Acts 3: 14). "The Righteous One; of whom ye have now become

betrayers and murderers" (Acts 7: 52). It was the light from
the empty tomb that explained the enigma of the Cross; it was
this that transformed apparent defeat into actual victory, and
tragedy into triumph. The resurrection was God's masterstroke to
prove beyond all doubt and for all time the deity of Jesus, for He
was "declared to be the Son of God with power . . . by the
resurrection of the dead" (Rom. 1: 4).

Apostolic preaching cannot of course be limited to the ministry
of the evangelist, separated for this special work. In revival it is
common to witness widespread evangelism through numbers of
believers possessed with the spirit of the first Christians, who when
"scattered abroad went about preaching the Word" (Acts 8: 4).
Paul wrote similarly to the believers of the Thessalonian church,
"From you hath sounded forth the word of the Lord, not only
in Macedonia and Achaia, but in every place your faith to Godward is gone forth; so that we need not to speak anything" (1
Thess. 1: 8). This explains the rapid and prodigious progress of
Christianity in the first century; and the same thing in lesser
degree has accompanied and followed almost every great movement of the Spirit.

It is said of the Moravian Revival, that in the thirty years
following the outpouring of the Spirit on the congregation at
Herrnhut (1727), the Moravian evangelists, aflame for God, had
carried the gospel not only to nearly every country in Europe,
but also to many pagan races in North and South America, Asia,
and Africa. Dr. Warneck, German historian of Protestant Missions, wrote, "This small church in twenty years called into being
more missions than the whole evangelical church has done in two
centuries." More than one hundred missionaries went forth from
this village community in twenty-five years.

Of the 1860 Revival in South India, the *Indian Watchman*
observed: "As in Ireland [Ulster Revival—1859], so here, the
recent converts, seized with irresistible spirit of evangelization,
were the means of carrying the wondrous influence from one
place to another." A missionary wrote, "There were indisputable
marks of a revival among the people, brought about by the influence of five men who had come voluntarily to preach the gospel
to heathen and Christians. . . . The effect of their proceeding
hitherto has been extraordinary. The heathen listen to them atten-
tively. Their doctrine is sound and pertinent, exhibiting a right

practical understanding both of law and gospel." Another says, "It is indeed a new era in Indian Missions, that of lay converts going forth without purse or scrip to preach the gospel of Christ to their fellow-countrymen, and that with a zeal and life we had hardly thought them capable of."

It will be seen that these features constantly emphasize what has already been remarked, that revival does not lead us forward to fresh stunts or unexplored methods to make the gospel more attractive and acceptable, but back to the old and often disused paths of apostolic evangelism. Would we be ready for revival?—then let us "ask for the old paths, where is the good way, and walk therein" (Jer. 6: 16). Where the Spirit of God is in complete control there is an inevitable return to the simple methods of the first century, and great is the surprise of many to discover that they not only still work, but that they still work the best. They are in fact the only channels capable of carrying the mighty rivers of blessing let loose in revival. We shall now see how great those rivers can be.

## Superabundant Blessing

"And there were added unto them in that day about three thousand souls" (verse 41). "And the Lord added to them day by day those that were being saved" (verse 47). "But many of them that heard the word believed; and the number of the men came to be about five thousand" (4: 4). "And believers were the more added to the Lord, multitudes both of men and women" (5: 14). "And the number of the disciples multiplied . . . exceedingly; and a great company of the priests were obedient to the faith" (6: 7). So reads the record of Pentecost and the days that followed. Here then is a further distinctive feature of revival, superabundant blessing. God had indeed fulfilled the promise of Malachi 3: 10; He had opened the windows of heaven and poured out such a blessing that there was not room enough to receive it.

If these recorded results of that outpouring of Pentecost were not part of inspired Scripture, we might have wondered whether the accounts were not exaggerated. Down the years, however, there have been seasons of revival when the blessing was, numerically at least, comparable with Pentecost. One wrote out of the midst of the New England Revival (eighteenth century), "The dispensation of grace we are now under is . . . in some circumstances so wonderful, that I believe there has not been the like since the extraordinary pouring out of the Spirit immediately after our Lord's ascension." Space does not permit giving here statistics of the great revivals of the church, even if accurate information were available. However, a few figures will be quoted, remembering that they are only estimates, but made when modesty and reserve in these matters were much more prominent than they are today.

It is estimated that 30,000 souls were converted through Whitefield's revivals in America. Of the revival in the same country in 1830, Dr. Henry Ward Beecher remarked to Charles Finney, "This is the greatest revival of religion that has been since the world began." It is computed that 100,000 were converted that year in the United States. In the great 1858 revival, conversions numbered 50,000 per week, and over the whole of the United States there could not have been less than 500,000 conversions, according to Finney's estimate in 1859, when the revival was still spreading. "In the year 1859 a similar movement began in the United Kingdom, affecting every county in Ulster, Scotland, Wales, and England, *adding a million accessions* to the evangelical churches" (J. Edwin Orr).

Far more significant to thoughtful minds than massive statistics is the estimate of what *proportion* of a community or district is savingly affected in these extraordinary seasons of blessing. Of the New England Revival (eighteenth century) Conant wrote : "It cannot be doubted that at least 50,000 souls were added to the churches of New England out of a population of about 250,000. A fact sufficient to revolutionize, as indeed it did, the religious and moral character, and to determine the destinies of the country." In Acts 9: 34, 35 there is the account of the healing of a palsied man which resulted in the wholesale turning to the Lord of a town, Lydda, and a populous district, the Sharon. Many similar instances could be given of communities swept by powerful revivals when it was most difficult, if not impossible, to find a single unconverted soul.

Of the revival in Northampton, Mass. (1735) Jonathan Edwards wrote : "There was scarcely a single person in the town, either old or young, that was left unconcerned about the great things of the eternal world. Those that were wont to be the vainest and loosest, and those that had been the most disposed to think and speak slightly of vital and experimental religion, were now generally subject to great awakenings. And the work of conversion was carried on in a most astonishing manner, and increased more and more; souls did, as it were, come by flocks to Jesus Christ." Similarly Finney wrote of the revival in Rome, N.Y.: "As the work proceeded, it gathered in nearly the whole population." Of the 1858 Revival in Sweden, an English minister resident in Stockholm reported, "I should be disposed to consider that at least 200,000 persons have been awakened out of a population not exceeding 3 millions." This would mean one out of every fifteen people. Another wrote of the same revival: "The awakening is so extensive that there is scarcely a town, a village, or a hamlet, where there is not a little company of believers united together, and edifying one another in love." Revival commonly leaves behind such groups, meeting on the simple ground of oneness in Christ, as did the early church. This leads us to the last feature of the outpouring of Pentecost.

## Divine Simplicity

"And they continued steadfastly in the apostles' teaching and fellowship, in the breaking of bread and the prayers. . . . And all that believed were together, and had all things common; and they sold their possessions and goods, and parted them to all, according as any man had need. And day by day, continuing steadfastly with one accord in the temple, and breaking bread at home, they did take their food with gladness and singleness of heart, praising God, and having favour with all the people" (verses 42–47). In those early days, the manner of life of the believers, their church order and fellowship were marked by divine simplicity and spiritual power. As faith and spirituality waned the power of the Spirit was gradually withdrawn. Soon it became necessary to substitute human arrangements, which could be worked without the Spirit's power, for the divine arrangements, which were dependent on that power. Thus by degrees the simple apostolic pattern ordained by the Spirit was abandoned in favour of the complex ways of man, and those concerned with the building up of the churches forgot the exhortation of God to Moses concerning His house, "See that thou make all things according to the pattern." Some asserted that God had revealed no pattern; others that the pattern did not matter, that every man could do that which was right in his own eyes. Since revivals bring a renewal of the power of the Spirit, they are commonly accompanied by a return to the simple apostolic pattern.

It is significant that many of the revivals of Old Testament days were characterized by a return to the divinely ordained worship of the house of the Lord. Asa, for example, "renewed the altar of the Lord", and "brought into the house of God the things that his father had dedicated" (2 Chron. 15: 8, 18). Similarly Josiah sent men "to repair the house of the Lord" (2 Chron. 34: 8). Hezekiah also "in the first year of his reign . . . opened the doors of the house of the Lord, and repaired them" (2 Chron. 29: 3). He then ordered the Levites to "carry forth the filthiness out of the holy place" (verse 5), which was of course essential to any further progress; but this was not all, for the rest of the chapter describes how "the service of the house of the Lord was set in order" (verse 35). It is needful, if the blessings of revival are to be preserved and maintained, that the cleansing of the house from sin, worldliness, and unbelief, be followed by the re-establishing of its order in divine simplicity. This passage in Acts 2 reveals that the outpouring of the Spirit was followed by steadfast continuance on the part of the believers in the four matters essential to their corporate life.

Firstly, there was the *apostles' teaching*. All the great movements of the Spirit that have affected the course of history have been accompanied and consolidated by spiritual teaching. Where this is not the case it is possible for a good movement to go off into error, peter out, or be dissipated in extravagance and fanaticism. The outpouring of the Spirit was never intended to be a substitute for such teaching, but rather to stimulate it. The one provides the dynamic and impetus; the other ensures that the power released continues to flow along the right channel. A missionary wrote of the converts of the 1860 Revival in South India, "One thing is very marked, their intense reverence for the word of God, and desire to be conformed to it in all particulars." What can do more to produce a hunger for God's word, foster a love for "sound doctrine", and check heresy of various forms than a mighty outpouring of the Spirit? Said R. A. Torrey, "A genuine, wide-sweeping revival would do more to turn things upside down and thus get them right side up than all the heresy trials ever instituted."

Secondly, there was the *apostles' fellowship*, in which they continued steadfastly. Not until the Holy Spirit was given at Pentecost, and these believers were fused into one body, the church, do we have this first mention of "fellowship", a sharing together; for though our fellowship is with the Father and Son, it is ever "the fellowship of the Holy Spirit", affected and maintained by Him. This fellowship of the early church was not only related to their spiritual experiences, but also to their material possessions, for they "had all things common" (verse 44). In this connection the following report from the 1860 Revival in South India is significant : "There are now in Christian Pettah alone, about one hundred who are bound together in the ties of Christian fellowship, and in the district of Arulappatoor there is about the same number, and very many more scattered about elsewhere. Sunday they make a day of special fasting and prayer, abstaining often from food till after the partaking of the Lord's Supper, which is partaken of every Sunday evening at 8. They appear to be living in much real simplicity, having all that they have in common, and working together for the common support" (Henry Groves). Steadfast continuance in fellowship involves the diligent cultivation of the corporate life, in which there is no provision for the free-lance or the "lone wolf". Here everything is sacrificed for the common good, and the unity of the Spirit is diligently preserved. Here the believers "consider one another to provoke unto love and good works" (Heb. 10: 24). Such a fellowship can only be maintained at the price of ceaseless vigilance, but it is characteristic of times of revival.

Thirdly, there was *the breaking of bread* in which they also continued steadfastly. The Lord's Supper was prefigured in Old Testament times by the Feast of the Passover, and it is significant that three outstanding revivals in the history of Israel were marked by a widespread return to the keeping of the Passover, under Hezekiah (2 Chron. 30), Josiah (2 Chron. 35), and Ezra (Ezra 6: 19). It is therefore not surprising to discover that revivals have ever quickened the desire of the church to obey the Saviour's command, "This do in remembrance of Me." Many a time the outpouring of the Spirit has coincided with the gathering of the saints to keep this simple ordinance. The glorious revival at Cambuslang, near Glasgow (1742) under the minister, William M'Culloch, culminated in two great communion seasons. Under the preaching of Whitefield, supported by that of this parish minister, the word was attended with remarkable results. Tens of thousands gathered on the hillside to hear the word of God, many being smitten down and carried into the surrounding houses. Thousands came to the communion tables, "sitting down by companies upon the green grass, as in Galilee of old". On both occasions the voice of prayer and praise could be heard throughout the night, mingling with the mourning of stricken hearts.

We read of the first communities touched by the Revival in South India, "They were very anxious to enjoy the Lord's Supper —every day if they could have it." Thus it was immediately after Pentecost, when the Lord's Supper was taken in the believers' houses in conjunction with the daily food: "breaking bread at home, they did take their food with gladness" (Acts 2: 46). It was in this manner that the Lord had inaugurated this simple ordinance in the upper room, and revival ever tends to bring us back to the apostolic pattern, divesting these things of the cloak of ecclesiasticism, and delivering us from the twin perils of ritualism and tradition. A modern writer has done well to remind us, "It is possible to reject traditions a thousand years old, and yet be slaves to traditions of scarcely fifty years standing" (W. W. Fereday).

Finally, there was steadfast continuance in *prayers*. As revivals are born out of prayer, so are they maintained by prayer; without it they cannot continue in purity and power. Soon after the outpouring at Herrnhut (1727) that commenced the Moravian Revival, it was determined that the voice of prayer should never be silent, neither by day nor by night, just as of old the fire was ever to be kept burning upon the altar. Twenty-four brethren and the same number of sisters divided the twenty-four hours between them into prayer watches. The number of intercessors increased, a spirit of prayer being poured out even upon the children. That prayer meeting went on without intermission, day and night, for 100 years, and was the source of power of the Moravian Missions.

When the revival in Adams, N.Y., that commenced with his own conversion, began to decline, Charles Finney read an article entitled, *A Revival Revived*. "The substance was, that in a certain place there had been a revival during the winter; that in the spring it declined; and that upon earnest prayer being offered for the continued outpouring of the Spirit, the revival was powerfully revived." He suggested to the young people that they should each pray in their rooms at sunrise, at noon, and at sunset for one week. Before the week was out a marvellous spirit of prayer was poured out on them, some lying prostrate on the floor during these seasons, praying for the outpouring of the Spirit. "The Spirit *was* poured out, and before the week ended all the meetings were thronged."

Prior to Pentecost it is recorded that the believers "continued steadfastly in prayer" (Acts 1: 14); after Pentecost the young church "continued steadfastly . . . in prayers" (Acts 2: 42); and when the rivers of blessing were flowing far and wide, and the work was so extensive that the apostles could no longer cope with it, we hear their solemn resolve, "We will continue steadfastly in prayer" (Acts 6: 4). Let it be burned upon our hearts by the Spirit of God that this mighty movement that turned the world upside down was not only born out of prayer, but that it brought forth prayer, and was maintained by prayer. Such praying, costly but indispensable, has ever characterized the great revivals of the past.

How simple were the channels along which the rivers of that first outpouring flowed. The corporate life of the first church was maintained by no methods or devices more complex than teaching, fellowship, breaking of bread, and prayers. These means were simple, but they were sufficient. When the Spirit of God is poured out again it will be seen that nothing more is needed. Other expedients are only called for when the power of the Spirit begins to wane. The local church is the only visible society that can adequately meet the varied needs of the believer, young or old. This is the design of God, though He raises up and uses other organizations when the local churches have failed. It is vital that the living stones quarried in times of revival shall not be left lying about, but shall be built into the house of God, and share the corporate life of the church. Therefore the form and condition of that local body are of great importance.

It is surely right that a soul converted in revival, when the Spirit was in complete sway, should be brought into a fellowship where, in the simplicity of apostolic church order, the Spirit continues to control, and where there is scope and liberty for each member of the body to exercise his or her spiritual gifts to the blessing of all. How often the flames of revival have been extinguished by the very structure in which it broke out. After the first inrush of the Spirit, the doors and windows were shut by the iron hand of ecclesiasticism, formalism, and tradition; the flame was suffocated; the Spirit quenched. The outgoings of revival are a key to the continuance of the work. If factory wheels are arrested by some outside agency, either the motive power is also arrested and all movement ceases, or else the link that joins the power to the wheels is broken. In a mighty movement of the Spirit sometimes the link is snapped, and the revival movement is severed from the old machinery and linked to new that is fit to receive and use the fresh output of power. It is the old principle of new wine causing the old wine-skin to burst so that the wine is spilled (Matt. 9: 17). New wine requires new wine-skins, and if the old are not prepared to be renewed and remodelled by the Spirit of God to meet the new situation, God has no alternative but to reject them. A movement of the Spirit can only be contained by the organization of the Spirit, and that organization is characterized by simplicity. As we scan that distant horizon, and watch the sun rising over that first church as it moved forward in the power of the Spirit, we are compelled to exclaim with Cowper,

> "Oh, how unlike the complex works of man
> Heaven's easy, artless, unencumbered plan!
> . . . . Majestic in its own simplicity."

Bend the church, and save the people.

MOTTO OF THE WELSH REVIVAL.

In breaking up your fallow ground, you must remove every obstruction. Things may be left that you think little things, and you may wonder why you do not feel as you wish to feel in religion, when the reason is that your proud and carnal mind has covered up something which God required you to confess and remove. Break up all the ground and turn it over. Do not *balk it*, as the farmers say; do not turn it aside for little difficulties; drive the plough right through them, beam deep, and turn the ground all up, so that it may all be mellow and soft, and fit to receive the seed and bear fruit a hundred fold.

CHARLES FINNEY.

## CHAPTER SEVEN

# THE PREPARED HEART

*"Break up your fallow ground*: for it is time to seek the Lord, till
He come and rain righteousness upon you" (Hos. 10:12).

FROM the characteristics of revival we must now proceed to
the conditions under which God is pleased to pour out this
blessing. Although God is the source of all revival, there are
conditions that He expects His people to fulfil before they are
ready to receive the outpouring of the Spirit. Hosea sets these
before us in one of the most comprehensive statements on the
way of revival to be found in Scripture. "Break up your fallow
ground"—that is heart-preparation; "for it is time to seek the
Lord, till . . ."—that is prevailing prayer; "He come and rain
righteousness upon you"—that is spiritual revival. Here then are
set before us the two all-inclusive conditions : heart-preparation
and prevailing prayer. We cannot rightly separate them, for, as
the verse suggests, they are intimately related. Sometimes when
souls truly seek God they are shown their sin and barrenness, and
heart-brokenness follows. With others, it is out of a time of heart-
brokenness that they really begin to pray.

From a group of missionaries in India seeking revival in 1940
there comes this personal testimony of one of them : "While living alone I got desperate. God showed me first that my life was
practically prayerless except for my anæmic morning and evening 'devotions'. I saw the need for intense and persistent intercession, so I gave myself to prayer. Then followed deep conviction of personal sin and backsliding. One thing after another had
to come out, and my heart was completely broken as time after
time I saw His wounds and heard His royal pardon. I marvelled
at His longsuffering, and trembled in case He should ever leave
me in anger at last. I felt this fear until I saw His crowning glory"
(*The Price They Paid*). This illustrates how these two conditions
may be related in experience. This needs to be borne in mind
when we separate them for the purpose of examining them in
detail. In this chapter we shall consider the heart prepared for

blessing, and in that which follows the heart that prevails in prayer.

### Fallow Ground

"Break up your fallow ground" is the figure that the prophet uses to impress this need of heart-preparation. What is fallow ground? It is not wilderness, and therefore we cannot apply his words to the unregenerate. It is not necessarily land that has returned to the wilderness state through being wilfully abandoned, so it is not the backsliders who are primarily in view. It is simply ground which has in the past yielded fruit, but has now become largely unproductive through lack of cultivation, land that is lying idle. Seed may be sown upon it in abundance, the heavens might pour out a copious rain, but what would be the good of either so long as the ground is in this uncultivated state? As we look out upon the state of the church today, as we look within at the condition of our own hearts, we cannot but admit the accuracy of Hosea's figure. Vast tracts of fallow ground in the hearts of professing Christians surely constitute the greatest barrier to the rain of revival. The characteristics of fallow ground must now be examined more closely.

Firstly, it is *hard*. The soil has become tightly packed; the clods are thick and coarse; men and animals have heedlessly crossed it so that it possesses a hard and brittle crust. Here is the way God describes the hearts of believers when they have become insensitive to the sins that grieve the Holy Spirit, and unresponsive to His still small voice. Here are hearts that have grown cold towards the Lord and His people, and indifferent towards the souls of the perishing. They are marked by formality in their fulfilment of spiritual obligations, and cold orthodoxy in their contention for the faith. This state of heart will often lead to a belligerent and graceless defence of minor points of doctrine, or to a holding fast the tradition of the elders. These are they who "strain out the gnat and swallow the camel" (Matt. 23:24); they "tithe mint . . . and pass over judgment and the love of God" (Luke 11:42). They profess much and possess little; they have all the right expressions but few of the right experiences.

In this state believers may diligently attend the ministry of God's word, the heart may be sown continually with the incorruptible seed, but there is no fruit unto holiness, for like the wayside ground in the parable, the seed lies upon the surface, and is quickly devoured by the agents of the Evil One (Matt. 13: 4). Such are "ever learning, and never able to come to the [experimental] knowledge of the truth" (2 Tim. 3: 7). Perhaps this is the main reason why there appears to be so little effectual result from so much ministry of the word. It is all too true of the church today, "Ye have sown much and bring in little."

This hardness of heart is also revealed by unbelief in the display of God's power. Mark gives four instances of this in the life and ministry of Christ (3: 5; 6: 52; 8: 17; 16: 14), and it is deeply revealing that in each of these cases, excepting the first, where there was a hardening of heart at the manifestation of Christ's power, it was amongst His own disciples. Are we who profess to be His disciples covering our unbelief about the possibility of revival by murmurings about "a day of small things", "the end times", or "the Laodicean age"? Let us search our hearts, lest He should say of us, "Ye do err . . . not knowing the power of God." Is it not evident that this state of heart must be dealt with before there can be a manifestation of God's power in revival? With the lesson of Israel before us (Heb. 3), who entered not into the promised land because their hearts were hardened in unbelief and disobedience (verses 18, 19), we do well to heed diligently these words of the Holy Spirit, "Today if ye shall hear His voice, harden not your hearts" (verse 15).

Secondly, fallow ground is *weed-covered*. One of the main objects in cultivation is to eliminate weeds that would overrun the good seed or the growing plants. Thorns and thistles are part of the curse and typify sin (Gen. 3: 18). Such weeds abound on fallow ground, so Jeremiah exhorts the people, "Break up your fallow ground, and sow not among thorns" (4: 3). Evidently they did not heed his words, for he said later, "They have sown wheat and have reaped thorns" (12: 13). Christ also described ground in the parable of the sower where thorns sprang up and choked the good seed. Where the diligent cultivation of the soul is lacking, one may be sure that thorns and thistles abound. As the gardener well knows, the weeds need not be wilfully encouraged in order to flourish; they are the product of sloth, indifference, and neglect. A greater than Solomon, even He that searcheth the hearts, might have to say of many, "I went by the field of the slothful . . . and, lo, it was all grown over with thorns" (Prov. 24: 30, 31).

There is only one way we can begin to deal with all that we know is grieving to God, checking our growth, and hindering revival, and that is by breaking up the fallow ground. It is time to cease excusing our sins by calling them shortcomings, or natural weakness, or by attributing them to temperament or environment. It is time to cease justifying our carnal ways and materialistic outlook by pointing to others who are the same. Those "measuring themselves by themselves, and comparing themselves with themselves, are without understanding" (2 Cor. 10: 12). We must face our sins honestly in the light of God's word, view them as He does, and deal with them as before Him. Until we do, it would be well that God should withhold the rain of revival, "for the land which hath drunk the rain that cometh oft upon it . . . if it beareth thorns and thistles, it is rejected and nigh unto a curse; whose end is to be burned" (Heb. 6: 7, 8).

Thirdly, fallow ground is of necessity *unfruitful*. Despite abundant sowing and copious showers, the ground remains largely barren because of its condition. The fruit that God expects the believer to bring forth is not religious activity, or even zealous Christian service, so much as Christ-like character as set forth in Galatians 5, verse 22: "The fruit of the Spirit is love, joy, peace, longsuffering, kindness, goodness, faithfulness, meekness, self-control (R.V. margin)." Fruit is practical holiness in thought, word, and deed; fruit is likeness to Jesus Christ. It is possible to be zealously active in Christian service, and yet, when a hungry Saviour comes to us as to the fig tree, yearning for fruit, He finds nothing but leaves. Who can measure His intense longing for fruit from those who are "God's husbandry"? All God's dealings with us, in mercy or in judgment, are designed to produce "fruit", "more fruit", "much fruit" (John 15: 2, 5). How much does He find? How much is choked by weeds? Peter explains clearly how to avoid becoming fallow ground, by "adding on your part all diligence" to produce the fruit of righteousness, "For", says he, "if these things are yours and abound, they make you to be not *idle nor unfruitful* unto the knowledge of our Lord Jesus Christ" (2 Pet. 1: 5–8).

## Breaking Up

If Hosea's figure of fallow ground is an accurate description of our own hearts, and if we are deeply concerned to remedy the situation, then we must face this command, "*Break up* your fallow ground." There is a sense in which God may break us in order to bless us, but here God places the onus upon us by commanding us to do it. It is as dangerous to expect God, by some sovereign act, to do for us what He has commanded us to do for ourselves, as it is to strive to do for ourselves what He has promised to do for us. In the path of spiritual progress there is no little emphasis in Scripture on the part the believer has to play. We read, "Cleanse your hands, ye sinners; and purify your hearts, ye doubleminded" (Jas. 4: 8), and again, "Let us cleanse ourselves from all defilement of flesh and spirit, perfecting holiness in the fear of God" (2 Cor. 7: 1). Thus it is with this question of heart-preparation; the responsibility is ours.

This is not only true in relation to revival, but in all Christian service and witness: "The preparations of the heart belong to man: but the answer of the tongue is from the Lord" (Prov. 16: 1). So there is our part and God's part. If we make it our business to have prepared hearts, God will make it His business to fill our mouths with arguments which our adversaries shall not be able to gainsay or resist. "Sanctify in your hearts Christ as Lord," says Peter, and you will be "ready always to give answer to every man that asketh you a reason concerning the hope that is in you" (1 Pet. 3: 15). God's contention with Israel was that they were "a stubborn and rebellious generation, a generation that prepared not their heart" (Ps. 78: 8, R.V. margin). If we are to have revival it must come from heaven, it must be the result of divine intervention, but how can we expect God to rain righteousness upon us before we have broken up the fallow ground? The words of Samuel should come as a challenge to the people of God today: "Prepare your hearts unto the Lord, and serve Him only: and He will deliver you out of the hand of the Philistines" (1 Sam. 7: 3). Are you ready to obey?

To "break up the fallow ground" of our hearts means to bring them to a humble and contrite state before God, for this is the only state of heart that God can revive, the only state that is ready for the rain of revival. "For thus saith the high and lofty One that inhabiteth eternity, Whose name is Holy; I dwell in the high and holy place, with him also that is of a contrite and humble spirit, *to revive the spirit of the humble, and to revive the heart of the contrite ones*" (Isa. 57: 15).

## The Humble

It was in the form of pride that sin first broke into the universe through the heart of Satan, and bore fruit at once in self-will and rebellion (Isa. 14: 12–14; Ezek. 28: 12–17). It was through temptation to pride that Satan first seduced Eve (Gen. 3: 6), and thus breathed this deadly poison into the human race. Pride finds expression in the lifting up of self and the justifying of self before God and man. It is the subtle, evasive influence behind many of the works of the flesh. It quickly leads to disobedience to God. When thwarted or humiliated it gives way to envy and bitterness. In order to justify itself it will not hesitate to slander, or speak evil of others. In the pursuit of its ends it may readily stoop to hypocrisy and deceit. Pride is fruitful of all manner of disorders and divisions amongst the people of God. It is perhaps the greatest enemy of revival, and the most difficult to diagnose and deal with. The most deceitful thing in the world is the heart of man, and only God can truly know it. Pride is woven into the warp and woof of it, and only the Spirit of God can expose it. We dare not try to search our own hearts, but can only cry to God with David, "Search me, O God, and know my heart : try me, and know my thoughts : and see if there be any way of wickedness in me " (Ps. 139: 23).

Many of the afflictions we are called upon to endure, whether spiritual, mental, or physical, are but the mighty hand of God upon us to bring us low before Him. "Thou shalt remember all the way which the Lord thy God hath led thee . . . in the wilderness, that He might humble thee, to prove thee, to know what was in thine heart" (Deut. 8: 2). Whether these wilderness experiences serve this divine purpose or not will depend on our attitude to the hand that afflicts us. If we can kiss that hand, and say, "In faithfulness Thou hast afflicted me", His purpose is surely being achieved. But the hand that softens one may harden another, just as the sun that melts the wax will harden the clay.

Are you resisting God's dealings with you? Remember, His powers of resistance are infinitely greater than yours. "God resisteth the proud, but giveth grace to the humble. Be subject therefore unto God" (Jas. 4: 6). If you are conscious of any spirit of pride, *now* is the time to deal with it. Before you read another page bow your knees before the Father and confess to Him all that you know of it. "Humble yourselves therefore under the mighty hand of God, that He may exalt you" (1 Pet. 5: 6). James reminds us that there must be transparent honesty, sincerity, and openness over this step, for he says, "Humble yourselves *in the sight of the Lord*" (Jas. 4: 10). If we simply did it in the sight of men we could be secretly proud of being humble; but there can be no trifling with God, for "the Lord looketh on the heart" (1 Sam. 16: 7), "and by Him actions are weighed" (1 Sam. 2: 3).

To humble ourselves is not to take a place lower than that which befits us, but simply to take our *rightful* place before God; not to think of ourselves more highly than we ought to think, but "to think soberly" (Rom. 12: 3). It means that we occupy that station that becomes us as creatures before our Creator, as sinners before our Saviour-God, as children before our heavenly Father. Are we willing to take that place? This is where breaking up the fallow ground begins. This is the first step, costly but indispensable, towards revival; and those unwilling to face it may as well cease to think or talk about revival any more. Do you acknowledge the importance of the step but feel that the exhortation does not apply to you? Then you may be the very one who most needs to heed the command. "If *My people*, which are called by My Name, shall *humble* themselves . . . then will I hear . . . forgive . . . and heal" (2 Chron. 7: 14). The revival under Josiah took place when the king gave the lead in abasing himself before God: "Thus saith the Lord . . . because thine heart was tender, and thou didst humble thyself before Me . . . I also have heard thee" (2 Chron. 34: 26, 27). This has ever been the pathway to blessing. When the people of God humble themselves in repentance, God will exalt them in revival.

## The Contrite

God not only revives "the spirit of the humble" but also "the heart of the contrite ones". When in humility we take our rightful place before God, He can then deal with us as He was unable to deal with us before. The heart is now ready for that breaking up out of which revival flows. To the soul humbled before God, or at least ready to be humbled, there comes a fresh revelation of the infinite holiness of God and the exceeding sinfulness of sin. Well may that one cry out:

> Eternal Light! Eternal Light!
> How pure the soul must be
> When, placed within Thy searching sight,
> It shrinks not, but with calm delight
> Can live, and look on Thee.
>
> T. Binney.

The light that streams from the throne illuminates the Cross. The heart is melted by that measureless love that found expression in the sacrifice of the Redeemer. The sin—one's own sin—that nailed Him there is seen in terrible contrast.

> In His spotless soul's distress
> I perceive my guiltiness;
> Oh, how vile my low estate,
> Since my ransom was so great!
>
> R. Chapman.

Nothing can more effectively bring a soul to that state of heart that God can revive than a vision of the Cross. It is in such an experience of God that the heart is broken over its sin, its unbelief, its coldness, and brought to repentance. The channel that God uses in revival is the channel of a broken heart.

When the armies of Judah and Israel were without water in the wilderness of Edom the word of the Lord came to them through Elisha, "Make this valley full of trenches. . . . Ye shall not see wind, neither shall ye see rain, yet that valley shall be filled with water" (2 Kings 3: 16). The hard crust of the soil had to be broken all over the face of the valley, that the trenches might be dug, and that the promised tide might find prepared channels. Readiness for revival involves this breaking up, this dealing with God over our sin. The Hebrew word translated "contrite" has the root meaning of "bruised" or "broken to pieces". Job uses it when defending himself against the accusations of his friends, "How long will ye vex my soul, and *break me in pieces* with words?" (19: 2). It would be well if the words of the Almighty would have this effect on our hearts, but this cannot be until there is a fresh dealing with God, as many instances in Scripture reveal. The geologists tell us that our garden soil is mainly rock, pulverized by the ceaseless action of the elements throughout the millenniums of the past. Similarly the con-

trite heart is that in which all that is rocklike and resistant to the
will of God has been reduced to powder, because submissive to
the action of His word and providences. "I will take away the
stony heart out of your flesh, and I will give you an heart of flesh"
(Ezek. 36: 26).

The God of glory so appeared to Abraham in Ur of the
Chaldees that he renounced the idolatry about him and "obeyed
to go out . . . not knowing whither he went" (Heb. 11: 8). God
revealed Himself to Moses in a flame of fire out of the midst of a
bush and said, "Put off thy shoes from off thy feet, for the place
whereon thou standest is holy ground" (Exod. 3: 2–5). As Captain of the Lord's Host He appeared to Joshua and brought the
same message, so that Joshua fell on his face to the earth (Joshua
5: 13–15). Early in his prophetic ministry Isaiah "saw the Lord
sitting upon a throne, high and lifted up", and the cry was wrung
from the lips of the prophet, "Woe is me, for I am undone" (Isa.
6). Although God boasted of Job, "There is none like him in the
earth, a perfect and an upright man", when there came to him
the revelation of God in His holiness he cried out, "I abhor myself, and repent in dust and ashes" (Job 42: 6). Just as there is
no state of soil more satisfying to the gardener than that which is
mellow and friable, crumbling to pieces at his touch, so there is
no heart more satisfying to God than that which breaks at His
touch, that crumbles under His mighty yet tender hand. "The
sacrifices of God are a broken spirit : a broken and a contrite
heart, O God, Thou wilt not despise" (Ps. 51:17).

Contrition involves repentance toward God, for all sin is
primarily against Him (Ps. 51: 4). There must be confession, without which there can be no forgiveness or cleansing (1 John 1: 9),
and to confess means to identify ourselves with our sin before
Him, to point to it and acknowledge, "Lord, that is mine". Often
our sin has not been a private matter between God and us; others
have been involved. For instance, the sin of which we are convicted may be that we have wronged another by some deceitful
or unkind act. It may be that bitter, wounding words were spoken
to or about another. It may be we have harshly criticized others,
secretly pulled their characters to pieces, exaggerated their
apparent faults, or presented them in the worst possible light. It
may be we have said or done no such thing, but our sin has been
in the attitude we have taken up towards another : we refuse to

forgive from the heart someone who we feel has wronged us; a spirit of envy, of bitterness, or of malice has dominated our thinking in relation to that person. Where the Holy Spirit convicts us of such sins against others, confession to God alone does not and cannot meet the case.

The Lord Jesus said, "If thou art offering thy gift at the altar, and there rememberest that thy brother hath aught against thee, leave there thy gift before the altar, and go thy way, first be reconciled to thy brother, and then come and offer thy gift" (Matt. 5: 23). God cannot accept and bless our gifts of worship, of service, or of substance, nor can He bestow upon His children His fatherly pardon until first we have dealt with such wrong relationships. The terms of Christ's command are plain : "first be reconciled" and then come to God. Full confession, and where necessary restitution must be made to the person or persons involved. Full confession, however, does not necessarily mean detailed confession. There are times when one must refrain from confessing the details of one's sin, as when one is moved to make public confession of moral impurity, when the minds of others— especially the young—may be defiled by even the confession. "But fornication, and all uncleanness . . . let it not even be named among you, as becometh saints" (Eph. 5: 3): or the details of evil-speaking which might grievously wound the one to whom confession is made.

Restitution means the restoring of that which we have wrongly obtained or retained. It means undoing, so far as possible, the result of every wrong that has affected others. Cases of evil-speaking, for example, necessitate not only confession before those *about* whom we have spoken, but also those *to* whom we have spoken, whose minds may have been wrongly influenced or even poisoned against that other through our words. We must go all lengths to put right every wrong, and the effect of every wrong, and let us remember, everything that is not dealt with now will be dealt with at the Judgment Seat of Christ to the detriment of our status in that day to come. Where a believer's sin has been against a community, such as dishonesty over church funds, or deceit as in the case of Ananias and Sapphira (Acts 5), or a course of action that has brought reproach on the Christian community or hindered blessing coming to others, then public confession must be made before the whole community thus wronged.

It matters not how long ago a sin was committed—weeks, months, or even years. If the Spirit of God convicts, then God is demanding that there be a confession, and we cannot refuse without sinning against our own soul and multiplying our guilt. "See that ye refuse not Him that speaketh. For if they escaped not, when they refused him that warned them on earth, much more shall not we escape, who turn away from Him that warneth from heaven . . . for our God is a consuming fire" (Heb. 12: 25, 29). Recently in a group seeking God for revival, a young brother restored from backsliding was convicted of a sin committed years before—that of defrauding the railway by travelling for a period with an invalid ticket. A special journey had to be made some distance to the railway junction concerned, where confession and restitution was made before the station-master and clerks. Yes, God may put tremendous pressure upon us that our lives may be adjusted to His holy will, and our willingness to go all lengths is the proof of a truly broken and contrite heart.

In the same revival prayer group a deeply devoted sister asked God to reveal anything in her life that was hindering revival. She wrote, "It was as though scales fell from my eyes, and I saw my heart as I had never yet seen it. I saw that although I had confessed all my sins to God, I had to confess something to one I had wronged years before. I wept for hours, cried to God for strength to confess, feeling that if I did not some calamity would come upon my home. After some days I confessed part, but not the whole. I had a measure of peace, but knew that God wanted absolute obedience." At the next prayer meeting the story of Ananias and Sapphira was read, the solemn account of two who "kept back part of the price" (Acts 5). The sister was moved, but thought that God was speaking to someone else. The following night she went to bed feeling wretched. In the early hours she awoke feeling God's hand upon her, and His holy presence filled the room. She cried aloud, "O Lord, I can't bear it! What must I do?" The Lord said, "Are you prepared to pay the price of revival?" "What is the price, Lord?" "A full confession," was the answer. She cried out, "How can I pay it, Lord?" Afraid to live and afraid to die, she spent the night in agony of soul. The next day this sister made full confession with tears to the one concerned, feeling that had she not done so her life would be taken away.

It is a deeply solemn matter to seek God's face for revival, for He may deal with us as He does not deal with others. From this incident let us learn to beware of applying to someone else what God is saying to us, and of feigning to fulfil the conditions while secretly keeping back part of the price. No sacrifice made in the interests of revival can be accepted as a substitute for implicit, unquestioning, whole-hearted obedience. "Hath the Lord as great delight in burnt offerings and sacrifices, as in obeying the voice of the Lord? Behold, to obey is better than sacrifice, and to hearken than the fat of rams" (1 Sam. 15: 22). Finney put his finger on the root of the matter when he described revival as "a new beginning of obedience to God". "Oh that My people would hearken unto Me, that Israel would walk in My ways! I should soon subdue their enemies, and turn My hand against their adversaries" (Ps. 81: 13).

Here then is the first great condition of revival, that brokenness of heart that is sensitive to the least touch of the Spirit, and that has only to know the will of God to do it. One may cross fallow ground and not see where the feet have trod—no impression has been made. But when the plough and the harrow have done their work, and the soil is soft and friable, then the print of the foot is clearly seen. When our hearts are sensitive, responsive, and impressionable to the movements of God across our lives, we may be sure that the fallow ground is broken. My reader, have you come to this point? Are you willing for God to bring you there? If so, the first step is with you. There must be, in the words of saintly Robert Chapman, "a looking back, and a dealing afresh with God respecting past iniquities". This is the way to a humble and contrite heart.

Having faced what is implied in this command to break up the fallow ground, let us nevertheless remember that ploughing is not reaping; that breaking up the fallow ground is not the coming of the showers; that repentance is not revival. The one is but the pathway to the other. The farmer has no interest in ploughing save as the indispensable means to the harvest. "Doth the plowman plow continually to sow? Doth he continually open and break the clods of his ground? When he hath made plain the face thereof, doth he not cast abroad the fitches, and scatter the cummin, and put in the wheat in rows. . . . For his God doth instruct him aright, and doth teach him" (Isa. 28: 24). In other words, the ploughman is not for ever ploughing and breaking up the ground. He does so until he has "made plain the face thereof", until the ground is smooth and soft and even, and then he moves on to the next operation, the sowing of the seed.

Brokenness is not revival; it is a vital and indispensable step towards it. To make it an end instead of a means is not only to miss that fuller end that God desires, but may also lead us into an unhealthy introspection, if not into definite bondage. But how are we to know when the breaking up has been done to God's satisfaction? He alone can reveal this to us, as Isaiah tells us—"For his God doth instruct him aright [in his judgment—Darby], and doth teach him" (verse 26). We cannot, of course, put these different processes of preparation into watertight compartments, for they are too intimately related, and dependent the one upon the other. As the man who is sowing or reaping now, will, in a few months hence, be ploughing once again; so God has often to bring the yielded servant back from his sowing or reaping to a deeper and more thorough ploughing. But with all these divine cycles there should be progress. Revival, however, is not ploughing or sowing, but the rain of ingathering. If a movement does not lead to reaping one may question whether it is revival in the full sense of the word.

The importance of heart-preparation becomes even clearer when seen in relation to prayer, the next vital step towards revival. The prepared heart becomes the praying heart that prevails with God.

When God intends great mercy for His people, the first thing He does is to set them a praying.

MATTHEW HENRY.

From the day of Pentecost, there has been not one great spiritual awakening in any land which has not begun in a union of prayer, though only among two or three; no such outward, upward movement has continued after such prayer meetings have declined.

A. T. PIERSON.

Early in the Welsh Revival (1904) a Wiltshire evangelist visited the meetings at Ferndale. He stood up and said, "Friends, I have journeyed into Wales with the hope that I may glean the secret of the Welsh Revival." In an instant Evan Roberts was on his feet, and with an uplifted arm towards the speaker he replied : "My brother—there is no secret ! Ask and ye shall receive !"

FROM AN UNPUBLISHED ACCOUNT
OF THE WELSH REVIVAL.

## CHAPTER EIGHT

# THE PRAYING HEART

*"Break up your fallow ground: for it is time to seek the Lord,* till
He come and rain righteousness upon you" (Hos. 10:12).

THE fallow ground while it is untilled seems to suggest to us a state of complacency and of permanency, as though it had always been in that barren condition and there was no likelihood of its being otherwise. But when the plough has done its work what a different aspect it presents! True, it is still barren, but instead of an air of complacency it has now an air of expectancy, of hope, of desire. Before, it held its moisture and had no need of or desire for rain, but now it has become thirsty, as though it would cry out to heaven for the showers. Thus the connection between breaking up the ground and seeking the Lord is clear. It is only out of a heart ploughed deep that there proceeds that kind of praying that prevails with God and brings revival.

A heart, resigned, submissive, meek,
    My dear Redeemer's throne;
Where only Christ is heard to speak,
    Where Jesus reigns alone.

A humble, lowly, contrite heart,
    Believing, true and clean,
Which neither death nor life can part
    From Him that dwells within.

A heart in every thought renewed,
    And filled with love divine;
Perfect and right, and pure, and good,
    A copy, Lord, of Thine.
                    CHARLES WESLEY.

Such a heart, in full sympathy with the heart of the Eternal, beating with the pulse-beat of heaven, was that of Nehemiah. It is laid bare for us in the first chapter of his book, when news is brought to him, far away in captivity, of the desolations of

Zion. "The remnant that are left of the captivity there in the province are in great affliction and reproach : the wall of Jerusalem also is broken down, and the gates thereof are burned with fire" (verse 3). This was the situation which drew forth such burdened praying from the heart of Nehemiah.

## Vision of the Need

Essential to the mighty intercession that is answered in revival is a clear vision of the need. What was it that so deeply moved this man of God? Firstly, it was the people of God "in great affliction and reproach". He saw "Ichabod" written across the nation, "the glory hath departed". The people who had been so mightily liberated by the outstretched hand of God were again in bondage. They had been so glorious and powerful and free in the eyes of men in the days that were past, and now they had been brought so low; this was the reproach that Nehemiah continually faced as he set to work to restore the situation. "They laughed us to scorn, and despised us" (2:19); "What do these feeble Jews?" (4: 2). "Hear, O our God; for we are despised : and turn back their reproach upon their own head" (4: 4). Since they were God's people and called by His Name, a reproach upon them was a reproach upon Him. The glory of God was involved. This is the situation today. God is jealous for His great Name because His church, which should be "fair as the moon, clear as the sun, terrible as an army with banners" (Song 6: 10), is all too often in bondage and affliction, the scorn and laughing-stock of the world.

Secondly, Nehemiah visualized "the wall of Jerusalem broken down". The wall was the line of demarcation, that which separated those within from those without. A city without walls was defenceless, an easy prey to every enemy marauder. In a great measure it is true today that the walls of the city have been broken down, the church has lost her mark of separation, her defences are departed from her, and she is vulnerable to every attack of Satan.

Finally, "the gates thereof are burned with fire". The gates were the key to the control of every city. In the gates sat the rulers of the city, the elders, the nobles, and the judges (Deut. 22: 15; Job 29: 7-10; Prov. 31: 23). When the gates were burned, authority and dominion were destroyed, and the people were subdued. In the days of the early church "the gates of the city" were intact. God's people knew the authority which was theirs in the Name of Jesus, and in their preaching and their praying and their working they used to the full that authority. How seldom is that authority or that power wielded today. How few there are of whom it may truthfully be said: "They shall not be ashamed, when they speak with their enemies in the gate" (Ps. 127: 5).

Before there can be a vision of the possibilities of the hour there must be a vision of the need of the hour. With many there is an unwillingness to face facts; the state of the church in general is so much the state of their own hearts that they are unmoved by the need of either. Such are "blind, seeing only what is near", to whom the Lord would say, "Thou sayest I am rich, and have gotten riches, and have need of nothing; and knowest not that thou art the wretched one and miserable and poor and blind and naked" (Rev. 3: 17). The need of the hour is for men of the stamp of Nehemiah to blow the trumpet in Zion and sound an alarm in God's holy mountain, to open our eyes that we may "see the evil case that we are in, how Jerusalem lieth waste, and the gates thereof are burned with fire", and to bring the challenge, "Let us build up the wall of Jerusalem, that we be no more a reproach" (Neh. 2: 17).

## Reaction to the Need

"And it came to pass, when I heard these words, that I sat down and wept, and mourned certain days; and I fasted and prayed before the God of heaven" (1: 4). In the reaction to spiritual need the state of the heart is revealed. The Saviour could not look upon the multitudes going astray as sheep not having a shepherd without being moved with compassion. He could not look out over the Jerusalem that had heard His word and witnessed His power and yet rejected His message without weeping. How we need to pray, "Lord crucified, give me a heart like Thine." Such a heart had Nehemiah. If it had been otherwise he might have quieted his conscience and soothed his feelings with the thought that Jerusalem was far away, that he was well cared for in Shushan the palace, and that the desolations of Zion were no fault of his, so why need he be concerned? He could have argued that this situation was in consequence of the people's sin —the *other* people's; and that it was up to them, not him, to remedy it. He might have fortified himself in his indifference by asserting that the end of the dispensation was at hand, that judgment on their departure from God was predicted, and therefore there was no hope of recovery or of revival until the coming of Messiah. But how different was his attitude !

If this was a time when Jerusalem was tempted to say, "Jehovah hath forsaken me, and the Lord hath forgotten me," then God was ready to answer with the tenderness of a nursing mother for her child, "Behold, I have graven thee upon the palms of My hands; thy walls [broken down though they may be] are continually before Me" (Isa. 49: 14–16). It was the man after God's own heart who was inspired to write long before, "Pray for the peace of Jerusalem : they shall prosper that love thee" (Ps. 122: 6). Because Nehemiah's heart was in sympathy with God he could not contemplate her afflictions without mourning, nor could he love her without weeping. Prevailing prayer requires a tender, compassionate heart, a deep solicitude for the glory of God and the good of His people. Nehemiah wept and mourned. While our praying is cold and formal and tearless we need not expect God to work for us as He did for Nehemiah. It is he that "goeth on his way weeping" who may expect to "come again with joy, bringing his sheaves with him" (Ps. 126: 6). "Blessed are they that mourn : for they shall be comforted" (Matt. 5: 4).

In the face of such a need heart-sorrow alone is not sufficient, for tears cannot remedy the situation. A godly sorrow, however, if it is created by the Spirit, will move the will to action. Said Nehemiah, "I fasted and prayed before the God of heaven." How seldom does the church of today turn in her overwhelming need to this old-fashioned, yet scriptural remedy. Other Old Testament saints like David (Ps. 109: 24) and Jehoshaphat (2 Chron. 20: 3), Ezra (Ezra 8: 21) and Daniel (Dan. 9: 3) did not hesitate to fast in times of great pressure or when the need of the hour demanded it. Jesus not only fasted Himself (Matt. 4: 2; John 4: 31–34), but gave us important teaching on the subject. It is needful to point out that the Saviour said, "*When* ye fast" (Matt. 6: 16), not "*if* ye fast". He took it for granted that there would be times when His followers would feel this need, and so He predicted, "the days will come, when the Bridegroom shall be taken away from them, and then will they fast" (Matt. 9:15).

The early church fulfilled this prophecy of Christ. It was out of a time of fasting that there proceeded those mighty church-founding tours of Paul that turned the world upside down. He and Barnabas were separated for their special ministry "as they [with the other prophets and teachers at Antioch] ministered to the Lord and fasted" (Acts 13: 2). It was with further fasting and prayer that they were sent forth by the church, and by the Holy Spirit (Acts 13: 3, 4). It was "in fastings often" that the apostolic group commended themselves as ministers of God that they might give no occasion of stumbling (2 Cor. 6: 3–5; 11: 27). "Be ye imitators of me," exhorts the apostle, "even as I also am of Christ" (1 Cor. 11: 1). Many mightily used in revival, as well as others whose names will never be known till the day of revealing, have followed the example of Christ and the apostles, and given themselves wholly to prayer in this way. No rule can be laid down since Scripture does not. Factors of health and strength and general circumstances must be taken into consideration. Each must be led in such a matter by the dictates of the Spirit. But let us remember that a desperate situation demands desperate measures. Fasting is an indication that we mean business with God. "Ye shall seek Me, and find Me, when ye shall search for Me *with all your heart* . . . saith the Lord" (Jer. 29: 13).

### Intercession for the Need

Nehemiah records the substance of the prayer he then offered, and it must surely be included amongst the greatest prayers of Scripture. Notice firstly how majestic is his conception of God. His appreciation of the greatness of Israel's need is more than matched by his appreciation of the greatness of his God to deal with it. But for the latter, the former would have driven him to despair. Listen then to his prayer: "I beseech Thee, O Jehovah, the God of heaven, the great and terrible God, that keepeth covenant and mercy with them that love Him and keep His commandments" (verse 5). Here is a heart that is filled with reverential awe for God, even that fear of the Lord which is the beginning of wisdom (Prov. 9: 10). Nehemiah had reason indeed to number himself amongst "Thy servants who delight to fear Thy

Name" (verse 11). How little is such an attitude towards God in evidence today, even amongst the saints. It is a mark of revival, however, and will be found wherever there are Christians who have paid the price for blessing; it is widespread when God comes down in power. Such a fear of God is possible only to those who have clear views of the majesty and holiness of the Lord on the one hand, and of His love and faithfulness on the other.

To Nehemiah God was not only "glorious in holiness, fearful in praises, doing wonders", but He was also "gracious and full of compassion", "the faithful God, which keepeth covenant and mercy with them that love Him" (Deut. 7: 9). Nehemiah was able to prevail in prayer because he held God to be faithful and pleaded His promises. He reminded Him of what He had cove-nanted to do (verse 8) and pressed Him to fulfil it. This is a spiritual lever that never fails to move the hand that moves the world. This great principle characterized the praying of Abraham, Moses, Elijah, and Daniel. All the mighty interceding of the ages that has ever shaken the kingdom of darkness has been based upon the promises of God. Why should we expect God to do what He has not agreed to do? Why should we expect Him to do less than what He has promised? Duncan Campbell says of those who were seeking God for revival in Lewis prior to the Awakening (1949), "They were possessed of the conviction that God, being a covenant-keeping God, must keep His covenant engagements. Had He not promised to 'pour water upon him that is thirsty, and floods upon the dry ground'? Here was something that for them existed in the field of possibility; why were they not actually experiencing it? But they came at length to the place where, with one of old, they could cry 'Our God . . . is able . . . and He will' " (*The Lewis Awakening*).

From this recorded prayer of Nehemiah two other important features emerge. Firstly, there is the earnestness and steadfastness which characterized his praying. "Hearken unto the prayer . . . which I pray before Thee at this time, *day and night*" (verse 6). We do not see here the passion or enthusiasm of the moment, soon to fade with the passage of time; nor yet the supplication that could be reduced to silence by reverses and disappointments. There was the will and the determination to win through, as we see by the fact that he prayed without ceasing. Here is surely an indispensable factor in prevailing prayer. Many who pray never obtain because they do not persevere. "In due season we shall reap, *if* we faint not" (Gal. 6: 9) is certainly true of prayer. Many, alas, faint and drop out of the battle who began so well, because the "due season" did not arrive as soon as they expected, or because the price proved to be more than they were prepared to pay. There can be no "praying through" without that strong purpose wrought in the heart by the Spirit. O, that God may grant us the steadfast continuance that marked the praying of the upper room (Acts 1: 14), and of the early church (Acts 2: 42; 6: 4). "It is time to seek the Lord *till* He come and rain righteousness upon you."

Secondly, there was the confession of Nehemiah mingling with his petitions. "*I confess* the sins of the children of Israel" (verses 6, 7). He did not tell God how hardly they were being treated, nor did he make mention of their affliction and reproach; instead he exposed the root of the trouble—the sin of the people, laying it open before God in confession. This was the condition for the turning again of their captivity (1 Kings 8: 46–49). There could be no restoration without repentance. Nehemiah could not force others to confess, but he could confess for them. This is an important feature in the work of intercession, identifying oneself not only with the need, but also with the sin of those for whom intercession is made. Moses did this (Exod. 32: 31, 32; 34: 9), and so did Daniel (Dan. 9: 4–14). But Nehemiah also confessed that both he and his circle were involved; for he says, "Yea, I and my father's house have sinned. We have dealt very corruptly against Thee." He was ready to acknowledge that he and his family had contributed their quota to the iniquities of God's people. Nor was he satisfied with generalizing, but stated wherein they had sinned, by uncovering the sorry tale of broken commandments, statutes, and judgments (verse 7). In our confessions we must be as specific and definite as in our petitions.

### The Divine Answer

When Nehemiah commenced to seek God he may have had little idea how his prayers were to be answered and the situation recovered. Of one thing he could be certain, God would be faithful to His promises. But as he continued to press his case in the courts of heaven there was borne in upon him by the Spirit the conviction that he himself was to be the instrument in the fulfilment of his own prayers, and that God had given him this place of influence in the Persian palace that he might use it for the good of Jerusalem. A new note comes into his praying: "Prosper, I pray Thee, Thy servant this day, and grant him mercy in the sight of this man. (Now I was cupbearer to the king)" (verse 11). This revivalist "sought the peace of Jerusalem; prayed for it; and was willing to sacrifice wealth, ease, safety, and even life itself, if he might be the instrument of restoring the desolations of Israel" (*Treasury of Scripture Knowledge*). Perhaps even Nehemiah did not anticipate all the difficulties and dangers, the afflictions and sorrows that were to beset his path before the vision was fulfilled, but he was prepared to go through with God, committing the unknown to Him. "If . . . God command thee . . . thou shalt be able" (Exod. 18: 23).

An intercessor cannot expect to prevail unless willing to be the instrument, if God should require it, in the fulfilment of the prayer. Moses had no doubt offered a thousand prayers for the deliverance of his people from Egyptian slavery, and how his heart must have been gladdened at the burning bush when the Lord said to him, "I am come down to deliver them" (Exod. 3: 8), but what a bombshell when He added, "Come now therefore, and I will send *thee* unto Pharaoh, that *thou* mayest bring forth My people" (verse 10). Similarly with the disciples, Jesus commanded them to pray that God would send forth labourers into the harvest, and then forthwith He sent out the twelve to become the answer to their own prayers (Matt. 9: 38–10: 1). Let all who would intercede for revival face up to the possible implications of their praying. Many a cherished ambition may be shattered. Many a smooth pathway of ease and safety may have to be exchanged for a thorny track, encompassed with dangers, afflictions, and reproaches. Do not pray for the outpouring of the Spirit unless, like Nehemiah, you mean to go through with God. Perhaps if some knew what was involved they would be imploring God *not* to send revival. "But the people that know their God [and can therefore trust Him] shall be strong, and do exploits" (Dan. 11: 32).

The writer was once asked at the conclusion of a meeting, "Do you think that *one* person can bring revival?" "Yes," was the reply, "for God says, 'I will pour water upon *him* that is thirsty, and streams upon the dry ground.' ". This first chapter of Nehemiah shows us "him that is thirsty", and the ensuing chapters describe "the streams upon the dry ground". Nehemiah was prospered before the king, and he came to Jerusalem to survey the ruins of the city. He gathered the nobles and rulers about him, and when he had put the case before them he said, "Come and let us build up the wall of Jerusalem, that we be no more a reproach" (2: 17). The waters had begun to flow out from the thirsty soul to the dry ground with their life-giving power. "Let us rise up and build", they responded. "So they strengthened their hands for the good work" (verse 18). The trowel is prepared, the sword is furbished, and the work begins. Many willing hands are grappling now with the situation, the purposes of God are moving forward apace, but let us not forget the prayers and the tears and the anguish of that one man who prevailed with God. We do not need the gifts of Nehemiah to prepare our hearts, seek the Lord, and prevail. It is thus that revival comes.

At a school for the sons of missionaries in Ootacamund, South India, there took place in 1930 a remarkable movement of the Spirit, notwithstanding that it was localized in its effect. R. T. Naish, the writer and speaker on prophetic subjects, was the instrument God used, although the work had begun before he arrived. Out of 130 boys in the school, 100 professed conversion, and with almost all of these there was deep conviction of sin and much brokenness. It all happened so suddenly as to take the staff completely by surprise, for they had no expectation of any such thing and were unable adequately to cope with it. One still on the staff of this school, who remembers this gracious movement of the Spirit, records that the boys seemed to sing all day, became Bible-conscious, and several were baptized. The last Sunday of the Mission eighty boys were at the Lord's table. But what was the explanation of the sudden movement? It was afterwards discovered that three boys under twelve years of age had been going out in the early morning to the edge of the jungle to pray. They had prevailed with God and He had answered by fire. "Out of the mouth of babes and sucklings hast Thou established strength, because of Thine adversaries, that Thou mightest still the enemy and the avenger" (Ps. 8: 2). If they prevailed, why may not we?

One further lesson from the story of Nehemiah is that there is nothing transient about the fruit of true revival. It is typified here by the figure of building. It is the purpose of God that something solid and stable, standing the test of time and eternity, shall emerge out of the spiritual upheavals of revival. The excitement will subside, certain features of the movement may pass away, but that building which is the workmanship of the Spirit, that which is God's real objective, will abide. In the excitement of the incidentals, it is vital to keep the divine purpose in view, and build according to the pattern. Nehemiah did not require an architect to plan where the walls should be. He had but to build upon the old foundations, and to reconstruct the walls and gates as they were of old time. So today God desires us to build according to the apostolic pattern. There are stones hidden by the accumulated rubbish of the centuries that are still waiting to be uncovered. "Will they revive the stones out of the heaps of rubbish?" asked the scornful and incredulous Sanballat (4: 2). They will—they did! "So the wall was finished . . . and all the heathen that were about us feared, and were much cast down in their own eyes : for they perceived that this work was wrought of our God" (6: 15, 16). Here then is the fruit of a praying heart—a work manifestly wrought of God.

The epic story of Nehemiah demonstrates what God may achieve through one man rightly related to Him. God is not looking for men; He is looking for a man. His methods have not changed since the day He said through Ezekiel, "I sought for a man among them, that should make up the fence, and stand in the gap before Me for the land" (Ezek. 22: 30). Is the reader concerned that no one else in the local church, the town, or the district seems burdened with the need of revival? Does the situation seem beyond hope? Give the Lord the channel of a thirsty soul, and there is no limit to what He may do. God is looking for a man, a woman, to stand in the gap; will you be that one?

I believe this gracious movement of the Holy Spirit—The Lewis Awakening in 1949—began in a prayer burden; indeed there is no doubt about that. It began in a small group who were really burdened. They entered into a covenant with God that they would "give Him no rest until He had made Jerusalem a praise in the earth". They waited. The months passed, and nothing happened, until one young man took up his Bible and read from Psalm 24: "Who shall stand in His holy place? He that hath clean hands and a pure heart . . . He shall receive the blessing from the Lord." The young man closed the Bible and, looking at his companions on their knees before God, he cried: "Brethren, it is just so much humbug to be waiting thus night after night, month after month, if we ourselves are not right with God. I must ask myself—'Is my heart pure? Are my hands clean?'"

DUNCAN CAMPBELL.

## CHAPTER NINE

# LIFTING UP HOLY HANDS

"I desire therefore that the men pray in every place, lifting up
holy hands without wrath and disputing" (1 Tim. 2: 8).

SINCE revival is the product of prevailing prayer, let us first
of all be quite clear as to what prevailing prayer is, and then
examine *the basic factors* which condition our approach to
God.

## Prevailing Prayer

Jacob's encounter with God at Peniel is the first instance in
which a man was said to prevail with God. "Let me go," said
the Stranger to Jacob, "for the day breaketh. And he said, I will
not let thee go, except thou bless me." Here was a man determined to be blessed, and he was blessed. "Thy name shall be
called no more Jacob, but Israel: for thou has striven with God
and with men, and hast prevailed. . . . And He blessed him
there" (Gen. 32: 24–30). Jacob prevailed with God because he
obtained from God the blessing he sought.

Prayer is a comprehensive word, and we may rightly think of
it in terms of communion, worship, thanksgiving, praise, confession and so forth. But here we are concerned with that aspect
of prayer that Scripture calls petition, supplication, or intercession. The great prayer promises are mostly related to this
aspect, and how definite they are:— "It shall be done for them"
(Matt. 18: 19); "ye shall have" (Mark 11: 24); "it shall be given
you" (Luke 11: 9); "that will I do" (John 14: 14); "it shall be
done unto you" (John 15: 7); "He will give it you" (John 16: 23);
"ye shall receive" (John 16: 24). James says, "Ye have not because ye ask not. Ye ask, and receive not, because ye ask amiss"
(Jas. 4: 2, 3). These and many similar passages confirm that it is
both the desire and intention of God that His children should
not only ask, but obtain what they ask; and if they are not obtaining, the purpose of God in their asking has not been fulfilled.
May this fact be as indelibly printed on every heart, as it is on

the pages of His word—God desires us to prevail in prayer. "Let us therefore draw near with boldness unto the throne of grace, *that we may receive* . . ." (Heb. 4: 16).

The expression "praying through", although not found in Scripture, is sometimes used for prevailing with God, and emphasizes an important aspect of the subject. It has been defined as "praying one's way into full faith, emerging while yet praying into the assurance that one has been accepted and heard, so that one becomes actually aware of receiving, by firmest anticipation, and in advance of the event, the thing for which one asks". This throws light on the paradox of Mark 11: 24, "All things whatsoever ye pray and ask for, *believe that ye have received* them, and ye shall have them." When in prayer we are brought to that point of faith where we believe that we have received, in spite of there being nothing outward to confirm it, then we have prevailed with God, or "prayed through". To continue in prayer for that object will now seem the height of folly and unbelief, since the heart is assured that the decree granting the request has gone forth from the throne, and will shortly be fulfilled.

In Hannah's prayer for a son Scripture gives us a clear example of "praying through". "She was in bitterness of soul, and prayed unto the Lord, and wept sore" (1 Sam. 1: 10), but when Eli said to her, "Go in peace: and the God of Israel grant thy petition" (verse 17), she received the assurance that she had been accepted and heard. When Hannah believed that she had prevailed with God, she wiped her tears and prayed no more. "So the woman went her way, and did eat, and her countenance was no more sad . . . and the Lord remembered her. And it came to pass, when the time was come about, that Hannah conceived, and bare a son; and she called his name Samuel, saying, Because I have asked him of the Lord" (verses 18–20).

This assurance of having "prayed through" before the answer is actually given is not essential in order to prevail with God. According to our definition we prevail whenever we obtain what we ask, and in many cases there is no assurance of having been heard until our eyes see the fulfilment of our prayers. It was thus with the release of Peter from prison, when "prayer was made earnestly of the church unto God for him" (Acts 12: 5). These prayers prevailed with God, and an angel was sent to bring him out. But when Peter knocked at the house of Mary, the mother of John Mark, the saints were still on their knees, and refused to believe the word of Rhoda "that Peter stood before the gate". If they had been praying in unbelief they could hardly have prevailed, for it is said of the doubter, "let not that man think that he shall receive anything of the Lord" (Jas. 1 : 6, 7). Perhaps in their desire to "continue steadfastly in prayer" they had forgotten the necessity of "watching therein with thanksgiving" (Col. 4 : 2). Be that as it may, one thing is clear, they prevailed with God without having any prior assurance of it. They knew not that they had been heard until Peter presented himself at the house.

When believers have an intolerable burden upon them so that they pray with strong crying and tears, and with groanings which cannot be uttered, as is often the case preceding a revival, it is very common for such intercessors to know beforehand that they have prevailed. A striking case of this is given by Charles Finney : "The first ray of light that broke in upon the midnight which rested on the churches in Oneida County, in the fall of 1825, was from a woman in feeble health who, I believe, had never been in a powerful revival. Her soul was exercised about sinners. She was in an agony for the land. She did not know what ailed her, but she kept praying more and more, till it seemed as if her agony would destroy her body. At length she became full of joy, and exclaimed, 'God has come ! God has come ! There is no mistake about it, the work is begun, and is going all over the region.' And sure enough, the work began, and her family were almost all converted, and the work spread all over that part of the country. Now do you think that woman was deceived? I tell you, no. She knew she had prevailed with God in prayer. She had travailed in birth for souls, and she knew it" (*Lecture II on Revivals of Religion*).

Praying through should ever be our objective, but God may permit us to see the answer before we are conscious of having prevailed. To prevail with God for revival is to "seek the Lord until He come" in revival blessing, whether that coming is, at first, only in the conviction of our hearts, as in the above case; or whether it be straightway in the full manifestation of divine power.

Alas, not all who pray, though their prayers be fervent and prolonged, succeed in prevailing with God. Of Moab we read, "when he wearieth himself upon the high place, and shall come

to his sanctuary to pray, that he shall not prevail" (Isa. 16: 12).
And the reason was not because Moab was outside the elect race
of Israel, but because God had seen "the pride of Moab, that he is
very proud" (verse 6). There are many such hindrances which
are set forth in Scripture as specific reasons for unanswered
prayer. It is these basic factors in our approach to God that must
now be considered.

## The All-Inclusive Condition

When David asked the question, "Who shall ascend into the
hill of the Lord? And who shall stand in His holy place?"—
and answered it by declaring, "He that hath clean hands, and
a pure heart" (Ps. 24: 3), he set before us the all-inclusive condition of our approach to God. This is true in all aspects of
prayer, but especially in that of intercession. He whose hands are
clean and whose heart is pure has fulfilled all the basic conditions
of prevailing prayer; he is a righteous man, and "the supplication
of a righteous man has much strength [to prevail] in its working"
(Jas. 5: 16 lit. trans.). To intercede is to plead in the court of
heaven against our adversary the Devil, to say with the widow in the
parable, "Do me justice of mine adversary" (Luke 18: 3, margin).
But that adversary is also in the court to oppose us as "the accuser
of [the] brethren" (Rev. 12: 10), and any unrighteousness he can
find in us will strengthen his case against us, and must lead to our
defeat. "The Judge of all the earth" cannot vindicate a law-
breaker, therefore the suppliant, if he would win his suit, must
have a case which bears investigation. The strength of his appeal
must lie in the fact that he has righteousness on his side. "The
eyes of the Lord are toward the righteous, and His ears are open
unto their cry" (Ps. 34: 15).

Who are the righteous? Who are the pure in heart? Only those
who have in repentance turned from their sin, abandoned their
own righteousness, and in faith subjected themselves to the righteousness of God (Rom. 10: 3–4). None other is deemed righteous by the great Judge, and none other has any right of appeal
whatsoever in the court of heaven. This however is not all. The
saving work of Christ in the believer is the ground, but not the
guarantee of heart purity. In other words, being born again does
not necessarily ensure that our hands are clean and our hearts

pure, in the sense of this passage. We may be true believers and yet not be qualified to "ascend into the hill of the Lord" as effective intercessors. Lot is described as "that righteous man" (2 Pet. 2: 8), but he had not the righteousness of the intercessor, and when God sought for a man to stand in the gap for Sodom that He might not destroy it, He had to turn to Abraham. It is worthy of note that Abraham did far more for Sodom from without than Lot ever did from within. The righteousness of the intercessor is not merely that which is *imputed*, or put to our account, when we believe (Rom. 3: 21–28), but that which is *imparted* and manifested in a holy life. This is the righteousness that a believer must seek (Matt. 6: 33), and after which he must hunger and thirst (Matt. 5: 6), to prevail as an intercessor. This necessarily involves an honest dealing with all in the life that is contrary to the righteousness of God, especially those unrighteousnesses that are specifically stated in Scripture to hinder prayer.

## Sin

Harbouring in the life that which we instinctively know to be sin will effectively prevent us praying through to God. "If I regard [or countenance] iniquity in my heart, the Lord will not hear" (Ps. 66: 18). All fellowship with God is rendered impossible by unjudged sin. This is obvious the moment we consider His character. "God is light, and in Him is no darkness at all. If we say that we have fellowship with Him, and walk in the darkness, we lie, and do not the truth" (1 John 1: 5). It was to the Lord's people that Isaiah had to say, "Your iniquities have separated between you and your God, and your sins have hid His face from you, that He will not hear" (Isa. 59: 2). The hands that are lifted up in the hill of the Lord must needs be "holy hands", lest God should have to say as He did to His ancient people, "When ye spread forth your hands, I will hide Mine eyes from you: yea, when ye make many prayers, I will not hear: your hands are full of blood" (Isa. 1: 15). But the situation was one they could remedy, and so the message continued, "Wash you, make you clean; put away the evil of your doings from before Mine eyes" (verse 16). The blood to cleanse and the water to sanctify are available today, and may be applied by confession and faith (1 John 1: 9; Acts 26: 18).

Is there one reading these lines with some sin of thought, word, or deed upon the conscience? Make no pretence of praying until that sin has been confessed and repented of, for God says, "Bring no more vain oblations; [your] incense is an abomination unto Me" (Isa. 1: 13). Such prayers are not only ineffective, they are an insult to the throne of God's holiness—an insult far greater than that of an earthly subject who appears in the august presence of his sovereign in torn or dirty clothes; or who, on being introduced, should stretch out a filthy hand. James was addressing Christians when he said, "Cleanse your hands, ye sinners; and purify your hearts, ye double-minded" (Jas. 4: 8).

### Idolatry

In addition to general sins and iniquities, there are some specific sins that are specially mentioned in Scripture as barriers to prevailing prayer, and these must be carefully watched. One is idolatry. Of some of the elders of Israel God had to say, "These men have taken their idols into their heart . . . should I be inquired of at all by them?" (Ezek. 14: 3). God will resolutely turn His face from the prayers of all who cherish idols in their hearts. In the very postures commonly adopted in prayer, the bowing of the head or the bending of the knee, the sovereignty of God is acknowledged. To submit to this proper relationship between the Sovereign and the suppliant is the foundation of all prayer. Idolatry, however, denies this very thing. How can we expect the One Whom we are commanded to love with all our heart, soul, mind, and strength, to grant our petitions when He sees in our hearts that which rivals His supremacy? Would a sovereign grant the petition of a subject he knew to be disloyal? Would a lover release her treasures to a beloved who she had discovered secretly cherished another more than her? Let us remember as we pray, "all things are naked and laid open before the eyes of Him with whom we have to do" (Heb. 4: 13). "Who [then] shall ascend into the hill of the Lord . . .? He that hath a pure heart"—cleansed from the pollutions of idols.

> Lord, I come to Thee for rest,
> Take possession of my breast.
> There Thy blood-bought right maintain,
> And without a rival reign.
>
> J. NEWTON.

An idol may be defined as any person or thing that has usurped in the heart the place of pre-eminence that belongs to the Lord. When a relationship with a friend or loved one is causing the spiritual life to wane we may suspect that that one has become an idol. When we are seeking first our business interests and vainly supposing that God will add to us the things of His kingdom, when in fact we are more concerned and anxious about material prosperity than spiritual prosperity, we should examine ourselves as to whether we are not joined to idols. When our homes and families become the be-all and end-all, and we are prepared to make a spiritual compromise to please them; when some pastime or recreational interest is our absorbing passion; when we are more concerned about our outward appearance than the state of our hearts; when our minds are perpetually full of some material possession or some human ambition, are we not as guilty of idolatry as any Israelite who bowed the knee to Baal? "What agreement hath a temple of God with idols?" (2 Cor. 6: 16).

> The dearest idol I have known,
>   What'er that idol be,
> Help me to tear it from Thy throne,
> And worship only Thee.
>                    W. COWPER.

It is true that where idols are detected they must be ruthlessly exterminated; but since prevention is better than cure it is vital to heed the exhortation, "guard yourselves from idols" (1 John 5: 21). A sure preventative is to maintain at all times the freshness of our "first love" toward the Saviour; to have, like Count Zinzendorf of Moravia, but "one passion—Jesus, Jesus only"; to cultivate His continual presence and live always in the sunshine of His smile. For as idolatry is an insuperable obstacle to prevailing prayer, just so is a personal, all-absorbing passion for Christ a mighty factor in praying through. "Delight thyself also in the Lord; and He shall give thee the petitions of thine heart" (Ps. 37: 4). Of the one who dwells in the secret place of the most High the Lord says, "Because he hath set his love upon Me . . . he shall call upon Me, and I will answer him" (Ps. 91: 14, 15). All the great intercessors of the Bible have been characterized by this intensity of devotion to the Lord. It was so with Abraham, "the friend of God"; Moses, "whom the Lord knew face to face";

David, the man after God's own heart; Daniel, the man greatly beloved; and Paul, who suffered the loss of all things and counted them as refuse that he might win Christ. No wonder they were princes who prevailed with God.

## An Unforgiving Spirit

Here is a common obstacle to prevailing prayer. Christ said, "Whensoever ye stand praying, forgive, if ye have aught against any one; that your Father also . . . may forgive you" (Mark 11:25). In the pattern prayer of the Lord, the fact that "we have forgiven our debtors" is cited as a ground upon which we ask God to "forgive us our debts" (Matt. 6:12). At the conclusion of the prayer the Lord further showed that the reverse was also true, that if we did not forgive we should not be forgiven. There are clearly two aspects of forgiveness in the New Testament, and they need to be distinguished. Failure to do this leads to confusion, and to the harmful theory that the teachings of Christ in the Gospels do not apply to this age (see Matt. 7:26; 28:20).

There is the initial forgiveness of the sinner, and there is the conditional forgiveness of the saint. The former is for ever ours when we repent and believe the gospel: "Repent ye and be baptized . . . unto the remission of your sins" (Acts 2:38; 3:19; 13:38, etc.). This, accompanied as it is by the new birth, brings the sinner into that relationship with God of Father and child. From then on conditional forgiveness applies. As children of God our fellowship with the Father is possible only as the sins we commit are confessed and thereupon forgiven (1 John 1:9). Where a believer does not confess he is not forgiven, though he is still a child of his Heavenly Father. A child who refuses to acknowledge his wrongdoing forfeits his father's forgiveness, ceases to enjoy his fellowship, and may, if he persists in his course, be disinherited, but he does not cease to be his child. He cannot be *un*-born. So it is in the spiritual relationship. This forfeiting of forgiveness concerns only those whose relationship to God is that of Father and child, as Christ showed when He said, "neither will *your heavenly Father* forgive you. . . ." While we regard the iniquity of an unforgiving spirit in our hearts, how can the Lord hear our confession of other sins, and bestow the forgiveness that we refuse to another? (see Matt. 18:21-35). "With what measure ye mete it shall be measured unto you" (Matt. 7: 2).

The importance of this teaching in relation to prevailing prayer cannot be over-emphasized. Many a time a bitter spirit maintained by one Christian towards another has been like a great dam holding back the river of blessing; only when the one concerned was broken down by the Spirit of God were the sluice-gates of blessing opened. The famous "four points" which Evan Roberts believed conditioned the outpouring of the Spirit were : (1) Dealing with unconfessed sin. (2) Dealing with doubtful things. (3) Implicit obedience to the Spirit. (4) Public confession of Christ. Under the second point he would commonly say: "Have you forgiven everybody, *everybody*, EVERYBODY? If not, don't expect forgiveness of your own sins. You won't get it."

## Sins of Omission

These are obvious hindrances to prevailing prayer. "Beloved, if our heart condemn us not, we have boldness toward God; and whatsoever we ask, we receive of Him, because we keep His commandments, and do the things that are pleasing in His sight" (1 John 3: 21, 22). Have we an uncondemned conscience concerning the things that God has commanded us to do? Have we kept His commandments? How can we stand before the throne with that boldness which prevails with God if our conscience is accusing us of disobedience? The particular command that the apostle has in mind here is that of loving one another in a practical way, for he has just said, "Whoso hath the world's goods, and beholdeth his brother in need, and shutteth up his compassion from him, how doth the love of God abide in him? My little children, let us not love in word, neither with the tongue; but in deed and truth" (verses 17, 18).

Failure to obey the supreme command of Christ to "love one another", and to do it "in deed and truth", and "out of a pure heart fervently", is an obvious cause of failure in prayer. This is even taught in the Old Testament. According to the law our whole duty manward is contained in the precept, "Thou shalt love thy neighbour as thyself"; but Solomon reminds us that, "He that turneth away his ear from hearing the law, even his prayer is an abomination" (Prov. 28: 9). Love cannot do other than minister to the needs of others according to its ability. "God so loved . . . that He gave." Believers who are mean and close with that which God has given them when there is need all around them, and the work of God is retrenching in many lands through lack of support, need not look far to see why their prayers do not prevail. "Whoso stoppeth his ears at the cry of the poor, he also shall cry, but shall not be heard." (Prov. 21: 13; see also Isa. 58: 7–9). After George Müller's death it was discovered that he had during his life given away, out of personal gifts designated to him, £81,490. He left £60, plus the value of his books and furniture, estimated at £100. Such sacrificial giving had without doubt a direct bearing on the extraordinary power he possessed to prevail with God in prayer.

Another common sin of omission relates to vows. "When thou vowest a vow unto God, defer not to pay it; for He hath no pleasure in fools: pay that which thou vowest" (Eccles. 5: 4). If we have made a vow to God and have not fulfilled it; if we promised that we would do something, and have not done it, we need not expect to prevail in prayer. As well may a man who has persistently refused to pay his just debts go to his creditor and ask for further credit. The hands we lift up in the sanctuary are not holy hands unless they have fulfilled the promises and vows our lips have uttered. A vow performed, however, gives us power with God. It is said of the Egyptians, in a day yet future, they "shall vow a vow unto the Lord, and shall perform it . . . and He shall be intreated of them, and shall heal them" (Isa. 19: 21, 22). And again, "Pay thy vows unto the Most High: and call upon Me in the day of trouble; I will deliver thee, and thou shalt glorify Me" (Ps. 50: 14; also 65: 1, 2). It was when Jonah said, "I will pay that which I have vowed" (Jonah 2: 9, 10), that his prayer prevailed, and he was delivered from the belly of the fish.

There are many other things that could be dealt with under this heading. Some of them are not covered by specific commands, but conscience tells us that they are among the "things that are pleasing in His sight" which we have failed to do. Let us put them right now if we would prevail in prayer.

## Unchristlike Relationships

These, especially between husband and wife, may be a serious hindrance to prevailing prayer. Husbands are commanded, "Dwell with your wives according to knowledge, giving honour unto the woman, as unto the weaker vessel, as being also joint-heirs of the grace of life; to the end that *your prayers be not hindered*" (1 Pet. 3: 7). Where a husband fails to show that due tenderness and consideration and unselfishness for the weaker vessel, or where the wife fails in her duty towards her husband, which is that "she doeth him good and not evil all the days of her life", and "the law of kindness is on her tongue" (Prov. 31: 12, 26), effective intercession will be greatly hindered. Failure on the part of either or both to see that the most intimate matters of their married life are pleasing before His all-seeing eyes and stamped with "holiness unto the Lord", may effectively prevent · their prevailing with God.

## Impure Motives

Whatever form our praying takes, if it be worship, confession, supplication, or intercession, it is vital that we "draw near with a true heart" (Heb. 10: 22), that is, in absolute sincerity, if we would really touch the throne. James speaks of two reasons why "ye have not" : firstly, "because ye ask not"; and secondly, "because ye ask amiss, that ye may spend it in your pleasures" (4: 2, 3); in other words, the motive in asking is selfish. When the motive in prayer is the satisfying of our own desires and pleasures, or when we desire the Almighty to pander to our own pride and love of reputation, or to act for our own convenience, the motive is clearly unholy, and God cannot and will not fulfil our petitions.

It is possible to pray for a right thing with a wrong motive. It is certainly pleasing to God that we plead for revival, but our prayer for revival may be displeasing to God because the motive is wrong. It is vital to examine our hearts on this matter. Let us pause a moment and ask ourselves, "Why do I want revival? How much does my own personal gain figure in my thinking and praying for it?" R. A. Torrey wrote in this connection, "Many prayers for revival are purely selfish. The churches desire revivals

in order that the membership may be increased, in order that the
church may have a position of more power and influence in the
community, in order that the church treasury may be filled, in
order that a good report may be made at the presbytery, or conference, or association. For such low purposes as these, churches
and ministers oftentimes are praying for a revival, and oftentimes,
too, God does not answer the prayer. Why should we pray for a
revival? For the glory of God, because we cannot endure it that
God should continue to be dishonoured by the worldliness of the
church, by the sins of unbelievers, by the proud unbelief of the
day, because God's word is being made void; in order that God
may be glorified by the outpouring of His Spirit on the church
of Christ."

Among those who seek God for revival, there may be few
who are, from the outset, wholly free from the admixture of selfish
motives in their petitions. This need not deter or discourage if
this condition of prevailing prayer is kept constantly in view.
When we are aware of being moved by anything less than a desire
for the supreme glory of God, let us avail ourselves of the cleansing of the blood by confession, and look to God in faith that He
may by the Spirit bring "every thought into captivity to the
obedience of Christ" (2 Cor. 10: 5). God uses the very activities
and heart exercises of prayer to effect this.

The diaries of David Brainerd, whose prayers and labours
brought revival in 1745 to the American Indians to whom he had
been sent, contain this entry: "I was wholly free from selfish
ends in my supplications for the poor Indians. . . . All my
cares, fears, and desires disappeared, and were of little more
importance than a puff of wind. I longed that God would get to
Himself a name among the heathen, and I appealed to Him with
the greatest freedom that He knew I 'preferred Him above my
chief joy'." Such selfless pleading is irresistible in the courts of
heaven. There is prevailing power in our intercessions when we
can pray with the sincerity of David, who said, "Give ear unto
my prayer, that goeth not out of feigned lips" (Ps. 17: 1); and
when we can truly append this desire to our petitions, "that the
Father may be glorified in the Son" (John 14: 13).

In view of the desperate need of revival, are we willing to
draw near to God and plead for this great thing? If so, we must
continually remember the way of approach that God has en-

joined. The priest of old, as he drew near to the sanctuary, came first to the altar, red with the blood of sprinkling, and then to the laver with its pure water. The altar would remind him that in approaching God the conscience must be purged from the guilt of sin, while the water, for the washing of his body, would speak of the cleansing of the outer life—the action of the Spirit applying the word, and effecting obedience to it in the life. This is "the washing of water [the Spirit] with the word" (Eph. 5: 26) to which the Psalmist also referred when he said, "Wherewithal shall a young man cleanse his way? By taking heed thereto according to Thy word" (Ps. 119: 9). Both the blood and the water would seem to cry out, "Be ye clean, ye that bear the vessels of the Lord" (Isa. 52: 11). So with us, only clean hands and a pure heart can qualify us for the sanctuary, and these necessitate the continual application of blood and water. "Purge me with hyssop [the blood], and I shall be clean : wash me [the water], and I shall be whiter than snow" (Ps. 51: 7).

> Let the water and the blood,
> From Thy riven side which flowed,
> Be of sin the double cure,
> Cleanse me from its guilt and power.
>                     A. M. TOPLADY.

The way into the holiest is open. The need of the hour is true intercessors. The goal of revival beckons us. "Let us draw near with a true heart in fulness of faith, having our hearts sprinkled [with the blood] from an evil conscience, and our body washed with pure water" (Heb. 10: 22).

When the glory of the Father
Is the goal of every prayer :
When before the throne in heaven
Our High Priest presents it there;
When the Spirit prompts the asking,
When the waiting heart believes :
Then we know of each petition
Everyone who asks receives.

AUTHOR UNKNOWN.

CHAPTER TEN

# THE DYNAMICS OF PRAYER

"Thou hast wrestled with God . . . and hast prevailed"
(Gen. 32: 28, Darby).

FROM the basic factors which condition our approach to God we now come to *the working factors*, the dynamics of prevailing prayer. These are the operations of mind and heart which give force to our praying. These are the conditions of prayer to which God has pledged Himself to respond.

> But there's a power which man can wield
>     When mortal aid is vain,
> That eye, that arm, that love to reach,
>     That listening ear to gain.
>
> That power is prayer, which soars on high,
>     Through Jesus to the throne,
> And moves the hand which moves the world,
>     To bring salvation down.
>                     J. A. WALLACE.

These principles are closely related to those just considered, for the state of one's heart in approaching God will largely determine the working of one's heart in the exercise of prayer. The New Testament contains six principles, and any one of them, if obeyed, will ensure that the prayer prevails. The first requires that we pray—

## In the Position of Abiding

"If ye abide in Me, and My words abide in you, ask whatsoever ye will, and it shall be done unto you" (John 15: 7). In the previous chapter the Lord Jesus had told the disciples that the Holy Spirit would come to them. "In that day," He said, "ye shall know that I am in my Father, and ye in Me, and I in you" (14: 20). In other words, the Spirit would reveal to them the true significance of the Son being "in the Father", and that they

139

were similarly in Him, and He in them. What He meant by being "in the Father" is fully unfolded throughout the gospel of John. The Father was His whole source and sphere of life. He had not come of Himself, but had been sent by the Father (John 7: 28; 8: 42). He had no teaching or words of His own, but spoke the words given Him by the Father (John 7: 16, etc.). He could do nothing of Himself, only what He saw the Father doing (John 5: 19). His very life depended on the Father (John 6: 57). He ever sought, not His own will or glory, but the Father's (John 5: 30; 8: 49). Because He chose to be limited by the Father's will, dependent on the Father's resources, seeking the Father's glory, He could truly declare, "I am in My Father".

To abide in Christ is to maintain in principle the same relationship towards Him that He maintained towards the Father. "He that saith he abideth in Him ought himself also to walk even as He walked" (1 John 2: 6). This means firstly, *a life of submission* in which we gladly consent to the limitations of "that good and acceptable and perfect will of God". We accept a bondage which we find to be perfect freedom. We pray, "Make me a captive Lord, and then I shall be free." This was truly His life who said, "I delight to do Thy will, O my God" (Ps. 40: 8); and again, "My meat is to do the will of Him that sent Me" (John 4: 34). It must be ours also if we would abide.

Then it must be also *a life of renunciation* of ourselves, our abilities, our resources. We have to come to the place of weakness and emptiness that His strength may be made perfect in us. This is the place of abiding. He is the vine, we are the branches. The vine has everything, the branch has nothing. "As the branch cannot bear fruit of itself . . . so neither can ye" (John 15: 4). This fact, obvious to the mind, does not easily sink down into the heart. Through the bitter experiences of failure we have to learn the lesson. Hudson Taylor said that when God decided to evangelize Inland China, He looked around to find a man who was *weak enough* for Him to use. The attitude of self-renunciation characterized the life of the Saviour. "The Son can do nothing of Himself" (John 5: 19, 30); "My teaching is not Mine" (John 7: 16); "neither have I come of Myself" (John 8: 42). We are called to follow Him. "Whosoever he be of you that renounceth not all that he hath, he cannot be My disciple" (Luke 14: 33).

Finally, abiding involves *a life of faith* which looks to Christ

for all, and finds its all-sufficiency in Him. Alongside the statement of Christ, "Apart from Me ye can do nothing" (John 15: 5),
we must put Paul's triumphant declaration, "I can do all things
in Him that strengtheneth me" (Phil. 4: 13). The Saviour revealed that His was a life of faith in dependence on the Father,
when He said, "I live because of the Father" (John 6: 57). But
He also declared, "Because I live ye shall live also" (John 14: 19),
and this requires the same attitude of faith that possessed Him.
Paul set forth the true life of renunciation and of faith when He
said, "I live; and yet *no longer I*, but Christ liveth in me . . . I live
by faith, the faith of the Son of God [Darby], who loved *me*, and
gave Himself up for me" (Gal. 2: 20). This is truly the abiding
life.

As well as abiding in Him, the condition requires that *His
words* abide in us. These He had earlier described as "spirit and
life" (John 6: 63), that is full of divine energy and life-giving
power. It is impossible to embrace those life-giving words without experiencing their spiritual and moral force. Christ had to
say of some, "My word hath not free course in you" (John 8: 37).
They rejected both Him and His message, to their own eternal
disaster. Others accepted the message joyfully, but did not allow
it to root fully in their hearts, so that the new growth withered
in the hour of persecution; or they allowed it to be choked by
worldly cares, and so to become unfruitful. These received the
word, but did not allow it to abide in them. There were those,
however, who allowed His word to make its home in their hearts,
to take deep root, and to spring up in spiritual fruitfulness. "They
have kept Thy word," He said of them to the Father (John 17: 6).
His words had already begun to abide in them, doing their quickening and fertilizing work.

There may be different grades or degrees of abiding, according
to our spiritual understanding and development. The principle,
however, does not change. When we can say from the heart, "To
me to live—Christ" (Phil. 1: 21), we are surely abiding in Him,
and this gives us a position of authority with God in prayer. So
long as we fulfil the condition, as it is revealed to us, the Lord
is pledged to answer whatever prayer we offer. So long as we
abide in Christ and His words abide in us, He can safely trust us
with a blank cheque drawn on the bank of heaven. "Ask whatsoever ye will, and it shall be done unto you."

In His holy humanity the Saviour's prayers were never refused by God, because He was ever abiding in the Father. "Father," He prayed, "I thank Thee that Thou heardest Me. And I knew that Thou hearest Me always" (John 11: 41). Seeking neither His own will nor His own glory, but ever the Father's, He had only to ask in order to receive. We shall be trusted in the same way when we fulfil the same condition. When the Father knows that it will be in His interests and for His glory that a certain petition is fulfilled, He cannot but respond to it. Such petitions ever flow from the life that abides in Christ. This suggests our next great condition of prevailing prayer. It must be—

### In the Will of God

"And this is the boldness which we have toward Him, that, if we ask anything according to His will, He heareth us: and if we know that He heareth us whatsoever we ask, we know that we have the petitions which we have asked of Him" (1 John 5: 14, 15). Notice that this verse is designed to give us a holy confidence before God, "this is the boldness which we have". Sometimes when a believer prays with boldness he is reproved by another, and reminded that he can only receive if it is God's will, and that he should pray with submission. The use that some make of this verse, always tacking on to their petitions, "if it be Thy will", would make the promise read, "This is the uncertainty that we have towards Him, that only if we should happen to pray according to His will is He at all likely to hear us." Thus would they make this word, given for the strengthening of their faith, a refuge for their unbelief.

Now notice the phrase, "anything according to His will". "Anything" gives the wonderful scope of the promise; "according to His will" gives the divine limitation. Someone has well said that nothing is beyond the reach of prayer, save that which lies outside the will of God. Prevailing prayer therefore involves a knowledge of the will of God. Then comes the assurance, "He heareth us." According to Scripture usage, for God to *hear* our prayer is for Him to accept it and fulfil the petition. To speak of God "hearing and answering prayer" is mere tautology. If God hears, He answers; if He does not answer, then He does not hear. "And if we know that He heareth us whatsoever we ask, we know that we have the petitions which we have asked of Him" (verse 15). "And if" shows that verse 15 is additional as well as conditional. We may pray according to God's will and so prevail without verse 15, without knowing that He has heard us or having the prior assurance that we have prevailed, until the answer comes. But where we have this assurance that He is hearing, where in fact we have "prayed through", we know we have in the purpose of God received the answer, and the petition will be fulfilled.

The vital condition, then, is that our petition is *in the will of God*. Is it possible to discover His will in the matters we bring before Him in prayer? There is much general praying we may do, viz. "for all men; for kings and all that are in high place" (1 Tim. 2: 1), where we may not know God's will, and yet do right to pray. But in the specific petitions that we offer, especially concerning ourselves, we have every reason to expect to know God's will. "Wherefore be ye not foolish, but understanding what the will of the Lord is" (Eph. 5: 17), "that ye may be filled with the knowledge of His will in all spiritual wisdom and understanding" (Col. 1: 9), "but be ye transformed by the renewing of your mind, that ye may prove what is the good and acceptable and perfect will of God" (Rom. 12: 2). But how may we know the will of God concerning our petitions?

*The word of God* may teach us His will. There are things for which we pray that are plainly revealed in Scripture to be His will for us. If we pray for holiness we may be sure that we pray according to His will because He has commanded us to be holy (1 Pet. 1: 15, 16), and because "this is the will of God, even your sanctification" (1 Thess. 4: 3). Are we praying for wisdom? "God . . . giveth to all liberally and upbraideth not" (Jas. 1: 5). Are we asking for the power and gifts of the Spirit? "How much more shall your heavenly Father give [the good things of] the Holy Spirit to them that ask Him" (Matt. 7: 11; Luke 11: 13). But what of revival? It has already been shown in chapter three that the promises in Scripture which reveal God's willingness to send revival are legion. Let us take them out of the show-case and turn them into fuel for prayer.

We may also be taught the will of God by *the operation of the Spirit* in our hearts. "And in like manner the Spirit joins also His help to our weakness; for we do not know what we should

pray for as is fitting, but the Spirit Himself makes intercession
with groanings which cannot be uttered. But He [God, Jer.
17: 10] Who searches the hearts knows what is the mind of the
Spirit, because He intercedes for saints according to [the will of]
God" (Rom. 8: 26, 27, Darby). Christ's intercession for the believer is effected apart from him. The Spirit's intercession for the
believer is effected through him. Verse 23 states that *we* groan,
verse 26 that He groans, but these are not two groanings but
one. Are you in ignorance of how and what to pray? You have
One within, "if so be that the Spirit of God dwelleth in you,"
who has perfect knowledge of the divine will, faultless intercom-
munication with the Father, and His almighty power in intercession is limited only by your own degree of preparation and
willingness and capacity for prayer. He is the gracious Paraclete
(Comforter), that is, the Advocate called to our side to present
our case and plead our cause in the courts of heaven. Let us allow
Him full play. Let us give Him opportunity to lead us, burden us,
and strengthen us, if we would pray according to God's will and
prevail.

It must ever be remembered that knowing the will of God
involves a heart in full submission to that will, whatever it may
be. "If any man willeth to do His will, he shall know . . ."
(John 7: 17). Secondly, it involves a patient waiting upon God in
prayer that the Spirit may enlighten us. We have to pray with
David, "Show me Thy ways, O Lord; teach me Thy paths. Guide
me in Thy truth, and teach me . . . on Thee do I *wait* all the
day" (Ps. 25: 4). The testimony of one of the greatest prayer
warriors of modern times illustrates the importance of these two
features, the willing heart and the waiting heart, in discerning the
will of God. After seven weeks of patient waiting upon God
regarding the building of two additional houses for his orphan-
age at a cost of about £50,000, George Müller of Bristol wrote:

"I have still day by day been enabled to wait upon the Lord
with reference to enlarging the orphan work, and have been during the whole of this period in perfect peace, which is the result
of seeking in this thing only the Lord's honour and the temporal
and spiritual benefit of my fellow-men. Without an effort could
I by His grace put aside all thoughts about this whole affair, if
only assured that it is the will of God that I should do so; and, on
the other hand, would at once go forward, if He would have it be

so. . . . After having for months pondered the matter, and having looked at it in all its bearings and with all its difficulties, and then having been finally led, after much prayer, to decide on this enlargement, my mind is at peace" (from *A Narrative of the Lord's Dealings with George Müller*). Thus may we also, by patient waiting upon God, pray our way through into the assurance of His will. This is the place of faith, which leads us to the next great principle. . . . Prayer to prevail must be—

## In Faith

"Jesus . . . saith . . . Have faith in God. Verily I say unto you, Whosoever shall say unto this mountain, Be thou taken up and cast into the sea; and shall not doubt in his heart, but shall believe that what he saith cometh to pass; he shall have it. Therefore I say unto you, All things whatsoever ye pray and ask for, believe that ye *have received* them, and ye shall have them" (Mark 11: 22–24; see also Matt. 21: 21, 22). "If ye have faith . . . nothing shall be impossible unto you" (Matt. 17: 20). "Let him ask in faith, nothing doubting" (Jas. 1: 6).

The faith that operates in prayer is not an uncanny "knack" or mysterious faculty which some saints have, but which it is not given to the rest to possess. "Have faith in God" is a command of Jesus Christ, and as such we are expected to obey it (Matt. 28: 20). The One Who commands us to believe is the One Who enables us to believe. Faith, however, cannot be worked up. No mere decision of the will can produce it. It is necessary to understand and obey the laws by which faith operates.

*The basis of faith* is a right heart condition before God. The deadliest enemy to faith in the heart is pride. This is a common reason for a weak faith, especially pride in spiritual things. A concern about our reputation in the eyes of men, rather than in the eyes of God; a jealous desire to guard our position, rights or dignity, though it be at the expense of the Lord's, may effectually destroy the spirit of faith in the heart. "How can ye believe, which receive glory one of another, and the glory that cometh from the only God ye seek not?" (John 5: 44). Effective faith in prayer is clearly impossible with such a heart condition.

It is deeply significant that the two who were commended by Christ in the Gospels for their outstanding faith were also outstanding for their humility. There was the centurion who said, "Lord, I am not worthy that Thou shouldest come under my roof," but of whom Christ said, "I have not found so great faith, no, not in Israel" (Matt. 8: 8–10); and there was the Canaanitish woman who alluded to herself when she said, "The dogs eat of the crumbs which fall from their master's table," to whom the Saviour said, "O woman, great is thy faith" (Matt. 15: 22–28). On another occasion when the apostles asked the Lord to increase their faith, He spoke of the servant ploughing, or feeding sheep, who had to learn to be humble as well as obedient towards his master. He concluded, "Even so ye also, when ye shall have done all the things that are commanded you, say, *We are unprofitable servants*; we have done that which it was our duty to do" (Luke 17: 5–10). An obedient humble heart is the first secret of the increase of faith.

Then *the instrument of faith* is the word of God, with its untold wealth of precious and exceeding great promises. It is the promises that quicken faith, and it is faith that apprehends the promises. We do not speak here of the gift of faith which is bestowed on a few (1 Cor. 12: 9; 13: 2), but the grace of faith which is open to all: all, that is, who are "the heirs of the promise" (Heb. 6: 17). Faith cannot look to God to do other than what He has promised. Since the very nature of faith is reckoning on the faithfulness of God, it is of necessity bounded by His promises. The faith of Abraham was just this, he "believed God" (Rom. 4: 3), believed that He meant what He said, and would fulfil it. "Looking unto the promise of God, he wavered not through unbelief, but waxed strong through faith, giving glory to God, and being fully assured that, *what He had promised*, He was able also to perform" (Rom. 4: 20). With his eyes fixed upon the promise of God, Abraham's faith grew strong, until at length it could cast aside even the mountain of physical impossibility, and grasp the promised blessing.

> Faith, mighty faith the promise sees
>     And looks to God alone,
> Laughs at impossibilities
>     And cries, "It shall be done."

"So faith then is by a report, but the report by God's word" (Rom. 10: 17, Darby). Faith grows exceedingly in the soul whose gaze is fixed upon the promises. Such faith is like the grain of mustard seed, so small in its beginnings, but containing within itself the life principle which can grow into something mighty under the quickening influence of the Spirit.

Finally there is *the exercise of faith,* even patience. The mark of a vital faith is that it endures. God desires that we may obtain the promises (Heb. 11: 33), but this requires a faith which has been purified and perfected through the exercise of patience. God is not only concerned that our praying should change things, but that it should change *us*; that through patient waiting upon Him our spiritual characters may be purified and deepened. God told Abraham that he would have an heir in his old age, a child of promise; but the years passed by and still there was no son. When the improbable had become the impossible, then Abraham's faith was made perfect, and he was certain that the promise would be fulfilled—and so it was. "And thus, *having patiently endured,* he obtained the promise" (Heb. 6: 15). But Abraham was not unique, for many have obtained in the same way. Let us then be "imitators of them who through *faith and patience* inherit the promises" (Heb. 6: 12).

"Believe that ye have received", is the Saviour's word to us, "and ye shall have." It is clear that during the waiting time Abraham believed that he had received, for the simple reason that he was "giving glory to God" in confident anticipation of the blessing. While still praying and waiting he was brought to the point of faith where he was as sure of the son that was to be given, as if he held the babe in his arms. To reach the same point should be our goal as we pray for revival. Referring to the outbreak of the awakening in Kilsyth, July 23rd, 1839, William Burns wrote : "Some of the people of God who had been longing and wrestling for a time of refreshing from the Lord's presence, and who had, during much of the previous night, been travailing in birth for souls, came to the meeting, not only with the hope, but with well-nigh the certain anticipation of God's glorious appearing." We cannot expect to reach this point without perseverance and patience. You may have prayed long and earnestly for revival. Your faith may have been sorely tried and tested. You may have been tempted to give up in despair. Hold on ! Hold on ! for He is faithful that promised. The very testing is effecting in you the will of God, and preparing you for the blessing. "Cast not away therefore your boldness, which hath great recompence of reward. For ye have need of patience, that, having done the will of God, ye may receive the promise" (Heb. 10: 35).

Then prevailing prayer must be also—

## In the Name of Christ

"And whatsoever ye shall ask in My Name, that will I do, that the Father may be glorified in the Son" (John 14: 13; other refs.: John 14: 14; 15: 16; 16: 23, 24, 26). There is an astonishing emphasis in the New Testament on the value and power of the Name of Christ. We call upon it for salvation (Rom. 10: 13); we are washed, sanctified, and justified in it (1 Cor. 6: 11); we are baptized into it (Acts 10: 48); and so come to hope in it (Matt. 12: 21). Further, in that Name we should meet together (Matt. 18: 20), give thanks (Eph. 5: 20), pray (John 14: 13), preach (Luke 24: 47), teach (Acts 4: 18–20), perform the supernatural (Mark 16: 17), in fact, do all things (Col. 3: 17). This is the Name we are privileged to bear, and for which we are called to suffer (Acts 9: 15, 16). It should be our supreme desire to see it magnified, as it was in Ephesus, in a time of powerful revival (Acts 19: 17). The Name of the Lord Jesus is the very sphere of our life and the very source of our authority. Can He be less than God who bears a Name of such significance? To deny the deity of Christ is to deny the divine authority which Scripture attaches to His Name.

What is the meaning of praying in His Name? When we speak today of acting in another's name we use the expression in much the same way as Scripture. Dr. Torrey put it thus: "If, for example, I should go to the First National Bank of Chicago, and present a cheque which I had signed for fifty dollars, the paying teller would say to me: 'Why, Mr. Torrey, we cannot cash that. You have no money in this bank.' But if I should go to the First National Bank with a cheque for five thousand dollars made payable to me, and signed by one of the large depositors in that bank, they would not ask whether I had money in that bank or in any bank, but would honour the cheque at once. So it is when I go to the bank of heaven, when I go to God in prayer. I have nothing deposited there, I have absolutely no credit there, and if I go in my own name I will get absolutely nothing; but

Jesus Christ has unlimited credit in heaven, and He has granted to me the privilege of going to the bank with His Name on my cheques, and when I thus go, my prayers will be honoured to any extent" (*How to pray*).

To pray for revival in the Name of Christ, is to pray as His representative, and the prayers are as effective as if it were His own blessed lips that framed them, and His own holy hands that were lifted up upon the throne of Jehovah. Therefore to pray in the Name of the Son is to pray with all the authority of the Son, who has Himself openly declared, "All authority hath been given unto Me in heaven and on earth" (Matt. 28: 18). In olden times a man might be rudely awakened in the night by a great knocking on his outer door, and a soldier's voice calling out, "Open in the King's name." It would not matter that the soldier was but a corporal, and that he had only a handful of men under him: if he was acting for the king, all the authority of the king lay behind his command, and none would be able to withstand it. "The king's word hath power; and who may say unto him, What doest thou?" (Eccles. 8: 4). How much more the word of the King of kings!

There are many prayers that have "in the Name of Jesus" appended to them which are not honoured in heaven. There may well be those who never pray without using this formula as a "rubber stamp", to whom the Saviour might truly say, "Hitherto have ye asked nothing in My Name" (John 16: 24). There are other prayers, however, that omit the expression and yet fulfil the condition, and so prevail. What does the condition involve, and how may we be sure that we are praying in the Name? It means that we pray as His representatives, that is, according to His mind and purpose. When in prayer we are moved by His compassions, motivated by His interests, weighed down by His burdens, reaching out towards His objectives, then we are praying in His Name. In a word, it involves being one with Him in will and purpose. When, prior to His death, the Lord Jesus spoke to His disciples about praying in His Name, He taught them that they had not yet prayed thus (John 16: 24), but that they would do so "in that day" (John 16: 26) referring to Pentecost (see 14: 16–20). Praying in the Name awaited the moment when they should receive the Spirit and be baptized into the body of Christ. They would thus be united in the Spirit with their risen Head.

"In that day," He declared, "ye shall ask in My Name." Thus the whole matter hinges on our experimental union with Christ. It is but the prayer activity of one who is abiding in Him, and presents yet another aspect of praying in God's will.

It has been shown that praying in His Name involves acting as His representative, but this applies not only to the asking, but also to the receiving. When we obtain what we ask in the Name of Christ, we are still bound by the fact that we are His representatives. It is still His desires and purposes that must ever be before us. If a landowner authorized his agent to collect the rental due from one of his tenants, the agent would go and ask for it in his master's name, and in that name would receive it. When, however, he has the money in his hand, he does not cease to be his master's agent. He is not free to spend the money as he likes, but to hold it in trust as a steward, disposing of it only according to the will of his master. It is so with us. We ask in His Name; we receive in His Name; we hold in His Name. Everything obtained is a trust, and one day we shall be called to give an account. This is directly connected with the question of right motives considered in the previous chapter. "Ye ask, and receive not, because ye ask amiss, that ye may spend it in your pleasures" (Jas. 4: 3). The Lord Jesus must take care to safeguard His rights, and our acting only in His Name is His safeguard.

"When Scripture speaks of men who have given their lives for the Name of the Lord Jesus or of one ready to die for the Name of the Lord Jesus, we see what our relation to the Name must be: when it is everything to me, it will obtain everything for me. If I let it have all I have, it will let me have all it has" (Andrew Murray). Let us take a final look at the opening verse, "Whatsoever ye shall ask in My Name . . . that the Father may be glorified in the Son." Here, then, is the acid test. We pray in the Name only when the supreme objective of our praying, colouring all our thoughts and desires concerning it, is that "the Father may be glorified in the Son". There is unlimited scope here to pray for revival, for when is the Father more glorified in the Son than when the Spirit is working in the midst of the church in resistless power?

Then, to prevail in prayer means praying—

## In the Spirit

Scripture speaks of "praying in the Holy Spirit" (Jude 20), and again, "praying at all seasons in the Spirit" (Eph. 6: 18). Since all saints without distinction are exhorted to pray thus, there can be no suggestion that this is an experience outside the reach of all but the most exalted believers. Paul not only expected the Ephesian saints to pray thus, but to do so "at all seasons". What does it mean to pray in the Spirit? It means, in a phrase, to pray in the realm of the Spirit. It is possible for praying to be vain talking, like the teaching of some whom Paul described (1 Tim. 1: 6), or like the vain repetitions of the heathen (Matt. 6: 7), neither of which is even intelligent. Such formalism is nothing more than an activity of the lips; it is praying in the realm of the body. It is possible, however, for our praying to be thoughtful and intelligent, and even scriptural in its phraseology, but nothing more. Such is praying in the realm of the mind, and this can never prevail with God.

The praying we are concerned with is that which may utilize the body, that is, the lips may express it; and that which demands the co-operation of the mind with all its faculties; but is essentially that which moves in the supernatural realm of the Spirit. This is but another aspect of praying in faith. Reason can take us so far, but faith reaches out into a realm where reason cannot go. "Where reason fails with all her powers, there faith prevails and love adores." Praying in faith is not irrational but super-rational. It is exactly thus with praying in the Spirit. It involves three things:

Firstly, *the Spirit has anointed the suppliant*. Without the anointing of the Spirit there can be no praying in the Spirit. In Old Testament times those who acted Godward for the people, the intercessors of Israel, were the priests. Before they could exercise this ministry they had to be anointed. The Lord Jesus promised the disciples that through the Holy Spirit, the promised Comforter, they would have a new insight into the mind of God: "In that day ye shall ask Me no question" (John 16: 23, margin); and they would be enabled to pray in His Name, obtaining whatever they asked: "If ye shall ask anything of the Father, He will give it you in My name" (John 16: 23). Thus praying in the Spirit is also related to praying according to God's will and praying in the Name of Christ. May the Lord raise up those who, like Stephen, shall be, "full of faith and of the Holy Spirit" (Acts 6: 5), that they may be mighty to *pray* in faith and in the Holy Spirit.

Secondly, *the Spirit is directing the prayer.* We are ignorant of the things for which to pray and how we ought to pray for them, but the omniscient Spirit helps our weakness by interceding on our behalf, and this intercession of the Spirit in us and for us is in perfect accord with the mind of God (Rom. 8: 26, 27). So here is another link with praying in the will of God. The mighty intercessions of the Spirit are dependent on the use of our yielded wills, minds, and desires. When we grant Him these, our praying is in fact His praying in us—we are praying in the Spirit.

Thirdly, *the Spirit is energizing the praying.* To pray in the Spirit is supremely to pray in the energy of the Spirit. There is perhaps no work that requires more energy than praying. There is a constant temptation to faint (Luke 18: 1). So great are the demands of the prayer battle, that "even the youths [with their energy and enthusiasm] shall faint and be weary, and the young men [in the prime of their strength] shall utterly fall : but they that wait upon the Lord [that they may be directed and energized by the Spirit] shall renew their strength; they shall mount up with wings as eagles [achieving the impossible]; they shall run, and not be weary [accomplishing the extraordinary]; they shall walk, and not faint [doing the humdrum]" (Isa. 40: 30, 31). Such will be found "praying at all seasons in the Spirit". Some may pray regularly and fervently. They may exercise a measure of faith. They may pray according to God's will. They may witness their prayers answered from time to time. But what is it that makes the praying of those who have become mighty in intercession so different? What is the secret of such astonishing energy and irresistible faith? How is it they can plead with such boldness, and are able with authority to cast mountains into the sea? Just this, they are praying with holy energy; they are praying in the Spirit.

Finally, prayer will prevail whenever believers pray—

### In Unison

"If two of you shall agree on earth as touching anything that they shall ask, it shall be done for them of My Father, which is in heaven" (Matt. 18: 19). The importance of acting in unison is clear enough in the natural realm. The power of a tug-of-war team depends, not so much on the total strength or weight of its members, but on the precision with which they pull as one. Said Solomon, "Two are better than one; because they have a good reward for their labour. For if they fall, the one will lift up his fellow : but woe to him that is alone when he falleth, and hath not another to lift him up. Again, if two lie together, then they have warmth : but how can one be warm alone? And if a man prevail against him that is alone, two shall withstand him" (Eccles. 4: 9-12). In other words, when it comes to the peril of stumbling, growing cold, or being overcome by the enemy, "Two are better than one."

This same principle was demonstrated by the Lord when He sent out the Twelve (Mark 6: 7) and later the Seventy (Luke 10: 1) "by two and two". When the ass and colt were to be brought (Matt. 21: 1), or the upper room prepared for the Passover (Mark 14: 13), He sent *two* disciples. There was the same principle when the Holy Spirit separated Barnabas and Paul for their special work (Acts 13: 2). When the partnership was broken by dissension the principle was still followed, "Barnabas took Mark", while "Paul chose Silas". There appear to have been few, if any, "lone wolves" or free-lance preachers among those early workers. The mighty ministry of these that "turned the world upside down" was characterized by team work. References to "Paul's companions in travel" (Acts 19: 29), his "fellow-workers" (Rom. 16: 21, etc.), his "partner" (2 Cor. 8: 23), his "fellow-soldier" (Phil. 2: 25, etc.), reveal what a vital part these played in the apostle's ministry. He seemed out of his element when he found himself without them (Acts 17 : 15, 16; 2 Cor. 2 : 13).

This wonderful prayer promise shows that the principle of united action has a special significance in the realm of prayer. "If two of you," that is the smallest possible combination, and therefore includes any larger, "shall agree . . . as touching anything that they shall ask", means very much more than general outward agreement concerning the objective of the praying, or the petitions offered. Two believers may pray for the same thing, using even the same words, without knowing the agreement spoken of here. The Greek word for "agree" in this verse might be transliterated "symphonize". From the cognate noun we get our word "symphony", translated "music" in Luke 15: 25. As in an orchestra different personalities, playing different instruments, with varying skill and ability are made to "symphonize", and so produce harmony pleasing to the ear, so in the realm of prayer, even when outward expression and manner of praying may be totally different, there can be a harmony of spirit that reaches the ear of God, delights His heart, and moves His hand to bestow the blessing desired.

How may this spiritual oneness in prayer be effected? Acts 15 records the controversy in the church at Jerusalem over the circumcision of Gentile converts. The whole assembly was concerned about this matter, and yet was divided upon it, some holding that it was necessary before they could be saved, others that it was not. One and another gave their judgment until the mind of the Spirit became clear, and the whole church was brought to see it. "It seemed good unto us, *having come to one accord*," ran the decree they then issued (Acts 15: 25). Many were the mistimed, discordant notes when the music began that day. How were they all brought to such perfect harmony before the assembly separated? An unseen Conductor controlled the orchestra, and the movement of His hand effected the harmony. Present there, though unseen to human eye, was "the hand of God to give them one heart" (2 Chron. 30: 12). The hand was the Spirit, and the harmony produced "the unity of the Spirit". The church was in submission to Him; there was the exercise of patience; and the seemingly impossible was achieved. "It seemed good unto us . . . it seemed good to the Holy Spirit, and to us" (Acts 15: 25, 28)—that was the secret. Although divided, they wanted the mind of God; they were miraculously brought to one mind; they knew that this one mind must be the mind of God.

This incident provides an illustration of much united prayer that has prevailed. Initial discord of spirit may be inevitable, but where hearts are earnestly seeking the mind of God, are open to the influences of the Spirit, and are prepared to wait patiently before the Lord, He is able, we know not how, to produce that "symphonizing" prayer which brings from heaven the answer, "It shall be done." By this wondrous working of the Spirit heaven and earth are linked in the fulfilling of the will of God. The Lord had said, "What things soever ye shall bind on earth shall be bound in heaven : and what things soever ye shall loose on earth shall be loosed in heaven" (Matt. 18:18); and then He added, "If two of you shall agree on earth . . . it shall be done . . . in heaven." Earth is characterized by discord and division, heaven by harmony and unity. When spiritual unity comes to those praying on earth, it has come from heaven through the operation of the Spirit, and such praying must return to heaven and be ratified there. To all such praying on earth, God will respond in heaven with His divine "Amen—it shall be done." What power He has put into the hands of His people! And yet how little used, how seldom proved!

Let us view this great truth from another aspect presented to us in Scripture, that of the Church being the body of Christ, the means by which the Head in heaven expresses Himself on earth. A child playing with a skipping-rope demonstrates the control of the mind over the body. By means of the spirit animating that child the head exercises control and causes the members to move in harmony. Even so with those who have been baptized into the body of Christ. When two or more are praying in spiritual unity it is because the Spirit of the ascended Head, sent forth to possess and empower the body, is effecting the harmony, that the will of the Head may be done. The Psalmist expressed the same truth when he said, "Behold, how good and how pleasant it is for brethren to dwell together in unity! It is like the precious oil upon the head, that ran down upon the beard, even Aaron's beard; that came down upon the skirt of his garments; like the dew of Hermon, that cometh down upon the mountains of Zion" (Ps. 133). This wondrous unity is "like the oil . . . like the dew", because both are typical of the Spirit, and this is "the unity of the Spirit". The oil *comes down* from the Head, even to those represented by the lowest extremity (or skirt) of the garments. The dew *comes down* from the exalted summit of Hermon, whose snow-clad peak is often hidden behind the clouds, to the lowlier mountains of Zion. Spiritual unity may be enjoyed on earth but it can only come from heaven.

Having likened the blessedness of this unity to oil and dew, the Psalmist concludes, "For there [where brethren dwell together in unity] the Lord commanded the blessing, even life for evermore." Once this unity is effected in prayer, the blessing is assured. Of the hundred and twenty in the upper room we read, "These all *with one accord* continued steadfastly in prayer" (Acts 1:14).

Through patient and steadfast waiting upon God they were brought to that symphony of prayer which knew no discordant note, and which brought from heaven the first great outpouring. When again believers "with one accord continue steadfastly in prayer" for such a visitation, the Spirit will surely be poured out again. The Lord has not withdrawn His promise. "If two of you shall agree . . . it shall be done." This unity is the crown of spiritual preparation. When the saints pray as one, revival is nigh, even at the doors.

Not only is revival the product of unity, but the producer of unity. It is characteristically a time when personal, social and sectarian barriers are thrown down, when hearts are melted and fused in the fires of the Spirit, and when believers see themselves as never before "all one in Christ Jesus". "They shall see, eye to eye, when the Lord returneth to Zion" (Isa. 52: 8). Perhaps there is no time when the yearning of the Saviour, "that they may be one" (John 17: 11) is more nearly fulfilled than in seasons of revival. They provide a blessed foretaste of a day yet future when the saints shall "all attain unto the unity of the faith, and of the knowledge of the Son of God, unto a full-grown man, unto the measure of the stature of the fulness of Christ" (Eph. 4: 13), and the Saviour's prayer be finally answered.

For the present let this great principle of spiritual unity be harnessed to the task of praying down the blessing. Are you praying for revival alone? Ask God to give you another of like mind with whom you may agree, that the power of your praying may increase manifold. Are you already praying with others? Look to God to bring all to that "one accord", that heart-agreement that ensures the answer.

### Steps to the Throne

It is recorded that "there were *six steps* to the throne" which King Solomon made (2 Chron. 9: 18). Through Christ we have access in prayer to a throne infinitely greater and more glorious than Solomon's. Praying in the position of abiding, in the will of God, in faith, in the Name of Christ, in the Spirit, and in unison are the six steps to the throne of God. They are all connected and inter-related, and any one of them is enough to lead us through to God in prevailing prayer. We have only to plant the foot of prayer upon one, and God has pledged Himself to grant us, not something, but the very thing that we ask. If we pray for revival, fulfilling any of these principles, we shall obtain revival. "Let us therefore draw near with boldness unto the throne of grace, that we may *receive* . . ." (Heb. 4: 16).

The next day they took Christian and had him into the armoury, where they showed him all manner of furniture, which their Lord had provided for pilgrims, as sword, shield, helmet, breastplate, *all-prayer*, and shoes that would not wear out. And there was here enough of this to harness out as many men for the service of their Lord as there be stars in heaven for multitude.

JOHN BUNYAN.

## CHAPTER ELEVEN

# WIELDING THE WEAPON

"After this manner therefore pray ye" (Matt. 6: 9).

P AUL, that outstanding soldier of Christ, has said that "the weapons of our warfare are not of the flesh, but mighty before God to the casting down of strongholds" (2 Cor. 10: 4). Although many will acknowledge that one of the greatest of these weapons is "all-prayer", comparatively few seem to be able to use it with real effect against the hosts of darkness. In addition to the vital principles just considered, there are other important features set forth in Scripture emphasizing the manner in which the weapon should be wielded for success.

Firstly, prevailing prayer necessitates that in our petitions we should be—

## Definite

Much ineffectiveness in prayer is caused by the vagueness of the request. If water is allowed to flow at random over a wide area it will dissipate its energy and produce only a marsh. If confined to a river-bed its power may be harnessed to turn a mill or generate electric power. There is, of course, a place for general praying, but the kind of praying that prevails is that which has been focused by the Spirit of God on a definite objective. There is a place and time in military strategy for general harassing tactics, but when the moment arrives for attack and advance, success depends on the concentration of force at the strategic points. If the vital objectives are seized, victory is assured.

When Bartimaeus cried out to Jesus to have mercy on him, the Saviour asked him, "What wilt thou that I should do unto thee?" (Mark 10: 51). Was it not obvious to the Saviour what he wanted? Of course, but the Lord was encouraging him to be definite in his petition, to change "have mercy upon me" to "Lord, that I may receive my sight." We often ask God to *bless* this or that; He might well answer, "What wilt thou? What exactly do you want Me to do for you?" Be specific, be definite in prayer. Let the prayer objectives be clearly defined.

If we want revival, let us plead the promise of the outpouring of the Spirit. Let us pray for the church to be quickened in love and life and power. Let us pray for believers to be filled with the Holy Spirit. Let us pray that conviction may seize the godless, and that there may be a great turning to God. Let us pray that the Lord alone may be exalted in that day.

Charles Finney recorded the following: "Some ladies had come over to New York, and were much struck with the progress of the revival movement there, particularly with some instances of remarkable conversions that had occurred in the case of individuals after special prayer made by Christians. They asked me a good many questions, and, among other things, wanted to know if I really thought it of any use for *them* to pray for a revival in *their* place. I related some facts to encourage them, and told them to go home and agree, together with other ladies of their acquaintance, to observe a closet concert of prayer for the outpouring of the Holy Spirit. They went home, and engaged some half-dozen of them for that purpose, at sunrise, at midday, and at sunset. Three times a day they prayed for the outpouring of the Holy Spirit on their place. *Now, mark, they had a definite object in their prayer*. They had no minister, but when the Sabbath came round the people assembled to hear a sermon read, and the conviction that the Holy Spirit was there that day was irresistible. At the close of the service no fewer than seventy individuals, who had been awakened, came together to be instructed by the deacons in regard to what they should do about the salvation of their souls, and a great revival followed."

Being definite in prayer not only concentrates spiritual pressure upon the vital objectives, but also serves to quicken faith in the heart of the suppliant. For Bartimaeüs to say before that crowd, "Lord, that I may receive my sight," not only required faith, but served to quicken faith that the Lord would do it. It is so with us. If we are definite in our prayer, God will be equally definite in His answering. "Jabez called on the God of Israel . . . and God granted him *that which he requested*" (1 Chron. 4: 10).

Secondly, our praying should be—

### Daring

This is a characteristic of faith in action—it is daring. The possibilities of daring prayer are not limited by the personality, imagination, or courage of the one who prays, but solely by what is revealed to that one of the power of God, the promises of God, the will of God. When the Spirit of Truth illuminates the histories and promises of Scripture, what scope there is for daring prayer. A quickened faith must truly exclaim, "With God all things are possible" (Matt. 19: 26). But the question that needs to be faced is this : is our praying in its very nature an acknowledgment of the omnipotence of our God and of His willingness to bless super-abundantly? Someone has well written, "we feel instinctively that our praying is mistaken when it has ceased to be daring—when-ever it has all tamed down to a decorous and decent asking for the very minimum of God's expenditure of power, and when our requests impose upon Him no requirement of action which is beyond our natural level of thought."

We can imagine the feelings of someone with exceptional power and ability, who is compelled to stand by inactive and watch another struggle in weakness and incompetence to fulfil some task that he could willingly do for him in an instant. It must be torture indeed to possess extraordinary powers and not be given the opportunity to exercise them. How often do we keep the Almighty standing by in silent inactivity, with all the power of the universe in His hands, yearning to intervene, to demonstrate His power and reveal His glory; while we toy with spiritual things, earthbound in our thinking, working, and praying! Well might the Lord say of us, "Oh that My people would hearken unto Me. . . . I should soon subdue their enemies, and turn My hand against their adversaries" (Ps. 81: 13), and again, "I will go and return to My place, till they acknowledge their offence, and seek My face" (Hos. 5: 15). On the other hand, a daring faith does not stagger at the promises of God; a daring faith can open the win-dows of heaven for revival; a daring faith delights the heart of God.

The Lord emphasized this same truth when he spoke in Luke 11: 5 of the man who knocked up his friend at midnight with the request, "Friend, lend me three loaves." Although he was refused at first, he eventually obtained all that he needed. How? "Though he will not rise and give him, because he is his friend, yet because of his importunity [shamelessness—Darby] he will arise and give him as many as he needeth." The rendering "impor-tunity" greatly limits the meaning; the word is shamelessness or impudence, and conveys the idea of the daring element in prayer.

He was daring because of *the hour when he made request*. It was midnight. This midnight hour which finds the church of Christ slumbering, and the world in spiritual darkness and need, is but a challenge to daring prayer. Are we bold enough to accept the challenge? He was daring because of *the measure of his asking*. The Eastern loaves were large and substantial. Could he not have made do with half a loaf till morning came and he could buy more? No, he was daring enough to ask for three, and by his boldness he obtained as many as he wanted. He was daring because *he persevered until he obtained*. He was met with a rebuff, "Trouble me not"; a shut door, "the door is now shut"; a hindrance, "my children are with me in bed"; a definite refusal, "I cannot rise and give thee" : but he persevered until the rebuff was withdrawn, the door opened, the hindrance removed, the refusal reversed. The Lord was careful to point out that it was not because of his friendship with the other, but because of his daring that he prevailed. "Let us therefore draw near with *boldness* unto the throne of grace" (Heb. 4: 16).

> Thou art coming to a King,
> Large petitions with thee bring;
> For His grace and power are such
> None can ever ask too much.
> J. NEWTON.

Thirdly, our praying should be—

### Intense

Peter was miraculously released from prison through such praying by the church. "Peter therefore was kept in the prison : but prayer was made *earnestly* of the church unto God for him" (Acts 12: 5). The word "earnestly" is derived from the verb "to stretch out", and suggests that they were drawn out in prayer to their utmost capacity. As an athlete straining for the tape, they were praying at full stretch. The apostle whose deliverance was effected by this kind of praying uses the word in the only other reference in the New Testament, "love one another from the heart *fervently*" (1 Pet. 1: 22; cf. Acts 26: 7; 1 Pet. 4: 8; Luke 22: 44). Perhaps the only English word that adequately conveys the meaning of the original is "intensively". A comparative form of the word is used to describe the praying of the Saviour in the garden, "And being in an agony, He prayed *more earnestly* [or more intensively]: and His sweat became as it were great drops of blood falling down upon the ground" (Luke 22: 44). This supreme example of intensive praying shows that it is related to soul agony, and those who enter this realm of prayer with their Lord must expect to know something of the fellowship of His sufferings.

"As soon as Zion travailed, she brought forth her children" (Isa. 66: 8). This might be a true description of the birth of many a revival. Movements of the Spirit are born out of soul travail, and no record shows this more clearly than the diaries of David Brainerd. E. M. Bounds says of him, "His whole life was one of burning prayer to God for the American Indians. By day and by night he prayed. Before preaching and after preaching he prayed. On his bed of straw he prayed. Retiring to the dense and lonely forests he fasted and prayed. Hour by hour, day after day, early morn and late at night, he was praying and fasting, pouring out his soul, interceding, communing with God. He was with God mightily in prayer, and God was with him mightily, and by it he being dead yet speaketh." Let us glance at a few entries in his diary three years before the visitation of the Spirit upon his labours, and see how this young warrior of only twenty-four years wielded the weapon of all-prayer.

His entry for Monday, April 19, 1742, reads as follows: "I set apart this day for fasting and prayer to prepare me for the ministry, to give me divine aid and direction, and in His own way to 'send me into His harvest'. In the forenoon, I felt the power of intercession for precious immortal souls; for the advancement of the kingdom of my dear Lord and Saviour in the world; and withal, a most sweet resignation, and even consolation and joy in the thoughts of suffering hardships, distresses, and even death itself, in the promotion of it : and had special enlargement in pleading for the conversion of the poor heathen. In the afternoon God was with me of a truth. Oh, it was a blessed company indeed! God enabled me so to agonize in prayer that I was quite wet with sweat, though in the shade and the wind cool. My soul was drawn out very much for the world; for multitudes of souls. I think I had more enlargement for sinners, than for the children of God; though I felt as if I could spend my life in cries for both."

Then on Monday, June 14, the same year, he wrote "I set

apart this day for secret fasting and prayer, to entreat God to direct and bless me with regard to the great work I have in view, of preaching the gospel. Just at night the Lord visited me marvellously in prayer: I think my soul never was in such an agony before. I felt no restraint; for the treasures of divine grace were opened to me. I wrestled for absent friends, for the ingathering of souls, and for the children of God in many distant places. I was in such an agony, from sun half an hour high, till near dark, that I was all over wet with sweat; but yet it seemed to me that I had wasted away the day, and had done nothing. Oh, my dear Jesus did sweat blood for poor souls! I longed for more compassion towards them."

If there are those who read such accounts of intensive praying only to reflect with a sigh, "It is too high, I cannot attain unto it," let them recall that "Elijah was a man of like passions with us", that he was overtaken by fear, despondence, and self-pity, and yet "he prayed fervently" (Jas. 5:17) and prevailed with God. Intensive praying, however, cannot be worked up; it is a burden that God places upon prepared hearts. When through the Spirit we are possessed with such a consuming desire for revival that we feel we must either pray it down or perish in the attempt, we may be confident that God is going to send it. When the cry of the church is, "Give me children or I die," then revival is nigh, even at the doors.

It is said that when Dr. Charles Goodell was sent to a run-down Methodist Church in New York city, his people said to him, "We hardly expect a revival here any more. We had them in years gone by, but times have changed." When Sunday came and he went into his pulpit and looked into the faces of his people, he said, "My brethren, they tell me you do not expect a revival here. I am telling you this morning that there *will* be a revival here, or there will be a funeral in the parsonage." The revival came, and a church dead and discouraged was quickened into life. Such an inflexible determination, inspired by the Spirit, is the underlying factor behind that intensive praying that prevails with God. It is this same determination that provides the next characteristic.

Fourthly, prevailing prayer must be—

## Importunate

We are exhorted to "pray without ceasing" (1 Thess. 5: 17). This means praying on in spite of delays and discouragements, and through weakness and fatigue, until prayer is answered. Importunate praying serves to build up spiritual pressure on the enemy until his defences crumble and the victory is won. Isaiah declared, "For Zion's sake will I not hold my peace, and for Jerusalem's sake I will not rest, until her righteousness go forth as brightness, and her salvation as a lamp that burneth"; and again, "I have set watchmen upon thy walls, O Jerusalem; they shall never hold their peace day nor night : ye that are the Lord's remembrancers, take ye no rest, and give Him no rest, till He establish, and till He make Jerusalem a praise in the earth" (Isa. 62: 1, 6). Here, then, is an inspired picture of importunate prayer in action.

If our spiritual battle is one of successive advance and retreat, it may very often be due to lack of persistence in prayer. It was the uplifted hands of Moses on the hill-top that swayed the battle waged by Joshua in the valley (Exod. 17: 8–13). The hand stretched out in conflict is immediately influenced by the hand stretched up in intercession. "When Moses held up his hand, . . . Israel prevailed : and when he let down his hand, Amalek prevailed" (verse 11). Charles Finney always said that when he lost the spirit of prayer he ceased to preach with power. "But Moses' hands were heavy" (verse 12); this is a sad yet fitting description of much of our praying. But before the day was done, Moses, supported by his companions, became importunate, "and his hands were steady until the going down of the sun. And Joshua prostrated [margin] Amalek and his people with the edge of the sword." May God give us the steadfast hands of importunate prayer.

Spiritual stamina in intercession is so rare, and the temptation to faint by the way is so great, that the Lord "spake a parable unto them to the end that they ought always to pray, and not to faint" (Luke 18: 1–8). The lesson of the parable is this : the widow, who was pleading in court for justice against her adversary, could not move the unrighteous judge by appeals to the law, though it catered for her protection as a widow, because the judge "feared not God". He was not moved by appeals to human sympathy or the thought of his reputation, for "he regarded not man". Where all factors and arguments failed, one consideration weighed so with the judge as to cause him to do her justice of her adversary—the fact that "she came *oft* unto him". Said he, "Because this widow troubleth me, I will avenge her, lest she wear me out by her *continual coming*." Because of the insistence of her pleading, and for no other reason, the judge changed his attitude, and the widow won her case.

"And shall not God"—Who, unlike the judge, is infinitely righteous, and ever ready to regard man in his weakness—"avenge His elect"—who stand in a special relationship to Himself—"which cry to Him day and night"—in importunate prayer —"and He is longsuffering over them"?—that patience may have its perfect work in them also—"I say unto you, that He will avenge them speedily." Here, then, is the moral : if a judge without pity or compunction could be moved by the importunate pleadings of a helpless widow, how much more shall God, righteous, merciful, longsuffering, be moved by the importunate pleadings of His elect.

In the little booklet *Vibrations*, Lilias Trotter of Algiers recounts the following, which should encourage every child of God to persevere in prayer : "One of the pillars that support the gallery of our old Arab house had fallen down into the court and lay shattered on the pavement, carrying with it a block of masonry and a shower of bricks. Down below, alongside of us, a native baker had installed himself six or seven years ago. For hours every night two men had swung on the huge see-saw which in some mysterious way kneads their bread, and every blow backwards and forwards had vibrated through our house, and now at last the result was seen in the shattering of masonry that had looked as if it would last as long as the world. . . . There is a vibrating power going on down in the darkness and dust of this world that can make itself visible in startling results in the upper air and sunlight of the invisible world, 'mighty through God to the pulling down of strongholds.' Each prayer-beat down here vibrates up to the very throne of God, and does its work through that throne on the principalities and powers around us, just as each of the repeated throbs from below told on the structure of our house, though it was only the last one that produced the visible effect. We can never tell which prayer will liberate the answer, but we can tell that *each one will do its work*."

As we may be called to pray on, week after week and month after week and month after month, for revival, let us be assured that each petition will play its part until the cumulative effect of our praying shall be manifested in the sudden demonstration of God's power. Let us therefore, like the early church, "continue steadfastly in prayer, *watching* therein with thanksgiving" (Col. 4: 2). Yes, with importunate praying there must be watching.

Fifthly then, prevailing prayer must be—

### Vigilant

There are two important words in the Greek of the New Testament meaning to watch. Both are used with the thought of *precautionary watching,* such as the watching of the sentry (Eph. 6: 18; Acts 20: 31). Both are also used with the thought of *anticipatory watching,* looking out for some expected event to take place, as watchmen for the morning, or servants for their returning lord (Mark 13: 33; Matt. 24: 42). Both these aspects apply in the realm of prayer. There must be precautionary watching because there are innumerable perils to be faced by the warrior who wields the weapon of all-prayer. There must also be anticipatory watching, for faith is continually expecting the fulfilment of its petition.

The need for *precautionary watching* must be plain when we remember that "our wrestling is not against flesh and blood, but against the principalities, against the powers, against the world-rulers of this darkness, against the spiritual hosts of wickedness in the heavenly places" (Eph. 6: 12). The prayer warrior faces an enemy with immense spiritual resources and centuries of experience in spiritual conflict. He is engaged in a battle to the death, and no quarter can be asked or given. When the Devil cannot carry the position by a frontal assault, he will use a flank attack or employ fifth-column tactics. Where he cannot intimidate us as a roaring lion, he will come as an angel of light to beguile us. What a need there is for vigilance!

Firstly, we must take precaution by *watching unto prayer*; that is, with a view to prayer. "Praying at all seasons . . . and watching unto this very thing" (Eph. 6: 18 Darby; cf. 1 Pet. 4: 7). In other words our approach to prayer requires constant vigilance. The Devil will do his utmost to keep us off our knees. He is a past master in the use of decoys and distractions. When the time comes for prayer, how many pressing duties suddenly clamour for attention! Is not this the activity of Satan? "We are not ignorant of his devices," we say; but are we not? Or is it that we succumb in spite of our knowledge? Even such a man of prayer as Andrew Bonar knew such continual attacks of Satan. "With me," he wrote in 1856, "every time of prayer, or almost every time, begins with a conflict." We are never likely to obey the exhortation to be "praying at all seasons", unless we are also "watching unto this very thing".

Secondly, we must take precaution, not only by watching *unto* prayer, but by *watching in prayer*. "Watch and pray that ye enter not into temptation." On the night of His betrayal the Saviour said to His apostles, "I will no more speak much with you, for the prince of the world cometh : and he hath nothing in Me; but that the world may know that I love the Father, and as the Father gave Me commandment, even so I do" (John 14: 30). The days of His flesh were drawing to a close, and the last momentous conflict with Satan was at hand. As the Saviour entered the garden of Gethsemane He took with Him that favoured trio, Peter, James, and John, that they might share His cup of sorrow, and watch with Him in that last great conflict.

As our Saviour penetrated the dark recesses of that garden in company with the three, it was as though all the forces of hell were let loose upon Him. The fact that "He began to be greatly amazed and sore troubled" suggests that even the Saviour Himself had not anticipated the unutterable horror of that hour. We can only estimate the intolerable pressure of evil upon His spirit by His own words, "My soul is exceeding sorrowful even unto death : abide ye here, and watch with Me" (Matt. 26: 38). In the hour of His deepest woe He sought the fellowship of these three disciples. It is doubtful whether we could find anywhere in Scripture a more striking contrast than the picture that is now presented to us. On the one hand we see the Son of God prostrate on the ground, agonizing for a world's redemption, the sod beneath Him wet with His sweat and tears; on the other hand we see the men who had pledged their allegiance to Him, had promised to go with Him to prison and to death, all unaware of the conflict and peril of the hour, in the oblivion of sleep. Tenderly He rebukes them, surprise and sorrow mingling with His words,

"What, could ye not watch with Me one hour? Watch and pray, that ye enter not into temptation" (Matt. 26: 40).

He who enters with his Lord the Gethsemane of prayer-conflict may expect to find himself "in the forefront of the hottest battle", and must not be surprised if he is a constant target of the Adversary. His only safety lies in ceaseless vigilance. Any who set themselves, like Nehemiah, to pray and work for revival may find, as that man did, that they have stirred a hornet's nest of Satanic opposition. Such counter attacks can only be met as Nehemiah met them. "We made our prayer unto our God, and set a watch against them day and night" (Neh. 4: 9). A military commander's decision to launch an attack is based largely upon military intelligence, the disposition and strength of the enemy, his morale, his movements and plans. Such information has been gleaned by thousands of watching eyes. Similarly, if we would wage war with the weapon of all-prayer, we must watch for the movements of the enemy; otherwise we shall be launching a blind offensive, which may give the enemy who is ever ready to counter-attack, the opening for which he has been waiting.

> Principalities and powers,
> Mustering their unseen array,
> Wait for thy unguarded hours :
>     Watch and pray.
>
> Watch, as if on that alone
> Hung the issue of the day;
> Pray, that help may be sent down :
>     Watch and pray.
>                         C. ELLIOTT.

Then the need for *anticipatory watching*, which looks for the expected answer, is suggested by the exhortation, "Continue steadfastly in prayer, watching therein with thanksgiving" (Col. 4: 2). One wonders whether there is any faith in the praying that is never followed by expectant watching. "We should watch daily," wrote Richard Sibbes, "continue instant in prayer; strengthen our supplications with arguments from God's word and promises; and mark how our prayers speed. When we shoot an arrow we look to its fall; when we send a ship to sea we look for its return; and when we sow we look for an harvest. . . . It is atheism to pray and not to wait in hope. A sincere Christian will pray, wait, strengthen his heart with the promises, and never leave praying and looking up till God gives him a gracious answer."

When God had answered by fire on Mount Carmel and the prophets of Baal had been slain, Elijah said to Ahab, "Get thee up, eat and drink; for there is the sound of abundance of rain. So Ahab went up to eat and to drink. And Elijah went up to the top of Carmel; and he bowed himself down upon the earth, and put his face between his knees. And he said to his servant, Go up now, look toward the sea. And he went up, and looked, and said, There is nothing. And he said, Go again seven times. And it came to pass at the seventh time, that he said, Behold, there ariseth a cloud out of the sea, as small as a man's hand" (1 Kings 18: 41). While Elijah persevered in prayer his servant persevered in watching for the answer. We might think that "a cloud . . . as small as a man's hand" was an insignificant token—the first sign of answered prayer is often like that—but to the watching eye of faith it was the harbinger of "a great rain". We say we are praying for the rain of revival, but are we watching for the cloud? Are we ready to act in faith when it appears? As Colossians 4: 2 suggests, watching in this way should ever be accompanied by thanksgiving.

This suggests our sixth feature. Prevailing prayer should be—

### Thankful

"In everything by prayer and supplication with thanksgiving" (Phil. 4: 6). In view of the Lord's abounding mercy towards His children, it is indeed becoming that they should "enter into His gates with thanksgiving, and into His courts with praise" (Ps. 100: 4), but this is by no means all. That the Lord has said, "Whoso offereth the sacrifice of thanksgiving glorifieth Me" (Ps. 50: 23) should be sufficient to move us all to do it, but we are concerned here with thanksgiving in its bearing upon prevailing in prayer. A praising and thankful spirit has a remarkable ability to quicken the faith of the suppliant, and to release spiritual power for the effecting of that for which we pray. This was so in the case of Abraham who "waxed strong through faith, *giving glory to God*" (Rom. 4: 20). Again, in the visions of Patmos, John tells us of those who overcame the dragon "because of the blood of the Lamb, and because of the word of their testimony" (Rev. 12: 11).

The praising "lips which make confession to His Name" (Heb. 13: 15) are a vital part of the word of testimony by which we overcome.

At the dedication of the temple by Solomon, the climax of the impressive ceremony was reached "when the trumpeters and singers were as one, to make one sound to be heard in praising and thanking the Lord; . . . then the house was filled with a cloud . . . so that the priests could not stand to minister by reason of the cloud: for the glory of the Lord filled the house of God" (2 Chron. 5: 13). It has been characteristic of the recent movement in the Hebrides, that on many occasions when the congregation united in a psalm of praise, the power of God came down, and "many were the slain of the Lord". When Jehoshaphat went out in battle against Ammon, Moab, and Mount Seir, "he appointed them that should sing unto the Lord, and praise the beauty of holiness, as they went out before the army, and say, Give thanks unto the Lord; for His mercy endureth for ever. And *when they began to sing and to praise*, the Lord set liers in wait against the children of Ammon . . . and they were smitten" (2 Chron. 20: 21). It is certainly true that they who have "the high praises of God in their mouth" have also "a two-edged sword in their hand" (Ps. 149: 6). It was thanksgiving as well as prayer that shut the lions' mouths for Daniel. Scripture records that "he kneeled upon his knees three times a day, and prayed, and *gave thanks* before his God" (Dan. 6: 10).

By precept and by practice Paul taught the churches that prayer and thanksgiving are two that God hath joined together, and no man ought to put asunder. He exhorts us to "pray without ceasing", and then, as though in the same breath, he adds, "in everything give thanks" (1 Thess. 5: 17). At the commencement of almost every epistle he writes in words like these: "We give thanks to God . . . praying always for you" (Col. 1: 3). When, at Philippi, he and Silas were arrested by the authorities for no other crime than delivering a captive of Satan, they had their garments rent off them, and their backs lacerated by many stripes of the rod. They were cast into the inner prison, and their feet made fast in the stocks. They were indeed "in the wars", but they were "the wars of the Lord", and these veteran warriors knew how to fight in them. Not by murmurings and recriminations, but by a spirit of prayer and praise they would conquer; and so the midnight hour found them "praying and singing hymns unto God", the other prisoners their silent, wondering audience (Acts 16: 25). The mighty earthquake that opened every prison door and loosed every man's bands, the attempted suicide of the jailer, his subsequent conversion with his whole house, and the eventual release of the apostles complete the wonderful story. How irresistible is the gospel war-chariot when drawn by the steeds of prayer and praise.

Finally, the seventh feature must be noted. To prevail in prayer we must be—

### Patient

That perseverance and vigilance are vital to prevailing prayer has already been stressed, but these qualities demand yet another which is basic to the whole ministry of intercession—patience. In prayer the self-discipline involved in patient waiting is one of the means by which God fits us to receive the answer, and this is especially true in revival. God will very likely keep us waiting much longer than we would have chosen or could have expected. The waiting period, whether short or long, is a time of indispensable preparation for the outpouring that God has purposed. The greater the blessing God intends, the longer the time, in all probability, that we shall have to wait, because the preparation needs co be correspondingly deeper. Therefore, discouraged prayer warrior, "let patience have its perfect work, that ye may be perfect and entire, lacking in nothing" (Jas. 1: 4) when at length God's hour shall strike.

Let us not think, as we plead for revival, that we have to move God to share our concern and burden about the matter. We feel as we do because God has stirred us to share but a fraction of His concern. Our longing is but a feeble, pale reflection of His own. Our exercise of patience should draw us into deeper fellowship with "the God of patience", who has manifested such longsuffering towards the sons of men. How long has He waited for us before we began to wait for Him? Let us also remember that for nigh on two thousand years the Son has been at the Father's right hand engaged in this very ministry of praying and waiting—"till His enemies be made the footstool of His feet" (Heb. 10: 13). "The Lord direct [our] hearts into the love of God, and into the patience of Christ" (2 Thess. 3: 5).

It has already been shown that the rains of Palestine, especially the former and the latter, are typical of the outpouring of the Spirit; and that these rains could only be expected at their appointed seasons, and so they had to *wait* for them, and they did so with eager anticipation. Job alludes to this in describing how men waited for his counsel: "They waited for me as for the rain; and they opened their mouth wide as for the latter rain" (Job 29: 23). "Are there any among the vanities of the heathen that can cause rain?" asked the prophet, "or can the heavens give showers? Are not Thou He, O Lord our God? Therefore we will *wait* upon Thee; for Thou hast made all these things" (Jer. 14: 22). Just as the first outpouring of the Spirit at Pentecost revealed the essential features of every subsequent outpouring, so the preparation for that outpouring constitutes a pattern for those that follow. The apostles were charged by Christ to "*wait* for the promise of the Father" (Acts 1: 4). They did so by continuing steadfastly in prayer until the day of Pentecost was fully come. All this shows us that waiting in prayer is not an incidental but an essential in the work of preparation. We cannot have revival when we like. We *can* have it if we fulfil the conditions, but one of these is that we continue patiently in prayer until God's time comes. Even God has to wait for the moment He has Himself ordained. "The husbandman waiteth for the precious fruit of the earth, being patient over it, until it receive the early and latter rain. Be ye also patient" (Jas. 5: 7).

If by the grace of God we are enabled to continue patiently in prayer for God's intervention, is it possible that we could be disappointed at last? Promises innumerable spring from the sacred page to deny such a thought. "Wait on the Lord, and keep His way, and He shall exalt thee" (Ps. 37: 34). "None that wait on Thee shall be ashamed" (Ps. 25: 3; cf. Isa. 49: 23). "The Lord is good unto them that wait for Him, to the soul that seeketh Him" (Lam. 3: 25). "Though [the vision] tarry, wait for it; because it will surely come, it will not delay" (Hab. 2: 3). "For ye have need of patience, that, having done the will of God, ye may receive the promise" (Heb. 10: 36). The experience of every patient and expectant soul is a testimony to "a God . . . which worketh for him that waiteth for Him" (Isa. 64: 4).

Few, if any, in modern times have demonstrated so forcibly the value of patient waiting upon God as George Müller. Referring to his daily prayer for the conversion of certain individuals, in some cases for many years, he wrote : "Still the answer is not yet granted concerning those persons, while in the meantime many thousands of my prayers have been answered, and also souls converted, for whom I had been praying. I lay particular stress upon this for the benefit of those who may suppose that I need only to ask of God, and receive at once . . . Patience and faith may be exercised for many years, even as mine are exercised, in the matter to which I have referred; and yet am I daily continuing in prayer, and expecting the answer, and so surely expecting the answer, that I have often thanked God that He will surely give it, though now for nineteen years faith and patience have thus been exercised."

Similarly, David Brainerd's diary not only reveals, as we have seen, the intensity of his praying, but how it pleased God to test his patience to the utmost. During his labours among the American Indians, he had often been uplifted by hopeful signs of a work of God among them, only to be disappointed when the effects seemed to fade away, so that he wrote on August 2nd, 1745, "My rising hopes, respecting the conversion of the Indians, have been so often dashed, that my spirit is as it were broken, and courage wasted, and I hardly dare hope." But though endurance was stretched to the full Brainerd continued to cling to God. The following day he records "a surprising concern" among the people as he preached. This increased daily, and in less than a week the Spirit of God was mightily poured out, and the revival had begun.

His reflections on this, in the conclusion of Part I of his journal, are deeply significant : "It is remarkable that God began this work among the Indians at a time when I had the least hope of seeing a work of grace propagated amongst them. I was ready to look upon myself as a burden, and began to entertain serious thoughts of giving up my mission. I do not know that my hopes respecting the conversion of the Indians were ever reduced to so low an ebb. And yet this was the very season that God saw fittest to begin this glorious work! And thus He ordained strength out of weakness, by making bare His almighty arm at a time when all hopes and human probabilities most evidently appeared to fail. —Whence I learn, that it is good to follow the path of duty, though in the midst of darkness and discouragement."

Be strengthened then, discouraged Christian, to "wait on thy

God continually" (Hos. 12: 6). In response to patient persevering prayer God will surely, in His own good time, open to you the windows of heaven.

> O living Stream—O gracious Rain,
> None wait for Thee, and wait in vain
> (TERSTEEGEN 1769).

The doorway of prevailing prayer lies open if we will but enter in. Abraham and Jabez, Hannah and Samuel, Daniel and Nehemiah, Moses and Elijah, Paul and Epaphras, and countless others whose names are known only to God, were men and women of like passions with us, but they prayed and prevailed. They became what they were by grace, in spite of what they were by nature, even as we read of Jacob: "In the womb he took his brother by the heel; and in his manhood he had power with God" (Hos. 12: 3). Their prayers ascended as incense to the throne. Through intercession they opened to a dying world the treasuries of grace. Who follows in their train?

For he shall be great in the sight of the Lord . . . and he shall be filled with the Holy Spirit. . . . And many of the children of Israel shall he turn unto the Lord their God. And he shall go before His face in the spirit and power of Elijah . . . to make ready for the Lord a people prepared for Him.

GABRIEL FORETELLING THE BIRTH OF JOHN
(Luke 1 :15).

## CHAPTER TWELVE

# PREPARING THE WAY

"The voice of one that crieth, Prepare ye in the wilderness the way of the Lord, make straight in the desert a high way for our God. Every valley shall be exalted, and every mountain and hill shall be made low: and the crooked shall be made straight, and the rough places plain: and the glory of the Lord shall be revealed, and all flesh shall see it together: for the mouth of the Lord hath spoken it" (Isa. 40: 3).

THESE familiar words of Isaiah set forth from yet another aspect the conditions and promise of revival. Firstly, there is *the forerunner* and his ministry, "The voice of one that crieth." Secondly, there is *the proclamation* he makes, heralding the approach of the Sovereign: "The King is coming! Prepare for the King!" Finally, there is *the promise* that when He comes, the state of the wilderness, with its valleys and mountains, its crooked and rough places, shall be transformed; and His glory shall be universally revealed.

It is characteristic of the Old Testament prophets to speak of revival in terms of a divine visitation. "His going forth is sure as the morning," declared Hosea (6: 3). Habakkuk described his vision of revival thus: "God came from Teman, and the Holy One from mount Paran . . . His goings were as of old" (3: 3, 6). If a sovereign should decide to visit some of his subjects unannounced, he would not be likely to use the occasion to demonstrate his majesty and glory. On a state visit, however, when he *does* come forth in royal splendour, it is essential that preparations in keeping with the grandeur of the occasion be made. It is indeed a state occasion when God comes forth in the splendour and power of revival, for it is a time, as Isaiah reminds us, when the glory of the Lord is revealed before the eyes of all. Suitable preparations must therefore be made, and first of all God has to find a man who will communicate to men His intentions. He raises up a herald for the hour of preparation. "Behold, I send My messenger, and he shall prepare the way before Me: and the Lord whom ye seek, shall suddenly come to His temple" (Mal. 3: 1).

## The Forerunner

In preparation for a great visitation, God may raise up many messengers, each preparing the way of the Lord in his own appointed sphere. This is surely a day when God is looking for forerunners to blaze the trail of revival; not smooth preachers, but rugged prophets: men of the stamp of Elijah, who, with the hand of the Lord upon him, girded up his loins and ran before the king to the entrance of the royal city (1 Kings 18: 46). Thus he demonstrated the spiritual work he was doing as a forerunner. On Carmel Elijah had prepared the way of the Lord, and now the Lord was coming "as the rain, as the latter rain that watereth the earth" (Hos. 6: 3).

Those whom God calls to such a ministry—and a call is essential—must be prepared for a pathway of unpopularity and misunderstanding. "Thou troubler of Israel" was the way Ahab addressed Elijah (1 Kings 18: 17), and so this prophet whom God had sent to deal with the "Achans in the camp" (see Joshua 7: 25) was himself accused of being one. John the Baptist demonstrates also this element in the ministry of the forerunner. Standing alone as the champion of righteousness, he unmasked the hypocrisy of the religionists and even denounced the sin of the king upon the throne. This man, who was "much more than a prophet", was called to seal his ministry with his blood, yet he succeeded in preparing the way of the Lord. "Among them that are born of women there hath not arisen a greater than John the Baptist" (Matt. 11: 11). A forerunner must needs be one who can say, "I truly am full of power by the Spirit of the Lord, and of judgment, and of might, to declare unto Jacob his transgression, and to Israel his sin" (Mic. 3: 8).

Jeremiah was another forerunner. In a day dark with declension and judgment his fearless ministry helped to check the evils of the time, and prepare the way for a reviving that he did not live to witness, under Ezra and Nehemiah. The commission given him of the Lord is deeply significant : "I have this day set thee over the nations and over the kingdoms, to pluck up and to break down, and to destroy and to overthrow; to build, and to plant" (Jer. 1: 10). It will be noted that there is twice the emphasis on the negative element as on the positive; two-thirds of his ministry was to be destructive, and only one-third constructive. This is characteristic of the work of a forerunner. Stumbling-blocks of iniquity have to be taken up (Isa. 57: 14) and stones of unbelief have to be gathered out (Isa. 62: 10) if the way of the Lord is to be prepared. The very word "prepare" contains this idea of casting out, emptying, and clearing as a field before planting. Destruction, ruthless and thorough, must precede the greater work of construction that is to follow. It takes a man who "fears no one but God and hates nothing but sin" to proclaim the message of the forerunner.

### The Proclamation

The first point to note in the proclamation of the forerunner is *the place of visitation*. It is obvious that one who prepares the way of the king must reveal what part of his domain the king is about to visit, and where it is that preparations are to be made. "Prepare ye *in the wilderness* . . . make straight *in the desert*," cries the prophet. We should not be surprised to discover that God does not often choose the well-watered garden, the fruitful field, or the luxurious forest as the scene of a divine visitation in revival, for they have no need. He chooses rather the dry and weary land, parched and barren, whose yawning cracks plead to heaven for showers; it is here that God is pleased to come in the rain of the Spirit. The promise that "the glory of the Lord shall be revealed" expresses the very nature and purpose of revival. God therefore chooses the place which provides the greatest scope for the demonstration of that glory. When the spiritual wilderness is transformed into a paradise men exclaim "this is the finger of God"; they acknowledge that "the exceeding greatness of the power" that has accomplished the miracle must be of God and not of men, and so the Lord alone is exalted in that day.

"Wilderness" is that which the farmer looks upon as unworkable, and therefore hopeless. Maybe that word is a fitting description of the sphere of your spiritual activities, that which has been for so long the scene of your travail and tears, your labours and longings. When it seems a sheer impossibility that there should be a work of God there, take heed to the command, "prepare ye in the wilderness . . . make straight in the desert", for God has promised that "The wilderness and the solitary place shall be glad; and the desert shall rejoice, and blossom as the rose" (Isa.

35: 1). Here is a message of hope for some discouraged servant. The God to whom no situation is impossible, has chosen the desert as the place in which to manifest His power and glory. "Strengthen ye the weak hands," continues the prophet, "and confirm the feeble knees. Say to them that are of a fearful heart, Be strong, fear not : behold, your God will come with vengeance, with the recompence of God; He will come and save you. . . . For in the wilderness shall waters break out, and streams in the desert. And the mirage [margin] shall become a pool, and the thirsty ground springs of water" (verses 3–7).

Before this wonderful work of transformation can take place a way must be prepared, a highway must be made straight. But who is to do it? *You!* "Prepare *ye* . . . the way of the Lord," cries the forerunner. But how is it to be done? There are perhaps four ways in which this command should be obeyed. Firstly, there are our own hearts; secondly, there are the hearts of our fellow-believers; thirdly, there are the hearts of the lost; and finally, there are the heavenly regions.

*"Beginning with me"* is the first step. "Blessed is the man whose strength is in Thee; in whose heart are the highways" (Ps. 84: 5). It is not necessary to add to what has been said in an earlier chapter on heart preparation, and what it involves. The Psalmist simply reminds us that the heart which is rightly related to God is a highway for Him. Isaiah's wonderful description of waters breaking out in the wilderness and streams in the desert (chap. 35) goes on to say, "And an high way shall be there, and a way, and it shall be called *The way of holiness*" (verse 8). We need only pause to ask ourselves again, Is my heart, is my life a highway of holiness for God? Have I swept away the stones of unbelief? Have the crooked places of unrighteousness been made straight? Have I taken up the stumbling-blocks of inconsistency, unreality, and worldliness? When the God of unsullied holiness moves in the irresistible power of revival, will He find in me the avenue He needs in this spiritual wilderness? If, my reader, you cannot answer "Yes" to these questions, lay down this book and seek the Lord *now*. When revival comes it may be too late.

It was said of David Brainerd, "God could flow unhindered through him. The omnipotence of grace was neither arrested nor straitened by the conditions of his heart; the whole channel was broadened and cleaned out for God's fullest and most powerful passage, so that God with all His mighty forces could come down on the hopeless, savage wilderness and transform it into His blooming, fruitful garden." Here was one who truly prepared the way of the Lord in his own life, and God saw to it that His glory was revealed in revival. When it comes to the mighty movements of the Spirit, every heart is either a highway or a hindrance.

"*Moving to others*" sums up the next sphere in which we must prepare the way of the Lord. Revival truly begins in us, but it does not end there. There must be a sense of responsibility towards our fellow-believers who do not yet feel the need or see the possibilities of the hour. "Write the vision, and make it plain . . . that he may run that readeth it" (Hab. 2 : 2). Until the vision is written others will never read; until others read they will never run, as men with a mission, as those sent of the Spirit. The vision must be written upon our hearts, upon our lips, upon our lives, if the way of the Lord is to be prepared in the lives of others. There must be expectancy in our praying, passion in our preaching, boldness in our planning, and holiness in our living if we are to stir the saints. We must be miniature forerunners, each in our own sphere; it is not enough to prepare the way in our own hearts, we must prepare the way in the hearts of others. This is a ministry which demands steadfastness of purpose, desire, and expectancy, for it is fraught with disappointments. Some seem to catch the vision at once, but set-backs, delays, or opposition take their toll, and they lose that vision. Others are slow to catch fire, but once aflame they are steadfast and irresistible in their burning.

"*Reaching the sinners*" suggests the third sphere in which the way of the Lord should be prepared. It is certainly true that in times of revival God very often takes the work right out of the hands of man and bids us stand still and see His salvation. But, note well, there is no standing still in preparing the way for revival, for it is a time of vital activity. We must heed the command, "preach the word; be instant in season, out of season" (2 Tim. 4 : 2) if we would prepare the way of the Lord in the hearts of sinners. There must be a tireless sowing of the seed. Every legitimate means and every available opportunity must be seized to make known the gospel of Christ.

Brainerd wrote of the revival among American Indians: "I never saw the work of God appear so independent of means as at this time. I discoursed to the people, and spoke what, I suppose, had a proper tendency to promote convictions; but God's manner of working upon them appeared so entirely supernatural, and above means, that I could scarce believe He used me as an instrument. . . . And although I could not but continue to use the means which I thought proper for the promotion of the work, yet God seemed, as I apprehended, to work entirely without them. I seemed to do nothing, and indeed to have nothing to do, but to 'stand still and see the salvation of God'." This is of course the mark of heaven-sent revival, but in contemplating such a glorious time of reaping, let us not forget those preceding years when Brainerd, despite bodily weakness, innumerable hardships, and constant discouragements, ploughed and sowed and fainted not. The work of God is not so independent of means as sometimes it appears.

"A few years ago a warm current called El Nina, which usually comes before Christmas, swept southward along the west coast of South America in greater volume than ever before. It brought with it torrential showers, which visited parts of South America which had not known rain since the year 1551. El Nina turned thousands of miles of desert into paradise in an incredibly short time, as it caused millions of hardy seeds which had lain dormant in the ground through decades of drought to sprout and grow with incredible vigour" (from *Rent Heavens* by R. B. Jones).

These remarkable facts are a salutary reminder that showers of rain alone can never turn a wilderness into a paradise. Rain must fall upon seed if there is to be a harvest. This has a most important bearing in the realm of revival. The hearts of the unconverted need to be well sown with the word of God in preparation for the outpouring of the Spirit. If we sow bountifully we may expect to reap bountifully, and if we sow sparingly we may expect to reap in like manner, when the rain of the Spirit comes. Many who seem in an awakening to be converted without any human agency, who "spring up among the grass, as willows by the watercourses", are very often the harvest of some bygone sowing that only needed the life-giving rain of the Spirit.

If we would prepare the way of the Lord in the hearts of sinners, then we must cover the ground with the incorruptible seed. We should of course desire and expect immediate results; but if these are delayed, let us not think they are denied. When the rain of the Spirit descends from heaven there will be a harvest above all that we could have asked or thought. "Wherefore, my beloved brethren, be ye steadfast, unmoveable, always abounding in the work of the Lord, forasmuch as ye know that your labour is not vain in the Lord" (1 Cor. 15: 58). Never mind if we seem to be prophesying unto the dry bones. Never mind if we seem to be ever sowing and never reaping. God's hour will strike. "Let us not be weary in well-doing : for in due season we shall reap, if we faint not" (Gal. 6: 9). We must be undaunted by spiritual weather conditions, we must persevere with this work, for "He that observeth the wind shall not sow; and he that regardeth the clouds shall not reap . . . In the morning sow thy seed, and in the evening withhold not thine hand : for thou knowest not which shall prosper, whether this or that, or whether they both shall be alike good" (Eccles. 11: 4, 6).

"But we are not all preachers," someone may say. That is sadly true, but the Lord expects us to be, though He may call but a few to a public ministry. In the early days of the church, when persecution broke out against the work in Jerusalem, it was as though the Devil had, in malice, kicked over the brazier of revival, and scattered the coals throughout Judaea and Samaria. But this did not extinguish the fire; it spread it. Wherever the live coals were cast new fires broke out. "They therefore that were scattered abroad went about preaching the word" (Acts 8: 4). But who were these who were scattered? "They were all scattered abroad . . . except the apostles" (8 : 1). All classes of believers in the church—the old and the young, the educated and the illiterate, the gifted and the not-so-gifted, the men and the women—were all, the apostles alone excepted, scattered abroad spreading the glad tidings. The extraordinary rapidity with which the movement spread may be traced to the fact that all the Christians of the early church were preachers, and so it should be with us. From place to place, and from door to door they went; in the streets and in the market-places, and wherever people were to be found, there were the Christians, testifying and exhorting, preaching and persuading, discussing and discoursing. They truly prepared in the wilderness the way of the Lord by scattering the land with the seed of the word, and we are called to do the same.

"*Preparing the Heavenlies*" is the final way in which we are to "make straight a highway for our God". The region immediately above the earth, called in Scripture "the heavenly places", is the sphere of spirit forces by which Satan controls the world. These demon powers are variously described as "principalities", "powers", "world-rulers of this darkness", "spiritual hosts of wickedness in the heavenly places" (Eph. 6: 12; cf. 3: 10). Though they work through human personalities, they are not themselves human, but Satanic. By their effective working the minds of men are darkened and their wills held captive to sin (2 Cor. 4: 4; 2 Tim. 2: 26, margin). Through their authority and agency "the whole world lieth in the evil one" (1 John 5: 19). This is literally true of the earth, for being spherical it is completely enveloped by these heavenly regions which are all enemy territory. Since the rain of the Spirit must come down through these lower heavenly places before there can be revival, and since this can only be in answer to prayer, Satan is prepared to throw everything into the conflict if he can only prevent or hinder this wondrous operation of the Holy Spirit. A way must therefore be prepared in the heavenlies for the Lord by "fighting-prayer". Says the apostle, "Our wrestling is not against flesh and blood, but against the principalities, etc. . . . in the heavenly places" (Eph. 6: 12). Therefore we cannot engage in this prayer warfare unless we are strong in the Lord, and have put on the whole armour of God (verses 10, 11).

There have been many occasions when it seemed certain to those watching and praying that God was about to visit them in revival, but on the very eve of the outpouring, or even after it had begun, the Enemy came in like a flood and swept almost everything away. Such instances confirm the reality of these powers of darkness which lie behind the stubborn wills and darkened hearts of men. We may be prayerful and spiritual, we may be courageous and determined, we may even be filled with the Spirit and succeed in breaking into "the strong man's house" and putting our hand upon his goods; but if we have not learned the secret of prayer warfare, and how to bind "the strong man", he will very likely return in fury and drive us out. Such a counter-attack can have a devastating effect on those who have been praying and labouring hopefully, and it can also supply opposers of the work with the ammunition they require.

If the work is to be safeguarded from such reverses, and if there is to be solid progress towards revival, the prayer warrior must set himself to win this battle in the heavenlies. Not until we have prepared a way up there can the Lord set before us down here "a door opened, *which none can shut*" (Rev. 3: 8). How we may overcome the Evil One in this prayer warfare was demonstrated to us by the life of the Son of God, and opened to us by His death and resurrection. Referring to Himself casting out demons, He spoke of first binding the strong one, and then entering into his house and spoiling his goods (Matt. 12: 29; Luke 11: 21). In every encounter with Satan the Lord Jesus manifested a superiority that was absolute. Though truly God, He overcame on earth as man filled with the Spirit, as He Himself was careful to point out: "If I *by the Spirit of God* cast out demons . . ." (Matt. 12: 28). With the last great encounter with Satan before Him, the Lord Jesus solemnly declared, "Now shall the prince of this world be cast out" (John 12: 31). Thus did He set His face as a flint to go to the cross, moving with sure and measured tread to His final conquest.

> Ride on ! Ride on in majesty !
> In lowly pomp ride on to die :
> Bow Thy meek head to mortal pain,
> Then take, O God, Thy power, and reign.
> H. H. MILMAN.

The victory of the cross was conclusive. It sealed for all time the doom of Satan, and the resurrection of Christ displayed that victory before the universe. The Saviour had returned from the dead as the risen conquering Son to claim the spoils of victory. The purpose of His mission, "that through death He might bring to nought him that had the power of death" (Heb. 2: 14) and "that He might undo [lit. trans.] the works of the devil" (1 John 3: 8), had been fulfilled. "Having put off from Himself the principalities and the powers, He made a show of them openly, triumphing over them in [the cross]" (Col. 2: 15). Having spoken with His mouth, He has with His own hand fulfilled it. The light that shines from the vacant cross and the empty tomb shows us our heavenly David with the head of Goliath in His hand. Behold the strong one, overcome by a stronger than he, stripped of the armour wherein he trusted, and bound with the cords of divine justice.

In spite of the reality of this victory, the fact remains that

Satan is still permitted to have great power. The divine sentence passed upon him at the cross is not yet executed. He knows that his time is short and that God will bruise him under our feet shortly. Meanwhile the conquest of Satan at Calvary only becomes effective when applied by faith, and this is done through wrestling in prayer. From our new vantage ground, risen with Christ and seated with Him in heavenly places (Eph. 2: 5, 6), we have to pin down and neutralize the enemy who has for so long dominated those regions. Pleading the victory of Christ we must wage war in prayer against the forces of darkness, using those principles of intercession already considered. Thus do we prepare the way of the Lord in the heavenly regions that He may come down in the majesty and power of revival.

### The Promise

When we have prepared the way of the Lord in our hearts, in the hearts of others, in the hearts of sinners, and in the heavenly places, then "Our God shall come, and shall not keep silence : a fire shall devour before Him, and it shall be very tempestuous round about Him" (Ps. 50: 3). We must expect a spiritual revolution if the wilderness is to be transformed into the garden of the Lord. God will see to the revolution if we will provide Him with the roadway. Herein lies the wonder of the promise. It is not our concern to transform the general situation, to deal with valleys and mountains, crooked paths and rough places, and whatever else may make up the spiritual wilderness. Give God a highway and He promises that "every valley shall be exalted, and every mountain and hill shall be made low : and the crooked shall be made straight, and the rough places plain : and the glory of the Lord shall be revealed, and all flesh shall see it together : for the mouth of the Lord hath spoken it". This is the revolution of revival : the wilderness turned upside down and inside out.

God is promising that this visitation will bring a reversal of values and a transformation of conditions. The valleys, abased and despised in the eyes of men, shall be exalted. The fear of God, obedience to His word, reverence for His day, love of righteousness and truth and equity, and all the things which have become valleys and depressions, matters of no account, in the foolishness of man's thinking, shall be exalted to a place of prominence according to God's original intention. Similarly, mountains of pride, unbelief, materialism, worldly cares, pleasures, ambitions and lusts of other things, all in fact which seems to present an insuperable barrier to the movements of God in our day, within the church and without it, shall flow down at the presence of the Lord. "The crooked shall be made straight" : crooked lives, characters, thoughts, words, habits, actions shall be made as straight as the woman whom Christ healed, who was bowed together and could in no wise lift herself up (Luke 13: 11). And the rough places of life, harsh and unrelenting and graceless, places that have never known the all-subduing tenderness of the love of Christ, shall be made smooth by the grace of the Lord. This is what God promises to do, in greater or lesser degree, in the visitations of revival.

Lastly, all the promise is gathered up and expressed in one final all-inclusive declaration, "And the glory of the Lord shall be revealed, and all flesh shall see it together." Here is the highest and holiest thing in revival, the manifestation of God, the shining forth of His glory before the eyes of men. It is the soul who, like Isaiah, has caught a glimpse of that effulgent glory—and one glimpse is enough to spoil him for all of earth—who will go forth, *whatever the cost*, to obey the divine command by preparing the way of the Lord, that men too may behold that glory and be changed (2 Cor. 3: 18). But what is the cost? That is a question that must now be answered.

"These things spake Jesus, and departed and did hide Himself" (John 12: 36). Is God hiding Himself because we are unwilling to face the implications of the cross? We want revival, but are we willing to pay the price? That price is death to the self-life. This surely is the place of victory and the price of revival. For the sake of our Lord, for the sake of perishing souls and the crown rights of our Redeemer, let us face the cross, and in the strength of His grace go through.

DUNCAN CAMPBELL.

## CHAPTER THIRTEEN

## PAYING THE PRICE

"Bring ye the whole tithe into the storehouse, that there may
be meat in Mine house, and prove Me now herewith, saith
the Lord of Hosts, if I will not open you the windows of
heaven, and pour you out a blessing, that there shall not be
room enough to receive it" (Mal. 3:10).

O N the conditions of revival much has been said of the
negative aspect, but there are certain positive factors that
must now be considered. It is an easy matter to pray for
revival without realizing what is involved, but it is quite another
thing to pray with a clear appreciation of the price that must be
paid. There may well be Christians praying for revival who, if
they knew the implications, would be crying to God *not* to send
it. With some there may be a willingness to face up to the question
of *sin*, but an unwillingness to face up to the question of *sacrifice*; yet the latter is as much bound up with the conditions
of blessing as the former. It is possible that some who oppose the
emphasis on revival have a clearer view of the cost than some
others who are in favour of it, and in this may be found the real
reason for their objections. Be that as it may, we cannot escape
from the fact that there is a price to be paid, for Scripture is
emphatic on the point.

### Robbing God

Through His prophet Malachi God had to say to His people,
"Return unto Me, and I will return unto you" (3:7). One can
almost hear their offended tone as the orthodox make answer,
"Wherein shall we return?" (verse 7). "*We* have not wickedly
departed from the Lord; why do you thus accuse us?" And the
Lord answers them, His voice vibrant with anger and yet
mellowed by grief, "Will a man rob God? yet ye rob Me . . .
in tithes and offerings . . . even this whole nation" (verses 8,
9). The closing days under the old covenant reveal that the sin of
God's people was that of robbing Him on a nation-wide scale.

What of the closing days under the new? Is history repeating itself? How many earnest Christians are irreproachable when called to "render unto Caesar the things that are Caesar's", but are verily guilty when it comes to rendering "unto God the things that are God's" (Matt. 22 : 21). Consciences are stirred when there is failure to settle debts with fellow-men, but there is often little or no concern that debts to the Lord remain unpaid. Such must face this accusation of God, "Ye rob Me."

The question, "How much owest thou unto my lord?"—which the unjust steward put to his lord's creditors (Luke 16 : 5)—is a pertinent question for us to ask one another today. Can we forget that there was a day when the only feeling we had in our hearts towards the God who gave us life and breath and all things, was one of enmity? He it was who had commended His love toward us while we were thus in rebellion against Him, by sending His Son to die for us. With what infinite longsuffering and relentless love He continued to pursue us, until He brought us with broken and contrite heart to the Saviour's feet. We cannot estimate the grace and the patience, the goodness and the mercy that have followed us all our life long unto this hour. In the light of all this and much more that is bound up in our inheritance, and reserved in heaven for us, let us face the question, "How much owest thou?"

> When I stand before the throne
> Dressed in beauty not my own,
> When I see Thee as Thou art,
> Love Thee with unsinning heart;
> Then, Lord, shall I fully know—
> Not till then—how much I owe.
> R. M. McCHEYNE.

However, we already know enough of the goodness of the Lord to answer, with the prompting of the Spirit, that we owe "a hundred measures". If we are able in any degree "to apprehend with all the saints what is the breadth and length and height and depth" of that love of Christ which passeth knowledge, we are bound to confess that nothing less than a hundred per cent should be the measure of our response. "Love so amazing, so divine, demands my soul, my life, my all." We may, however, acknowledge in theory that everything belongs to the Lord, and yet utterly fail in the practical outworking of it. The lip-service we pay to the truth of "full surrender" may all too easily cover a practical failure to render to the Lord His due.

Under the old covenant God claimed absolute possession of all that belonged to His people, and indeed of everything that He had created. "The silver is Mine, and the gold is Mine, saith the Lord of Hosts" (Hag. 2: 8). "The earth is the Lord's, and the fulness thereof; the world, and they that dwell therein" (Ps. 24: 1). "For every beast of the forest is Mine, and the cattle upon a thousand hills" (Ps. 50: 10). This did not, however, relieve His people of their responsibility to honour the Lord with their substance, and with the firstfruits of all their increase (Prov. 3: 9), to be faithful and diligent in the rendering of their tithes and offerings. When David blessed the Lord for the free-will offerings that the people had brought for the building of the temple he said, "But who am I, and what is my people, that we should be able to offer so willingly after this sort? For all things come of Thee, and of Thine own have we given Thee" (1 Chron. 29: 14). It was this people to whom God had to say later, "Ye rob Me . . . in tithes and offerings." Let us now consider four ways in which the church of Christ may be guilty of doing the same.

### Devotion

It is possible that we are robbing God of the love and devotion which are His due. Of all the offerings we may bring to the Lord, the expression of our heart's affection is supreme. He cannot accept any substitute for this. He may have blessed us with many human loves, but He demands the firstfruits of our devotion for Himself, for the firstfruits are holy unto the Lord. These were not only first in sequence, but first in quality. He is not content to accept the second best. He will brook no rival for that first place in the heart. "He that loveth father or mother [or anyone else] more than Me is not worthy of Me" (Matt. 10: 37). He, who has poured out His love upon the sons of men in measureless fulness, is He likely to be satisfied with that pittance which is all too often confined to Sunday mornings, offered from cold hearts, and which we dare to call "worship"?

The following is another extract from *The Price They Paid*, an account of a movement of the Spirit among missionaries in India: "We were directed to Malachi 3: 10, 'Bring ye all the tithes into the storehouse', and found that one tithe was worship and praise of Christ. The Lord brought our past lives into review before us, and we saw how continually we had denied Him fellowship, praise, and love, for which He is longing. We spent a good deal of time in those days just worshipping and glorifying the Lamb upon the throne. Our eyes were continually brought to focus on the cross." The Lord is commanding us also, "Bring ye the *whole* tithe into the storehouse, that there may be meat in Mine house." Again and again He comes to His house hungry for the meat-offering of our devotion, thirsty for the drink-offering of our love; He meets us there to receive His portion, and receives it not. Do we wonder that the heavens are shut up and there is no rain? "Return unto Me," He says, "with the warmth of true devotion, and I will return unto you with the rain of the Spirit."

## Time

Are we robbing God of that portion of our time that He expects us to yield to Him in a special way? It is true that *all* our time is His, whether occupied with secular or domestic duties, or even with social or recreational activities, and that all should be done to His glory. But over and above this, God expects us to preserve time from the incessant claims of temporal things to devote utterly to Him and His interests, in the same way as He expected the Israelite not only to acknowledge that all he possessed was God's, but to give a proportion specifically and wholly to God. There is much land to be possessed in the spiritual realm, there are priceless treasures to be sought and obtained, and these can only become ours when we are prepared to give time to seeking them with undivided attention. "Ye shall seek Me, and find Me, when ye shall search for Me with all your heart" (Jer. 29: 13). How can we do this when pressed down with the cares of this life, legitimate though they may be? Whether our responsibilities are great or small, as followers of Christ we are to obey His command, "Seek ye first His kingdom, and His righteousness; and all these things shall be added unto you" (Matt. 6: 33).

At a certain missionary training college the students are required to account for every minute of their day, that they might learn self-discipline in the use of time, and how to use the mo-

ments to the best advantage. It may be a revelation to the reader
to put pencil to paper in a similar way and account for the past
week and how many of its 168 hours have really been devoted
to God. Whether we care to submit to such a test or not, it is
certain that it will all be revealed at the judgment seat of Christ
when "each man's work shall be made manifest : for the day shall
declare it" (1 Cor. 3: 13). Had some remembered what it was
they were to "seek first", even God's kingdom and righteousness,
they might have halted the expansion of their businesses; they
might have refused the more lucrative job that robbed God of
the time they had been giving Him; they might have been content with the smaller house or the less congenial surroundings,
instead of moving away from the sphere where God was using
them. To many a Christian swamped with business God has to
say, "Ye rob Me of My time." Such might argue that we fail to
understand the situation, the cost of living, the needs of a growing
family, and so on. Perhaps this is so, but the Saviour understands,
and He answers, "All these things shall be added unto you." No
one ever sacrificed anything for Christ's sake and lost out by it.

The founder and head of an immense and prosperous factory,
having listened to an address by a servant of God, wrote to him
as follows:

> "Your words may save a soul from death.
> Early days—I was out and out
>     The Spirit of God was mighty.
>
> I.  Obedience to Him was a delight.
>     His word was illuminated.
>     It was the chief delight.
>     His service was supreme.
>     Everything was done by prayer.
>     Great distress and crises in business.
>     Remarkable deliverances.
>
> II.  Tide turned.
>     Prosperity dawned.
>     Responsibilities increased.
>
> III.  Prayer time shortened.
>     Practically nil today.
>     Experience of His presence gone.
>     Life no longer on the heights.
>     Foundations of things on low level.

Impossible through sheer impotency.
Habits have the grip.
Will power gone.

IV. The truth and force of your words realized, but case hopeless.
With the outline of your address I can fill in practically
all you said : it shall be my close study and may be the
recovery of my soul."

With this solemn case before us, let us take heed to the apostle's
words, "Look therefore carefully how ye walk, not as unwise, but
as wise; *redeeming the time,* because the days are evil" (Eph.
5: 15). May we never have to regret the hours that we might have
devoted to Him, but squandered on ourselves and our selfish
interests. Time lost can never be reclaimed.

Take time to be holy, the world rushes on;
Spend much time in secret with Jesus alone.
By looking to Jesus like Him thou shalt be;
Thy friends, in thy conduct, His likeness shall see.
                                W. D. LONGSTAFF.

If we truly desire that God shall open the windows of heaven
and pour us out the blessing of revival, then we must render to
Him forthwith the tithe of our time. Do we already give a little?
God says, "Bring ye the *whole* tithe into the storehouse."

## Gifts

Here is another sphere in which God is robbed by His people.
Gifts may be natural endowments which God desires to purify
and set apart as holy unto Himself, or they may be spiritual gifts
which are the manifestations of the Holy Spirit received by faith
(1 Cor. 12). In either case they are gifts from God, for "a man
can receive nothing, except it have been given him from heaven"
(John 3: 27). This fact should keep every believer humble. It was
to those who were zealous of gifts that Paul had to say, "Who
maketh thee to differ? and what hast thou that thou didst not
receive? but if thou didst receive it, why dost thou glory, as if
thou hadst not received it?" (1 Cor. 4: 7). As the farmer scatters
his seed in the expectation that it will return in harvest, even so
does "the Father of lights", from whom cometh down "every

good gift" (Jas. 1 : 17), expect that each shall return to Him again, bringing an increase of honour and glory to His Name.

It has been the continual objective of Satan to frustrate the purpose of God, and so to rob Him of His portion in His people. All too often he has succeeded, and believers have been, though often unconsciously, ready tools in his hand. Where human talents are made to serve selfish interests, to minister to our promotion, popularity, social prestige, or material prosperity, his evil purpose has in that measure been achieved, and the divine purpose has failed. It is inevitable that talents retained for ourselves will serve the Devil's purposes more than God's; yielded to Him, however, their powers and influence are transformed and multiplied beyond measure. When Stenburg, already famous as a German artist, was converted to Christ he longed to serve His newly found Saviour. What could he do? He had no gifts in preaching or speaking. It flashed into his mind that since he could paint, his brush must declare the love of God and glorify His Saviour. As he laid his wondrous artistic power at the feet of His Lord, his natural ability was purified, quickened, and inspired by the Spirit; and thus the brush of the artist led many a soul to Christ. "What is that in thine hand?" asked the Lord of Moses (Exod. 4: 2). It was only the humble rod of the shepherd; cast down it became a serpent; taken up in faith it became the rod of God by which signs and wonders were done in Egypt. If we yield that shepherd's staff to Him, He will transform it into the rod of God.

As with natural gifts, so with the spiritual. Even these may be prostituted to fulfil the desires of the flesh. The carnal man will seize with grasping fingers the choicest spiritual flower that God has placed in his garden, only to discover too late that he has shed the bloom. When God invests spiritual gifts in men He looks for His investment to return with eternal dividends. Where, however, such gifts become a means of ministering to the flesh, an occasion for pride and ostentation, the opportunity of obtaining the praise of men, then that which should return to God is retained for self, and God is thus robbed of His portion. But we may rob God also by neglecting our spiritual gifts, as well as by abusing them. The servant who hid his lord's talent in the earth was as guilty of robbing him as if he had invested it and misappropriated the dividends. Have we allowed temporal things so to swamp us, or personal considerations so to weigh with us,

that our gifts have run to seed? Let us own at once that we are
guilty of robbing God, and take heed to the apostle's words,
"Neglect not the gift that is in thee" (1 Tim. 4: 14), "Stir up the
gift of God, which is in thee" (2 Tim. 1: 6); and let all who
desire to bring the whole tithe into the storehouse that the windows of heaven may be opened observe well the words of Peter,
"According as each hath received a gift, [minister] it among
yourselves, *as good stewards* of the manifold grace of God" (1
Pet. 4: 10).

### Money

Primarily, the verse in Malachi suggests that God's people had
been robbing Him in the matter of their material giving. The
Israelite was commanded to honour the Lord with his substance
and with the firstfruits of all his increase (Prov. 3: 9). This involved, firstly, returning a tenth (or tithe) to the Lord (Gen.
28: 22; Deut. 14: 22). Over and above this proportion that was
*owed,* the Israelite had opportunity to give free-will and other
offerings. It would appear that an Israelite's giving did not com-
mence, strictly speaking, until he had paid his tithe. Here in
Malachi God accuses His people of robbing Him in both tithes
and offerings (3: 8). They were speaking and acting as though
they had fulfilled their obligations while they were giving God
short measure, imagining that they would escape detection, and
that no one would know. They were despising God by offering Him
beasts that were blind, lame, or sick, that they would not offer to
their governor (1: 6–8). "But cursed be the deceiver, which
. . . sacrificeth unto the Lord a blemished thing: for I am a
great King, saith the Lord of Hosts, and My Name is terrible
among the Gentiles" (1: 14).

How is it with us under "the better things" of the new covenant? Does God expect less from His people under grace than
He demanded from His people under law? Shall we who live in
the full blaze of Calvary and Pentecost, who are blessed with
every spiritual blessing in the heavenly places in Christ, and who
are looking for that blessed hope—shall we give less than they
who only knew "a shadow of the good things to come"? It is
true that we are not under law, and that there is no specific
command in the New Testament that we must give a tenth or any
other definite proportion of our income to God. You may re-

joice in this freedom, "only use not your freedom for an occasion to the flesh" (Gal. 5: 13). Remember, God's love was measured by His giving (John 3: 16; Eph. 5: 25) and so is ours. The teaching of the New Testament is, "Give, and it shall be given unto you; good measure, pressed down, shaken together, running over . . . for with what measure ye mete it shall be measured to you again" (Luke 6: 38). This is but a re-statement of that Old Testament proverb, "There is that scattereth, and increaseth yet more; and there is that withholdeth more than is meet, but it tendeth only to want" (Prov. 11: 24). God's ways have not changed.

Our heart attitude to our money and possessions may be a very real index to our spiritual state. "Lay not up for yourselves treasures upon the earth . . . but lay up for yourselves treasures in heaven . . . for where thy treasure is, there will thy heart be also" (Matt. 6: 19–21). Since it is obviously impossible for our hearts to be in two places at once, we cannot lay up treasure on earth, and at the same time lay it up in heaven. Which are we doing? The command of Christ is, "Sell that ye have, and give alms; make for yourselves purses which wax not old, a treasure in the heavens that faileth not" (Luke 12: 33). Are we obeying it? It is a spiritual tragedy when God's stewards feel free to lavish what has been entrusted to them on needless and even harmful luxuries while the interests of God's kingdom in many lands are declining through lack of means. Is it not clear that such Christians do not look upon their money as God's but as their own to use as they please? "Let each one of you lay by him in store, *as he may prosper*" (1 Cor. 16: 2), is the New Testament standard of giving, and it is certainly no lower than the Old Testament. It means in a word that instead of *living* up to our income we are *giving* up to our income. When John Wesley commenced his ministry he found he could manage to live on his meagre stipend. As God prospered him and his income increased he resisted the temptation to raise his standard of living; instead he continued to live in simplicity and gave the rest away. Since he gave the Lord His due, is it any wonder that the heavens were opened on his ministry?

Have we not here one vital reason why so often today "the heaven is stayed from dew, and the earth is stayed from her fruit" (Hag. 1: 10), even that many of God's people are more wrapped up in their own earthly interests, than in those of His heavenly kingdom? Before the fall of Jericho God had said, "The city shall be devoted, even it and all therein, to the Lord" (Joshua 6: 17). This was not only because of its wickedness, but because it was the firstfruits of Israel's conquest of Canaan, and therefore belonged to God. "All the silver, and gold, and vessels of brass and iron, are holy unto the Lord: they shall come into the treasury of the Lord" (6: 19). It will be remembered that Achan committed a trespass in the devoted thing, in that he secretly retained for himself that which should have been devoted to God. This one man's sin resulted in the Lord's anger being kindled against all Israel, so that they turned their backs before their enemies and were smitten at Ai. The judgment that befell Achan and his family teaches us how solemnly God views this sin of robbing Him of His due, and suggests a possible explanation for some of the reverses sustained by God's people in the wars of the Lord.

Much the same lesson is repeated in the story of Ananias and Sapphira (Acts 5). The church had been obeying the command of Christ, "Sell that ye have and give alms," "for as many as were possessors of lands or houses sold them, and brought the prices of the things that were sold, and laid them at the apostles' feet" (Acts 4: 34). But these two desired "to make a fair show in the flesh", to give the appearance of utter consecration while they "kept back part of the price". Deceit is anathema to God at all times, but more particularly when it is planned deceit in relation to holy things. No one had compelled them to sell the land— "Whiles it remained, did it not remain thine own?"; and when sold no one had forced them to devote the money to God— "after it was sold, was it not in thy power?" (5: 4). But they wanted the blessings of consecration without paying the price. In their sin and folly they thought that they were only dealing with the church; they did not perceive that it was the Head of the church with whom they had to do. Their end reminds us that "it is a fearful thing to fall into the hands of the living God" (Heb. 10: 31).

This solemn act of divine judgment is recorded for our warning. It is better not to vow unto the Lord than to vow and not pay (Eccles. 5: 5); it is better that we should openly fail to pay our tithes, than pretend to do so while withholding part of what is due; it is better that we should not seek revival, if, while we appear to mean business, we keep back part of the price. Let us face it now; let us face it on our knees before God : REVIVAL IS COSTLY. If it were otherwise the people of God would be more ready for it than they are, and perhaps God would send it more often. God is saying to us, "Bring ye the whole tithe into the storehouse." Whether it be our devotion, our time, our gifts, our possessions, or whatever else it is we have not been rendering to Him, He demands nothing less than "the whole tithe". If the windows of heaven are to be opened the price must be paid in the coin of sacrifice.

> Speak to us, Lord, till shamed by Thy great giving,
> Our hands unclasp to set our treasures free;
> Our time, our love, our dear ones, our possessions,
> All gladly yielded, gracious Lord, to Thee.
>
> ANON.

### Prove Me Now

That the blessing may be poured out God not only says, "Bring ye the whole tithe", but also, "Prove Me now herewith." The one is the divine challenge to sacrifice, the other is the divine challenge to faith. We cannot prove God until all the tithes are in, for they constitute the "herewith", the ground on which we prove Him. The bringing in of all God's due does not necessarily secure the outpouring, for there must also be the exercise of faith. When faith is made perfect, when in the words of this passage we can prove God now, He will surely respond in a way which shall be worthy of His promise of a blessing which shall overflow our capacity to receive it. Perhaps there are those who have, according to their knowledge and ability, laid all at His feet, yet the blessing tarries, and they have wondered why. It is evident that they have not yet arrived at an unwavering faith that can prove God now.

The need for patient waiting upon God has already been emphasized. This factor needs to be balanced by remembering that the time must come when God says, "Prove Me now." Let us beware that as we pray for revival we do not in our thinking defer it for ever to some remote time in the future, when God may be saying, "Now is the accepted time." It is an imperfect

faith that always relegates the desired blessing to a tomorrow
that never comes. If we would see revival, we must sooner or
later deal with this procrastination of unbelief. Deeply significant
are the words of the Lord to Ezekiel: "Son of man, behold, they
of the house of Israel say, The vision that he seeth is for many
days to come, and he prophesieth of times that are far off. Therefore say unto them, Thus saith the Lord God: There shall none
of My words be deferred any more, but the word which I shall
speak shall be performed, saith the Lord God" (Ezek. 12:27).
The acid test of a faith that is made perfect is the ability to prove
God *now*. When we find it in our hearts to do this, revival will be
nigh, even at the doors. In the words of Charles Finney, "If
God should ask you this moment, by an audible voice from
heaven, 'Do you want a revival?' would you dare to say 'Yes'?
'Are you willing to make the sacrifices?' would you answer 'Yes'?
'When shall it begin?' would you answer, 'Let it begin tonight—
let it begin here—let it begin in my heart *now*.'?"

All over the world Christian people of all denominations are expecting something. We may not all dream the same dream. We may not all express in the same way the new-born hope that has arisen in our hearts of God's *something* that is on the way. It may be when the veil is drawn asunder, when the church has been made ready, when the time has come for God to act, and to take the cataract off the eyes of the nation, that the mode and the method of the great ministry of the Spirit of God, for a great out-pouring, shall be very different from what we see and feel and hear today. But I care not how it comes; I care not through whom it comes; I care not what method is adopted so long as that method is in accordance with the will of the Divine Spirit of God. I feel the day is drawing swiftly near when men shall sink their differences, and shall come together to a place called Calvary, and there repent of their own foolishness of the days gone by, and, looking up into the face of God's anointed, shall say, "Thy kingdom come."

WILLIAM REID.

Hark what a sound, and too divine for hearing,
Stirs on the earth and trembles in the air!
Is it the thunder of the Lord's appearing?
Is it the music of His people's prayer?

From F. W. H. MYER's *St. Paul.*

## CHAPTER FOURTEEN

# THE SOUND OF MARCHING

"And it shall be, when thou hearest the sound of marching in
the tops of the mulberry trees, that then thou shalt bestir
thyself: for then is the Lord gone out before thee to smite the
host of the Philistines" (2 Sam. 5: 24).

SOON after David had been established king over Israel, the
Philistines came up and occupied the valley of Rephaim.
David inquired of the Lord, and was told to go up against
them. A bold frontal assault carried the day, and the Lord delivered them into his hand. Some time after, the Philistines
repeated the manœuvre, but David, without presuming on earlier
guidance or relying on past success, inquired of the Lord again.
This time he was told to make a detour, take up a position behind
them by the mulberry trees, and wait till he heard *the sound of
marching*. This was to be the sign that "God's host" (Gen. 32: 1, 2)
was on the move, and that the powers of heaven were being
thrown into the conflict to secure overwhelming victory.

These two battles help to illustrate the difference between God's
method in normal evangelism on the one hand, and His method
in revival on the other. In the first it is man's activity with divine
aid that is prominent, in the second it is God who goes into battle,
and man has only to move in the train of His victory and gather
the spoils. For the moment we are only concerned to notice that
preceding this remarkable operation in which God went forth
for the salvation of His people, there was "the sound of marching". This warning sign, this harbinger of revival was heard only
by those in the battle, the right men in the right place at the right
time.

Just as there are recorded in Scripture signs that are to
warn the watchful of the imminence of Christ's return, so there
are also signs given to us by which we may discern that God is
about to fulfil His promise to pour out the Spirit. "Behold, the
former things are come to pass, and new things do I declare:
before they spring forth I tell you of them" (Isa. 42: 9). This

"sound of marching" must be analysed and described so that if it is now present our ears may be attuned to hear it, or if it should come in the future we may be quick to recognize it. Let us take heed that we do not look at the wrong factors for evidence of impending revival. General Booth of the Salvation Army, writing to his eldest daughter, "the Maréchale", when much discouraged during the early days of her work in Paris, advised her to keep her eyes off the waves and fix them on the tide. To be occupied with the waves, with the ebb and flow of the spiritual battle, is to be alternately uplifted and downcast, elated and dejected. It is the unconquerable power of the tide that matters. The factors that reveal the quiet but irresistible trend of God's purposes are the true index. "Look! the tides are rising", Finney used to exclaim, and he was seldom wrong. Are they rising today? Here are some factors that may help us to answer the question. If we can discern them today we may be quite sure there is "the sound of marching in the tops of the mulberry trees".

### A Spirit of Lawlessness and Deadness

It is strange but true that the prevalence of lawlessness in the world and of deadness in the church is often an indication of impending revival. Said the Psalmist, "It is time for the Lord to work, for they have made void Thy law" (Ps. 119: 126). "The wave of spiritual progress recedes, but even in receding it is gathering in power and volume to return, and to rush further in . . .; when the night is at its darkest the dawn is on the way" (James Burns). They make a big mistake who always expect to see revival heralded by a decreasing of wickedness or by a marked and widespread improvement in the spiritual state of the church. The very reverse is often the case. Those who look for such improvement may shake their heads at a time when God is about to pour out His Spirit, and declare that there is no hope of a revival. Said Finney, "The prevalence of wickedness is no evidence at all that there is not going to be a revival. That is often God's time to work."

In an address on the eighteenth-century revival Dr. P. V. Jenness said: "Every student of history knows that the dawn of the eighteenth century was a time of material prosperity in England. The colonies were pouring their new wealth into the mother country. It was a day of luxury, dishonesty, speculation, and extravagance, and was followed by a severe panic when the South Sea bubble collapsed. It was a time of increased intellectual activity and expression. The freedom of worship secured through the Reformation had degenerated into licence to defy all authority, human and divine. Hobbs and Locke made infidelity popular. Gibbon and Hume devoted their talents to discrediting the church. Bolingbroke and Shaftesbury* among statesmen helped to create an atmosphere of spiritual chill. The church seemed helpless. The Reformation was a spent force. The ministry was largely corrupt. Blackstone, author of the *Commentaries on Law* writes as a young man that he sought in vain for a sound gospel preacher in London. The Sabbath was a day of general carousal. Public blasphemy was common. Current literature and common conversation was lascivious and corrupt. God was openly defied. The outlook was dark indeed. Here and there a few godly men and women were crying unto God for reformation and revival. Then the Lord 'made bare His holy arm in the eyes of all the nations, that the ends of the earth might see His salvation.' Three men were born in one year, 1703, John Wesley in England, Gilbert Tennent in Ireland, and Jonathan Edwards in Massachusetts. Eleven years later George Whitefield was born. These four men were the human agents of the great spiritual awakening that broke, like a storm, over England and America just two hundred years ago."

This extraordinary fact, that the river of blessing is often flowing at lowest level prior to a time of awakening, could be confirmed from history again and again. Jonathan Edwards in his *Thoughts on the Revival of Religion in New England* (1742) wrote: "Who that saw the state of things in New England a few years ago, the state that it was settled in, and the way that we had been so long going on in, would have thought that in so short a time there would be such a change?" And again, "How dead a time it was everywhere before this work began."

Shortly after the 1904 Revival broke out, the correspondent of the *Liverpool Daily Post* wrote in that paper: "If I had been asked a month ago whether a revival was probable in Wales, I should have answered, 'No'. It seemed to me that the 'higher

---

* Not to be confused with the famous Christian philanthropist of the nineteenth century.

criticism' had wrecked the ordinary machinery of a revival, and that, until theology had been reshaped in accordance with its conclusions, nothing would happen to disturb the prevailing apathy" (from *Rent Heavens* by R. B. Jones).

Prevailing deadness among believers and abounding lawlessness in the world are not an indication that revival is impossible, but that it is imperative. The hopelessness of the situation was to the Psalmist one of the strongest arguments in favour of divine intervention, for he saw therein a challenge that an omnipotent God could not ignore. To him the very need of the hour cried out, "It is time for the Lord to work."

## A Spirit of Dissatisfaction

This second factor may be widespread among peoples of all classes, or it may be confined to a few of the people of God who are being quietly prepared for what God is about to do. James Burns writes that the period preceding a widespread awakening "is characterized by a profound sense of dissatisfaction awaking in many hearts. A period of gloom sets in, a weariness and exhaustion invade the heart, the pleasures of the world no longer satisfy, they set up a deep distaste and satiety. Sick in soul, men turn with a sigh to God; dimly they wake to the consciousness that, in bartering heavenly for earthly joys, they have encountered irremediable loss; that in the decay of spiritual vision the world has lost its soul of loveliness. Slowly this aching grows, the heart of man begins to cry out for God, for spiritual certainties, for fresh visions. From a faint desire this multiplies as it widens, until it becomes a vast human need; until in its urgency it seems to beat with violence at the very gates of Heaven" (*Revivals, their Laws and Leaders*).

Though this widespread dissatisfaction is almost always there in measure, it cannot always be discerned until the movement is under way. But a sure mark of impending revival is where this spirit of dissatisfaction becomes apparent among believers. It may not be widespread, but here and there among different groups there is a growing thirst for a fuller, richer, and deeper experience of God than they have known. This spiritual restlessness, this holy dissatisfaction that is wrought in their hearts by God causes them to reach out with a great longing for that life more abundant that they know is theirs in Christ. Here are the birth pangs of that new thing that God is about to do, the travail out of which revival is born. "I will pour water upon him that is thirsty, and streams upon the dry ground" (Isa. 44: 3). "Blessed are they that hunger and thirst after righteousness : for they shall be filled" (Matt. 5: 6). Thank God for every thirsty, dissatisfied heart in a day when coldness, apathy, and complacency abound.

This profound dissatisfaction with which these believers view themselves and the work of God around them is nothing less than *a thirst for God*. "As the hart panteth after the water brooks, so panteth my soul after Thee, O God. My soul thirsteth for God, for the living God" (Ps. 42: 1). There is a thirst for the holiness of God, for the power of God, for the manifestation of God, for the truth of God.

There is a thirst for *the holiness of God*. A longing fills the soul for victory over sin and deliverance from the corruptions of the carnal man; for hearts of flesh instead of hearts of stone; to be wholly sanctified and conformed to the image of God's Son; to walk, like Enoch, in unbroken fellowship with God, and to be well-pleasing in His sight.

There is a thirst also for *the power of God* in personal experience. Believers begin to view with growing concern the ineffectiveness of their own efforts to serve the Lord. They are conscious of the reproach of the ungodly that God is not amongst them, even as was David, when he confessed in the same Psalm. "My tears have been my meat day and night, while they continually say unto me, Where is thy God?" (Ps. 42: 3). The more they examine the pages of the New Testament, and the lives of those whom God has used, the more convinced they become that they too ought to be clothed with power from on high, filled with the Spirit, and speak the word with boldness.

There is a thirst for *the manifestation of God,* to see His power and glory displayed before the eyes of men. It is this that David expresses in another Psalm, "My soul thirsteth for Thee, my flesh longeth for Thee, in a dry and weary land, where no water is . . . to see Thy power and Thy glory" (Ps. 63: 1). That their beloved, yet rejected Lord should be vindicated before the eyes of men becomes the passion of their souls. As in that first recorded prayer-meeting of the early church, they long that God would stretch forth His hand to heal and that signs and wonders may be done in the name of Jesus, so that He may be glorified and the hearts of the people may be opened to Him.

> Lord, we are few, but Thou art near;
> Nor short Thine arm, nor deaf Thine ear :
> Oh, rend the heavens, come quickly down,
> And make a thousand hearts Thine own.
>
> COWPER.

There is a thirst too for *the truth of God*. Believers begin to crave for a deeper understanding of God's word; they search for it as for hid treasures, and rejoice in it as one that findeth great spoil. There is often a healthy unwillingness to accept without question all that is taught and accepted as orthodox. A spirit of inquiry and discernment necessitates a fresh examination of what Scripture has to say. There is often a purging of the floor of truth, which scatters the chaff of human tradition and interpretation. James Burns points out one of the curious facts connected with the human mind—"its power to see only that which corresponds with current opinion, and of failing to see, not by conscious rejection, but by a strange incapacity, all that opposes it. Every age is imprisoned in its own conceptions, and has to be set free by the master minds which refuse to be enslaved." Such are often raised up preceding or during times of revival, when hearts have been unconsciously made ready to receive fresh light from God.

### A Spirit of Sin-consciousness

Like the spirit of dissatisfaction, this sensitivity to sin will be in evidence here and there among the people of God, where hearts are being made ready. It will be seen that most of these signs of impending blessing anticipate in the hearts of the few that which is to characterize all who will be affected when revival comes. Just as a cloud "as small as a man's hand" betokened to Elijah on Carmel the sound of abundance of rain, and was to him the earnest of "the heaven black with clouds" (1 Kings 18: 44, 45), so does this growing sensitiveness to sin in the hearts of the few indicate to the watchful eye that the day is at hand when God shall be revealed in holiness, and men shall repent in dust and ashes. The God who dwells in "the high and holy place" has promised "to revive the heart of the contrite ones" (Isa. 57: 15). A spirit of contrition among the saints is therefore a strong indication that revival is coming.

This conviction of the conscience regarding personal sin is usually manifested by confession. Christians are not easily brought to the point where they are prepared to obey the exhortation, "Confess therefore your sins one to another" (Jas. 5: 16), to apologize and ask forgiveness, and to make restitution. Where this happens, and there is a deep desire on the part of the saints to walk in the light with God, and in love one with another, it is evident that the Spirit of God is working, and hearts are being prepared for the outpouring of the Spirit. "A revival of religion may be expected when Christians begin to confess their sins one to another. . . . when there is an ingenuous breaking down, and a pouring out of the heart in making confession of their sins, the floodgates will soon burst open, and salvation will flow over the place" (Finney).

## A Spirit of Tender Concern

Where this is found in the hearts of believers it is a strong indication that revival is at hand. "Thou shalt arise, and have mercy upon Zion: for it is time to have pity upon her, yea, the set time is come. For thy servants take pleasure in her stones, and have pity upon her dust" (Ps. 102: 13, 14). When the harsh, unfeeling criticism with which believers often speak of the state of the church or the sin of the world gives place to a deep solicitude and tender concern which manifests the strong compassion of the Son of God, then we may be sure that the hour of revival is near. When believers feel as though they could cry out with the weeping prophet, "Oh that my head were waters, and mine eyes a fountain of tears, that I might weep day and night for the slain of the daughter of my people!" (Jer. 9: 1), then it is evident that the fountains of the great deep are being broken up, that the windows of heaven may be opened (Gen. 7: 11). When the saints mourn before the Lord, as did Hannah, Nehemiah, and Daniel, the answer of heaven will be as near to them as it was to those of a bygone age when they wept in the secret place.

## A Spirit of Expectancy

This is a further mark of coming revival, when found in the hearts of God's people. To find groups of Christians in different places, meeting independently of one another, with no denominational or other connection, and yet possessing the same spirit of desire and expectancy throbbing in their hearts, is presumptive evidence that it has been created by the sovereign Spirit, that out of the fulness of His loving heart God may abundantly satisfy it. The measure of expectancy may vary greatly; with some it is little more than a vague presentiment that something, they hardly know what, is going to happen; with others it is a clear and definite expectation of the outpouring of the Spirit. But however dim or definite it may be, it is the beginning of that spirit of faith that rises like the waters within the lock gates, until it has reached the required level, and the ship of revival moves forward on its divinely appointed way.

News of stirrings of the Spirit or even outpourings of the Spirit in other parts is a means God commonly uses to foster this spirit of expectancy. Every evidence of God's willingness to bless in other places should be to every longing soul a most hopeful sign of impending revival. "If God has done it there, may He not do it here also?"—this is the simple but reasonable ground of optimism. There is nothing more calculated to quicken desire and expectancy in prepared hearts than the news of what God has done or is doing elsewhere. When there comes news of striking conversions, of local movements of the Spirit, of touches of revival—if we may call them such—here and there, longing hearts will beat with quickened expectancy, and opened ears will hear God saying through these unusual events, "I will work, and who shall reverse it?" (Isa. 43: 13, R.V. margin).

### A Spirit of Unity

When this is manifest among various believers it is a strong indication that revival is at hand. "With one accord" marked the preparation of those early believers for the first outpouring of the Spirit, and so it has been in every subsequent outpouring. In spite of the prayer of the Son of God, "That they all may be one," sectarianism, exclusivism, and an attitude of spiritual superiority have everywhere split the people of God. Churches and groups act as though they and they alone were the rightful recipients of divine blessing. The Lord's servants outside their circles, although they may be signally used of God, have evidently nothing to impart to them. They only desire ministry from the man who, in the realm of theology, will dot all their "i"s, cross all their "t"s, and subscribe to all their shibboleths. They have, it would seem, the monopoly of truth and spiritual illumination. They feel that God ought to favour them in a special way; and when, as is often the case, He blesses elsewhere, they are at a loss to know why, and all too often try to disparage or belittle what God has done.

When, however, such barriers are thrown down, and believers come together in true humility and on the common ground of their love for Christ and desire for souls; when denominational pride and jealousy are slain, and there is a willingness, without compromising personal convictions, to learn in meekness one of another, to receive light and impart light, then there is evidence indeed that revival is coming. "Behold, how good and how pleasant it is for brethren to dwell together in unity! . . . For there the Lord commanded the blessing" (Ps. 133).

## A Spirit of Prayer

Finally, the infallible sign of impending revival is a spirit of prayer for it. When you see this in evidence among the people of God, you may be sure "it is time to seek the Lord, till He come and rain righteousness upon you" (Hos. 10: 12). It has been well said that "Satan laughs at our toil, mocks at our wisdom, but trembles when we pray". Therefore we may be confident that where a true spirit of prayer for revival exists, it does not proceed from the Devil. Such a spirit of prayer leads to humbling before God; to confession of sin, coldness, and unbelief; and to the consecration of oneself to the Lord: therefore we may be certain it has not issued from the flesh. Therefore it has come from God; and if God has created and maintained in the hearts of His children that spirit of prayer for revival, however few and feeble they may be, there can be but one logical explanation—He intends to *send* revival.

This spirit of prayer need not be widespread before it constitutes a sign of impending blessing. It may be but a small group of earnest souls; it may be but a single intercessor who has caught the vision of what God is about to do, and refuses to let Him go until He does it. Such was a case recorded by Finney: "There was a woman in New Jersey who was very positive there was going to be another revival. She wanted to have conference meetings appointed. But the minister and elders saw nothing to encourage it, and would do nothing. She saw they were blind, and so she went forward, and got a carpenter to make seats for her, for she said she would have meetings in her own house. There was certainly going to be a revival. She had scarcely opened her doors for meetings, before the Spirit of God came down with great power. And these sleepy church members found themselves surrounded all at once with convicted sinners. And they could only say, 'Surely the Lord was in this place, and we knew it not.' The reason why such persons understand the indication of God's will is not because of the superior wisdom that is in them, but because the Spirit of God leads them to see the signs of the times . . . that converging of providences to a single point, which produces in them a confident expectation of a certain result."

### Signs of the Times

"When ye see a cloud rising in the west, straightway ye say, There cometh a shower; and so it cometh to pass . . . Ye know how to interpret the face of the earth and the heaven; but how is it that ye know not how to interpret this time?" (Luke 12: 54). Thus Christ spoke to the multitudes probably less than a year before that first great outpouring of the Spirit. They were quick to perceive the cloud in the sky, but were blind to that which heralded the spiritual shower. How easy it is to miss the signs of the times, and fail to recognize what God is about to do.

Let us pause a moment and look into our own hearts. Let us look about us. Let us strain our ear to catch any sounds wafted by the wind of the Spirit from distant parts. Is there abroad a spirit of lawlessness and deadness that challenges the Most High, and cries out, "It is time for the Lord to work"? Is there a spirit of dissatisfaction, of soul thirst among the people of God? Can we find those with a deep consciousness of the holiness of God and the sinfulness of sin, with a readiness to confess the sin and put things right? Are there those with a deep and tender concern for the state of the church and the need of the world? Can we discern a spirit of expectancy, a conviction or premonition that God is about to do a new thing? Do we find anywhere a new spirit of unity among the people of God, a breaking down of sectarian barriers, and a meeting together on common ground to seek after God? Is there a new spirit of prayer appearing among believers, that cannot be limited to the weekly prayer-meeting, but which is seen in groups of Christians on bended knee in cottage or mansion, in school or business premises? Are some seizing for prayer the hurried moments of the lunch hour, praying on into the night, or wakening the dawn with their cries?

If we can answer "yes" to these questions, it matters not that the sun still shines out of an azure sky—we have seen the cloud rising in the west. "Is the seed yet in the barn? Yea, the vine, and the fig tree, and the pomegranate, and the olive tree hath not brought forth; from this day will I bless," saith the Lord (Hag. 2: 19). Above the incessant noise of human activity we have heard "the sound of marching" that tells us God is on the move.

A revival of religion is indispensable to avert the judgments of God from the church. . . . The fact is, Christians are more to blame for not being revived, than sinners are for not being converted. And if Christians are not awakened, they may know assuredly that God will visit them with His judgments. How often God visited the Jewish church with judgments because they would not repent and be revived at the call of His prophets.

CHARLES FINNEY.

It is most significant that since the Reformation, revivals have recurred with increasing frequency. Again and again God has rescued that which had gone beyond all human aid : what could have saved the church but these gracious interventions of almighty power? The need can but grow more urgent as the age draws to its close. When revivals cease to flow from the mercy of God, judgment must come.

D. M. PANTON.

## CHAPTER FIFTEEN

## THE SOLEMN ALTERNATIVE

"For the time is come for judgment to begin at the house of God: and if it begin first at us, what shall be the end of them that obey not the gospel of God?" (1 Pet. 4:17).

### *The Divine Purpose*

GOD has a grander and greater purpose for this age than simply saving souls from hell; He is bringing "sons unto glory" (Heb. 2:10). He is not now concerned with improving the world, but with gathering out of it a people for His Name. He is forging an instrument, glorious and holy, that shall rule and administer the world in the coming age under the sovereignty of His Son. In this age it is the angels, "sons of God" by creation, who govern the universe. In the age to come it will be the saints, "sons of God" by redemption, who shall judge the world and angels (1 Cor. 6:2, 3; Heb. 2:5). Thus God is now displaying through the church His manifold wisdom to those heavenly powers soon to be replaced by the church (Eph. 3:10). We can hardly contemplate these tremendous events without realizing that something radical must take place in the church as we see it today, if it is ever to be worthy of association with the Son of God in such a capacity, if in fact it is to be "a glorious church, not having spot or wrinkle or any such thing; but . . . holy and without blemish" (Eph. 5:27).

If an exiled monarch had hopes of returning in power to judge the usurper, claim his throne, and set up again his kingdom, he would surely choose his ministers and administrators from among those who had shown unswerving loyalty towards him, and where possible he would train them in advance to fulfil their future functions. How could he promote to such executive positions those whose devotion to his cause had been lukewarm, who had been ashamed to side openly with him in his rejection, or who had been more concerned in his absence to serve their own selfish interests than his? It is such a picture that Christ paints in the

parable of the pounds (Luke 19: 11), in which He teaches us that
His servants are on probation in this age, being trained and fitted
for their function in the age to come. With Christ "the saints of
the Most High shall receive the kingdom, and possess the kingdom" (Dan. 7: 18, 22). But how are they to be made fit? There
must of necessity be a purifying, a making white, a refining, as
Daniel also foretold (Dan. 12: 10). In the larger scheme of things,
God has commonly effected this purifying by—

## Revival or Judgment

Strange though it may seem, there are distinct similarities between the ways of God in revival and in judgment. Throughout
the prophets the thought of *a divine visitation* is used to describe
blessing and revival on the one hand (Jer. 27: 22) and a season
of judgment on the other (Jer. 50: 31). Likewise *the overflowing
rain* could picture a time of spiritual revival (Ezek. 34: 26) or of
divine judgment (Gen. 6: 17). Another figure used of the mighty
operation of the Spirit in revival is *fire from heaven* (1 Kings
18: 38; Acts 2: 3), but it is also typical of the judgment of God
(2 Kings 1: 10). All this may be partly explained by the fact that
there is an element of judgment present in every revival. But it
is also true that judgment is the solemn alternative to revival.
The purifying and quickening of the people of God are a moral
and spiritual necessity. Because of His very nature, God cannot and
will not permit spiritual decline to continue unchecked. He is ever
halting and reversing the trend of the times by means of revival—
or judgment. Where His people are not prepared for the one,
they shut themselves up to the other.

Some may wonder whether there can be any question of divine
judgment upon a true child of God or a true church of God, since
the Saviour declared that a believer "hath eternal life, and cometh
not into judgment, but hath passed out of death into life" (John
5: 24). There can certainly be no question of judgment for being
dead in trespasses and sins, because those who believe have passed
once for all out of the realm of death into that of life, and there
is "no condemnation to them that are in Christ Jesus" (Rom.
8: 1). Subsequent unbelief and disobedience are another matter,
and if persisted in must sooner or later evoke the chastisement
of the Father.

The Egyptians did not hear Moses' word, nor did they believe on Him who sent him, therefore they came into judgment culminating in the death of the firstborn. The Israelites who heard and believed did not come into judgment, but passed out of death into life. Once redeemed, however, God began to deal with them as a father with his children, and thereafter they suffered chastisements and judgments, some of them severe, at His hands. The apostles drew valuable lessons from this for the warning of the church (Jude 5; 1 Cor. 10). Paul showed that not only the sins of redeemed Israel (1 Cor. 10: 6), but the judgments that befell them were "by way of example; and they were written for our admonition" (verse 11). There are also New Testament illustrations of the truth that "the Lord shall judge His people" (Heb. 10: 30).

We see from the history of Israel, in Canaan as well as in the wilderness, that God has always worked in His people through revival and through judgment. A time came, however, when there was no remedy and God could revive them no longer as a nation, but shut them up to the overwhelming judgments of the captivities. Even in the midst of these desolations of Zion we hear the cry of the faithful remnant, "Turn again our captivity, O Lord, as the streams in the South" (Ps. 126: 4), and we witness the mercy of God in granting to a few under Ezra and Nehemiah "a little reviving in [their] bondage" (Ezra 9: 8).

The close of the New Testament revelation brings again the message of revival or judgment. Before Paul laid down his pen and sealed his faith with his blood, that great sweep of the Spirit that began at Pentecost had begun to wane, with accompanying signs of spiritual decline. John, writing at the close of the first century, conveys to a small circle of seven churches a personal message from the risen Christ (Rev. 2 and 3). Five of them are charged by the Head of the church with sins of departure and commanded to repent. The "germs" which Paul had diagnosed years before, and about which he had faithfully warned the churches (Acts 20: 29), were now an epidemic. The Lord showed these five churches that there could be no reviving without repentance, and if they were unwilling for this, the alternative was judgment. Doubtless then, as now, the Lord longed to pour out His Spirit, but how could He do this greater thing until they were willing for personal reviving? In these five letters the need of this reviving is laid bare, the way to it is marked out, and the solemn alternative is set forth; it is only these points in the letters we need now consider. If ever there was a message to the churches of today it is here in Revelation 2 and 3.

## Love

"I have this against thee, that thou didst leave thy first love" (Rev. 2: 4). The Lord's contention with His people at Ephesus centred in this terse and pointed accusation.

The life of God that comes into the centre of a newborn soul does not always or at once influence, as it should, the whole circumference of the outer life; hence the exhortations to true believers not to lie, steal, commit fornication, bite and devour one another, etc. Conversely, spiritual decay may be at work in the heart of a believer or a church without the signs of decline being at once manifest. The rosy apple with unblemished skin may be rotting at the core. It was so with Ephesus. The glowing commendation of verses 2 and 3 might lead one to suppose that here was a church that left nothing to be desired. This was no doubt man's verdict, but it was not God's; "for man looketh on the outward appearance, but the Lord looketh on the heart" (1 Sam. 16: 7). Those eyes which were as a flame of fire, piercing through every veneer and searching the hidden depths, had perceived in this church, despite its orthodoxy and its activity, the symptoms of spiritual decline. Ephesus, to whom Paul had declared "the whole counsel of God" (Acts 20: 27), to whom had been committed the sublimest truths in the New Testament regarding the church as the bride-to-be of Christ (Eph. 5: 22–32), had declined in that very relationship: she had left her first love.

How true is the saying, "Christianity is a religion of the heart." It is not a religion of the head, though it is essentially rational. It is not a religion of the hand, though it is essentially practical. It is a religion of the heart: for what a man is in his heart that is he in the sight of God. Christ taught that the thoughts, words, and actions that go to make up the life, proceed from the heart (Matt. 12: 34; 15: 19). Since the heart is the very fountain of man's personality, it is ever the object of Satan's attack. If he can but corrupt the heart he will soon defile the whole life. Solomon was wise to warn us, "Keep thy heart with all diligence; for out of it are the issues of life" (Prov. 4: 23). He would have been wiser still had he practised what he preached. Implicit in this heart condition of Ephesus were solemn possibilities that only Christ could see. He had diagnosed in the heart of this church that deadly germ which is responsible for all spiritual decline. Such a condition, threatening as it did the very life of the body, called for drastic action by the Surgeon. Hence the sternness and solemnity of Christ's words to these believers.

What is this "first love" that Ephesus had forsaken? It is the love of her whose every fear and prejudice and reserve have been broken down; whose heart has been utterly captured, she knows not how; and who presents herself to her beloved as his, and his for ever. It is the love of betrothal. It was this love that drew Israel out of the bondage of Egypt into a covenant relationship with the Lord, anticipating a day when He should say to them, "thy Maker is thine husband; the Lord of Hosts is His name" (Isa. 54: 5). Alas, they too left their first love, and sorrowfully God had to remind them of it: "I remember for thee the kindness of thy youth, the love of thine espousals; how thou wentest after Me in the wilderness, in a land that was not sown. . . . My people have committed two evils; they have forsaken Me the fountain of living waters, and hewed them out cisterns, broken cisterns, that can hold no water. . . . My people have forgotten Me days without number" (Jer. 2: 2, 13, 32). Thus this church of the New Testament, heedless of that which had been recorded for her admonition, was repeating the sin of "the church in the wilderness".

Not only is a first love towards Christ one of the most precious and sacred and beautiful things under heaven, but it is vital to a deeper life and growth in the things of God. When the love wanes, the life will soon decline. Is this the reason why the life of the church today is so low, and the need for its reviving so great? As we consider some of the characteristics of "first love", let us ask ourselves whether the church, whether we ourselves, are guilty of the sin of having left it, or the greater sin of never having had it.

It is *pure* love, without the taint of worldly attraction, and unweakened by ulterior motive. It is the love of the "pure virgin", uncorrupted "from the simplicity and the purity that is toward Christ" (2 Cor. 11: 2, 3). It is a *tender* love, sensitive to the smallest thing that might bring grief or displeasure to the Beloved, ever seeking to be well-pleasing unto Him who said, "If ye love Me, ye will keep My commandments" (John 14: 15). It is a *supreme* love that has conquered all other loves and brought them into subjection, according to His own word, "He that loveth father or mother, etc. . . . more than Me is not worthy of Me" (Matt. 10: 37). It comes from a heart that can sing:

> Jesus, Thy boundless love to me,
> No thought can reach, no tongue declare;
> Oh, knit my thankful heart to Thee,
> And reign without a rival there.
>                               P. GERHARDT.

It is a *sacrificial* love, because it partakes of the very nature of the love of God and of Christ. "God so loved . . . that He gave His only begotten Son." "Christ loved the church and gave Himself up for it." And this "first love" is but the offspring of the divine love, which ever brings forth after its own kind. It is a love that gives itself up and pours itself out. This had once been the love of the Ephesian church. This was the love she had forsaken.

These are not so much the words of an offended Lord as of a wounded Lover, "I have this against thee, that thou didst leave thy first love." The toil, the zeal, and the orthodoxy of this church could never compensate for the loss of that first love. Her need, more desperate and urgent than she could know, was for a *revived love*. Is it not the need of the church today? Is it that many believers have lost, or is it that they have never known the freshness and fervency of "first love"? How easy it is to be deceived over this matter. One may perform the same exercises, pray with the same words, sing the same hymns, as one has always done, and yet the whole be no longer an exercise of the heart, but simply a matter of form or of duty. Said Christ, "This people honoureth Me with their lips; but their heart is far from Me" (Matt. 15: 8).

John in his first epistle brings the matter of love for the Lord down to a very practical issue by showing that the measure of a believer's love for God is the measure of his love for his brother, that much and no more (1 John 4: 11–21). The Saviour said that His disciples were to be known by their love for each other (John 13: 35); instead they have become marked before the world by their strifes and divisions. Is there any need for further evidence that the first love of the early church, who were of "one heart and one soul", and of whom men had to exclaim, "Behold how they love one another," has been largely lost by the church of today?

Compassion for the perishing is another expression of this first love. Most are prepared to pay lip-service to the need of the lost, but with how many is there practical indifference? How few are the churches today with a heart like the church of the Thessalonians, to whom Paul said, "From you hath sounded forth the word of the Lord . . . in every place . . . so that we need not to speak anything" (1 Thess. 1: 8). Is it not evident that we need a revived love?

The One who still walks in the midst of the lampstands, and before whose eyes every heart is laid bare, not only reveals the condition, but also the cure. Here are the three steps to a revived love: "Remember . . . repent . . . do the first works" (verse 5). "*Remember* from whence thou art fallen." Christ is not addressing the individual; He is addressing the church. There had been corporate failure, and the Lord calls for corporate action. As a church they had lost their first love; as a church they had fallen; and therefore as a church they needed to remember, that is to go back in thought to their beginning, and realize how great their fall was. The church of today must do the same. Only through an honest comparison of the love of the early church with the love of the church today can we appreciate the greatness of our fall. Then "*Repent*". Long have we urged the sinners to do it: now the Lord commands us to do it ourselves. This involves a change of attitude, a change of heart, a humbling before God, who has promised to revive the heart of the contrite ones. Finally, "*Do the first works.*" The church must go back to the beginning, and tread again the pathway of the first love. Of the Macedonian churches we read, "First they gave their own selves to the Lord" (2 Cor. 8: 5). This in a phrase is doing the first works. There must be a renewed dedication, presenting ourselves afresh to our Beloved as "in the day of His espousals, and in the day of the gladness of His heart" (Song 3: 11).

If the church was not willing to pay the price of a revived love, there could be but one alternative—He would visit her in judgment: "Or else I come to thee, and will move thy lampstand out of its place, except thou repent.". The lampstand is the proper place for the light. "Neither do men light a lamp, and put it under the bushel, but on the stand [or lampstand]; and it shineth unto all that are in the house" (Matt. 5: 15). The threatened judgment upon Ephesus was that of having the lampstand removed, so that the lamp of corporate testimony would cease to shine. Her organization, her activities, and even her form of witness might continue, but there would be no light there. Can any greater tragedy overtake a church than to lose its testimony? Souls would stumble and perish in the darkness because the light was not shining where it ought to be. Ships that might have found the haven of this church would make shipwreck because the harbour light was not in its place. They shall perish in their iniquity, but their loss God will require at the church's hands—the church that lost her light because she lost her love.

"He that hath an ear, let him hear what the Spirit saith to the churches" today. If the church is not willing to return to her first love, can we expect God to pour out His Spirit?—can we expect Him to withhold His judgment? As we face the alternatives, let us pray individually:

> Oh, grant that nothing in my soul
> May dwell but Thy pure love alone;
> Oh, may Thy love possess me whole,
> My joy, my treasure, and my crown :
> All coldness from my heart remove;
> May ev'ry act, word, thought, be love.
> P. GERHARDT.

### Truth

"I have a few things against thee, because thou hast there some that hold the teaching of Balaam . . . of the Nicolaitans . . . thou sufferest the woman Jezebel . . . and she teacheth and seduceth my servants" (Rev. 2: 14–20). These were the charges Christ brought against the churches of Pergamum and Thyatira. Since they had much the same condition and need, they can be considered together. Their spiritual decline was manifest in an attitude of complacency towards the truth. Where Ephesus had stood firm, intolerant of evil men and judging those who posed as apostles (2: 2), these two churches had slipped. They had not apostatized as a whole, in fact Pergamum earned the commendation, "Thou holdest fast My Name, and didst not deny My faith" (2: 13), but both were guilty of an easy-going attitude towards false teaching within the fellowship. Unlike Ephesus, these churches had become tolerant where their Lord was intolerant (2: 6). They were treating those teaching error with weak indulgence, when they had been told to "contend earnestly for the faith" (Jude 3). By failing in the exercise of discipline, they revealed that they were no longer jealous for the truth. They were busying themselves about "the house of God, which is . . . the pillar and ground of the truth" (1 Tim. 3: 15), unconcerned about the men who were tampering with its foundations.

What was this error that had reared its head in these churches? It was the teaching of Balaam that led those holding it "to eat things sacrificed to idols, and to commit fornication" (Rev. 2: 14, 20). Nothing definite appears to be known about the teaching of the Nicolaitans, but the fact that it was linked with the teaching of Balaam, and that there were those holding it "in like manner" (verse 15), is an indication that it may have been the same evil, though perhaps in a different form. Similarly with the self-styled prophetess in the church at Thyatira; Jezebel was probably a figurative name which described her character, but her teaching was that of Balaam (cf. verses 14, 20). In Numbers (chaps. 25 and 31: 16) the origin of the teaching is recorded. It began in the heart of a covetous man who loved the hire of wrong-doing; thus the motive was evil gain. Balaam, whom God had compelled to bless Israel instead of cursing them, counselled the Moabites to seduce the Israelites into the licentious idolatry of Baal-peor. It was a teaching of guile (Num. 25: 18) that succeeded all too easily in seducing a people whose strength lay in being separate and undefiled in comparison with the other nations. Balaam himself had testified of this: "It is a people that dwell alone, and shall not be reckoned among the nations" (Num. 23: 9); and again, "He hath not beheld iniquity in Jacob, neither hath He seen perverseness in Israel" (Num. 23: 21).

The epistles disclose that two principal threats to the life of the New Testament churches were: firstly, the teaching of Judaism with its return to the bondage of ceremonies and rituals; and secondly, this teaching of Balaam in various forms, with its return to the bondage of the world. The council at Jerusalem (Acts 15) had the delicate task of marking out for the guidance of the churches the middle path between these two extremes of error. It refused to put the yoke of Judaism upon the neck of the disciples by insisting on circumcision and the keeping of the ceremonial law. But it warned them to abstain from that which would lead to the bondage of the world, such as, "things sacrificed to idols . . . and fornication", which was the teaching of Balaam.

This doctrine of worldliness under the guise of Christianity was gaining momentum in the latter part of the first century. In his second epistle, Peter devotes almost the whole of chapter 2 to those teachers who "followed the way of Balaam", and it is the burden of Jude's whole epistle. These two give us a clear view of the character of the teachers and their doctrine. They despised dominion. They were revellers, adulterous, and covetous. They enticed unsteadfast souls. As Balaam may have justified his evil counsel by arguing that, since God had promised to bless Israel and no one could reverse it (Num. 23: 19), therefore they could sin with impunity, so were these Balaam teachers of the New Testament guilty of "turning the grace of our God into lasciviousness, and denying our only Master and Lord, Jesus Christ" (Jude 4). In other words, they followed and taught a worldly policy of self-indulgence under the cloak of grace, denying thereby the Lordship of Christ. They argued that they were no longer under the bondage of the law, and therefore could do as they pleased. Their motto might have been, "Let us continue in sin that grace may abound," or "Let us do evil that good may come." They held out a way of escape from the strait gate and the narrow way, offering the wavering believer a new "liberty", while they themselves were "slaves of corruption" (2 Pet. 2: 19).

Down the centuries all the seductive skill of Satan has been employed in seeking to break down the fence that God has placed around His people. He has used his evil genius to thwart those glorious purposes that can only be achieved through "an elect race, a royal priesthood, a holy nation, a people for God's own possession" (1 Pet. 2: 9). Paul told the Corinthian believers, "I espoused you to one husband, that I might present you as a pure virgin to Christ" (2 Cor. 11: 2). No wonder James addresses the worldly Christians thus : "Ye adulteresses, know ye not that the friendship of the world is enmity with God?" (Jas. 4: 4). Let us face it now : a teaching that encourages conformity to the world, though it takes to itself the name of Christian, and though it works under the orthodox evangelical phraseology, is a doctrine of Balaam. "For if, after they have escaped the defilements of the world through the knowledge of the Lord and Saviour Jesus Christ, they are again entangled therein and overcome, the last state is become worse with them than the first" (2 Pet. 2: 20). It were better never to have had opportunity to be espoused to the Lord, than having been betrothed to play the harlot with the world.

The woman who has lost her first love for her husband is the one most open to the temptation of being unfaithful. It is not such a big step from the sin of Ephesus to that which threatened the life of Pergamum and Thyatira. Who can estimate the devastating effect upon the church today of the teaching of Balaam? It is finding its way into circles which one might have thought were for ever immune. This modern form of the pollutions of idols and committing fornication with the world is one of the greatest scourges among the people of God. As with these two churches, God holds responsible those who, though they have not been deceived and do not follow the teaching, countenance it being taught, and with a criminal indulgence allow it to be followed. The Lord is here contending with those who tolerate that which He has specifically stated He hates (Rev. 2: 6). It is they who are commanded to repent. It is they who must judge this evil thing. *The reviving of the truth* that the church is set apart as holy for her Lord is in their hands.

"Repent therefore; or else I come to thee quickly, and I will make war against them with the sword of My mouth" (verse 16) "And I gave [Jezebel] time that she should repent; and she willeth not to repent of her fornication. Behold, I do cast her into a bed, and them that commit adultery with her into great tribulation, except they repent of her works. And I will kill her children with death; and all the churches shall know that I am He which searcheth the reins and hearts: and I will give unto each one of you according to your works" (verses 21–23).

Once again the alternatives are clear. The Lord was calling these churches to repentance with a view to their being purified and revived. They must deal with this complacency towards worldliness in their midst and the teaching that fostered it. If they refused to exterminate this evil the Lord would visit them, not in revival but in judgment. What the Lord said to His people long ago in the visions of Patmos, He is saying to His people to-day, "If you will not purge away the harlotry of the church, I will do it in judgment."

Pergamum and Thyatira were guilty of the sin of Eli, whose covetous and licentious sons made themselves vile in the priest-hood and *he restrained them not,* concerning whom the Lord said, "I will judge his house for ever, for the iniquity which he knew" (1 Sam. 3: 13), and because he refused to repent at the warning of God. But when the time came for judgment to begin, the thing was not done in a corner, but before all Israel. God was fulfilling His word, "Behold I will do a thing in Israel, at which both the ears of everyone that heareth it shall tingle" (1 Sam. 3: 11). So the Lord warns these New Testament believers, "I will deal with this thing," and "all the churches shall know that I am He which searcheth the reins and hearts". His visitation in judgment would be vindicated before the eyes of all.

When, through the counsel of Balaam, Israel began to commit whoredom with the daughters of Moab, there was one in the camp of Israel who saved the situation by drastic discipline. Phinehas felt as God did about the matter: "He was jealous with My jealousy among them," declared the Lord, therefore "behold, I give unto him My covenant of peace . . . the cove-nant of an everlasting priesthood; because he was jealous for his God" (Num. 25). The God who cut off the house of Eli because of his tolerance of this evil, perpetuated for ever the house of Phinehas because of his holy intolerance. The truth must be revived that a holy God requires a holy people. Where are they who may, like Phinehas, save the churches of today from the wrath of the Lord's jealousy?

There was another in a similar day of apostasy, who was "very jealous for the Lord, the God of Hosts" (1 Kings 19: 10). He acted as drastically as his forebear to purge out the idolatry and fornication from the midst of God's people. In his jealousy for the Lord Elijah averted the fire of divine wrath and brought down the fire of revival. He slew the worshippers of Baal and opened the windows of heaven. "The God that answereth by fire" is still God. Shall it be the fire of judgment or of revival?

## Life

"I know thy works, that thou hast a name that thou livest, and thou art dead" (Rev. 3: 1). This was the divine estimate of the church in Sardis. Since Scripture clearly teaches that a church is composed only of "living stones", those who have been spiritually quickened and possess life in Christ, how could Christ say of this church, "Thou art dead"? . . . Clearly it was meant in a relative sense, not in an absolute sense. If this company had never possessed life Christ would never have exhorted them to "stablish the things that remain". Since He obviously addresses them as believers, He teaches us that there is a sense in which believers may be dead. Christ's statement follows from His absolute knowledge of their works, "I know thy works, that . . . thou art dead." In essence they had life, but when it came to manifestation or "works", they were dead. This church was like the boy whom the Lord delivered from an unclean spirit of whom it is recorded, "the child became as one dead; insomuch that the more part said, He is dead" (Mark 9: 26). The life was there, but it was not being manifested.

There is no suggestion that these believers were dead because of an absence of works. Here is not the deadness of inactivity, for Christ clearly stated that they *had* works, that He knew them, and that He had found them unfulfilled. Nor is there any suggestion that they were dead because they held heterodox teaching, for though Christ had many things to judge of them, He never implied that they had departed from the faith. Here, then, we are faced with the anomaly of a church which is evangelically orthodox, manifestly active—but *dead* in the estimate of the Lord. In His address to these believers, the Lord discloses the reasons for their state, and marks out the way whereby the life of the church may be revived.

Firstly, Sardis was a church *relying on her past reputation*. "Thou hast a name that thou livest." Here was evidently a company with a great spiritual tradition, that had succumbed to the temptation of looking backwards in pride instead of looking upwards in humility and dependence. Doubtless there had been a day when the eyes of this church were truly fixed on Christ, seeking to do all as unto Him; thus had she become great in spiritual power and influence, and had a name among the churches. Now, alas, she had taken her eyes off the Lord and fixed them upon men, more concerned with their commendation than His, striving to live in the borrowed glory of a day that had passed.

Men are impressed by externalities, the Lord only by realities. When the saints at Sardis lost that "single eye" that was set on pleasing the Lord, they became occupied with maintaining forms and traditions, "sadly contented with a show of things". Activity and organization continued, but life and power waned. The church had striven to maintain appearances, and she had succeeded—"Thou hast a name that thou livest," but at the cost of her life—"Thou art dead." Sardis had become like the Necropolis of Cairo, whose streets and houses appear from a distance like those of a thriving community, but when viewed from within it is discovered that the houses are roofless, and in place of the hearthstone there is a tombstone.

Secondly, Sardis was a church *not fulfilling her works.* "Be thou watchful, and stablish the things that remain, which were ready to die : for I have found no works of thine fulfilled before My God" (Rev. 3: 2). It has already been pointed out that the deadness of Sardis was not to be accounted for on the ground of her inactivity. It was the quality rather than the quantity of her works that revealed that she was dead. "The Lord is a God of knowledge, and by Him actions are weighed" (1 Sam. 2: 3). The output of this church, when placed upon the balances of the sanctuary, was found to be deficient of that vital element, "the spirit of life". Here was the activity of converted men without the activity of God. Here was action without unction. Here was a form of religion that, despite its orthodoxy, denied the power thereof.

Thus with all the energy put forth there was no consummation and no fruition. Before God the works were unfulfilled, that is, the divine purpose in them was not being achieved. There was gospel testimony with no conversions; prayer gatherings with no spirit of intercession and no answers from heaven; ministry of the word with no enrichment to the church; much being done but nothing being achieved. "I have found no works of thine fulfilled." Unless the life of the Spirit was pulsating through her activities, how could there be fulfilment so as to satisfy the eye of

God? She was working in the energy of the flesh, and it is always true that "they that are in the flesh cannot please God" (Rom. 8: 8). The case of Sardis is a vivid illustration of the truth that "the mind of the flesh is death" (Rom. 8: 6). She was sowing to the flesh, and thus she could not reap fruition and fulfilment, only corruption (Gal. 6: 8). Well might the Lord have said to Sardis what He said to Israel years before: "Consider your ways. Ye have sown much, and bring in little; ye eat, but ye have not enough; ye drink, but ye are not filled with drink; ye clothe you, but there is none warm; and he that earneth wages earneth wages to put it into a bag with holes" (Hag. 1: 5, 6).

Thirdly, Sardis was a church *not living up to her privileges*. "Remember therefore how thou hast received and didst hear; and keep it, and repent" (verse 3). She is now reminded by the Lord of how she had received the truth. It is possible that she had been entrusted with a fuller measure of spiritual light than many other churches; and that this was why she had "a name", a reputation among the others. At the first she had accepted in humility and obedience this sacred trust, for Christ reminds her, "Thou . . . didst hear." She had become "obedient from the heart" to that which she had received. The truth had been embraced. As Ephesus had to be reminded that she had lost her first love, so Sardis had now to be reminded that she had lost her first obedience. Privileged beyond many, and with a reputation surpassing most, she had become careless of her holy stewardship: God had given these believers light that they might walk in it, not boast about it. Every privilege brings an attendant responsibility. Failure to live up to the light received had brought this church to a worse state than if she had never had that fuller light. "If the light that is in thee be darkness, how great is the darkness!" (Matt. 6: 23).

Christ had now to command this church to "keep" that which she had at the first received and heard, and to "repent" of her failure to do so. She had let the truth slip, not mentally perhaps, but experimentally. Have we done the same? "Therefore we ought to give the more earnest heed to the things that were heard, lest haply we drift away from them" (Heb. 2: 1). It is a most solemn thing to receive and not to keep. If there are churches today who, like Sardis, have a name that they live, who speak of the greater light that they have received, they would do well to ponder what Paul would describe as "sound words, even the words of our Lord Jesus Christ" (1 Tim. 6: 3), when He spoke of our accountability as servants in view of the privileges we have received: "That servant, which knew his Lord's will, and made not ready, nor did according to His will, shall be beaten with many stripes. . . . And to whomsoever much is given, of him shall much be required: and to whom they commit much, of him will they ask the more" (Luke 12: 47, 48).

Finally, Sardis was a church *failing to maintain her purity.* The heart-attitude of these believers resulted in defilement as well as deadness. There were only " a few names in Sardis which did not defile their garments" (Rev. 3: 4). These garments speak of the outer life, that which is plain for all to see. These who were resting on a past reputation, who were satisfied to think that they had been privileged to receive the fuller light, had grown careless about their outward purity. The garments of glory and of beauty had been defiled by the works of the flesh. Instead of "hating even the garment spotted by the flesh" (Jude 23), they were hardly conscious of any defilement there, or that the outer garments were any less pure than they ought to have been. It was clearly taught in the Old Testament that where there was death there was defilement (Lev. 21: 1, 11, etc.). Had these Christians been full of life they would have been vigilant, and so have avoided the spotting of their garments. Only he who watches can expect "to keep himself unspotted from the world" (Jas. 1: 27). The moment of decline was when they ceased to watch. The Lord had thus to bring them back to the point of departure in order to show them the way to recovery, to the reviving of their life.

"Be thou watchful, and stablish the things that remain, which were ready to die : for I have found no works of thine fulfilled" (Rev. 3: 2). The things that remained in Sardis were her incomplete works. These spiritual activities were a mere shell devoid of the kernel of life, and now even the shell was about to pass away. That which remained could only be saved from final decay and stablished by a new inflow of divine life. For this the church must awake. There must be a new spirit of vigilance, of obedience, of repentance.

"If therefore thou shalt not watch, I will come as a thief, and thou shalt not know what hour I will come upon thee." Once again the solemn alternative is set forth. If the church was not willing to watch that her life should be revived Christ would visit her in judgment. The words of the Lord to these believers, "I will come as a thief," had evidently no immediate reference to His return, although His second advent is thus described elsewhere. This coming was not a promise but a warning, and its fulfilment was contingent upon the failure of the church to watch—"if . . . thou shalt not watch, I will come," implying that vigilance could avert it. It was a coming of Christ in judgment—"I will come *upon* thee." And finally, whatever application the warning may have for believers today it applied primarily to this church in Sardis, who Christ knew would no longer exist when He should come again. If the church did not repent Christ must fulfil His word.

The thief comes to dispossess his victim of the precious things in his keeping. In such a manner would Christ come upon this church in judgment if she did not repent and watch. Did these believers boast that they had a name that they lived? He would come and take it from them, and all the churches would know that Sardis was dead. Were they still making much of "the things that remain", the works that were unfulfilled? He would come and these things that were "ready to die" would pass away. Were they satisfied with the light that they had received? He would come and take this from them so that the light that was in them would become darkness. As for the garments that were spotted and defiled, He would come and strip these from them, and their nakedness would be seen by all. "Behold, I come as a thief. Blessed is he that watcheth, and keepeth his garments, lest he walk naked, and they see his shame" (Rev. 16: 15). In a word, this church lacked the one thing needful, the spirit of life; and if she would not remedy the situation He would come to fulfil His own words spoken here on earth, "whosoever hath not, from him shall be taken away even that which he hath" (Matt. 13: 12).

Not only would Christ come to do the work of a thief, but He could come in the manner of a thief. "Thou shalt not know what hour I will come upon thee." As a thief comes stealthily, secretly, silently, so would Christ come upon this church in judgment. Unheralded He would arrive, undetected He would go. Her precious things would be taken from her without her realizing it. As Samson "awoke out of his sleep, and said, I will go out as at other times. . . . But he wist not that the Lord was departed

from him" (Judges 16: 20); so would she awaken, all unconscious that "the thief" had visited her in her slumbers and that
which she should have held fast till He came (Rev. 2: 25) had
gone.

As we have weighed up the Lord's description of the church
in Sardis, has there risen up before us those churches that we
know? Have we seen our own spiritual lives mirrored in the condition of these first century Christians? Then we can be assured
the warnings apply to us also. It is ours to determine whether He
shall come unto us as the rain, or as the thief, to quicken or to
judge.

### *Zeal*

"Thou are lukewarm, and neither hot nor cold" (Rev. 3: 16).
This was the Lord's appraisal of Laodicea. What is the spiritual
significance of being hot, cold, or lukewarm? The final command
of the Lord to this church was, "*Be zealous* therefore and repent" (verse 19); He had evidently been registering the zeal or
fervour of this church. Now zeal is not enthusiasm, though it may
contain it. There is, however, a fleshly enthusiasm in spiritual
things which is the offspring of pride, and which bears no relation
to spiritual zeal. To be fervent and to be zealous both convey in
the original the idea of heat, of intensity of feeling. Zeal also
contains the thought of a jealous concern: "zealous" and "jealous" being interchangeable words in Scripture. A jealous concern
for God's glory is the motive of true spiritual zeal. It was jealousy
for God's honour that moved the Saviour to purge the temple,
but it reminded the disciples of the Scripture, "The *zeal* of Thine
house shall eat me up" (John 2: 17).

Registering the temperature of this church's zeal, the Lord says
to her, "I would thou wert . . . hot." The zeal that God looks
for is "boiling hot", for this is what the word means in the original.
How many there were in the sacred records who were "hot" in
their zeal for God. Said David, "My heart was hot within me;
while I was musing the fire kindled: then spake I with my
tongue" (Ps. 39: 3). Jeremiah declared, "If I say I will not make
mention of Him, nor speak any more in His Name, then there is
in mine heart as it were a burning fire shut up in my bones" (Jer.
20: 9). But who among the sons of men ever exceeded the zeal
of him who described himself as "the least of the apostles", but

who "laboured more abundantly than they all" (1 Cor. 15: 9, 10). "I am ready," he could say, "not to be bound only, but also to die at Jerusalem for the Name of the Lord Jesus" (Acts 21 : 13). Paul's Christianity was not a pastime but a passion. The zeal that was once engaged in persecuting the church had been reclaimed for God, purged and sanctified; and now, fed by the Spirit of God and burning with holy intensity, it was ever urging him forward "toward the goal for the prize." One can only imagine the feelings of the Saviour as He looked sorrowfully at this church of Laodicea and said, "I would thou wert . . . hot."

"I would thou wert cold." This does not suggest an unregenerate state, for Christ could not have wished that these Laodicean believers had never been redeemed, unless He thereby denied the value of His redemptive work in them. No, the state here described is that of the backslider, who has slipped so far as to reveal no concern at all for the things of Christ. He has opened his life to the world with its icy blast. He has become manifestly cold towards the One to whom he once yielded allegiance. The cares, riches, and pleasures of this life have frozen his soul. There is not even a pretence of zeal; he is cold. But this was not the state of the Laodiceans.

"Thou art lukewarm," that is, the state between the two. Laodicea had neither the spiritual intensity of the hot, nor the spiritual honesty of the cold. The hot are fervent, the cold are indifferent, but the lukewarm are complacent. According to her confession, this church was "hot", for she professed so much: according to her condition, this church was cold, for she possessed so little. These believers were tepid because they had not the concern, the passion, the zeal which would make them hot; and because they were too self-respecting to be numbered with those who were openly cold. "Tepid is that condition in which conviction does not affect conscience, heart, or will" (Campbell Morgan). Whatever convictions these Christians had, they did not lead to action.

"I would thou wert cold or hot." That the Lord would rather they were hot than lukewarm we can readily understand, but why would He rather they were cold than lukewarm? *Firstly,* because a lukewarm state is a mixture of hot and cold, and the Lord abhors mixtures. Mixture is the work of Satan and spells chaos. This was the state of the creation as we find it on the first page of Scripture (Gen. 1 : 2), and God set to work to renovate and restore by dividing the things that were different, the light from the darkness, the waters beneath the firmament from those above, the seas from the earth, etc. The same lesson was enshrined in the law. "Thou shalt not let thy cattle gender with a diverse kind : thou shalt not sow thy field with two kinds of seed : neither shall there come upon thee a garment of two kinds of stuff mingled together" (Lev. 19 : 19). "Thou shalt not plow with an ox and an ass together" (Deut. 22 : 9–11). Divine order necessitates the separation of those things which by their very nature are irreconcilably distinct.

*Secondly,* the Lord prefers the cold, because there is an element of hypocrisy in the lukewarm state that is not so with the cold; and the Lord abhors hypocrisy. The profession of those believers, "Thou sayest, I am rich," was denied by their true condition, "and knowest not that thou art . . . poor." When a man's condition denies his profession, that is hypocrisy, even though he may be blind to it. It is the same in the realm of salvation: compare the attitude of Jesus to the self-confessed sinner, tax-gatherer, and harlot with his attitude to the hypocritical, self-righteous Pharisee. To the former He said, "Come unto Me, all ye that labour" (Matt. 11 : 28); to the latter, "Ye offspring of vipers, how shall ye escape the judgment of hell?" (Matt. 23 : 33). Though the Laodiceans were hardly conscious of their hypocrisy, they were not thereby absolved from it.

*Finally,* the Lord prefers the cold because there is more hope for the recovery of the cold than of the lukewarm. There was more hope for the son (representing the tax-gatherer) who said, "I will not", but afterwards repented and went, than for the son (representing the Pharisee) who said, "I go, sir," and went not. To the latter Jesus said, "the publicans and the harlots go into the kingdom of God before you" (Matt. 21 : 31). It was to these two classes that the parable of the prodigal was directed (Luke 15 : 1–3). Today we may rightly use the story to preach the gospel to sinners, but it has a more poignant application to those who are already sons of the Father, especially in relation to the elder brother in the plot. If the prodigal who openly left the home be taken to represent the cold backslider, and the elder brother who stayed at home, professing that he had never transgressed and yet who never possessed his possessions (verse 29), be regarded as the lukewarm believer, the story will live. How would we expect a lukewarm, complacent Christian to react to a backslidden brother who not only returns to the Father's house, but into a fulness of joy and blessing that the other has never known? How would we expect him to behave when he is entreated to come in and share these good things? Just as did the elder brother: "He was angry, and would not go in" (verse 28). Ah, there is more hope for the recovery of the cold than of the lukewarm.

The Lord now proceeds to define this lukewarm state. "Because thou sayest, *I am* . . . and knowest not that *thou art* . . ." This was the whole situation in a nutshell. Even the hot could hardly be in a better state than rich, having gotten riches, and having need of nothing. Even the cold could be little worse than wretched, miserable, poor, blind, and naked. They aspired to be among the hot, whereas in all but name they were among the cold.

Their claim was threefold. Firstly, they boasted of their *spiritual inheritance* : "I am rich." They made much of the great objective side of truth, their spiritual riches in Christ, without realizing that such is vain unless backed up by the subjective or experimental side. In other words it was no use talking about being spiritual millionaires, while they were living like spiritual paupers. It was no use congratulating each other that they were "Blessed with all spiritual blessings . . . in Christ", or that they were "in everything . . . enriched by Him", if they were manifestly not living in the good of their inheritance.

Then they spoke of their *spiritual increase* : "I have gotten riches." They thus included riches gained by them as well as riches given to them. It is right and proper that riches received as an inheritance should be increased by proper use. The faithful servant who has received five talents will gain other five talents. Light obeyed will increase. God deals to each man a "measure of faith", but it may grow exceedingly. "Unto everyone that hath shall be given, and he shall have abundance" (Matt. 25: 29). This boast might have been true, but was in fact a sad delusion. They mistook increased apprehension for increased appropriation.

Finally, they asserted their *spiritual independence* : "I have need of nothing." They were self-sufficient. No minister of the word, no servant of God could impart anything to them. They knew it all, and they had it all. The exceeding riches of God's grace were not flowing through to meet the need of this poverty-

striken church because she had "need of nothing". The Lord
has no wealth for the rich, no food for the full. "The hungry He
hath filled with good things; and the rich He hath sent empty
away" (Luke 1 : 53). Did someone suggest an extra church prayer
meeting to implore God's blessing? They had no need of such a
thing. Was mention made of a day to be set apart for humiliation
and confession in view of the prevailing deadness? It was quite
uncalled for—things were going well. Was concern expressed
that the gospel service was not reaching the people, or resulting
in conversions? The gospel service had always been quite adequate, and the results must be left with God. Did someone dare to
suggest that there was a suspicion of coldness in the service of
worship? The gatherings were all that could be desired.

Such was the claim of these believers; but what had the Lord
to say of their actual condition? "And *knowest not* that thou
art . . ." They were oblivious of their true condition before God.
Spiritual insensibility is always a mark of lukewarmness. They
had not "their senses exercised to discern good and evil" (Heb.
5 : 14). So much had they emphasized their standing and so little
their true state that they were virtually saying, "Everyone that
doeth evil is good in the sight of the Lord, and He delighteth in
them" (Mal. 2 : 17). "Thou art the wretched one and miserable."
"Wretched" indicates the state of one in the midst of trouble or
frustration, as when Paul cried out in the midst of his failures,
"O wretched man that I am." "Miserable" means in a state to be
pitied, an object of mercy. Paul used this word also to describe
what a believer would be without the hope of resurrection : "If
in this life only we have hoped in Christ, we are of all men most
*pitiable*" (1 Cor. 15: 19). Where they had thought to be con-
gratulated they were in fact to be commiserated. Why were these
believers wretched and miserable, though unconscious of it? Because they were "poor and blind and naked".

"Thou art . . . *poor*." They could talk about "the unsearch-
able riches of Christ", they could admire them as though they
were their own, but they failed utterly to possess them. This
church stands in striking contrast to that of Smyrna whom the
Lord consoled in all her tribulation and poverty with the reminder, "But thou art rich" (Rev. 2: 9). She had learned the
secret of "having nothing, and yet possessing all things" (2 Cor.
6: 10).

"Thou art . . . *blind.*" Not only is there a blindness which affects the minds of the unbelieving (2 Cor. 4: 4), but of the believer also. Peter reminds us of those spiritual virtues that God has granted to us as believers, and how they may become ours; but he adds, "He that lacketh these things [who, like the church of Laodicea, does not possess his possessions] is blind, seeing only what is near" (2 Pet. 1: 3–9). These believers were "short-sighted" (2 Pet. 1: 9, Darby), seeing only the temporal and transitory things of the passing world, and without the heavenly vision for "the things that are above, where Christ is" (Col. 3: 1). These believers were indeed "wretched and pitiable", as was sightless Samson, grinding in the prison house.

"Thou art . . . *naked.*" As God looked at this church all that He could see was "flesh". "In my flesh dwelleth no good thing" (Rom. 7: 18). "They that are in the flesh cannot please God" (Rom. 8: 8). The eye of God can only find pleasure in looking upon one clothed with "the new man" which we are commanded to put on (Col. 3: 10). If these believers had ever "put on", then they had certainly failed to keep on. "Blessed is he that watcheth, and *keepeth* his garments, lest he walk naked, and they see his shame" (Rev. 16: 15). Yes, there is an inevitable shame attached to nakedness in the spiritual as well as the natural realm, and this reproach was upon the Name they bore as well as upon themselves. Little wonder their Lord was deeply concerned that "the shame of [their] nakedness be not made manifest" (Rev. 3: 18).

Despite this pathetic picture the Lord had not yet despaired, even of these believers. He outlines the pathway to recovery: "I counsel thee to *buy of Me* . . ." This meant, firstly, they must renounce their boast to "have need of nothing", for clearly he who has no need, has no need to buy. Secondly, they must be prepared to pay the price, for all buying costs. This must be paid in humility, repentance, diligence, and sacrifice. Finally, they must buy of *Him.* In Christ Jesus their Lord were all the resources and blessings they could need to meet their poverty, blindness, and nakedness.

For their poverty He offered them "*gold refined by fire*". Gold means purchasing power. There is practically nothing material beyond the grasp of the natural man if he has gold. There is no spiritual blessing that is beyond the grasp of the spiritual man who has this gold that Christ offers. They needed everything, and they could have everything, if they had "gold refined by fire", that is, a purified faith. "The proof of your faith, being more precious than gold that perisheth though it is proved by fire" (1 Pet. 1: 7). Faith is the great purchasing power of the believer. "Believing, ye shall receive" (Matt. 21: 22) is an eternal principle of the ways of God. All things are within range of the one who believes (Mark 9: 23). If the Laodiceans' claim to be rich meant that they were well-to-do they were certainly devoid of *this* gold. Smyrna in her material poverty, however, had much of it (Rev. 2: 9). It is indeed seldom that material gold and spiritual gold are found together in any quantity. "Did not God choose them that are poor as to the world to be *rich in faith*?" (Jas. 2: 5). "Buy of Me gold." The gold was in Christ and of Christ. They could henceforth, if they would, "live by faith, *the faith of the Son of God*" (Gal. 2: 20, Darby), just as a pauper, receiving a vast inheritance, would start to live by his newly acquired wealth.

For their nakedness He offered them "*white garments*". These were also to be bought of Him. If the gold was the faith of Christ, then these garments were the righteousness of Christ; not the imputed righteousness which is the portion of all who believe, but the imparted righteousness, seen in the practical outworking of holiness day by day. They were to "put on the new man". But what is meant by this? The passage goes on to explain, "Put on therefore . . . a heart of compassion, kindness, humility, meekness, longsuffering," and so on (Col. 3: 10, 12). "The fine linen is the righteous acts of the saints" (Rev. 19: 8). The flesh was to be covered with the white garments of Christlikeness. Not only had they to buy the garments, but also don them, "that thou mayest *clothe thyself*", as the R.V. rightly renders it. This is in keeping with the teaching concerning "the new man" which the saints themselves had to put on, and also concerning the Bride of whom we read, "It was given unto her that she should *array herself* in fine linen" (Rev. 19: 8). Only thus could the shame of their nakedness be covered.

Finally, for their blindness He offered them "*eyesalve to anoint [their] eyes*". Of the three things mentioned here, vision is perhaps the most difficult to recover, once it has been lost. Samson recovered his great strength before he died with the Philistines, but he never recovered his vision. In Christ there is an eyesalve, more wonderful than that which He once made of clay to anoint the eyes of a man born blind (John 9: 6). That day Christ "anointed on" the eyes for outer sight. This eyesalve they themselves had to "anoint [or rub] in" that the inner sight might be restored. As the Anointed One, there rested upon Christ "the spirit of wisdom and understanding, the spirit of counsel and might, the spirit of knowledge and of the fear of the Lord" (Isa. 11: 2). The same anointing of the Spirit from Him could bring healing virtue to the blinded vision, causing these believers to know and to be taught concerning all things (1 John 2: 20, 27). Thus would they receive " a spirit of wisdom and revelation in the knowledge of Him; having the eyes of [their] heart enlightened" (Eph. 1: 17); thus would they see the wondrous ways and purposes of God.

> That blessed unction from above
> Is comfort, life, and fire of love,
> Enables with perpetual light
> The dullness of our blinded sight.
> FROM LATIN OF NINTH CENTURY.

Having sharply reproved these Christians, nauseating in their lukewarmness, the Chief Shepherd tenderly adds, "As many as I *love* I reprove." What matchless grace is this! In spite of everything He loved them still. Since He had not abandoned them, there was still hope of their recovery. "Be zealous therefore and repent" was His last exhortation. In place of their lukewarmness there must be a revived zeal accompanied by a thorough-going repentance in view of what they had professed to be, and what in fact they were.

If the Laodiceans were not willing to heed the command of their Lord they would face the solemn alternative of a judgment more imminent than anything He had already issued. "Because thou art lukewarm, and neither cold nor hot, I am about to spue thee out of my mouth" (Darby), as one would vomit out food disagreeable to the palate. If words have any significance, Christ was warning this church of some kind of imminent rejection. Paul was urging the Corinthians to be hot in their zeal for God when he said, "Know ye not that they which run in a race run all, but one receiveth the prize? *Even so run that ye may attain.*" Then he added, "I therefore so run . . . lest by any means . . . I myself should be *rejected*" (1 Cor. 9: 24–27). This solemn warning to Laodicea is also a warning to every lukewarm church or

Christian, that though their final salvation cannot be imperilled, they are in grievous danger of being rejected as to the prize. Paul took no chances. "Brethren, I count not myself yet to have apprehended : but one thing I do . . . I press on toward the goal unto the prize of the upward calling of God in Christ Jesus" (Phil. 3: 13, margin).

How would Christ reject this church? "I am about to spue thee *out of My mouth*." It was from the mouth of the Lord that this church would be rejected, if unrepentant and unrevived. He had once said, "Everyone therefore who shall confess Me before men, him will I also confess before My Father which is in heaven. But whosoever shall deny Me before men, him will I also deny before My Father which is in heaven" (Matt. 10: 32). If the promise concerning confession applies to true believers, so does the warning concerning denial. The lukewarm Laodiceans, wretched, miserable, poor, blind, and naked, with Christ standing outside the door, were virtually denying Him. He was about to reject them from His mouth by denying them before His Father, with all the loss that that would involve. "*If* we died with Him, we shall also live with Him: *if* we endure, we shall also reign with Him : *if* we shall deny Him, He also will deny us" (2 Tim. 2: 11).

As we have contemplated this final message of the risen Christ, dare we say that the spirit of Laodicea is not abroad today? Is there no trace of it in our own hearts? Are we prepared to pay the price of a zeal revived, ablaze for God? Are we ashamed to be fervent in our devotion to the Lord? Have we faced the solemn alternative? What a need to cry,

> Revive us, Lord ! Is zeal abating
> While harvest fields are vast and white?
> Revive us, Lord, the world is waiting,
> Equip Thy church to spread the light.
>                                         B. P. HEAD.

The words of Christ shut us up to the reviving of our love, our truth, our life, our zeal—or to certain judgment. "He that hath an ear, let him hear what the Spirit saith to the churches."

Revivals are supernatural demonstrations of God's power. When will we learn to let God work in His own way? When will we spend more time in seeking to know what His way is than we do in devising human plans and methods which only bring us a sense of failure and loss? We need a revival. The church needs a revival. The world—hungry, restless, sin-cursed, dying—needs a revival. God wants us to have it. Let us make every effort to meet the divine conditions and let us expect Him to answer by fire.

P. V. JENNESS.

# CONCLUSION

"Who knoweth whether thou art not come to the kingdom
for such a time as this?" (Esther 4:14).

IT was an hour of crisis. A situation had arisen in which the
destiny of the elect nation seemed to hang in the balance.
Ahasuerus, the despotic monarch of Persia, had consented
to sign a decree at the request of Haman, the adversary of God's
people, that on a certain day all Jews throughout his vast domain
were to be slain. It seemed that certain judgment was about to
overwhelm God's people, and that the lamp of Israel would be
quenched for ever. But in the wondrous providences of God a
Hebrew orphan girl had been brought into a unique relationship
with the king. Ahasuerus had chosen Esther as his bride, set the
royal crown upon her head, and made her queen (2:17). God had
so ordained that she should come to the kingdom for such a time,
that out of desperate weakness His people might be made strong.
He had determined that through Esther He would make the
wrath of man to praise Him, so that in an hour of impending
judgment and calamity there might arise relief and deliverance
to the captive daughter of Zion.

It is such an hour of crisis today. Satan, the "Haman" of the
people of God, knows that his time is short. From within and
from without he is making a last desperate bid to overwhelm the
church. Materialism, Communism, Mahomedanism, Romanism,
and Spiritism are making rapid advances. If figures recently
issued are reliable, the increasing world population is swallowing
up the efforts of the church to evangelize to a finish by preaching
the gospel to every creature. "The population of the world in-
creases at a rate of 44 millions per year. There are 400 millions
more on earth today that have not been reached with the gospel
than there were a generation ago. During the last generation
alone, 750 millions went into eternity who had never heard one
word about Christ and His salvation" (L. Steiner). It must be
obvious to every thoughtful mind that the situation is desperate.
Time is running out. World events are moving fast. The nations
are lining up for the last great conflagration. Only revival, a last

great sweep of the Spirit can meet the need. This is indeed the hour of crisis, and "who knoweth whether *thou* are not come to the kingdom for such a time as this?"

### The Call to Intercede

"Charge her that she should go in unto the king, to make supplication unto him, and to make request before him, for her people" (4: 8). Thus Mordecai, Esther's guardian, answered the messenger whom she had sent. She was to use her unique relationship with the king for the deliverance of her people. She was to "go in unto the king, to make supplication unto him" who alone could alter the situation. A breach had been made in the defences of God's people, and the enemy was about to rush in for the kill. But there was one who had the ear of the king, who could therefore stand in the gap, and turn the tide of calamity that would engulf both her and her people.

Like Esther, many of God's people today are oblivious of the breaches in our defences that leave us wide open to the enemy. They look upon the Mordecais of today who foresee the perils, as pessimists. Like Esther, they would like to take from these realists the sackcloth of their gloomy outlook, and clothe them with the bright garments of their own wishful thinking (4: 4). The church needs to be awakened to the perils of the hour and the possibilities of revival.

Down the years God has ever looked in the hour of crisis for intercessors. Sometimes He has looked in vain. Has He to say to His people today what He said long ago through Ezekiel: "Ye have not gone up into the gaps, neither made up the fence for the house of Israel, to stand in the battle in the day of the Lord"? (Ezek. 13: 5). The word of God, the need of the church, the plight of the world, the possibility of revival, the shortness of the time, would unitedly urge us "to go in unto the King". God forbid that He should have to say of His people today: "I sought for a man among them, that should make up the fence, and stand in the gap before Me for the land, that I should not destroy it : but I found none" (Ezek. 22: 30). Today God is seeking for a man, a woman. Will you be that one? "Who knoweth whether *thou* art not come to the kingdom for such a time as this?"

## The Challenge to Sacrifice

"All . . . know, that whosoever, whether man or woman, shall come unto the king into the inner court, who is not called, there is one law for him, that he be put to death, except such to whom the king shall hold out the golden sceptre that he may live" (Esther 4: 11). Mordecai was in fact urging the young queen to take her life in her hands by going into the presence of the king unbidden. He was in fact asking her to cast aside all thought of self-preservation, and to be willing to sacrifice herself for the life of her people. A desperate situation demanded desperate measures.

Is not the situation desperate today? Where are those who are willing to sacrifice themselves that they may go "up into the gaps . . . to stand in the battle in the day of the Lord"? Where are those who will put their lives in jeopardy that they may "turn back the battle at the gate"? God is looking for the intercessor who will live the life of crucifixion, laying down his life daily for the cause of Christ. Such was a saintly woman who lived in the West Country and who passed away but a few years ago. Although in failing health she had a clear vision of the need of revival and a great prayer burden for it. Her sister declared that she probably hastened her end by her agonizing in prayer for the windows of heaven to be opened. Such are the Esthers who turn the tide for God. Paul said of himself, "I hold not my life of any account, as dear unto myself, so that I may finish my course" (Acts 20: 24), and of Epaphroditus, "for the work of Christ he came nigh unto death, hazarding his life" (Phil. 2: 30). Who follows in their train?

## The Issues at Stake

"Think not with thyself that thou shalt escape in the king's house . . . For if thou altogether holdest thy peace at this time, then shall relief and deliverance arise to the Jews from another place, but thou and thy father's house shall perish" (Esther 4: 13, 14). In the face of the sacrifice she was being called upon to make Esther hesitated. She was counting the cost. The reply of Mordecai, however, set forth with unmistakable frankness the issues at stake. Esther might refuse the call to intercede, trusting to her relationship with the king to save her skin if the worst happened. In a word Mordecai shatters such a thought. "Think not with thyself that thou shalt escape." To hold her peace at such a time would not bring disaster to her people, but to herself. God would certainly deliver His people. He was not shut up to Esther or anyone else. If she failed in this hour of desperate need and of great opportunity, if she shirked the issue, relief and deliverance would arise to the Jews from some other quarter, but she and her house would perish.

Many are convinced that God is going to revive His people; that there is scriptural ground for that conviction has already been shown. The Lord is now calling for intercessors; it may be that some have heard the call through reading this book. If we fail, God will bring relief and deliverance from some other quarter. "For the Lord of Hosts hath purposed, and who shall disannul it? and His hand is stretched out, and who shall turn it back?" (Isa. 14: 27). We must, however, face the consequences of our refusal. Sometimes the issue is not one of "Revival or Judgment" but of "Revival *and* Judgment". The very tide of blessing may sweep away those who will not obey, or will not believe. It was so in the siege of Samaria. Elisha brought the promise of imminent deliverance, declaring that on the morrow fine flour and barley would be sold at normal prices in the gate of Samaria. The king's captain replied, "Behold, if the Lord should make windows in heaven, might this thing be?" (2 Kings 7: 2). Said Elijah, "Behold, thou shalt see it with thine eyes, but shalt not eat thereof," and so it came to pass. In the stampede for food he was trodden to death. Relief and deliverance came to the people, but he perished in his unbelief. It is a major tragedy when a soul lives to see revival, but not to partake of it, because of disobedience or unbelief.

Do we believe? We cannot have a true expectation of revival while refusing the call to intercede. Our apathy denies our belief. The solid and practical proof of faith in this matter is a readiness to lose our lives in this ministry of intercession, that we may find them in revival. To fail to do so when God calls is to bring upon ourselves a curse instead of a blessing. Deborah and Barak in their song of victory over the hosts of Sisera, praised God "For that the leaders took the lead in Israel, for that the people offered themselves willingly" (Judges 5: 2); but they also pronounced an anathema upon the inhabitants of Meroz because they failed to do so. It was an hour of crisis and of opportunity, but they refused "to stand in the battle in the day of the Lord." "Curse ye Meroz, said the angel of the Lord, curse ye bitterly the inhabitants thereof; *because they came not to the help of the Lord, to the help of the Lord against the mighty*" (verse 23). It is a grievous thing to stand aloof in pride, or to hold back in fear or unbelief, when the Spirit of God is moving. The Lord will surely require it. Shall we then hold our peace, or shall we go in unto the King?

## The Solemn Resolve

"So will I go in unto the king, which is not according to the law: and if I perish, I perish" (Esther 4: 16). Moved by the desperate need, awed but not intimidated by the peril involved, convinced that she had come to the kingdom for this very hour, the young queen came to this solemn resolve to lay herself upon the altar of sacrifice, to stand in the gap in the hour of crisis, to go in unto the king, and if she perished, she perished. She had faced the challenge, counted the cost, and had thus come to a steadfast determination to deliver her people by her intercession, or die in the attempt. She went in unto the king. He held out to her the golden sceptre, thus accepting her person. He said, "What wilt thou, queen Esther? And what is thy request?" She prevailed with the king for her people. She reversed the situation, and so turned the day of distress into the day of deliverance, and the day of judgment into the day of revival.

When the breaches were wide, and the wrath of God ready to sweep us to hell, the Son of God stood in the gap, and interposed His precious body to save His people from their sins. He is Himself the guarantee of God's willingness to send the revival so desperately needed, for "He that spared not His own Son, but delivered Him up for us all, how shall He not also with Him *freely give us all things*?" (Rom. 8: 32)—revival among them. The appalling need of this hour is only matched by its unique opportunity to afford a display of the power and glory of God. Many a faithful intercessor of the past has desired to see the things which we are about to see, and has not seen them. In His matchless grace, God has brought us to the kingdom for such a time as this. The Saviour calls us to follow His steps in the pathway of intercession.

Shall we—dare we disappoint Him?
    Brethren, let us rise!
He who died for us is watching
    From the skies—

Watching till His royal banner
    Floateth far and wide,
Till He seeth of His travail—
    Satisfied!

                    A. J. JANVRIN.

"Now unto Him that is able to do exceeding abundantly above all that we ask or think, according to the power that worketh in us, unto Him be the glory in the church and in Christ Jesus unto all generations for ever and ever. Amen" (Eph. 3: 20, 21).

# A PRAYER FOR REVIVAL

O GOD, send us the Holy Ghost! Give us both the breath of
spiritual life and the fire of unconquerable zeal. O Thou
art our God, answer us by fire, we pray Thee! Answer us
both by wind and fire, and then we shall see Thee to be God indeed. The kingdom comes not, and the work is flagging. Oh, that
Thou wouldst send the wind and the fire! Thou wilt do this when
we are all of one accord, all believing, all expecting, all prepared
by prayer.

Lord, bring us to this waiting state! God, send us a season
of glorious disorder. Oh, for a sweep of the wind that will set the
seas in motion, and make our ironclad brethren, now lying so
quietly at anchor, to roll from stem to stern!

Oh, for the fire to fall again—fire which shall affect the most
stolid! Oh, that such fire might first sit upon the disciples, and
then fall on all around! O God, Thou art ready to work with us
today even as Thou didst then. Stay not, we beseech Thee, but
work at once.

Break down every barrier that hinders the incoming of Thy
might! Give us now both hearts of flame and tongues of fire to
preach Thy reconciling word, for Jesus' sake! Amen!

C. H. SPURGEON.

# BIBLIOGRAPHY ON REVIVAL

THIS list of works on revival is far from exhaustive, but it is hoped it may prove comprehensive. The larger Historical Section shows the narratives covering various revivals according to their century. The smaller Doctrinal Section contains those works unfolding the principles of revival. The rarer volumes may be found in The Evangelical Library, 78 Chiltern Street, London, W.1.

> "The works of the Lord are great, sought out of all them that have pleasure therein. . . . He hath made His wonderful works to be remembered" (Ps. 111: 2, 4).

## I. HISTORICAL SECTION

### EIGHTEENTH CENTURY

1. *Britain and America.*

*The Journal of David Brainerd.* American Indian revival (1745). The rise and progress of a remarkable work of grace amongst a number of Indians in the provinces of New Jersey and Pennsylvania.

*The Distinguishing Marks of a Work of the Spirit of God,* by Jonathan Edwards (1741–2). An account of the work of God at Northampton, Mass. Also *Thoughts on the Revival in New England.*

*Memoirs of Howell Harris* (1714–73), by John Bulmer. The life and religious labours of the first itinerant preacher in Wales.

*Howell Harris and the Welsh Revivalists* (1711–93), by H. Elvet Lewis.

*Narrative of the Revival of Religion* (1742), by James Robe. Revivals at Kilsyth, Cambuslang, and elsewhere.

*Christian History* (1743–4), by Thomas Prince. Accounts of eighteenth-century revivals in Great Britain and America.

*Revivals of the Eighteenth Century in Scotland,* particularly at Cambuslang, by D. Macfarlan.

*The Great Awakening,* by Joseph Tracy. A history of the revival of religion in America under Edwards and Whitefield.

*The Revival of Religion in England in the Eighteenth Century,* by John S. Simon. Describes the conditions, social, moral, and religious which preceded the revival, and the influence of the Religious Societies.

*Christian Leaders of the Last Century,* by J. C. Ryle (1869). Including Whitefield, Wesley, Grimshaw, Romaine, Rowlands, Berridge, Venn, Walker, Hervey, Toplady, Fletcher.

*Showers of Blessing,* by Robert Young (1844). An account of revivals among the Methodists from the time of Wesley to 1834.

*The Journals* and sundry biographies of *Wesley and Whitefield.*

2. *Moravian Revival*

*The Moravians,* by E. R. Hassé. Showing the relationship between the Moravian revival and the eighteenth-century revivals in England.

*Life of Nicolas Lewis Count Zinzendorf,* by A. G. Spangenberg. Translated from the German.

*Revival under Zinzendorf*, by J. E. Hutton.

*Power from on High*, by John Greenfield (published 1950). The Moravian revival as illustrating the need and effect of the anointing of the Holy Spirit.

## NINETEENTH CENTURY

*The Autobiography of Charles G. Finney* (1821–68). Perhaps the most remarkable account of one man's labours in revival since apostolic times.

*The Revival of Religion* (1839), by Andrew Reed. An account of a revival that broke out in Wycliffe Chapel, East London.

*Memoir of Rev. Wm. C. Burns*, by Islay Burns (1869). Containing accounts of the revivals in Kilsyth, Dundee, St. Andrews, Perth, etc. (1839–40).

*The Revival in Ulster* (1859), by R. M. Sibbeth. Being the life-story of a worker (W. M. Speers).

*A Visit to the Scenes of Revival in Ireland* (1859), by J. W. Massie. In four parts.

*The Year of Grace* (1859), by Wm. Gibson. An account of the Ulster revival. The author was that year Moderator of the Presbyterian Church of Ireland.

*The Great Revival in Ireland* (1859), by Samuel Moore.

*The Revival in its Physical, Psychical, and Religious Aspects*, by W. M. Wilkinson. An inquiry into the physical and psychical phenomena manifested in the Ulster and other revivals.

*The '59 Revival in Wales*, by J. J. Morgan. Some incidents in the life and work of David Morgan, the revivalist.

*The Welsh Revival: Origin and Development* (1859), by Thomas Phillips. An account by one who witnessed the movement.

*The Second Evangelical Awakening in Britain* (1859), by J. Edwin Orr. A fully documented account of the movement in Ulster, Scotland, Wales, and England. (Published 1949.) With complete Bibliography.

*The History and Diaries of an Indian Christian*, by G. H. Lang. Containing an account of the revival in the Tinnevelly district of South India (1860).

## TWENTIETH CENTURY

*The Awakening in Wales* (1904–5), by Mrs. Penn-Lewis. Glimpses into some of the hidden springs.

*Rent Heavens—The Revival of 1904*, by R. B. Jones.

*Living Echoes of the Welsh Revival* (1904–5), by Robert Ellis. A modern account centring in the work of seven leaders in the movement.

*I Saw the Welsh Revival* (1904–5), by David Matthews.

*By My Spirit*, by Jonathan Goforth. An account of the revivals under his ministry in Manchuria and China (1906–9).

*The Revival in Manchuria* (1908), by James Webster.

*Road to Revival—The Story of the Ruanda Mission* (1916–46), by A. C. Stanley Smith. Tracing the beginnings and the development of the Ruanda revival.

*John Sung—Flame for God in the Far East*, by Leslie Lyall. Revivals in the Far East (1934–39) under the ministry of this unique evangelist.

*The Price They Paid*, by Norman Grubb. A booklet based on letters received from a group of missionaries in India (1940–1), giving an intimate picture of their experiences in seeking revival, and the result.

*The Lewis Awakening* (1949–53), by Duncan Campbell.

*This is That*, by the General Secretary of W.E.C., being an account of the revival in the Belgian Congo (1953) edited from missionaries' reports.

### GENERAL NARRATIVES

Accounts of revivals in more than one century.

*Historical Collections*, by John Gillies with supplement by H. Bonar. Accounts of labours in the gospel and revivals from earliest times to nineteenth century.

*Narratives of Revivals of Religion* (1623–1839), by Glasgow Revival Tract Society. Accounts of revivals in Scotland, Ireland, and Wales.

*Revivals*, by William Brock. A brief review of revivals up to 1859.

*Stories of Great Revivals*, by Henry Johnson. Revivals from eighteenth century to beginning of twentieth century.

*Old Time Revivals*, by John Shearer. Brief accounts of revivals from the time of the Puritans to 1859.

*The History of Revivals of Religion*, by William E. Allen. Outlines of revivals from earliest times to the present day.

*Revivals, Their Laws and Leaders*, by James Burns. Some of the laws governing revivals, and accounts of the movements under Francis of Assisi, Savonarola, Luther, Calvin, Knox, and Wesley.

## II. DOCTRINAL SECTION

*The Revivals of the Bible*, by Ernest Baker. Lessons from 18 movements of the Spirit in Scripture.

*History and Character of American Revivals*, by Calvin Colton (1832). Emphasizes use of appropriate means.

*Lectures on Revivals of Religion*, by William Sprague (1833). A comprehensive discussion of revival doctrines.

*Lectures on Revivals of Religion*, by Charles Finney (1835). In spite of its controversial nature, the influence exerted by this book on revival movements has been unique, especially Lectures I–VII.

*Lectures on Revivals of Religion*, by Ministers of the Church of Scotland (1840), including one by William Burns.

*Handbook of Revivals*, by Harry C. Fish (1873). A manual covering various aspects of revival.

*Revivals How Promoted*, by Thomas Payne.

*Apostolic Christianity and How it Turned the World Upside Down*, by Thomas Payne.

*Personal Declension and Revival*, by Octavius Winslow. Emphasizing the need of personal reviving.

*The Revival We Need*, by Oswald Smith.

*Revive Us Again*, by Philip E. Hughes.

# *Classics* from KINGSWAY

The Kingsway Classics series presents favourite best-selling titles by well-known authors in special omnibus editions, for the same price as a single-volume paperback.

---

**Classics from Jamie Buckingham**
*Risky Living, Where Eagles Soar* and *A Way Through the Wilderness*.

**Classics from Arthur Wallis**
*Living God's Way, Going On God's Way* and *Into Battle*.

**Classics from Watchman Nee Vol 1**
*The Normal Christian Life, Sit Walk Stand* and *Changed Into His Likeness*.

**Classics from Watchman Nee Vol 2**
*A Table in the Wilderness, Love Not the World* and *What Shall This Man Do?*

**Classics on Prayer**
*Learning the Joy of Prayer* by Larry Lea, *Pray in the Spirit* by Arthur Wallis and *Praying Together* by Mike and Katey Morris.

**Classics on Worship**
*Worship* by Graham Kendrick, *The Believer's Guide to Worship* by Chris Bowater and *To the Praise of His Glory* by Dave Fellingham.

**Classic Real-Life Stories**
*Vanya* by Myrna Grant, *Blood Brothers* by Elias Chacour and *Streetwise* by John Goodfellow.

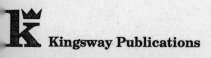

**Kingsway Publications**

# *Classics* from KINGSWAY

Don't miss the following exciting titles in the series due for publication in 2001:

---

**Classics from Merlin Carothers**
with *Power in Praise, Bringing Heaven into Hell* and *What's On Your Mind.*

**Classic Stories: Women of Faith**
includes *No Greater Love* by Joy Bath, *Living Under the Volcano* by Christine Perillo and *I Dared to Call Him Father* by Bilquis Sheikh.

**Classics from Doreen Irvine**
includes *From Witchcraft to Christ, Set Free to Serve* and *Spiritual Warfare.*

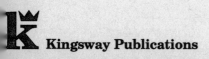
**Kingsway Publications**